3ds Max 2008

Architectural Visualization

Beginner to Intermediate

Brian L. Smith

3ds Max 2008 Architectural Visualization
Beginner to Intermediate

ISBN-13: 978-0-9792811-1-2

ISBN-10: 0-9792811-1-3

Printed in China

Distributed to the book trade worldwide by 3DATS, LLC, 1188 N. Tamiami Trail, Suite 205, Sarasota, FL 34236. 3DATS is a subsidiary of 3DAS.

Phone 1-941-953-3323, fax 1-8666-258-5534, e-mail 3dinfo@3das.com, or visit www.3dats.com.

The downloadable content for this book is freely available to readers at www.3dats.com\books in the Downloads section.

Credits

Technical Reviewer
Mark Gerhard

Contributing Authors
Brian Zajac
Padhia Romaniello

Compositor
Dina Quan

Cover Image Designer
Padhia Romaniello

3D Models Provided by
Alex Gorbunov, Intero Visuals

Contributing Graphic Artists
Panorama01
Visarty

The inspiration for everything I do in the 3D world has always been my wonderful wife Shari and our two kids Laken and Kegan. I would not be doing what I do without their support.

Contents at a Glance

Contents

PART 1 Getting Around Inside 3ds Max

PART 2 Modeling

CHAPTER 4 **The Critical Compound Objects Types (Loft, Boolean, Pro Boolean, Terrain, and Scatter)**   **4-1**

PART 4 **Lighting**

PART 5 **Cameras and Animation**

Appendixes

About the Author

Since 1997, **Brian Smith** has worked as a CAD manager and animation specialist in architectural, engineering, and landscaping firms in southwest Florida. He started his own company in 2001, specializing in the production of architectural animations and renderings in 3ds Max. He is the cofounder of 3DAS in Sarasota, Florida, and its subsidiary training company 3DATS. He is currently an instructor for 3DATS and VisMasters, where he teaches 3ds Max, AutoCAD, and V-Ray. A portfolio of his work can be seen at www.3das.com.

Brian graduated from the U.S. Military Academy at West Point with a major in aerospace engineering. He served on active duty, and later in the Florida Army National Guard, including two years as a battery commander, responsible for a short range air defense battery of over 100 soldiers. Following 9/11, he served in Washington, D.C. as an air defense artillery fire control officer, working closely with the US Secret Service, the US Air Force, and the FAA to provide air defense coverage of our nation's capital. In 2005, he deployed numerous times with his unit to provide humanitarian relief to hurricane victims along the Gulf Coast.

About the Contributing Authors

Brian Zajac received his B.F.A. from Bowling Green State University in Ohio and began working in the field of 3D in the mid 90s. At that time, a typical workstation cost as much as $100,000 and ran at a fraction of the speed of today's computers. He left 3D and turned his sights towards a career in web design where he wouldn't have to wait so long to see the fruits of his labor. In 2002, Brian started his own company EyeMagination (www.eyemagination.us) with the goal to build the best possible web-based solutions and internet marketing for small businesses. Brian has worked with several hi-profile organizations, such as the PGA, American Golf and the New York Yacht Club.

After establishing his web-based business, Brian noticed that the 3D world of technology had become much faster, produced better results, and was finally cost-effective. So, along with his business partner Brian Smith, he formed 3D Architectural Solutions (3DAS) – a 3D architectural visualization facility that creates stunning photorealistic renderings and animations. He also co-authored the world's first book ever written for architectural visualization and is currently co-authoring additional books in the architectural visualization area. A portfolio of his work can be seen at www.3das.com.

Padhia Romaniello is an artist and graphic designer who stumbled upon the 3d world in 1997. Immediately entranced by the infinite possibilities of using 3d as a medium, she moved from Long Island to Fort Lauderdale to continue her education and receive two separate B.S. degrees in computer animation and graphic design. She continued even further in her education by spending time at Mesmer Animation Labs, a former Alias Wavefront certified training center in Seattle.

Originally focused on character design and animation as well as the creation of digital sets, Padhia discovered that to earn a living in this field, she would really need to relocate to another state. Not ready to leave this new tropical paradise, she began freelancing in architectural visualization and later founded Avocado Digital Design in 2001. Success required several years of what she refers to as "mental boot camp", during which time she became self-taught in business strategy, web design, commercial print, and many crucial software packages.

Seven years later, Avocado Digital Design is a thriving 3D visualization company working on 3D production, web design, branding, and collateral materials of projects across the country and abroad. In 2006, her company joined in a strategic partnership with 3DAS.

About the Technical Reviewer

Mark Gerhard serves as a Media and Entertainment application engineer for IMAGINiT Technologies. He has worked with 3ds Max since its inception as 3D Studio DOS in 1990 and was the first artist hired to test the software while collaborating with the original development team including Gary Yost, Tom Hudson and Dan Silva. He was one of the first 3D Studio instructors, training most of the original dealers and educators around the world (Ted Boardman was one of his very first students!) He served as a product manager for the 2D animation products, Animator Pro and Animator Studio. He was also the first application engineer at Autodesk dedicated to the multimedia products. Mark spent the last six years of his Autodesk tenure as the lead writer for the tutorials that shipped with 3ds Max versions 3 through 6. He currently serves as an Autodesk web board forum assistant for the 3ds Max forums.

He has served as technical editor on numerous books on 3D Studio, including the "Inside 3ds max" series for New Riders, and the Mastering Visually series for Wiley (now Sybex). He has also taught 3D Modeling and Animation at Napa Valley College, Santa Rosa Junior College, Sonoma State University, Academy of Art University and Digital Media Academy (at Stanford University) since 2001. He has worked for NIIT (New Delhi) and created online courses on for the Art Institute Online and Westwood College. He has freelanced doing design visualization for numerous clients including Marin Solar, Leinow and Associates and the Cities of Cloverdale, Novato and Santa Rosa.

Beyond his 3D and teaching, he holds a degree in Painting and Sculpture from UC Berkeley, where he wrote and illustrated a children's book, The Elf of the Shelf Sees Himself, as part of an honors independent study program in Art.

Mark has also had a longterm involvement with India, studying classical North Indian music with Ali Akbar Khansahib, Shankar Ghosh and Jnan Prakash Ghosh from 1970 to 1998, and has performed on the tabla with Allen Ginsburg, Jai Uttal, Geoffrey Gordon, and Babukishan Das Baul. He can be heard on the albums "Love, Serve, Remember", and "Swaha" featuring Bhagavan Das and Amazing Grace. He has lived in India and studied Bengal folk music with Baidyanath Das Baul, and is a proficient player of the gubgubi (khammok), khartals (manjira), dholak, khanjeera, and harmonium. He speaks a passable Hindi and can cook a pretty aloo gobi curry as well.

He has 4 children and one grandchild. When he isn't teaching 3D, he enjoys modeling, animating and rendering, as well as character rigging. Just kidding...he hates character rigging.

Acknowledgments

Thanks to Dina Quan for single-handedly doing the compositing and layout design of this book.

Thanks to Mark Gerhard for his meticulous work as the technical reviewer.

Thanks to my good friends Nadiya and Volodymyr at Visarty (www.visarty.com). For many years now they have provided unwavering 3D production support through many difficult projects. They are two of the best in the business. One of these days, we will actually make it over to Ukraine to visit you both.

Thanks to the crew at Panorama01 (www.panorama01.com) in Argentina for their 3D production help and for help in preparing much of the graphics found through this book. They too are some of the best 3D artists around.

Thanks to Padhia Romaniello for her great taste in colors and fonts, as well as the front cover design. If you dislike any of these, it's her fault. ☺

Thanks to Brian Zajac for picking up my slack in all areas of our business. If there's anything else wrong in this book, it's his fault. ☺

Thanks to Alexander Gorbunov for providing many of the models used in this book. Alexander is arguably the best furniture modeler in the world and he has become an invaluable asset to our business. You can see his work at www.interovisuals.com.

Thanks again to my mom for beating proper English into me.

Finally, thanks to the entire crew at VisMasters that has supported 3DAS and 3DATS in more ways than we can possibly recall. Pictured left to right are Magnus Lindqvist, Jeff Mottle, Padhia Romaniello (3DAS), Randall Stevens, Dee Fife, myself, Brian Zajac (3DAS), Nathaniel McConathy, Jon Anderson (not pictured).

Brian L. Smith

Foreword

AFTER STRUGGLING FOR MANY YEARS and countless long hours, it was a series of very fortunate events that led me to meet Mr. Brian Smith…and to my current position of having him as a mentor, friend, and strategic business partner.

After graduating with a BS in Computer Graphics, I came to realize the obvious truth that my college instructors avoided addressing…that there are few character animation jobs in the state of Florida. It was at this time that the south-east Florida real estate boom was ascending to its peak and I began seeing 3D renderings of pre-construction projects popping up everywhere. And so, attempting to apply my education, I built my first 6-bedroom home in Maya, entirely out of NURBs (if this foreword had an accompanying laugh track, I would push that button here). I can still see it gleaming proudly in my mind, with its bizarre perspective and slightly inappropriate roundedness in places. As a testament to my indefatigable determination, I did manage to earn a living for while in this fashion. It was 2001 that I decided to explore the possibility that I could earn a living in architectural visualization and graphic design full-time. It is now almost 2008, and my company is flourishing. Having been asked to write this foreword, gives me the opportunity to acknowledge the place Brian Smith holds in all of this.

As Maya was my first true love, for way too long of a time, I refused to listen to the voice of reason within the various chat forums I subscribed to; that perhaps there might just be another piece of software out there that better suited for architectural visualization. I had invested so much time in the solutions that I so painstakingly developed (to model the projects, create realistic shadows, and fake color bleeding, etc.), that the thought of throwing it all out and starting from scratch was a really overwhelming thought. I wince at the thought of my old workflow, and feel unimaginable inner pain every time I open my big old box of Maya & mental ray training DVDs.

That went on for several years, until one day I couldn't deny it any longer…that 3ds Max & V-Ray produced far superior results than I was able to achieve with Maya & mental ray, and apparently in a fraction of the time. I couldn't fully comprehend, having not yet learned in the software, but it seemed that using 3ds Max & V-ray would simplify tasks which were, for me, unbearably tedious.

For awhile I tried to learn 3ds Max & V-ray in my spare time, but because of my then current methodology, I had no spare time. It became apparent that I needed to make the break in the middle of a project and under the pressure of the deadline, or it just wasn't going to happen. And so I sat at my computer and went through the entire 1252-page 3ds Max Bible cover to cover. I scoured the web like a search-bot and went through every online resource available about 3ds Max or V-Ray. It was in the course of this research that I came across Brian's first book, which I still to this day keep by my desk as an invaluable resource. Despite all of my self-education, I was continually plagued by scene crashes and very slow render times. I located a training center only a few hours away, which offered the opportunity for custom training, and I signed up for an 8 hour one-on-one class with a V-ray & 3ds Max instructor. Almost as if it were a reward for all my years of struggle and long hours of work, the instructor turned out to be none other than Brian Smith, author of the very informative book which I had recently finished.

In addition to the obvious reasons, using Maya for architectural visualization also plagued me because it was incredibly lonesome. There was not much of an online community and few resources available when I needed help. The thought of meeting someone face to face who was an expert in this field and who had published a book on these topics, brought me hope that I would not spend the rest of my working days struggling & suffering alone.

I brought some of my scenes with me, which I had so carefully constructed (more like con-cocted) per the various settings and instruction of a slew of tutorials. I began explaining what I had done and why, as I proceeded to take out my giant stack of printed tutorials. What happened next is pretty funny, though at the time I was a little offended.

Brian completely interrupted me, pushed the tutorials aside, opened a fresh Max scene, and created a simple box. He proceeded to spend the next 8 hours meticulously explaining the most efficient workflow, basic concepts, and procedures for optimization. He began way beneath the sur-face of the Max & V-Ray interfaces, explaining things, which to this day, I still wonder how he figured out. Instead, He explained what the calculations were based on, what the range of values would yield, and most importantly why. I have a degree in graphic design and another in computer anima-tion & digital media. I went to Mesmer Animation Labs in Seattle and completed a certification program in character animation from Alias Wave front. Never has anyone given me such a thorough education or understanding of anything. Brian's ability to dissect the core concepts of 3ds Max, V-Ray, and 3D rendering in general, is rivaled only by his ability to teach. He seems to switch into another mode, where his thoughts become clearly organized, and he is able to see ten steps ahead, much like the game of chess. He lays the foundation, and a solid one at that and then he builds…and builds…and builds. He said that he never forgets what it was like knowing nothing about 3D and likes showing others how not to make all the mistakes he made and how not to learn everything the hard way.

One of the most valuable aspects of learning from Brian is that he is not someone who theo-rizes about these things, but someone who is involved everyday in implementing these concepts, exploring new possibilities, and continually expanding his knowledge in the 3D production of large architectural projects. His successful visualization firm, 3DAS, is a testament to the fact that he is a master of the concepts he educates about.

Anyone involved in this industry understands that although it is a global industry, it is very small and interconnected. I often reflect that Brian deserves proper acknowledgement not only for his contribution towards education in this community, but also for setting such an enormously positive tone. His "lead-by-example attitude" of sharing information and supporting growth as a global team, makes competition friendly and spreads the sentiment of being a part of something on a larger scale. Deserving equal weight in acknowledgement is his commitment to continually offering infor-mation outside of things he profits from, such as in continuously updated amazingly in-depth, free columns online & free webinars.

At first I found his attitude puzzling. Wasn't the goal in 3D and life in general to figure out as much as you could, keep it to yourself and guard it with your life? I was under the impression that this was what would give me a leading edge in life. Through his example, Brian has taught me to see a much bigger picture…. a picture that extends beyond the reach of my wireless mouse, and that has led me to realize that the 3D architectural visualization community is one entity working together on a global scale. He stressed that it wasn't until the turn of the century that architects, developers, builders, and other clientele really started believing in 3D…and that one of the reasons why it took so long to catch on is that nobody did 3D…and since nobody did 3D, it wasn't the norm and it wasn't expected or demanded. He said that the more our 3D community grows, the more it's expected and demanded. As an example, numerous cities in Florida, and I'm sure around the globe, have already required or are considering the requirement of 3D models and/or renderings to be submitted along with building applications. This is a monumental advancement from just a few years ago and something that wouldn't be possible if our community wasn't growing. In addition, the more our community grows, the more support we can expect from software manufactures and the faster we will see all the wonderful programs we know will eventually come.

Brian's attitude that "there is enough work for everyone in this industry, and far more good comes from sharing knowledge and ideas", clearly sets a tone in the community of wanting to connect with each other and share knowledge and experiences, even though this small community is divided by many bodies of water & time zones. It is my hope that in some small way, writing this foreword gives me the opportunity to acknowledge his positive contributions and applaud his attitude towards sharing work and knowledge. Even things that at first glance might seem like "trade secrets" he unselfishly publishes online & for free. Inherently, computer based fields lead to long hours of isolation, but his actions are a source of inspiration for connecting despite logistics & practicality. Since meeting Brian, I have begun instant messaging with people all around the world.

And so now having switched over to 3ds Max and V-Ray, and having been taught from a true master, I now find architectural visualization an enjoyable and rewarding process; whereas before, it was a constant struggle to stay afloat.

One of the truest things Brian always emphasizes is that it is just as important to know how to optimize a scene, as it is to be able to create it. The first few times I heard him say this it went right past me, but through his training and later working with him on large projects, I have come to realize how true that statement is. When work is well organized and efficiently constructed, things just seem to come together and work the way they are supposed to. Programs don't crash, renderings don't take forever, and clients don't scream at you for their work. And it's then that architectural visualization becomes more than just a line of work. . .it becomes an enjoyable, gratifying, and profitable trade.

Cheers to Brian Smith, and his contributions to the world-wide architectural visualization community,

Padhia Avocado Romaniello
Founder, Avocado Digital Design Inc.
Strategic business partner, 3DAS

Who is this Book For?

THIS BOOK IS A PARTIAL rewrite of the book *Foundation 3ds Max 8 Architectural Visualization*, published by Friends of ED in April 2006. This time around, I've decided to publish it directly through my 3D training company 3DATS, which gives me far greater control and flexibility over the design and style. Unlike the first book, this edition is printed in full color, which makes illustrations far easier to understand, and this time around I have used far more architectural based models in the illustrations.

This book is written primarily for beginners and students and is designed to take readers to an intermediate level. I have made every attempt to simplify the program and break it down to the most simple and easy to understand language, and whenever possible, I have included personal experiences to provide relevancy to the features being discussed. It is a fairly comprehensive book, which is to say I believe it covers everything a beginner or student needs to know to land a job with a visualization company. The companion to this book, *3ds Max 2008 Architectural Visualization - Intermediate to Advanced*, is designed to take intermediate level users to the advanced level, not by teaching more advanced features but rather by teaching practical application and time-saving techniques of the tools covered in this book. These techniques are the combined result of many years of trial and error by me and many of the peers with whom I share tips and tricks.

Introduction

I BEGAN TEACHING MYSELF 3D after landing my first architectural drafting position. At the time, I couldn't afford the program, so the only time I could practice was during lunch breaks on a shared computer that 3D Studio Release 4 was installed on at the office I worked at. I bought almost every book available on the program but since I could only practice with the program occasionally at work, most of the reading I did was without the benefit of being able to immediately practice what I was reading. I was continually frustrated with every book I read because the material in each book was not presented in simple enough language so that I could understand it without following along on a computer. It was for this reason that when I started writing this book, I decided that I would write it in language so simple that the average reader wouldn't even have to follow along with a computer to understand. Ironically, when I wrote this book, I didn't even have a computer to use myself to test the procedures of which I was writing. I didn't even have a computer to type the words on.

I had wanted to write a book on 3ds Max for several years but the opportunity didn't present itself until I was sent to Washington, D.C. with my National Guard unit. My unit was a specialized air defense unit and we were sent to provide short-range air defense of Washington D.C. in 2004. I did not look forward to being removed from the 3D world but the job was quite interesting to say the least and a far better duty than most of the military was assigned to. My job was to serve as the 'Air Defense Artillery Fire Control Officer', which simply meant that I worked in a room that looked like a small version of NORAD and monitored all flights in and out of the capital while communicating with other government agencies to evaluate and repel any potential air threats. We worked side-by-side with the FAA, Secret Service, and had direct communications with all major intelligence agencies.

During this tour, I had the good fortune of being assigned a nighttime shift which ran from early evening to early morning and because there are virtually no aircraft flying around Washington between 12am and 5am, everyone on shift between those hours had little to do to occupy their window. I decided to put my time to good use by starting to write this book, but because of the classified nature of everything in the room, no one was allowed to bring computers or recording devices inside. Since I couldn't use a computer, not only could I not use 3ds Max for reference while I wrote, I had to write everything by hand and then transfer it to computer when I was off-duty. So the majority of this book was written by hand in the late night hours of my tour in Washington while sitting in a room full of high-ranking officers and state-of-the-art surveillance equipment. And because I was forced to write from memory, I believe it helped me write with a simplicity and clarity that I could not have otherwise achieved.

But the idea for writing this book started almost immediately after I began teaching myself 3D. I was amazed at all the books available for users in the entertainment industry, yet not one could be found for those of us in the visualization industry. I wasted countless hours learning things I found out only later that I didn't need to know, and I made up my mind that if someone else didn't have a visualization book on the market when I had learned the program, I would write one myself.

As I mentioned in the first edition of this book, I feel fortunate to be part of the 3D world at a time when it appears that the real world is completely embracing our work. My business partner Brian Zajac started in the 3D business a long time ago, when a typical workstation cost $100,000, and a simple animation that today would take only minutes to render took weeks. He gave up 3D and turned his sights to a career in web design where he wouldn't have to wait so long to see the fruits of his labor. Many architectural visualization companies struggled to survive these early days of 3D, when the software lacked the quality that many clients demanded, and the cost of equipment was a great a burden to manage. But just like the conversion from hand-drawn architectural blue-prints to computer-aided drafting in the 90s, 3D visualizations have gained the necessary backing to make our work the norm. Now anyone with enough drive and desire can start a 3D visualization business from their own home with just a single computer. With computers becoming faster and faster each year, the near future promises even greater power for all of us to build better scenes and render them in a fraction of the time it takes today. Before you know it, we will be able to render our scenes in real time!

Tutorial and Layout conventions

The tutorials within the chapters are designed to maximize the clarity of selected features and the speed at which you can learn the material. Whenever possible, you'll be asked to reset 3ds Max and create scene elements from scratch, rather than simply opening preconstructed scenes. By taking you through a tutorial that starts from scratch rather than a preconstructed scene, you'll be apt to feel a greater sense of confidence that the steps in the tutorial work independently of any pre-arranged settings or elements. Also, I've kept the complexity of the tutorials to a minimum and incorporated mostly simple objects (such as primitives) so that you can gain a greater sense of clarity of what exactly is going on. The end result is a tutorial that maximizes the transfer of knowl-edge in a minimal amount of time.

To keep this book as clear and easy to follow as possible, the following text conventions are used throughout:

Bold text is used to draw your attention to on-screen elements in the 3ds Max interface and the first appearance of important words or concepts.

Menu commands are written in the form **Menu ➤ Submenu ➤ Submenu**.

Downloadable Files

Some of the tutorials in this book require files that can be downloaded from the book's web page at www.3dats.com\books. As I can, I will add additional content to this web page that should serve useful to beginner-intermediate level 3ds Max users. Check back from time to time to see what's been added!

When I was almost 4 years old, my mother took me to a doctor because she was worried about the fact that I didn't ever try to talk. She thought something was wrong with me because I just wouldn't say anything. The doctor told her that I was perfectly fine and that 'your boy will talk when he has something important to say'.

She often laughs about that and reminds me of how far I've come from the time when apparently I had nothing important to say.

PART 1

Getting Around Inside 3ds Max

An underlying theme of this book is to teach you what you need to learn to be productive in an architectural visualization firm and avoid learning too many features that serve no purpose or function. Although I have always strived to learn as many new features as I can, my first priority has always been to perfect the tools that truly pay off in a production environment.

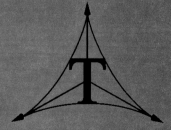

CHAPTER 1

Navigating the 3ds Max Interface

THE 3DS MAX INTERFACE HAS seen a great deal of change since its early days as a DOS based program released in 1990 under the name 3D Studio. By today's standards, the 3D Studio interface, shown in Figure 1-1, was quite simple and easy to learn. Needless to say, the 3ds Max 2008 interface is a little more complicated.

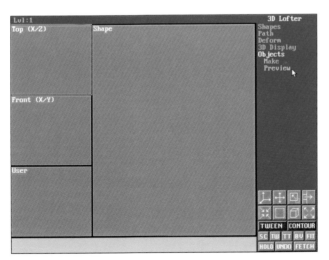

Figure 1-1. The interface of the original DOS based 3D Studio program released in 1990

The interface of any computer program is the means with which you command the program to perform a task. It stands to reason, therefore, that an interface should be designed in a way that allows the user to command the program as quickly and efficiently as possible. Did Autodesk succeed in creating that perfect interface? They did a great job; however, the default interface was created to benefit all 3ds Max users, not just those specializing in architectural visualizations. This chapter shows you how to best make use of the interface provided, and Appendix A demonstrates how to pick up where Autodesk leaves off, by showing you how to customize the 3ds Max interface to your specific needs.

Why put customization in an appendix at the end of a book? Simple. Until you have a firm grasp of at least the fundamentals, you won't know how to best customize the interface, and you'll probably end up changing it anyway. That being said, this chapter will focus on how to interact with the program as it is.

Autodesk did an outstanding job of making the 3ds Max interface user-friendly and efficient. As with many programs, there are numerous ways to tell the program to do the same thing. The trick is knowing which way is best—and this 3ds Max user defines *best* as the way that's fastest. It's a cliché, but time is money.

The interface elements

There are eight main screen interfaces through which to communicate with 3ds Max and get your work done, as shown in Figure 1-2. They include the Menu bar, toolbar, Command panel, viewport, Lower Interface bar, quad menu, floater, and dialog box. But before you can even use them, you have to work through at least one of two other interfaces: the keyboard and the mouse. Most users rely almost completely on the mouse—at least at first—and although using the mouse is a must in many ways, you should never overlook the power and usefulness of the keyboard.

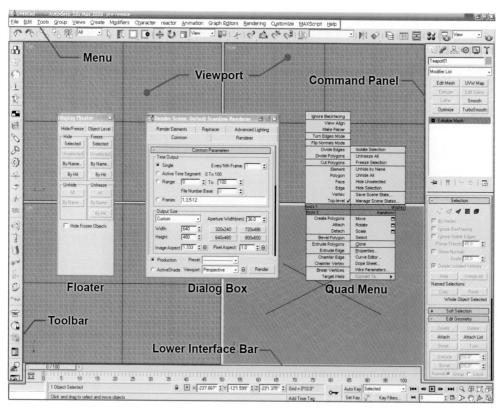

Figure 1-2. The eight main screen interfaces of 3ds Max

Most commands in 3ds Max can be executed with shortcut keystrokes. For example, to change the active viewport from Top view to Left view, simply press L. Keyboard shortcuts make using the keyboard a fast and efficient way of executing commands. If you find yourself using the screen interfaces to execute the same commands over and over again, it would be wise to invest a small amount of time learning the keyboard shortcuts for those commands and try using them for a while to see how beneficial they can be. Refer to Appendix D to see a list of all of the keyboard shortcuts relevant to architectural visualizations. If a shortcut doesn't exist for a particular command, Appendix C will show you how to create your own.

The mouse is also a critical interface through which you work. One feature on a mouse that's an absolute must, as any serious user would agree, is the scroll button (often in the form of a wheel between the left and right buttons). This additional feature allows you to pan and zoom, which are probably the two most frequently used commands in 3ds Max. Without the scroll button, you have to interrupt other commands to execute a zoom or pan.

A scroll button gives you two additional benefits. First, you can easily rotate your view by dragging the mouse while holding the Alt key and the scroll button on your mouse. Second, if you press and hold both Ctrl and Alt, you can zoom in and out of your scene by dragging the mouse up or down.

Menus

Although most commands in 3ds Max can be executed through the use of menus, the time needed to execute this way is much greater than with other interfaces. With the exception of a few tools not found in any other interface, I don't use the menus at all.

Notice the underlined letters in the default menus shown in Figure 1-3. You can use the keyboard to quickly open a menu by holding the Alt key and pressing the key of the letter that's underlined. You can then execute a command by pressing the key for an underlined letter of a submenu command. Holding the cursor over a submenu command that has an arrow to the right of it opens another sub-menu for that command. I dislike menus so much because it takes several keystrokes or precise and slow movements of the mouse to get to the command you want. There are better ways. For this reason, I avoid using menus whenever possible and won't spend time covering them here. Certain features that can only be accessed through the menus, however, will be discussed in the chapters that cover those features.

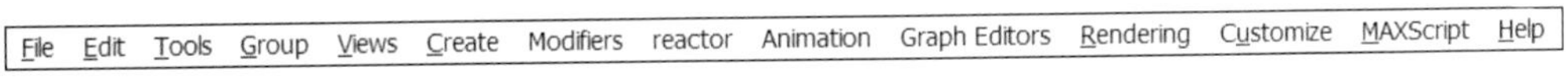

File   Edit   Tools   Group   Views   Create   Modifiers   reactor   Animation   Graph Editors   Rendering   Customize   MAXScript   Help

Figure 1-3. The default 3ds Max menus

Toolbars

Toolbars contain groups of icons that require only a single click of the mouse for command execution. However, with the exception of the **Main** toolbar (shown in Figure 1-4), I avoid using toolbars almost entirely because they simply require more time to use than keyboard shortcuts. Icons require moving the mouse cursor and your eyes away from the object or Command panel feature that you're working with, and making a precise selection over a small area of screen space. I prefer using keyboard shortcuts because I can keep my eyes on the object, and with one hand already resting on the keyboard, I can execute the command in a fraction of the time—without the risk of selecting the wrong command and having to spend time backing out of it when I do. Although the difference in time between the two interfaces may seem insignificant, when you consider that you may execute several thousand commands in one day, it becomes very significant.

Figure 1-4. The Main toolbar

The Command panel

The Command panel, shown in Figure 1-5, is an immense and complex interface with which to execute commands. It features six tabs at its top that you can click to access other panels. Each of these panels contains a vast array of features that sometimes are found only here. The Command panel, like toolbars, can be undocked and redocked—however, undocking results in a partial blockage of the viewports, and for that reason, I don't recommend undocking the Command panel.

Figure 1-5. The Command panel

Viewports

Viewports are the windows through which you can view your creations. By default, 3ds Max loads with a Front, Left, Top, and Perspective viewport. The arrangement of viewports and what you see within them can be easily changed or customized, as you'll learn later in this chapter.

The Lower Interface bar

Along the bottom of 3ds Max is a collection of some of the most important and frequently used controls in 3ds Max (Figure 1-6). These controls include the Time slider and the Track bar, as well as animation playback and viewport navigation controls.

Figure 1-6. The Lower Interface bar

Quad menus

Quad menus are quick-access menus that appear when you right-click within the active viewport. The menus change depending on what type of object (if any) is selected, as well as the cursor location. An example of a quad menu is shown in the right-hand side screenshot of Figure 1-7.

Floaters

Floaters are a type of interface that can remain open anywhere on the screen while you work. They're only available for certain commands, but for those they apply to, the benefit is that they don't take up too much screen space and you can continuously execute the same commands without having to leave other interfaces or open and close dialog boxes. An example of a floater is shown in the left-hand screenshot of Figure 1-7.

Dialog boxes

Many commands in 3ds Max open another type of interface, called a dialog box. Dialog boxes can contain their own menus, toolbars, spinners, or other means of user input. An example of a dialog box is shown in the center screenshot of Figure 1-7.

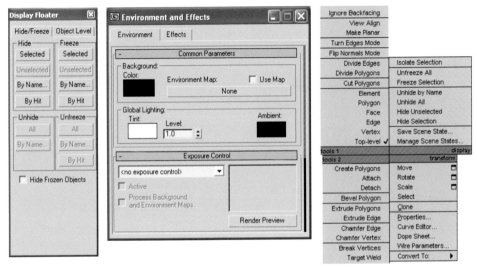

Figure 1-7. From left to right, an example of a floater, dialog box, and quad menu

Using the Command panel

With the exception of the viewports, you'll find that there's no area on the screen where you spend more time than the Command panel. Within the Command panel are six other panels that you access through tabs immediately under the Command panel header. The six tabs are **Create, Modify, Hierarchy, Motion, Display, and Utilities.** Each panel contains areas in which common controls are grouped together in what's called a rollout. To access a rollout's controls, the rollout must first be opened. Some rollouts are by default open, and some are closed. To the left of each rollout is a plus or minus sign—the plus sign indicates that the rollout is closed, and the minus sign indicates that the rollout is open. You can open or close a rollout by clicking on the rollout title. If the entire rollout exceeds the screen space available to the rollout, a small vertical scrollbar will appear to the right of the rollout—you can use this scrollbar to access the part of the rollout that can't be seen. Alternatively, if you move the cursor over an area of the rollout where no controls appear, a hand symbol will appear, which you can click and drag to scroll up or down. You can also click and drag the left edge of the Command panel to expand its width. Doing so can eliminate the need to pan. Like many options, this is a matter of personal preference.

The Create panel

When you click the **Create** panel tab, seven other icons will appear below it, as shown in Figure 1-8. Clicking these icons allows you to add all of the following categories of objects to your scene: **Geometry, Shapes, Lights, Cameras, Helpers, Space Warps, and Systems**. Immediately under the category icons is a subcategory drop-down list. Each subcategory displays an **Object Type** rollout, as well as a **Name and Color** rollout. Different subcategories display different objects available for creation. Immediately under the **Object Type** rollout is the **Name and Color** rollout, which allows you to change the default object name and color.

Figure 1-8. The Create panel

Creating an object

This exercise demonstrates use of the **Create** panel by creating a simple teapot. The teapot is a special object type often used for demonstration purposes.

1. Reset 3ds Max by selecting **Reset** from the **File** menu.

2. In the Command panel, click **Create** ➤ **Geometry** ➤ **Standard Primitives** ➤ **Teapot.**

3. Click and hold the left mouse button and drag anywhere in the Perspective view to place the teapot and increase its radius. Release the mouse button to complete the creation.

The Modify panel

There are several ways to modify an object, the most obvious of which is with the **Modify** panel (see Figure 1-9). When you select an object and click the **Modify** panel tab, the object name appears immediately below. Below the name is the **Modifier** drop-down list. Clicking this list opens all the available modifiers for the selected object. Modifiers are functions that contain parameters and change the appearance or structure of an object. Each type of object has a specific set of modifiers that can be applied. Below the **Modifier** drop-down list is the **Modifier Stack,** which contains the history of all modifiers applied to an object. Once applied, you can change the parameters of the modifier using the controls found in the **Parameters** rollout, located directly below the **Modifier Stack.**

Figure 1-9. The Modify panel

Modifying an object

This exercise demonstrates use of the **Modify** panel by adjusting the teapot's radius parameter and then adding a simple modifier.

1. Continue from the previous exercise or reset 3ds Max and create a teapot of any size in Perspective view.

2. Click the **Modify** tab.

3. With the teapot object still selected, click and hold the up arrow to the right of the **Radius** field to increase the radius of the teapot.

4. Click the **Modifier** drop-down list, scroll down, and select **Spherify** to add the **Spherify** modifier to the teapot. The teapot becomes more spherically shaped

5. Click the **Undo** icon to undo the command and remove the modifier. The Undo icon is the leftmost icon in the Main toolbar and it looks like a counterclockwise arrow.

The Hierarchy panel

The **Hierarchy** panel, shown in Figure 1-10, contains three buttons that give you access to several new rollouts and controls for an object. These buttons are **Pivot, IK** (Inverse Kinematics), and **Link Info**. The **Pivot** button gives you access to an extremely vital set of tools for creating architectural visualizations. The rollouts contain controls that allow you to change the location and orientation of an object's pivot point—the point about which transformations are applied. The **IK** button gives you access to controls that create inverse kinematics, which is a term describing the way motion is inherited up the hierarchy of a linked system of a body of objects, from the extremity objects to the objects closer to the body. The use of IK in architectural visualizations is very limited and the only use I've ever found for it is to simulate the motion of trees swaying in a wind (as such, I won't be covering IK in this book). Finally, the **Link Info** button gives you access to rollouts that contain locks, which simply prevent objects from being transformed (moved, scaled, or rotated) along a specific axis.

Figure 1-10. The Hierarchy panel

Changing an object's pivot point

This exercise demonstrates use of the **Hierarchy** panel by changing an object's pivot point.

1. Continue from the previous exercise (or reset 3ds Max and create a teapot of any size in Perspective view).

2. Select the teapot if it's not already selected.

3. Click the **Hierarchy** tab.

4. From the **Adjust Pivot** rollout, click the **Affect Pivot Only** button.

5. Click the **Center to Object** button. This moves the teapot's pivot point from the bottom of the teapot to the center of the teapot.

The Motion panel

The **Motion** panel, shown in Figure 1-11, simply provides access to tools that control the motion of objects or sub-objects. Within the panel are two buttons, **Parameters** and **Trajectories**. The **Parameters** button opens rollouts that allow you to assign controllers that affect the translation of objects in preset ways, or assign constraints that limit the translation in certain ways. The **Trajectories** button opens a single rollout that gives you access to parameters that govern animation paths. If this sounds confusing, don't worry, it can be—and we won't cover that until Chapter 12.

Figure 1-11. The Motion panel

The Display panel

The **Display** panel (shown in Figure 1-12) is perhaps the simplest and most straightforward of the six panels that make up the Command panel. This panel controls how objects are displayed within the viewports. You can change the display of individual objects or change the display of all objects at once. Clicking the **Display** panel takes you to six rollouts. The two that you'll most often use are the **Hide** and **Freeze** rollouts.

I'd also like to make brief mention of the **Display** floater, which is a handy feature (found in the **Tools** menu) that contains most of the same features found in the **Display** panel. It should be no surprise that the only things you see when you first open the **Display** floater are the **Hide** and **Freeze** features, which, as mentioned, you'll be using often. Good use of the **Hide** and **Freeze** features are essential for efficient work in 3ds Max.

Figure 1-12. The Display panel

Changing the display of an object

This exercise demonstrates use of the **Display** panel by hiding all scene geometry, including the simple teapot.

1. Continue from the previous exercise or reset 3ds Max and create a teapot of any size in Perspective view.

2. Click the **Display** tab.

3. In the **Hide by Category** rollout, click the **Geometry** option. All of the geometry in the scene will be hidden from view, including the teapot.

4. In the **Hide by Category** rollout, click the **Geometry** option again. The teapot will reappear.

5. In the **Hide** rollout, click the **Hide Unselected** button. All unselected objects will be hidden from view.

6. In the **Hide** rollout, click the **Unhide All** button. All scene objects will be unhidden and once again visible.

The Utilities panel

The **Utilities** panel (shown in Figure 1-13) is the last of the six that make up the Command panel. It contains a large assortment of utilities that do many different things. If you ever add a plug-in to 3ds Max, access to that plug-in might only be found by clicking the **More** button, which opens a dialog box with many other utilities. With the exception of specific plug-ins that I have installed, the only utility I've found useful on a regular basis is the **Asset Browser,** an extremely useful tool that allows you to scan your computer or the Internet for files. A couple of others tools will be discussed later, but for now, the **Asset Browser** is the only one you should concern yourself with. Almost all others require extensive knowledge of the program and only do very specific tasks that simply aren't needed in architectural visualizations.

Figure 1-13. The Utilities panel

The **Asset Browser** opens to a display much like Windows Explorer; however, the **Asset Browser** has many more features. It can display thumbnails of many file types related to graphics, such as files with the .tga extension. The **Asset Browser** also allows you to filter and display specific file types and choose from three different thumbnail sizes to display file content. You can double-click an image file to display it at full size, drag-and-drop files into your 3ds Max scene, and explore online content with many of the same types of buttons that you would find within Windows Explorer.

As you'll soon start to realize, there's an enormous portion of 3ds Max that you don't need to spend time learning if you're working strictly on architectural visualizations.

Using the Asset Browser

This exercise demonstrates use of the **Utilities** panel by utilizing the **Asset Browser** feature.

1. Reset 3ds Max.
2. Click the **Utilities** tab.
3. Click the **Asset Browser** button.
4. After a few seconds, a message will appear; when you see it, click **OK.**
5. Explore the directories within your computer to view thumbnails of your files.
6. Select **File ➤ Exit** from the **Asset Browser** menu to close the **Asset Browser.**

Using the viewports

There's no other place in 3ds Max where you'll spend more time than in the viewports. Viewports are the windows to your 3D world, through which all your work is performed. The importance of learning efficient use of viewports can't be overemphasized. Like all interface elements in 3ds Max, viewports have numerous settings that allow for customization; however, this section will focus on the fundamentals of viewport usage. You can refer to Appendix C at any time to learn how to customize the 3ds Max interface.

If you find learning a 2D CAD program difficult, then you'll probably find learning a 3D CAD program impossible. Adding that third dimension changes everything, and weeds out many 2D users who aren't up to the challenge of conceptualizing their creations in a third dimension. Most 2D CAD users operate through only one viewport, but in 3ds Max that's not even an option. Luckily, 3ds Max has developed a highly effective viewport interface that enables you to view your creations from four different perspectives at the same time. This section will show you how to work in viewports in ways that will maximize your efficiency in manipulating your creations.

Perspective and axonometric views

All viewports in 3ds Max show one of two types of views, perspective or axonometric. **Perspective views** mimic how your eyes perceive the real world, in which objects in the distance converge to a single point (as shown in the top pane of Figure 1-14). **Axonometric views** show objects from an infinitely distant perspective so that an object's parallel lines remain parallel regardless of the distance from the observer (see the bottom pane of Figure 1-14). In a perspective view, for example, a street that an observer stands on would vanish in the distance with both sides of the street converging to a single point, whereas in an axonometric view, both sides would remain parallel all the way to the horizon. In 3ds Max, the only perspective views are the Perspective, Camera, and Target Light views. All others, including the default views of Top, Left, and Front, are axonometric views.

Figure 1-14. Perspective view (top) and axonometric view (bottom)

Learning the viewports

The default viewport layout shows four viewports, with the currently active viewport marked with a yellow border. In the top-left corner of each viewport is the viewport type, which you can right-click to bring up a menu, as shown in Figure 1-15. You can change the viewport type by selecting **Views** from this menu and selecting the view type from the flyout menu that appears.

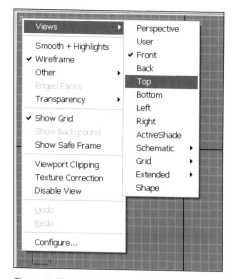

Figure 1-15. Viewport types

Several viewport types have shortcut keys that can be used to change the current viewport to a desired viewport type. These include **T** (Top view), **B** (Bottom view), **F** (Front view), **L** (Left view), **P** (Perspective view), and **U** (User view). Notice that when a Target Light or Camera is present in a scene, you can change a viewport to show the view from the perspective of either. The shortcut for Target Light view is **$** (Shift+4), and the shortcut for Camera view is **C**.

Another way to change the viewport type is by selecting one of the viewport navigation controls, such as **Arc Rotate or Pan**. Using these tools will automatically change, for example, a Front view into a User view. User views are axonometric views that aren't constrained to a single axis and can show the scene from any location—but unlike perspective views, all parallel lines remain parallel.

Changing views within a viewport

This exercise demonstrates how to change the view of a viewport to some of the most commonly used view types.

1. Reset 3ds Max and create a teapot of any size in Perspective view.
2. Within any viewport, type "**T**" to change to Top view.
3. Type "**L**" to change to Left view.
4. Type "**U**" to change to User view.
5. Type "**P**" to change to Perspective view.
6. Right-click any viewport name and select **Views** ➤ **Front** from the drop-down menu to change the viewport to Front view.

Zooming, panning, and rotating in a viewport

You'll probably spend a significant amount of time changing your perspective within a viewport to get a better look at an object. The three methods available to do so are zooming, panning, and rotating your view. Table 1-1 lists and describes each of the different icons on the Lower Interface bar that allow you to zoom, pan, and rotate. If you use these three tools as often as I do, it would be wise to perfect their use.

Table 1-1. Viewport navigation controls

Icon	Name	Description
	Zoom (Alt+Z)	Zooms in and out of a viewport
	Zoom All	Zooms in and out of all viewports at the same time
	Zoom Extents (Ctrl+Alt+Z)	Zooms to the extents of all objects in the scene
	Zoom Extents Selected	Zooms to the extents of a selected object
	Zoom Extents All (Ctrl+Shift+Z)	Zooms all viewports to the extents of all objects

Continued

Table 1-1. Viewport navigation controls *(Continued)*

Icon	Name	Description
	Zoom Extents All Selected	Zooms all viewports to the extents of the selected object
	Region Zoom (Ctrl+W)	Zooms to a specific area that's selected by dragging the mouse
	Pan (Ctrl+P)	Pans within a viewport when the mouse is dragged
	Walk Through	Lets you move through a viewport by pressing a set of shortcut keys, including the arrow keys (similar to navigating in many 3D video games)
	Field of View	Changes the width of a Perspective or Camera view
	Arc Rotate (Ctrl+R)	Rotates the view around the world origin
	Arc Rotate Selected	Rotates the view around a selected object
	Arc Rotate SubObject	Rotates the view around a selected sub-object
	Maximize Viewport Toggle (Alt+W)	Toggles between one maximized viewport and four smaller viewports

Although there are keyboard shortcuts that allow you to zoom, pan, and rotate within a viewport, and I am an outspoken advocate of keyboard shortcuts, I would be doing you an injustice to endorse keyboard shortcuts in this particular instance. By far, the most effective way to move around inside a viewport is with the use of a mouse scroll button that has zoom, pan, and rotate capabilities. With such a mouse, zooming in and out of a view can be accomplished by simply scrolling the mouse wheel up or down. Alternatively, you can zoom in and out by dragging the mouse while pressing and holding its scroll button and the Alt and Ctrl keys on the keyboard. Panning is accomplished by simply dragging with the mouse while holding down its scroll button. Rotating is accomplished by dragging the mouse while holding its scroll button and the Alt key. If the scroll wheel on your mouse isn't working, check the settings in the **Viewports** panel in the **Preference Settings** menu.

Let's examine the viewport navigation icons a little more closely, because you may find that while there are some you may never use, there are some you can't live without. You can refer to Table 1-1 as you read. First, as I mentioned, I recommend avoiding the **Zoom** and **Pan** icons altogether, but they're there if you desire to use them. The very bottom-right icon, the **Min/Max** toggle, makes the active viewport larger (it takes up the space of all viewports combined), thus giving you an enlarged view of the active viewport.

To the left of the **Min/Max** toggle is the **Arc Rotate** icon. If you click and hold this icon, you're presented with two other flyout icons: **Arc Rotate Selected** and **Arc Rotate SubObject**. **Arc Rotate Selected** rotates about the pivot point of any object or objects selected. **Arc Rotate SubObject** allows you to rotate about an individually selected sub-object, such as a vertex or a multiple selection of sub-objects. When either of these icons is selected, a rotation guide appears in the active viewport.

This guide looks like a circle with a square located at each quadrant. Clicking either the left or right squares rotates the view from side to side, while clicking either the top or bottom squares rotates the view up or down. Clicking inside this circle allows you to rotate about a point without tilting or banking the view from side to side. Clicking outside the circle allows you to rotate about a point while simultaneously causing the view to tilt or bank; however, tilting your view is usually unwanted in the visualization industry, and you should be careful not to tilt your view accidentally.

To the left of the **Pan** icon is the **Region Zoom** icon, which allows you to zoom in to a specific area by dragging the cursor over the region of the viewport that you want to zoom in to. When a viewport is in Perspective mode, this icon has a flyout icon called the **Field of View** icon. The **Field of View** icon lets you change the width of a view much like changing the lens of a camera. Unlike the **Zoom** feature, increasing or decreasing the field of view distorts the perspective, just as a wide angle or telescopic lens does.

The very top-right icon is the **Zoom Extents All** icon, which zooms all viewports to the extents of all visible objects in the scene until the objects fill each viewport to its entirety. This icon has a flyout, the **Zoom Extents All Selected** icon, which zooms all viewports to the extents of all selected objects.

To the left of the **Zoom Extents All** icon is the **Zoom Extents** icon, which zooms to the extents of all visible objects in the active viewport. This icon also has a flyout icon, the **Zoom Extents Selected** icon, which zooms to the extents of all selected objects in the active viewport.

To the left of this icon is the **Zoom All** icon, which simply zooms in to or out of all the viewports simultaneously, which is achieved by dragging the cursor in any of the viewports.

Navigating within a viewport

This exercise demonstrates how to use some of the important viewport navigation tools.

1. Reset 3ds Max and create a teapot of any size in Perspective view.

2. In the Lower Interface bar, click and hold the **Arc Rotate** icon, and select **Arc Rotate Selected** from the flyout menu.

3. Click and drag inside the rotation guide that appears in the active viewport. The view should rotate around the selected teapot.

4. Right-click inside any viewport to end the command. To reinitiate the command, you can use the keyboard shortcut Ctrl+R.

5. Click the **Min/Max Toggle** icon (Alt+W) to change views from four small viewports to one large one.

6. Click the **Zoom Extents** icon (Ctrl+Alt+Z) to zoom to the extents of all objects in your scene.

Grids

When 3ds Max opens to its default views, a grid appears in each viewport. The grid is simply a guide to help you establish your bearing in the viewports. Grids consist of lines that represent increments of space. You can change the lines within a grid to appear closer together or farther apart, and you can change the value that each increment represents. This book, however, won't cover this form of customization, as it's not crucial to the content of the book. I usually find myself disabling this feature before I even start a project, as it appears to clutter the viewport more than it benefits me to keep it active. You can disable the grid in the active viewport by pressing G.

Viewport refreshing and disabling

When you work in a program like 3ds Max, it's easy to build scenes that quickly get out of control in terms of file size and scene complexity. Although it's optimal to work in a way in which you don't have to wait on the computer to crunch the numbers, this is not always possible. Fortunately, 3ds Max gives you several ways of displaying objects in viewports that lessen the graphical burden on the computer. Each of these ways changes how quickly objects can be regenerated or refreshed in a viewport, which translates into how long you must wait to see the changes.

By default, all viewports in 3ds Max are **active.** (Don't confuse this word with the same term that describes which viewport is current, though.) When you make a change to your scene, every viewport that displays the part of the scene that gets changed has to be updated. Some changes are small and don't burden the computer. Other changes can take several seconds to refresh in each viewport. You can disable a viewport to prevent such updates by pressing D. You can also right-click the viewport name and select **Disable** from the pop-up menu.

Another setting that you can change to increase the viewport update speed is the **Update During Spinner Drag** option from the **View** menu. Spinners are the up and down arrows that appear next to an object's parameters. Every time you drag on a spinner to change an object's parameter values, each viewport that displays the object is updated. For complex objects, changing a spinner rapidly can cause even a powerful computer to crash. By disabling this option, you force the viewports to wait for the spinner to stop changing before updating the display.

Rendering levels

Another way to speed up viewport refresh rates is to reduce the rendering levels. Rendering levels describe the level of detail and display provided by a view. Several rendering level choices are available for each viewport, as shown in Figure 1-16, but I've found that there are only three I typically need to use: **Smooth + Highlights, Wireframe, and Bounding Box. Smooth + Highlights** is the highest-quality viewport display—it shows smooth surfaces with all lighting highlights. This rendering level takes the longest to regenerate. The second level that I use is **Wireframe,** which shows polygon edges only, and is somewhat quicker to regenerate. Lastly, the **Bounding Box** level, which is the quickest to regenerate, just shows a box in place of the object whose extents would completely enclose the object.

By default, 3ds Max opens with four viewports, three of which have a **Wireframe** rendering level. The fourth viewport, which displays the Perspective view, is displayed in **Smooth + Highlights** mode. Good management of rendering levels is critical for working efficiently in large scenes, and can prevent you from having to wait long periods of time for viewport regenerations.

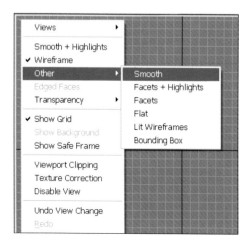

Figure 1-16. Rendering levels

I'll rarely have more than one viewport showing a **Smooth + Highlights** level, and that's usually the one displaying the Perspective or User view. As I develop very large scenes, I try to view as many objects as I can with the **Bounding Box** level. You'll probably find it rare to get any benefit out of turning the rendering level for an entire viewport to **Bounding Box** because you won't be able to recognize which objects are which (and you might even have trouble remembering which way is up). A much better use of the **Bounding Box** option is to view select *objects* in **Bounding Box** mode. These objects should be the most complex objects in your scene, and should remove a substantial burden from your graphics card. They should also be objects that you won't have to manipulate regularly. As I said, other levels are available for your use, but their benefit in architectural visualizations is questionable. Knowing when and how to use the three levels mentioned here will suffice.

Changing a viewport's rendering level

This exercise demonstrates how to change a viewport's rendering level to enhance object visibility within a scene. It also demonstrates the importance of rendering level management in maintaining acceptable viewport regeneration time.

1. Reset 3ds Max.

2. In the Perspective viewport, create a teapot.

3. Place the cursor over the Perspective viewport, click and drag using the mouse's scroll button, and pan around the viewport. With only one object in the scene, containing only a small number of faces, panning should be very smooth.

4. Click the **Modify** tab and change the segments to a maximum possible value of **64.**

5. In the Perspective viewport, create 5 more similar teapots, each with 64 segments. After the first teapot is changed to 64 segments, each successive teapot will be made with 64 segments automatically.

6. Pan around the Perspective viewport again. Panning should now be very choppy in a shaded viewport with this many faces visible.

7. Right-click the Perspective viewport name and select **Other ➤ Bounding Box** from the drop-down list.

8. Pan around the Perspective viewport one more time. Panning should now be smooth again because 3ds Max doesn't have to work hard to regenerate the viewport.

Enabling Fast View

Another way of achieving quicker viewport refreshing is to enable the Fast View option. I've made a point to avoid highlighting too many configuration options in this book, but this is one configuration feature that's too valuable to pass up. This option speeds up refreshing by displaying only a fraction of the faces in a scene. To enable this option, right-click the viewport name (or select the **Customize** menu) and select **Viewport Configuration**. Within the **Rendering Options** section of the **Rendering Method** tab, select **Fast View Nth Faces** and set its value to **5,** as shown in Figure 1-17. To change all the viewports in the same way, select the **All Viewports** option from the **Apply To** section of the same tab.

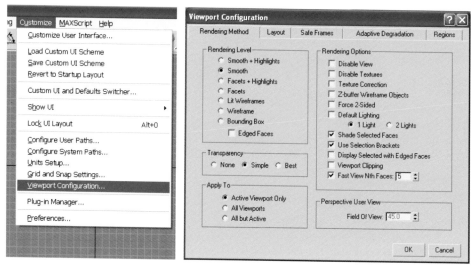

Figure 1-17. Enabling Fast View

Enabling Fast View within a viewport

This exercise demonstrates how to enable Fast View within a viewport to speed up viewport regenerations.

1. Continue from the previous exercise.

2. Right-click the Perspective viewport name and select **Wireframe** from the drop-down list.

3. Pan around the Perspective viewport. Even though the viewport is in **Wireframe** mode, panning should be choppy with such a large number of faces displayed.

4. Right-click the Perspective viewport again and select **Configure** from the drop-down list. The **Viewport Configuration** dialog box will open to the **Rendering Method** tab.

5. In the Rendering Options section, enable the Fast View Nth Faces option.

6. Click **OK** to close the **Viewport Configuration** dialog box. Now, only every fifth face will be visible inside the Perspective viewport.

7. Pan around the Perspective viewport one more time. Panning should now be smooth again because 3ds Max doesn't have to work as hard to regenerate just one-fifth of the previous number of faces.

The viewport layouts

At times you may decide you want to change the number or arrangement of your viewports, or you may want to quickly change their size or aspect ratio. The default layout displays four equally sized viewports, which can easily be changed by right-clicking the viewport name, clicking **Viewport Config-uration** from the menu, and selecting **Layout**. Choose from any of the available layouts (as shown in Figure 1-18). An even easier way to change the size or arrangement of your viewports is to click at the intersection of two viewports and drag the edge to a new location. You can return to the original layout by right-clicking any of the viewport borders and selecting **Reset Layout** from the pop-up menu.

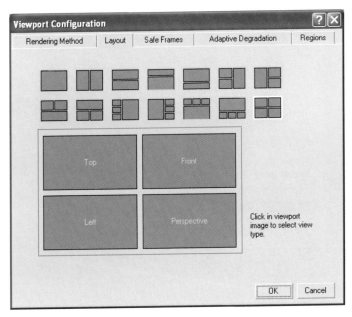

Figure 1-18. The viewport layouts

Changing the viewport layout

This exercise demonstrates how to change the viewport layout to suit your particular needs.

1. Reset 3ds Max.

2. Right-click the Perspective viewport name and select **Configure** from the drop-down list.

3. Select the **Layout** tab.

4. Select any of the 14 different viewport layout options and click **OK.** The viewport will change to match the option you selected.

5. Place your cursor over the border of any two viewports. Arrows will appear.

6. Click and drag any viewport border to resize any two viewports. You can also click and drag the border of any three or four viewports at one time.

7. Place your cursor over the border of any two viewports and right-click.

8. Select **Reset Layout** to reset the layout to the default 3ds Max layout.

Undoing and saving view changes

In the course of a project, you're bound to make several inadvertent changes to a viewport's display. When this happens, you can simply undo the view change by pressing **Shift+Z** or right-clicking the viewport name and selecting **Undo View Change** from the bottom of the pop-up menu, as shown in Figure 1-19. The menu will display the actual view type that can be changed. In the example in Figure 1-19, the user can undo the view rotate feature just implemented.

You can also save a specific view in any viewport by selecting **Save Active Viewport** from the **Views** menu. To restore this view later, select **Restore Active Viewport.** I don't find much use in this feature, however, because only one view can be saved per viewport.

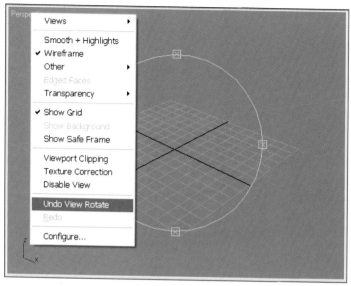

Figure 1-19. The Undo View Change command

Summary

By now you should know that 3ds Max is simply too large a program to learn comprehensively and that it's wise to focus on those features that are relevant to your industry. An underlying theme of this book is to teach you what you need to learn to be productive in an architectural visualization firm and avoid learning too many features that serve no purpose or function. Although I have always strived to learn as many new features as I can, my first priority has always been to perfect the tools that truly pay off in a production environment.

This chapter has covered the basics of navigating the 3ds Max interface, with a strong emphasis on efficient viewport navigation and keyboard shortcuts. Hopefully, you're ready to take the next step— working with objects!

CHAPTER 2

Working with Objects

NOW THAT YOU UNDERSTAND THE basics of the 3ds Max interface, it's time to learn how to work with objects in a scene. The concepts discussed in this chapter are critical because they represent the most common tasks that most 3ds Max users will perform: selecting objects, displaying objects, and transforming objects. There are numerous tools available and a seemingly infinite number of ways to accomplish the same task in 3ds Max. However, no task can be performed without utilizing the concepts covered in this chapter. Efficient use of the select, display, and transform features can save you countless hours over the course of any architectural visualization.

Selecting objects

Selecting objects in your scene is one of the most common and repeated tasks you will perform in 3ds Max. It would make sense, therefore, to ensure that the method you use to select an object is efficient and time-effective. Fortunately, 3ds Max gives you several different ways to select objects.

The Select icons

The easiest way to select an object is by simply clicking the object in one of the view-ports. You can do so with any of four different select icons found on the **Main** toolbar and shown in Table 2-1. If you are in the middle of a command, pressing Esc once or twice or clicking the right mouse icon in the active viewport will end the command and return you to whatever select mode was last active.

Table 2-1. The Select icons

Icon	Name	Keyboard Shortcut
	Select Object	Q
	Select and Move	W
	Select and Rotate	E
	Select and Scale	R

The first icon, which looks like an arrow, is the **Select Object** icon, which can be enabled by pressing Q. This is the only icon of the four that does not allow you to perform a transform with the same click of the mouse used to select the object. The importance of this cannot be overemphasized. The reason it is so important, as you will probably learn many times the hard way, is that it is very easy to inadvertently transform an object when all you intend to do is select the object. In some instances, you may not notice it until it's too late. The undo feature in 3ds Max recycles itself after every 20 commands or actions performed. If the 20th action you performed is an accidental select-andmove command, you won't be able to undo the mistake because the undo queue will be erased and all previous actions will be unavailable for undo. The consequences of this could be very time-consuming to fix. One technique that I recommend when continuously selecting objects without applying a transform is to activate the **Select Object** icon so that you cannot transform an object accidentally. If anything other than the **Select Object** icon is active, you cannot rush the selection of an object without eventually getting burned.

When you do select an object, the selected object turns white and is enclosed in what are called selection brackets. The transform gizmo also appears at the object's pivot point. You can deselect an object by simply clicking anywhere in a viewport where there's not an object.

As a scene becomes crowded, it may become difficult to select the object you want. If two objects lie on top of each other from the perspective of the viewport you're selecting in, clicking the object that's already selected will cause it to be deselected and the other object selected. With many objects lying on top of one another, it may take several clicks of the mouse before you select the object you want.

The Select From Scene dialog box

When you need to select one or more objects in your scene, and you can not easily do so by clicking on the object(s) inside a viewport, the next best option is to use the **Select From Scene** dialog box, shown in Figure 2-1.

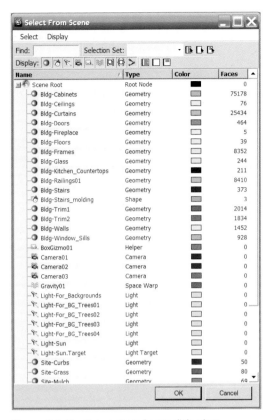

Figure 2-1. The Select From Scene dialog box

This dialog box can be accessed by clicking the **Select By Name** icon (Figure 2-2) on the main toolbar, or by pressing the keyboard shortcut **H**.

Figure 2-2. The Select From Scene dialog box

This dialog box is a read-only version of the more sophisticated **Scene Explorer** feature (Figure 2-4), which is a fantastic feature new to 3ds Max 2008. The Select From Scene dialog box provides a quick and easy way to select objects from a list of all the currently unhidden and unfrozen objects. When opened, no other work in 3ds Max is allowed until the dialog box is closed.

The **Select From Scene** dialog box contains icons along the top that allow you to turn on and off the display of objects in the list according to their object type. For example, if you want to turn off the display of all the lights in the list, simply click on the light icon. All object types are checked by default and therefore displayed in the name list.

To highlight an object, simply click the name of the object. To select multiple objects hold down Ctrl and click on multiple object names. Holding down Shift allows you to select every object that lies between two objects that you select. Double-clicking any object name closes the dialog box and selects that object.

Above the display icons is a search field in which you can type to help locate objects of a particular name. As you type, all of the objects with names that begin with the same letters that you type are highlighted in the name list. For example, if you type the letter **w** in the list, all objects with names that begin with **w** will be highlighted. If you add the letter **a**, then an object with the name **Wall** will remain highlighted, while an object with the name **Window** will no longer be highlighted.

Two wildcard characters can be used within the field to help locate and select objects. The wildcard character ***** can be used to replace multiple characters, and the character **?** can be used to replace a single character. If you type **Wa***, all objects that begin with **Wa** (such as **Wall** and **Water**) will be highlighted, while objects such as **Window** and **Willow** will not. If you type **?all,** all four-letter object names in which last three letters are **all** will be selected (e.g., **Wall** and **Ball**).

It should be noted that while wildcards are effective for locating objects, you should strive to avoid being in a position that warrants using them. By maintaining a good naming system, you'll save a great deal of time when trying to find objects in large scenes. A good naming system is like a seatbelt—it takes about the same amount of time and can save you a lot of grief. Wildcards are something that I rarely use, as I spend more of my time naming my objects in a way that makes them easy to find and select.

Within the dialog box you have numerous columns that display characteristics of each object, such as color and face count. This is good information, but if you right-click any of the column headers, you are presented with a menu that contains a feature called **Column Chooser**, shown in Figure 2-3, which allows you to display many more columns and much more information about each object. When the Column Chooser is open, simply drag the new column type into the header area where you want the new column to be displayed. By clicking on the header of any column, you can sort all of the objects in the dialog box in ascending or descending order of any particular object characteristic listed.

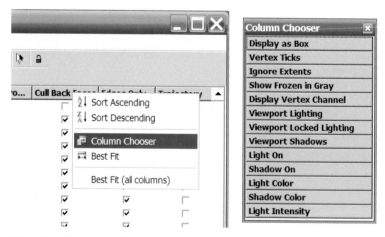

Figure 2-3. The Column Chooser

An additional feature within 3ds Max that will be discussed later in this chapter is selection sets, which allows you to name a selection of multiple objects and then quickly recall that selection at any time by selecting the name from the list here in the Select From Scene dialog box or from the Main toolbar. Again, this feature will be discussed shortly.

As a final note about the information in this dialog box, I find the **Faces** column particularly useful. Good scene management is critical to efficient workflow and I like being able to keep an eye on the face count of objects in a scene so that I can better manage the display of objects and see which objects might need further optimization.

Selecting an object by name

This exercise demonstrates the use of the Select From Scene feature.

1. Reset 3ds Max.
2. Create two spheres, two boxes, and two teapots in any viewport.
3. Click the **Select by Name** icon in the **Main** toolbar, or press **H**, to open the **Select From Scene** dialog box (shown in the following image).

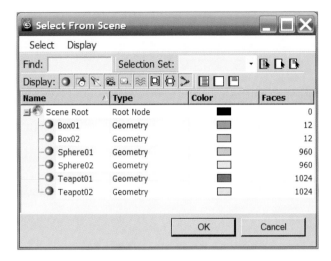

4. In the empty field to the right of **Find**, type **S**. All the object names that begin with the letter **S** are highlighted.
5. Click **OK** to complete the selection of the two sphere objects.
6. Open the dialog box again and click the **Geometry** icon. All the **Geometry**-type objects in your scene will disappear from the name list.
7. Reselect the **Geometry** option.
8. Click the column header labeled **Name** to list the objects alphabetically by name.
9. Highlight **Box01,** hold the **Shift** key, and select the **Sphere02** object. The objects between the two names you selected should now be highlighted.
10. Click **Cancel** to end the command.

Scene Explorer

With the release of 3ds Max 2008, Autodesk presents us with a great new feature called the **Scene Explorer**, shown in Figure 2-4. This feature is a modeless and editable version of the Select From Scene dialog box and provides users with a new way to control the selecting and displaying of objects. Because it's modeless, the Scene Explorer can remain open at all times while you work in other interfaces and because it's editable, you can change numerous different qualities about an object or even a group of objects all at the same time.

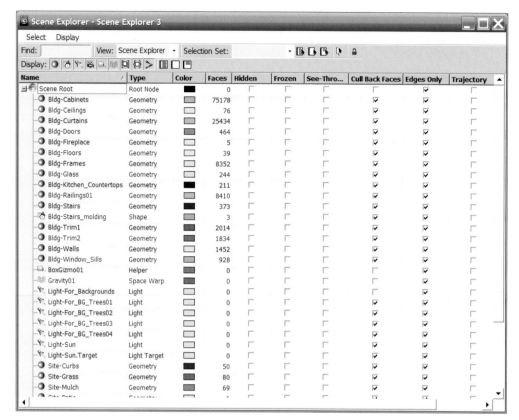

Figure 2-4. The Scene Explorer dialog box

This feature can be accessed through the **Tools** menu or by pressing the keyboard shortcut, **Alt+Ctrl+O**. You can create and maintain numerous different scene explorer windows, though I don't personally find any need to have more than one version of this feature used in a scene.

Because the Scene Explorer can take up so much screen real estate, it's best used when you have a second monitor with which to work. If you don't have a 2nd monitor, you might be better off using other features to do the things that you can do within the Scene Explorer, especially when you consider that this kind of feature becomes more practical as your scenes grow in size, which means more objects taking up more real estate. Nonetheless, it is a powerful and well designed feature that offers you an alternative way of controlling the selection and display of objects.

Select by region

Besides clicking objects directly, you have the option of creating windows with which to define a region of selection. There are two types of window selections: window and crossing. The icon that allows you to toggle between these two options is called the **Window/Crossing** icon (see Figure 2-5); this icon is located on the **Main** toolbar to the left of the **Select and Move** icon.

Figure 2-5. The Window (left) and Crossing (right) selections of the Window/Crossing icon

To make a selection, simply click anywhere in the active viewport away from the object or objects you want to select, drag the mouse, and click somewhere else away from the object(s), so that the drag outline created with the mouse movement either intersects or completely encloses your selection. After the second click of the mouse, the objects will be selected. When the **Window/Crossing** icon is toggled to the **Window** selection option, all objects must be completely enclosed within the selection outline for them to be selected. When toggled to the **Crossing** selection option, an object is selected when any portion of the selection outline touches the object. Let's look at the difference in action.

Notice that in the left image of Figure 2-6, a selection is made that partially encompasses the chair and foot rest. Since the **Window/Crossing** icon is toggled to **Crossing,** both objects become selected, as shown in the image on the right.

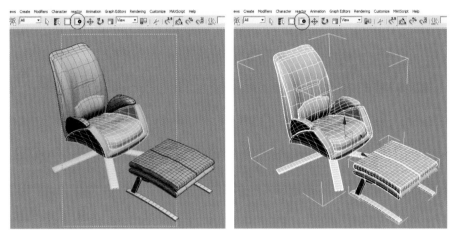

Figure 2-6. A crossing selection

Notice in the images in Figure 2-7 that the **Window/Crossing** icon is toggled to **Window.** This time, the selection outline in the image on the left completely encompasses the chair and partially crosses the foot rest. Since the **Window/Crossing** icon is toggled to **Window,** only the chair becomes selected, as shown in the image on the right.

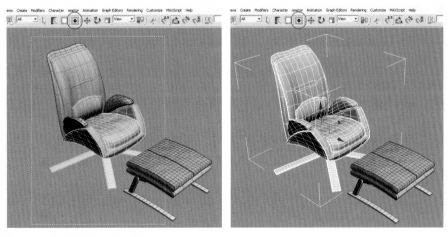

Figure 2-7. A window selection

To the left of the **Window/Crossing** icon is the **Selection Region** icon. This icon is a flyout menu that contains four other shape selection icons that can be used to create other shapes to define selection regions. Figure 2-8 shows the five available shapes. The first icon on the top, **Rectangular Selection Region,** uses a rectangle to define the selection region, and involves two clicks of the mouse—one for each corner of the rectangle. The next icon, **Circular Selection Region,** creates a circular selection region that grows from the center outward. The third icon, **Fence Selection Region,** lets you draw a shape of any kind with multiple clicks of the mouse that define the corners of the shape. The fourth icon, **Lasso Selection Region,** lets you draw a selection region freehand. The last icon, **Paint Selection Region,** lets you select objects by placing the cursor over an object.

Figure 2-8. The Selection Region flyout menu

You can cycle through the five available **Selection Region** icons by pressing Q repeatedly.

In addition to the select-by-region method, you can select many objects at a time by holding Ctrl while clicking all the objects you want individually, or by using the Select By Region feature to add objects to your current selection. To deselect objects individually, hold Alt and select the objects. You can also use the select-by-region method while holding Alt to deselect multiple objects.

Selecting an object by region

This exercise demonstrates use of the Selection Region command to select objects in your scene.

1. Continue from the previous exercise or reset 3ds Max and create two spheres, two boxes, and two teapots in any viewport.

2. Toggle the **Window/Crossing** icon to **Window.** The **Window/Crossing** icon will turn yellow.

3. Click the **Rectangular Selection Region** icon (shown at the top of Figure 2-8).

4. Select either teapot object in your scene by clicking and dragging around the entire object in any viewport.

5. Hold **Ctrl** and select the other teapot object to add it to the current selection.

6. Hold **Alt** and select either teapot object to remove it from the current selection. You can also hold Ctrl again to remove an object when you select it.

Selection filters

The **Selection Filter,** shown in Figure 2-9, is a great feature you can use to specify which object types are selectable. If you have a complex scene with hundreds of objects of various types, and all you want to do is modify the lights without hiding all other objects, then applying a filter would be helpful. With a **Light** object selection filter applied, no other object type can be selected, and you can work with the light objects without worrying about inadvertently selecting a different object type.

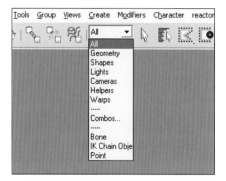

Figure 2-9. The Selection Filter

To enable the **Selection Filter,** select the desired object type from the drop-down list.

Named selection sets

Selecting objects in your scene can be very time-consuming, especially when your scene becomes large and cluttered. If you spend any significant amount of time selecting a group of objects to work on in some way, and you know you're going to need to select the same group of objects again for some other modification, then creating selection sets can save a great deal of time. With just two clicks of the mouse, you can bring back that previously saved selection that took much longer to create the first time. To use the **Named Selection Sets** dialog box (shown in Figure 2-11), click the **Edit Named Selection Sets** icon located on the **Main** toolbar (shown in Figure 2-10).

 Figure 2-10. The Edit Named Selection Sets icon

The Create New Set icon at the top-left of the dialog box creates a new set that you can name and add objects to or subtract objects from, using the icons that resemble a plus and minus sign. The Select Objects in Set icon (third from the right) selects within the dialog and within the scene all of the objects in that set. The Select From Scene dialog box is also available from here. The Highlight Selected Objects icon (far right) highlights within the dialog box all of the objects that are currently highlighted within the scene. You can drag and drop objects from one set to another. You can also drag one set name onto another to combine all of the objects of both sets into the second set name. Double-clicking a set name selects all of the objects within that set. Sub-object selection sets can also be made and selected, but only when in sub-object mode. Sub-object mode is covered in greater detail in Chapter 3.

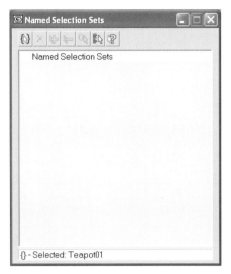

Figure 2-11. The Named Selection Sets dialog box

An easier way to create a selection set after selecting the objects to include is to type the name of the new set inside the **Named Selection Sets** drop-down list next to the **Edit Named Selection Sets** icon, as shown in Figure 2-12. To recall a selection, click the same drop-down list and select the name.

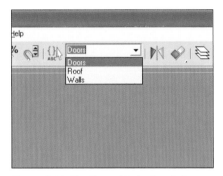

Figure 2-12. The Named Selection Sets
drop-down list

Named selection sets highlight the point that I made earlier in the chapter—that you should take whatever time necessary to name the objects in your scene in a way that makes them easy to find and select later on. If you work with others on the same project, this becomes even more important. Someone unfamiliar with your scene can find it extremely difficult to select objects when all the objects are left with the original names, such as **Sphere01, Sphere02, Cylinder01,** and so on. It becomes very frustrating, for example, to work in a scene with fifty doors that were created as copies of a box and still have the default names **Box01, Box02, Box03 . . . Box50.**

Using named selection sets

This exercise demonstrates use of named selection sets with the **Named Selection Sets** dialog box and the **Named Selection Sets** drop-down list.

1. Continue from the previous exercise or reset 3ds Max and create two spheres, two boxes, and two teapots in any viewport.

2. Deselect all the objects in your scene.

3. Select the two teapots in your scene.

4. Click the **Edit Named Selection Sets** icon (shown in Figure 2-10). The **Named Selection Sets** dialog box will open.

5. Click the **Create New Set** icon.

6. Type the name **Teapots** in the field that appears.

7. In any viewport, select one of the sphere objects.

8. In the **Named Selection Sets** dialog box, click the **Add Selected Objects** icon (shown in the following image). The sphere will be added to the named selection set you just created.

9. In the **Named Selection Sets** dialog box, click the **Subtract Selected Objects** icon (shown in the following image). The sphere will be subtracted from named selection set.

10. Close the **Named Selection Sets** dialog box.

11. Deselect all the objects in your scene.

12. Click the down arrow on the **Named Selection Sets** drop-down list, as shown in Figure 2-12. All the named selection sets you created will be displayed.

13. Select the set called **Teapots.** The two teapot objects in your scene will become selected.

Selection lock

A handy feature that lets you quickly lock your selection is the **Selection Lock** toggle icon, shown in Figure 2-13. When this feature is enabled, the current selection cannot be changed. You cannot add objects to or remove objects from the selection no matter where you click. This feature is enabled by clicking the **Selection Lock** toggle icon, an icon that looks like a lock and is located on the Status bar in the Lower Interface bar. You can also use the method I prefer: pressing the space bar. When the feature is enabled, the **Selection Lock** toggle icon turns yellow and stays yellow until the icon is toggled off.

Figure 2-13. The Selection Lock toggle, disabled (left) and enabled (right)

Using the Selection Lock feature

1. Continue from the previous exercise or reset 3ds Max and create two spheres, two boxes, and two teapots in any viewport.

2. Click the **Selection Lock** toggle. The toggle will turn yellow.

3. Try selecting any new objects in your scene (you will be unable to).

4. Click the **Selection Lock** toggle again. The toggle will return to its previous state.

Other ways to select objects

There are a few other interfaces with which to select objects in a scene, such as the **Material Editor,** Track view, and Schematic view. Selecting objects with the **Material Editor** will be covered in Chapter 6, and selecting objects with Track view will be covered in Chapter 12. The Schematic view interface is a relatively little used feature in visualization and is not covered in this book.

Isolate selection

Finally, there is a feature that first appeared in 3ds Max 6 that I would simply find difficult to work without now: **Isolate Selection**. This feature is available through the **Tools** menu or the keyboard shortcut Alt+Q. Enabling this feature hides all objects except the currently selected object. What's more, it zooms to the extents of the object in the active viewport. In the left image of Figure 2-14, an object is selected and the Isolate Selection command is activated. Notice in the image on the right that all other objects disappear and the active viewport is zoomed in to the extent of the single object. It also brings up a small dialog box that has a single icon to exit you out of isolation mode.

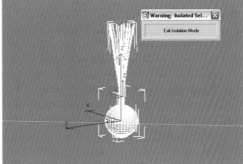

Figure 2-14. Isolating a selection

Using Isolate Selection

This exercise demonstrates use of the Isolate Selection feature.

1. Continue from the previous exercise or reset 3ds Max and create two spheres, two boxes, and two teapots in any viewport.

2. Select the two spheres in your scene.

3. Press **Alt+Q**. The two spheres will be isolated and all other objects in your scene will be temporarily hidden from view.

4. Click the **Exit Isolation Mode** message that appears. All of the previously hidden objects will return to view.

Displaying objects

3ds Max gives you great flexibility over the display of objects. How you display objects in your scene can greatly affect your speed and efficiency. If you're like me, you hate having to wait on your computer to do anything. Well, if you're not smart about how you display objects in 3ds Max, you can end up doing a lot of waiting.

There are several interfaces that control the display of objects, but as with all areas of the program, you should strive to use the most effective and efficient ones. Undoubtedly, those would have to be the **Display** panel, the **Display** floater, and as usual, the keyboard. The **Display** panel and **Display** floater are very similar in function. In fact, the only features on the panel that don't exist on the floater are the **Display Color** and **Link Display** rollouts, which are of little importance in architectural visualizations and are not discussed in this book.

The two most important and frequently used display features in 3ds Max are located on the **Display** panel and **Display** floater. They are **Hide** and **Freeze.**

Hide simply turns off the display of an object, and **Freeze** locks an object so that it cannot be modified in any way. Objects that you don't need to work and don't need to see, should be hidden. Objects that do not need to be worked on, but still need to be displayed as a reference, should be frozen. Freezing is a great feature when you need to view an object as a reference but don't want to have to worry about inadvertently transforming or modifying it. Frozen objects are displayed in light gray so that they don't stand out and make it difficult to see other objects.

The Display floater

The **Display** floater contains two tabs, **Hide/Freeze** and **Object Level,** which are identical in content to four of the rollouts in the **Display** panel; **Hide, Freeze, Hide By Category,** and **Display Properties** (see Figure 2-15). Both give you the ability to hide, unhide, freeze, and unfreeze selected or unselected objects. The **By Name** option opens the **Select From Scene** dialog box so that you can apply the display change to objects you select by name. The **By Hit** option lets you pick objects in a viewport to apply the display change to. Additionally, the **Display** floater and **Display** panel have a **Hide By Category** option, which lets you quickly hide all scene objects of a certain type (e.g., lights or cameras).

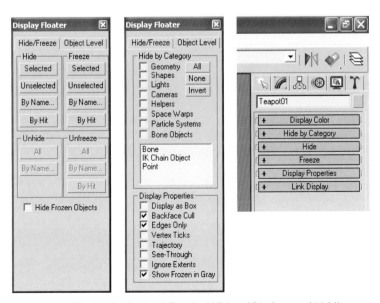

Figure 2-15. The Display floater (left and middle) and Display panel (right)

The **Display** floater and **Display** panel also contain a section that lets you change other display properties. These options, shown in the **Object Level** tab in Figure 2-15, can prove to be invaluable display aids as you work.

- **Display as Box:** This option is disabled by default; enabling it turns any object into a box just large enough to enclose the object. This is used to reduce the display of high polygon models to simple boxes that are easier for your computer to display. In architectural scenes with numerous trees containing tens of thousands of polygons, this can be an invaluable option. Without converting these trees to simple boxes, it wouldn't take many of them to bring your graphics cards to a screeching halt.

- **Backface Cull:** This option is enabled by default; disabling it makes the hidden faces on the backside of an object be displayed.

- **Edges Only:** This option is enabled by default; it causes only the edges of polygons to be displayed. Disabling it causes the shared edge of every face that is not a polygon edge to be displayed.

- **Vertex Ticks:** This option is disabled by default; enabling it causes all vertices in an object to be displayed without having to be in vertex sub-object mode. This can be a nice visual aid at times.

- **Trajectory:** This option is disabled by default; enabling it causes the path that an animated object follows to be displayed as a spline.

- **See-Through:** This option is disabled by default; enabling it causes shaded objects to appear transparent. This does not affect the rendered image, only the viewport display.

- **Ignore Extents:** This option is disabled by default; enabling it causes the object to not affect the zoom extents. If an is object a large distance away from the rest of your scene, such as a light representing the sun, enabling this option will disregard the light and allow the zoom extents to zoom in closer to the extents of the main area of the scene. I use zoom extents constantly and enable this feature whenever I use far-away lights.

- **Show Frozen in Gray:** This option is enabled by default and should be left enabled; disabling it causes frozen objects to appear as if they're not frozen.

As with all areas of 3ds Max, I highly recommend the use of keyboard shortcuts in the display of objects. These shortcuts exist as toggles, so that one press of a key makes the objects disappear and another press makes them reappear. Objects that utilize hide and unhide toggles include cameras (Shift+C), geometry (Shift+G), grids (G), helpers (Shift+H), lights (Shift+L), particle systems (Shift+P), shapes (Shift+S), and space warps (Shift+W).

Finally, the **Object Properties** dialog box is another interface that displays some of the options you just read about and many more. These options are more advanced and will be covered later.

Using the Display floater

This exercise demonstrates use of the **Display** floater.

1. Continue from the previous exercise or reset 3ds Max and create two spheres, two boxes, and two teapots in any viewport.

2. Select the two box objects in your scene.

3. From the **Tools** menu, select **Display Floater**. The **Display** floater will appear, as shown in the left image of Figure 2-15.

4. From the **Display** floater, select **Hide** ➤ **Selected.** The two boxes will disappear from view.

5. Select **Unhide** ➤ **All.** The two boxes will reappear.

6. Press the keyboard shortcut **Shift+G**. All the geometry in the scene disappears.

7. Press the keyboard shortcut **Shift+G** again. All the geometry in the scene reappears.

Layers

When I first started using layers, I remembered the old encyclopedias that showed the anatomy of a frog using pieces of cellophane to show the different layers of the frog. If you want to see just under the skin, turn the page; if you want to see deep under the muscles, turn a few more. Layers in 3ds Max are similar to this kind of display. They provide an easy way to display specific objects or groups of objects.

Using the Layer Manager

Layers are created and managed through the **Layer Manager** dialog box, shown in Figure 2-16. This dialog box is a floater, and thus can remain open while you work. It is accessed through the **Layer** icon on the **Main** toolbar, or the same icon on the **Layers** toolbar. The **Layer Manager** can take up a lot of screen real estate, which for a short period of time is fine. If you're like me and prefer to maximize screen real estate, I suggest turning on the **Layers** toolbar so that you can do many of the same things that you can in the **Layer Manager** without having to open it.

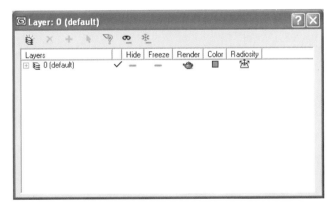

Figure 2-16. The Layer Manager

The **Layer Manager** includes seven icons along the top (as shown in Figure 2-16) that allow you to do the following, respectively, from left to right:

- Create a new layer (containing selected objects)
- Delete highlighted empty layers
- Add selected objects to a highlighted layer
- Select highlighted objects and layers
- Highlight selected objects' layers
- Hide/unhide all layers
- Freeze/unfreeze all layers

Also within the **Layer Manager** are columns for **Hide, Freeze, Render, Color,** and **Radiosity** (covered much later in the book). You can change these options for an individual object; or, by highlighting the layer name, you can make changes to all of the objects on a certain layer. If a property is enabled, an icon is displayed. If the property is disabled, a dashed line is displayed. If you want an object to derive its display options from the layer, then click the appropriate icon until a dot icon is displayed. Objects within a layer can have different display options enabled or disabled. By clicking the column heads, you can sort objects and layers according to the status of the display icons.

The following are some important things to remember about layers:

- Newly created objects are added to the current layer.
- You cannot delete a layer if any objects are assigned to the layer or if it is the current layer.
- Creating a new layer automatically makes it the current layer.
- Each object can be assigned to only one layer.
- All layer names must be unique.
- Layer 0 is the default layer that objects are added to, and this layer cannot be deleted.

Using layers

This exercise demonstrates use of layers in your scene.

1. Continue from the previous exercise or reset 3ds Max and create two spheres, two boxes, and two teapots in any viewport.
2. Select the two teapot objects in your scene.
3. Click the **Layer Manager** icon in the **Main** toolbar. The **Layer Manager** dialog box will open (see Figure 2-16).
4. Click the **Create New Layer** icon.
5. Click the yellow highlighted word **Layer 01** that appears.
6. Type the name **Teapots** and press **Enter**.
7. Click the plus sign to the left of the new layer named **Teapots.** The two teapots that were selected when you created the layer are now on a layer called **Teapots.** All other objects are on the layer named **0,** by default.

Transforming objects

Transformation is a term used to describe a change in an object's position, size, or orientation in 3D space. Technically, you could argue that you could transform an object with any of the hundreds of available tools in 3ds Max; however, in 3ds Max the term is only actually applied to the use of the Move, Rotate, and Scale commands. These commands are three of the most powerful and critical commands used in 3ds Max. Let's look at each a little more closely to see what they do, before moving on.

Move

The move transform allows you to move any object anywhere in 3D space, along any of the three axes or xy, xz, or yz planes. There are several ways to perform a move transform. In each case, you must first select the object and click the **Select and Move** icon (or press W).

You can click, hold, and drag on the transform gizmo within the active viewport. Placing the mouse over a single axis of the transform gizmo causes that axis to become highlighted in yellow, and restricts transformation to just that axis. Placing the mouse over the area between any two axes causes a rectangle lying in the plane of those two axes to become highlighted and any transformation to become restricted to that plane. Figure 2-17 shows an example of both. In the image on the left, the cursor is placed over the y axis, which becomes highlighted; in the image on the right, the cursor is placed between the y and z axes, which causes the yz plane indicator to become highlighted.

You can use the cursor icons to move an object in small increments, although this is not a preferred method because it is not precise. If you right-click any of the transform icons (**Select and Move**, **Select and Rotate**, or **Select and Scale**) in the **Main** toolbar, you'll bring up the **Transform Type-In** dialog box, which is discussed in further detail later in this chapter.

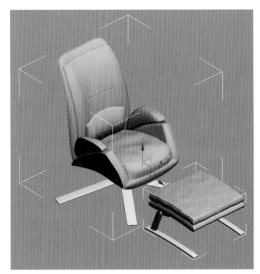 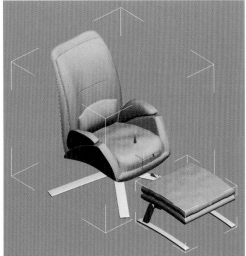

Figure 2-17. The transform gizmo

Scale

The scale transform allows you to increase and decrease the size of an object about its transform gizmo. The scaling of an object's three dimensions, x, y, and z, is uniform by default. You have the option, however, to perform a non-uniform scale, in which one or two dimensions are scaled while the other one or two remain constant. You can also perform a squash scaling operation, in which one dimension is increased in scale and the other two dimensions are decreased in scale.

To access these additional two scaling options, click and hold the **Scale** icon and select either option from the flyout menu, as shown in Figure 2-18. You can also press R repeatedly to cycle through all three scaling options. You can right-click any transform icon to bring up the **Transform Type-In** dialog box.

Figure 2-18. The Scale flyout menu

An example of the non-uniform scale and the squash feature is shown in Figure 2-19, in which the couch on the left is first reduced in scale non-uniformly along just the vertical axis (middle couch), and then squashed along the same axis (right couch).

Figure 2-19. Uniform scale, non-uniform scale, and squash scale, shown left to right

Rotate

The rotate transform allows you to spin an object around any axis of its transform gizmo. To perform the rotate transform, select the object, click the **Select and Rotate** icon (or press E) and click, hold, and drag the transform gizmo within the active viewport. You can also right-click any of the transform icons to bring up the **Transform Type-In** dialog box. By placing the transform gizmo in selective locations, you can spin an object any way you want. Rotations are measured in degrees by default; 360 degrees equals a full rotation.

Performing move, scale, and rotate transforms

This exercise demonstrates how to perform move, scale, and rotate transforms.

1. Continue from the previous exercise or reset 3ds Max and create two spheres, two boxes, and two teapots in any viewport.
2. Select one of the objects in your scene.
3. In the **Main** toolbar, click the **Select and Move** icon (or press W).
4. Place your cursor over one of the axes on the transform gizmo that appears. The axis your cursor is over will turn yellow.
5. Click and drag on the highlighted axis. The object will move along the highlighted axis only.
6. Click the **Select and Scale** icon (or press R).
7. Within the Perspective viewport, place your cursor in the middle of the transform gizmo. The center triangle should become highlighted.
8. Click and drag on the transform gizmo. Dragging upward will scale the object up and dragging downward will scale the object down.
9. Click the **Select and Rotate** icon (or press E).
10. Place your cursor over one of the rotation rings and click and drag to rotate the object around the highlighted axis.

The Transform Type-In dialog box

The **Transform Type-In** dialog box, shown in Figure 2-20, is a great tool that can be used to transform objects precisely. This dialog box is available for all three transforms and can be accessed by right-clicking any of the transform icons (or by pressing F12). The dialog box opens to whatever transform icon is enabled, regardless of which icon you right-click. The dialog box is also modeless, which means you can leave it open while you continue to work. You can also switch between the three transforms while you work.

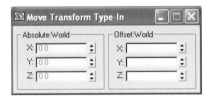

Figure 2-20. The Transform Type-In dialog box

When the dialog box first opens, two columns are displayed: **Absolute:World** and **Offset:World**. The **Absolute:World** column displays the x, y, and z values of the selected object's pivot point position. The pivot point of an object marks the one exact position of the object, even though the pivot may not even lie within the volume of the object, and can in fact be moved far away from the object. By typing a value of **0** for each of the **X:**, **Y:**, and **Z:** boxes while the move transform is active, you are telling 3ds Max to move the object to the world origin (or at least the object's pivot point).

The **Offset:World** column always displays a value of 0 for x, y, and z (unless you are currently typing). This column allows you to transform the object relative to its current position, orientation, or size. For example, when the move transform is active, typing a value of 10 for the z value in the **Offset:World** column will move the object 10 units in the z direction, while typing the same value in the **Absolute:World** column will move the object to a point 10 units from the world origin in the z direction.

Using the Transform Type-In dialog box

This exercise demonstrates use of the **Transform Type-In** dialog box and its effectiveness in transforming objects precise amounts.

1. Continue from the previous exercise or reset 3ds Max and create two spheres, two boxes, and two teapots in any viewport.

2. Select one of the objects in your scene.

3. Right-click the **Move** icon in the **Main** toolbar. The **Move Transform Type-In** dialog box will appear.

4. Double-click the number in the **X:** field under the **Absolute:World** section. The number will become highlighted.

5. Type a new value, slightly larger than the one shown, and press **Enter**. The object will move to that new x location in the scene.

6. Double-click the **0** inside the **Offset:World (X:)** section of the **Transform Type-In** dialog box. Type the number **1** and press **Enter**. The object will move exactly 1 unit in the x direction.

Status bar type-in fields

The Status bar type-in, shown in Figure 2-21, allows you to do the same thing as the **Transform Type-In** dialog box: transform an object with absolute or offset values. To transform the object with absolute values, toggle the **Transform Type-In** icon to Absolute mode—for offset, toggle to Offset mode. This icon is located to the left of the **X:** field. The benefit of this tool is that it's docked and out of the way of the viewports. The Status bar is also just that—a bar that shows the status of the object's position, orientation, or scale, depending on which transform is active.

 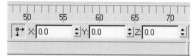

Figure 2-21. The Status bar type-in fields

Summary

This chapter has covered the essential concepts of selecting, displaying, and transforming objects. If you understand the concepts presented in this chapter, you will be able to work with objects effectively and efficiently.

Now that the essential concepts of working with objects have been covered, it's time to discuss how to create new objects. The next chapter looks at the basics of modeling, and it begins by discussing how to set up 3ds Max for efficient use.

PART 2

Modeling

Whether you are trying to create terrain from an engineering drawing of contour lines, scatter leaves along the branches of a tree, or erect complex walls capable of easy modification, compound objects can do the job.

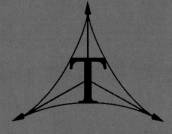

CHAPTER 3

Modeling Basics

3DS MAX GIVES YOU ENORMOUS modeling power to create just about anything you can dream up. There are numerous ways to create the same model, and every user seems to have his or her own technique and approach. But in the world of architectural visualizations, there are a few basic modeling types no user can do without: splines, shapes, and meshes. This book does not deal with NURBS, patches, or many of the other powerful modeling types because their usefulness is extremely limited at best.

The building block of any architectural scene is line work. Ideally, an architect or some other professional in the design process will provide this line work in the form of 2D CAD drawings; but occasionally, the 3ds Max user will have to create it from scratch using hand drawings or some other media. Whether the line work is created in 3ds Max or imported from a 2D CAD program, it will end up in the form of a spline or shape, which can be used to create primitives, compound objects, or numerous other object types. All of these object types can then be used to create the editable mesh, which is the powerful and versatile object type prevalent in all architectural scenes.

Before beginning the modeling of any project, however, you should set up 3ds Max for efficient and accurate work. Since 3ds Max was not geared toward any one industry, you should also set up the work environment for architectural work. I'll begin this chapter with scene setup and discuss the many important factors that you should be aware of before beginning any project.

This chapter focuses on how to set up 3ds Max for efficient and accurate architectural work, and how to work with splines, shapes, and meshes.

Setting up the work environment

Setting up your work environment before beginning any project can save you valuable time and prevent unnecessary grief. Although there are an enormous number of settings that control the behavior of the 3ds Max interface, there are only a few important ones that you need to know about. They include units, display drivers, configure path settings, and select preference settings. Some of these need to be changed for each new scene, while others need to be changed only after 3ds Max is installed.

Units

An important setting that should be looked at before you even start setting up a scene is the **System Units** setting. Units are simply a standard of measure, and in 3ds Max they dictate what the true value of any number entered or displayed really means. Since you will be working on architectural visualizations, it only makes sense to use architectural dimensions. Also, since much of your work will originate in AutoCAD with drawings set to architectural dimensions, there's no reason to set your units to anything else.

To change the unit settings, choose **Customize ➤ Units Setup.** The **Units Setup** dialog box (shown in Figure 3-1) opens with a default **Display Unit Scale** of **Generic Units.** Check **US Standard** and ensure the drop-down menu is set to **Feet w/Decimal Inches.** These are display settings, which means any value displayed in 3ds Max is expressed in feet and decimal inches, or ' and ".

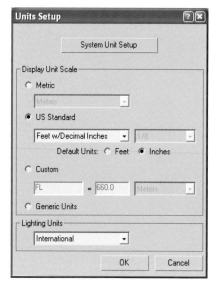

Figure 3-1. The Units Setup dialog box

Next, ensure **Default Units** is set to **Inches,** as shown in Figure 3-1. This means that any number entered into any field will be considered a number expressed in inches if it isn't followed by a unit designation. Therefore, if you change the radius of a sphere to 20 without following it with an apostrophe, the radius becomes 20 inches. But because the display settings are set to **Feet w/Decimal Inches,** the radius will actually change to read 1'8". You can also enter 1'8" yourself; or, even easier, 1'8. An apostrophe (') indicates feet and a double quote mark (") indicates inches.

The reason I suggest changing the **Default Units** to inches is that when you want to enter a certain number of inches into a field, such as 4.5", you won't have to do any math to figure out what the number is expressed in feet (0.375' in this case). It simply saves time. In addition, **AutoCAD** uses inches as its default units, and it can be confusing when working in two programs with two different default unit types.

Last, click the **System Unit Setup** button and ensure that the **System Unit Scale** is set to **1 Unit = 1.0 Inches,** as shown in Figure 3-2. Changing this to read **1 Unit = 1.0 Feet** will cause your entire scene to be scaled up twelve fold. The objects won't actually change in size, they will simply be given new units. A sphere that was expressed as 5 inches will now be expressed as 5 feet.

This also means that when you import an AutoCAD drawing with default units set to inches, all imported objects will remain their original size. If you change your **System Unit Scale** to read **1 Unit** = **1.0 Feet,** then a sphere with a radius of 5 inches in AutoCAD will change to a sphere with a radius of 5 feet when imported into 3ds Max.

Figure 3-2. The System Unit Setup dialog box

There are no other settings that need to be altered with the **Units Setup** dialog box; however, I would like to make a note of the bottom half of the **System Unit Setup** dialog box. These values control how accurate 3ds Max is in the use of numerical values. Basically, the closer objects lie to the origin of the World Coordinate System (i.e., 0,0,0), the more accurately objects are displayed and parameters computed. The values in this dialog box indicate that objects would have to be more than 16 million inches away from the origin in order to be inaccurate to an inch. Although this may seem to be more than accurate enough, problems can still arise, as I once learned the hard way. I was once knee-deep in the modeling of a very large project for a golf course community with site elements (streets, lakes, etc.) that I created straight from the line work of an engineering firm's site plan that I imported from AutoCAD. I inserted all my individual objects, such as houses, streetlights, cars, etc. What I didn't realize is that for some reason the drafter had placed all the line work in the AutoCAD file at an incredibly great distance from the origin. So when I inserted all the objects, they too were a long way from the origin and were no longer accurate. I didn't catch it at first, and couldn't figure out why all my modeling operations were messed up. With 3ds Max being 1 inch off at a distance of 16 million inches from the origin, you can't move or modify objects in increments less than one inch. This won't cut it for architectural models. So now the absolute first thing I do with any AutoCAD drawing that I'm going to use is move all line work so that it's centered on the world origin. The moral of the story is to always keep your scene centered on the origin.

One final and very important note about units is that engineering firms typically produce site drawings for architects using engineering scales. In engineering scales, the unit of measure is 1 foot, which means that an object 12 feet long will actually appear only 12 inches long when its line work is imported into 3ds Max. Therefore, you must scale site plans 1200% prior to or immediately after importing.

Setting up 3ds Max with architectural units

This exercise demonstrates how to set up 3ds Max for architectural units.

1. Reset 3ds Max.

2. Click the **Customize** menu and select **Units Setup**. The **Units Setup** dialog box will open, as shown in Figure 3-1.

3. Select **US Standard** and make sure that the drop-down list below is set to **Feet w/Decimal Inches** and **Default Units** is set to **Inches**, as shown in Figure 3-1. Your units will now be set up correctly for architectural work, but for this drawing only. Any new drawing will require the units to be changed again.

Display drivers

When you start 3ds Max for the first time, the **Graphics Driver Setup** dialog box appears (Figure 3-3). This dialog box allows you to either keep the default display driver (by keeping the **Software** option selected) or use other more powerful drivers, such as OpenGL or Direct3D. You can only use OpenGL, Direct3D, or any other driver if your graphics card supports the driver you want to use. To use a customized driver, select **Custom** and choose an installed driver from the drop-down list. If you are unsure of whether your graphics card supports a specific driver, you should use the default software driver. If you change the display driver, you will need to restart 3ds Max.

Figure 3-3. The Graphics Driver Setup dialog box

You can also make display driver changes within the **Viewports** tab of the **Preference Settings** dialog box (Figure 3-4). In the **Display Drivers** section, click **Choose Driver** to change the **Currently Installed Driver.** The **Configure Driver** option opens a dialog box that allows you to make changes to the settings associated with the currently installed driver. One important setting in this dialog box is the **Download Texture Size** setting, which controls the size of the bitmaps displayed in your viewports. Larger maps result in better but slower viewport displays. Each display driver configuration setting represents a trade-off between display quality and display speed, and will require experimentation on your part to optimize for your specific hardware and needs.

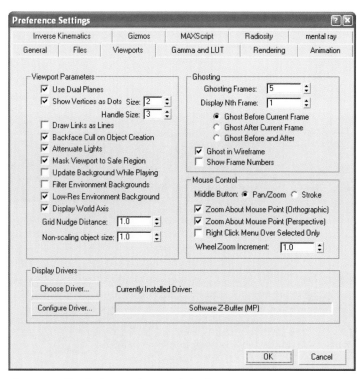

Figure 3-4. The Preference Settings dialog box

Configure paths

When 3ds Max is installed, every file is placed in a specific location for future retrieval. Sound files are placed in the Sounds folder, fonts in the Fonts folder, scripts in the Scripts folder, and so on. All of these locations, also known as paths, can be modified within the **Configure User Paths** and **Configure System Paths** dialog boxes of the **Customize** menu, as shown in Figure 3-5. External files are important path types that you may need to update from time to time—they can be found on the **External Files** tab, which is the first tab that appears when you open the **Configure User Paths** dialog box. This is really not one path, but many paths—one for each folder on your computer where you want 3ds Max to search for images that you want to use to texturize your scenes. By default, 3ds Max creates a path for each of the directories within the Maps folder. To add additional folders in which you want 3ds Max to look for images, click the **Add** button within the **External Files** tab. Select **Browse**, locate the directory you want to add, and select **Use Path.**

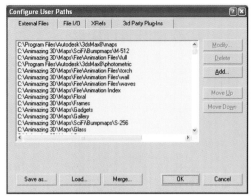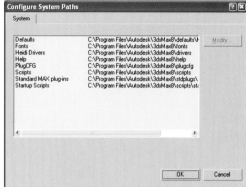

Figure 3-5. The Configure User Paths and Configure System Paths dialog boxes

Once you assign an image to a material, 3ds Max will start all future searches for the image in whatever location you specified when you first assigned the image to the material. If you delete or move the image from the folder to which it was first assigned, during the render process 3ds Max will search for the image in each of the folders (paths) listed in the **External Files** tab of the **Configure User Paths** dialog box. It will start the search in the first folder specified at the top of the list and continue looking in additional folders, in the order the paths are listed. To move a specific path closer to or farther from the top of the paths list, highlight the path and select **Move Up** or **Move Down.** Continue clicking until the path is in the desired location in the list. The result of moving a path higher up on the list is that the path will be searched sooner.

Creating a good directory structure for maps is essential for assigning images efficiently. If you have to spend more than a minute just trying to find where you stored an image on your computer, you're spending too much time and should reorganize your images. Personally, I keep all maps in a separate directory outside of the directory in which 3ds Max was installed. This keeps the maps from being erased or overwritten when 3ds Max is uninstalled or updated. Additionally, I like to create very explicit folder names to make finding a particular image as quick and easy as possible. Figure 3-6 shows a screenshot of what my map directory structure looks like.

Figure 3-6. My personal map directory structure

Configuring paths in 3ds Max

This exercise demonstrates use of the configuring paths feature by changing one of the many folders that 3ds Max searches for a specific file type in.

1. Reset 3ds Max.
2. Click the **Customize** menu and select **Configure User Paths**. The **Configure User Paths** dialog box will open to the **External Files** tab.
3. Click the **File I/O** tab.
4. Scroll down and click **Scenes**, as shown in the following screenshot.

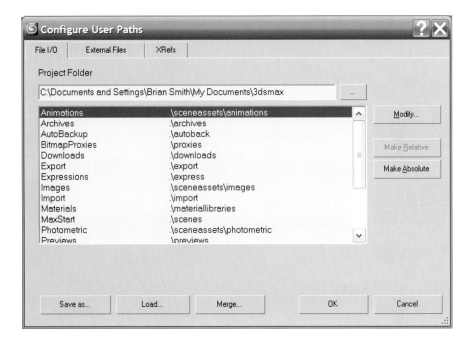

5. Click the **Modify** button.
6. Find another folder in your computer's directory to set as the Scene directory. This will be the folder that 3ds Max starts in when you want to open an existing 3ds Max file.

Preference settings

There are several hundred settings available within the **Preference Settings** dialog box, and for a new user they can be very confusing. Even as an experienced user, I find little need to change the majority of these settings. There are, however, a few important settings that you need to know about. Beyond these, I would discourage you from spending too much time trying to learn as many as you can unless you are an experienced 3ds Max user.

This first critical setting is **Backup Interval (minutes)** in the **Auto Backup** section of the **Files** tab (shown in Figure 3-7). 3ds Max automatically makes a backup file of the file you work in every 15 minutes. When working in 3ds Max, there is nothing I hate more than losing work; even just a few minutes worth. Therefore, I keep this setting at 5 minutes as much as possible. However, the larger a scene becomes, the longer it takes for these automatic backups to complete. When 3ds Max runs the auto backup, you cannot do anything with the program and must wait until the backup is complete. When your scenes become so large that you are waiting longer than you like on these backups, change this setting so that the backups occur at greater intervals.

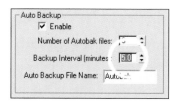

Figure 3-7. The Auto Backup settings

Also within the **Files** tab is a setting called **Zoom Extents on Import,** as shown in Figure 3-8. This setting is enabled by default, but as a personal preference, I always disable it. Leaving this option enabled means that every time you import an object into your scene from another file, 3ds Max will automatically perform the **Zoom Extents** command within every viewport. I find this very annoying, especially when I have just spent time zooming into a specific location in my scene that I want to focus on.

Figure 3-8. Disabling the Zoom Extents
on Import option

The last setting you should ensure is set properly is **Middle Button** in the **Mouse Control** section of the **Viewports** tab, as shown in Figure 3-9. The middle mouse (scroll) button is best utilized when set to control the panning and zooming within a viewport. When zooming with the mouse, it is ideal to have the zooming centered on the cursor of the mouse. To set up 3ds Max this way, enable **Zoom About Mouse Point (Orthographic).** This option controls the zoom for viewports with orthographic views, such as Top, Left, User, etc. You can also enable the option for perspective viewports.

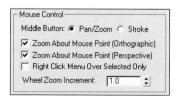

Figure 3-9. Options controlling the zooming
and panning capabilities of the mouse

These three settings I have mentioned are the only ones I make a point to change whenever I install 3ds Max. I would never discourage exploring and experimentation within 3ds Max, as that is often the only means some users have to learn, but I do not think new users should attempt to learn every setting, as it may only confuse and frustrate. The 3ds Max programmers have done an excellent job optimizing the default Preference settings for the majority of users; for the most part, the settings are optimal for those of us in the visualization industry. Generally, if you get to the rare point at which you decide there has to be a better setting for a particular feature being used, you will probably know enough to be able to figure out where to find the setting and how to change it.

Changing critical preference settings

This exercise demonstrates the changing of three critical settings found in the **Preference Settings** dialog box.

1. Reset 3ds Max.
2. Click the **Customize** menu and select **Preference Settings**.
3. Click the **Files** tab.
4. In the **Auto Backup** section, change **Backup Interval (minutes)** to **10.0**. This will cause 3ds Max to create a backup file of your current scene every 10 minutes. The file will be found in the **AutoBak** directory within 3ds Max.
5. Deselect **Zoom Extents on Import**, as shown in Figure 3-8. This will prevent 3ds Max from performing the **Zoom Extents** command every time a file is imported.
6. Click the **Viewports** tab.
7. In the **Mouse Control** section, enable the **Zoom About Mouse Point** option for both orthographic and perspective views, as shown in Figure 3-9. This will allow you to zoom in and out of a scene wherever the mouse is placed.

Customization

Experienced 3ds Max users often find it helpful to customize the 3ds Max interface to their specific style of work, and 3ds Max contains very powerful customization features that make this possible. However, customization can be a complex endeavor, and placing a discussion of the subject at the beginning of a book would be inappropriate because new users aren't familiar enough with the capability and power of a program like 3ds Max to know the best way to customize. Trying to customize 3ds Max before learning at least some of the program is putting the cart before the horse, as the saying goes. Because of this, I have placed an explanation of customization in Appendix A, near the end of the book.

Working with shapes and splines

When creating architectural visualizations, you will almost always work with drawings that originate in a 2D CAD program such as AutoCAD (see Figure 3-10). Why is this? Because someone will undoubtedly want to build the project you create in 3ds Max, and to do so, someone must submit construction drawings to their respective local governments in order to obtain the required building permits. These days, almost all architectural construction drawings are created with CAD software, and unlike other applications for 3ds Max—such as character animation, which incorporates more creativity and artistic interpretation—architectural modeling is very precise, and what you see is what you need to create.

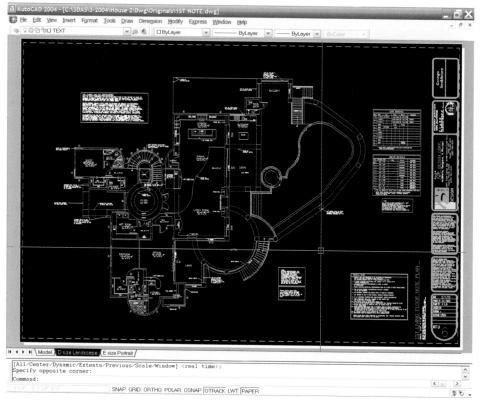

Figure 3-10. Example of a floor plan drawing in AutoCAD

That being said, unless someone hands you a few sketches and says "Show me what this looks like in 3D," you will usually be at the mercy of the drafter that put the drawings together. In fact, with the exception of one project in which the client said exactly that, every one of the 100-plus 3D projects I have worked on began with AutoCAD drawings. Knowing how to interpret architectural drawings is a must, and knowing how to work with them in AutoCAD is equally important.

If you ask a 3ds Max user in any field other than architecture what the building blocks of 3D are, chances are he or she will tell you primitive solids (i.e., spheres, boxes, cylinders, etc.). With architectural visualizations, however, the building blocks are shapes and splines. Primitive solids are a great supplement, but your work will truly begin with a mass of shapes and splines.

Shapes and splines defined

So what are shapes and splines? Essentially, they are both made up of the same ingredient: lines with curves defined by mathematical equations. Shapes are simply tools to facilitate the arrangement of line work into a certain pattern, such as text. How laborious would it be to write your name in 3ds Max with individual lines that have to be curved, bent, and shaped just right? With the text shape, writing your name can take just a few seconds. Figure 3-11 shows several examples of shapes.

Figure 3-11. Examples of shapes in 3ds Max

Splines are different from shapes in that splines are not created from scratch; they are converted from other objects—most commonly shapes. Take, for example, the simple circle. The circle is a shape with one basic parameter, the radius value. You can't do very much with a simple circle; but convert it to a spline and you can suddenly turn that circle into almost any type of line imaginable. Since splines usually begin with shapes, I will first discuss shapes, and then cover how to manipulate those shapes once converted to splines.

Shape basics

Figure 3-12 shows an example of each of the shapes available for creation. In creating 3D architectural structures, you will probably find only an occasional use for such shapes as the star, donut, or NGon— but four shapes that you won't be able to do without are the line, circle, arc, and text.

Figure 3-12. Available shapes
in 3ds Max

Most of the shapes have several common rollouts: **Name and Color, Rendering, Interpolation, Creation Method, Keyboard Entry,** and **Parameters** (as shown in Figure 3-13). They are very similar for all shapes.

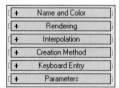

Figure 3-13. Typical shape rollouts

Within the **Object Type** rollout (see Figure 3-12) are the **AutoGrid** and **Start New Shape** options. By checking the **AutoGrid** option, you can set the creation point for a shape on the surface of an existing object. When you do so, the new shape's normal is aligned with the normal of the face your cursor is over when the shape is created. This causes the new shape to be aligned with the surface of the object.

Figure 3-14 shows an excellent example of the **AutoGrid** feature. With one click of the mouse, you can place a text shape of the word **YIELD** on the surface of a triangle-shaped street sign without having to create the shape and execute the move and rotate commands several times.

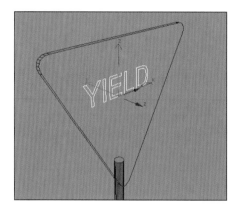

Figure 3-14. Using AutoGrid to place a shape on the surface of an object

Using the AutoGrid feature

This exercise demonstrates use of the **AutoGrid** feature by placing text on the surface of a box.

1. Reset 3ds Max.

2. In the Perspective view, create a box with a length, width, and height of 500.

3. Click the **Shapes** icon within the **Create** panel.

4. Enable the **AutoGrid** feature.

5. Click the **Text** button and move the cursor over one of the sides of the newly created box. A reference gizmo appears, with the z axis aligned with the normal of the face the gizmo is over.

6. Click one of the sides of the box to place the text object on the surface of the box. Repeat the process for the two other sides visible in the Perspective view, as shown in the following image:

The **Start New Shape** option is checked by default; it makes every newly created shape a separate object. When not checked, each additional shape created becomes another part of a single object.

The **Creation Method, Keyboard Entry,** and **Parameters** rollouts need no real explanation. Personally, I can't recall a time that I've ever used anything other than the default creation method, and I can't recall ever using the **Keyboard Entry** feature because it's simply too slow. The two rollouts that warrant discussion are **Rendering** and **Interpolation,** and we'll look at these next.

The **Name and Color** rollout simply gives you a place to change the default name and color that is used upon creation.

The Rendering rollout

Shapes by default are not rendered, but by selecting the **Enable In Renderer** option in the **Rendering** rollout (see Figure 3-15), the shape will be included in the rendering. The lines that make up the shape will appear tubular, with a thickness and number of sides that you specify. The minimum number of sides possible is three, which creates a triangular cross-section. This feature has limited use in architecture, but there are times when you may find its use invaluable, such as creating the branches of a tree. The benefit of this feature is that while the shapes appear to be solids when rendered, and thus can significantly increase render times, they are still displayed as lines within the viewports and do not significantly increase viewport refresh rates. You can, however, show the shapes in the viewports as they will appear when rendered. To do so, select the **Enable In Viewport** option.

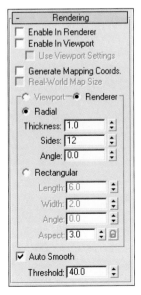

Figure 3-15: The Rendering rollout

Creating renderable shapes and splines

This exercise demonstrates how to make shapes and splines renderable.

1. Reset 3ds Max.

2. Create a circle in the Perspective view with a radius of **100**.

3. In the **Rendering** rollout, check the **Enable in Renderer** and **Enable in Viewport** options, as shown on the left in the following image.

4. Change **Radial Thickness** to **10.0**. The circle is now renderable and can be seen in the viewport the same way it will be when rendered, as shown on the right in the following image:

 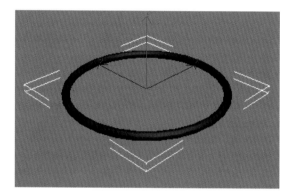

5. Save your work for use in the next exercise.

The Interpolation rollout

In the next rollout, **Interpolation** (Figure 3-16), you can control the smoothness of curves within a shape. By definition, interpolation means inserting or introducing between other elements or parts. Increasing the number of steps increases the number of vertices and makes the curves in the shape appear smoother. Different shapes require a different minimum number of vertices and segments to be defined.

Figure 3-16. The Interpolation

Take, for example, the circle shown in Figure 3-17. The circle is defined by four initial vertices and thus has four initial segments. Without any additional steps to define its curve, the circle resembles a diamond, as in the rollout image on the left. If the number of steps is increased to 1, one additional vertex (or step) is inserted in each of the original four segments, as shown in the middle image. If the number of steps is increased to 2, two additional vertices are inserted in each of the original four segments, as shown in the image on the right. As the step value is increased, the curves in the path become smoother. The default value of 6 provides a fairly smooth curve, but in many cases you will need to increase this number significantly.

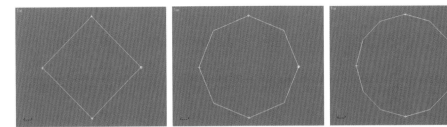

Figure 3-17. From left to right, a circle with zero, one, and two steps

The **Optimize** option removes any unnecessary vertices in a shape, such as multiple vertices in a straight section of a shape. Figure 3-18 shows the effect of using **Optimize** on a simple extruded spline with two straight segments and a curved segment. With **Optimize** disabled, the straight segments receive just as many additional steps as the curved segments. The **Optimize** option should always remain enabled, except in some specialized circumstances.

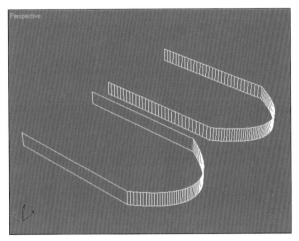

Figure 3-18. A spline with Optimize enabled (left), and the same spline with Optimize disabled (right)

The **Adaptive** option automatically places vertices in the locations necessary to produce a smooth look at all curved sections of a shape. When the **Adaptive** option is enabled, the **Optimize** option becomes disabled—it is no longer necessary since 3ds Max determines the correct number of vertices to use for each segment. Figure 3-19 shows the effect of using the **Adaptive** option on the extruded letter "S." Notice that the straight segments receive no unnecessary steps, while the more curved areas receive as many steps as needed to produce decent curves. The **Adaptive** option can be very handy when you work on large splines that would be too time-consuming to manage segment by segment.

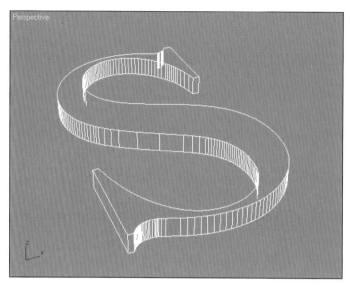

Figure 3-19. The letter "S" with the Adaptive option enabled

Using Interpolation with Shapes and Splines

This exercise demonstrates how to use interpolation to make curved segments of shapes and splines smoother.

1. Continue from the previous exercise.

2. Open the **Interpolation** rollout and type **0** in the **Steps** field. This causes the circle to be square-shaped because it has no steps to define the curved segments between the original four vertices.

3. Increase the **Steps** value to **12**. The circle now becomes smooth.

4. Decrease the **Steps** value to **0** once again.

5. Enable the **Adaptive** option in the **Interpolation** rollout. This option causes 3ds Max to automatically place vertices in the locations necessary to produce a smooth look at all curved sections of the shape. The circle is now smooth again.

Spline basics

Once a shape is converted into a spline, a wealth of features are made available that give you tremendous modeling power. With the tools provided, you can manipulate the individual segments or vertices of a spline with great precision and versatility. Many of the critical tools in the spline rollouts are similar to those explained in the next section of this chapter, "Working with meshes and polys," and are also used in the next two modeling chapters. Therefore, you will gain a solid understanding of splines throughout the course of the remaining discussion on modeling.

It wasn't long ago, pre-3ds Max, that users were forced to create many architectural elements, such as walls, roofs, and doors, from scratch using primitive solids. I remember creating walls by extruding shapes or stacking one shape on top of another, much like working with LEGOs. While there are still situations in which this may be the optimal way of modeling, dramatic improvements in shapes and splines have enabled users to achieve the same result in a fraction of the time with far more flexibility in making modifications as their work progresses. If you want to create architectural visualizations at warp speed, then a good understanding of how to work with shapes and splines (also known as 2D modeling) cannot be overemphasized. For now, let's take a look at the next important step in the modeling process: 3D modeling.

Working with meshes and polys

Mesh and poly objects will comprise the vast majority of objects you will create in architectural visualizations. In large, complex scenes, you may have (and should strive to include) such finer details as particle systems, environment effects, or even third-party plug-in objects, such as RPCs (Rich Photorealistic Content, www.archvision.com). The meat and potatoes of your scenes, however, will be mesh and poly objects.

Meshes and polys have several advantages over other modeling types. They are easy to work with and manipulate, they lend themselves to more exact and precise modeling, and they are perhaps the most common modeling type, supported by a large number of 3D packages.

Editable mesh and editable poly objects are very similar, yet they have many distinct differences. **Editable Poly** provides several unique features unavailable with **Editable Mesh**, and is generally more advanced. Learning the characteristics and capabilities of the poly object becomes much easier with an understanding of the mesh object, and at the end of this chapter is a short comparison between the capabilities of the Edit Mesh and Edit Poly objects.

Creating mesh and poly objects

Mesh and poly objects cannot be created from scratch. They can only be converted from other objects. The **Create** panel allows for the creation of various types of models, such as primitives, shapes, compound objects, patches, and NURBS. Nowhere, however, is there a create button for mesh objects. On the other hand, all of the objects discussed in this chapter could be converted to meshes.

There are several ways to convert an object to a mesh or poly (see Figure 3-20). One way is to right-click the object in the active viewport and select **Convert To: Editable Mesh** or **Convert To: Editable Poly** from the pop-up quad menu. Another way is to right-click the object within the **Modifier Stack**. You can also add the **Edit Mesh** or **Edit Poly** modifier to an object, and finally, you can collapse an object by selecting **Collapse** from the **Utilities** menu.

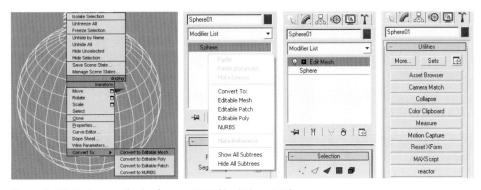

Figure 3-20. Various methods of converting objects to a mesh

Creating mesh objects

This exercise demonstrates a few of the ways to create mesh objects.

1. Reset 3ds Max.

2. Create a sphere in the Perspective view.

3. Right-click in the Perspective view to bring up the quad menu.

4. Move the cursor over the **Convert To** option and select **Convert To: Editable Mesh**. The sphere is now a mesh object.

5. Click the **Undo** icon to return the object to a sphere.

6. In the **Modify** panel, click the **Modifier List** drop-down list and select **Edit Mesh**. This adds the **Edit Mesh** modifier to the sphere. The object is now a mesh again.

7. Save your work for use in the next exercise.

Editing mesh objects

You can change the structural appearance of an object in several ways: with transforms, modifiers, utilities, controllers, and even materials. But no method of changing an object's structure is as powerful and versatile as the **Edit Mesh** feature. All mesh editing occurs at one of the five sub-object levels: vertex, edge, face, polygon, or element. Sub-objects are the components that make up a mesh. Once you convert an object to an editable mesh, you can enter sub-object mode in a few different ways, as shown in Figure 3-21. For example, you can select **Edit Mesh** in the **Modifier Stack,** click the small plus sign to its left to show the five sub-object levels, and then click the sub-object you wish to work on. Another way is to click one of the sub-object icons listed in the **Selection** rollout directly below the **Modifier Stack.** You can also right-click an object in the active viewport and select a sub-object level from the quad menu. Yet another way is to press a number key from 1 to 5 when **Edit Mesh** is listed at the top of the **Modifier Stack** (as shown in Figure 3-21). Press 1 for the **Vertex** sub-object level, 2 for **Edge,** 3 for **Face,** 4 for **Polygon,** and 5 for **Element.**

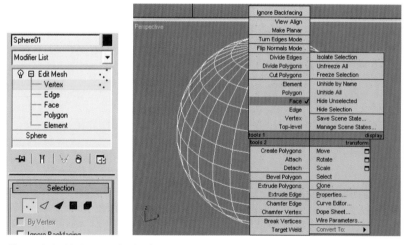

Figure 3-21. Various methods of entering sub-object mode

When you enter a sub-object level, the sub-object icon in the **Selection** rollout and the sub-object name for the level that you enter both turn yellow. To exit sub-object mode, you can click the same icon or the name of the level again. Clicking other features in 3ds Max, such as a different panel within the **Control** panel, can cause the sub-object mode to close automatically. Until sub-object mode closes, you cannot select any other object in your scene.

Once in sub-object mode, you can select individual sub-objects by clicking them, or multiple sub-objects by holding down Ctrl while clicking them, as shown in the left image of Figure 3-22. Notice the plus sign that appears below the cursor when holding down the Ctrl key, indicating the next selection will be added to the current selection. Holding down Ctrl while clicking sub-objects which have already been selected will cause them to be deselected. Holding down Alt while clicking selected sub-objects will also cause the sub-objects to be deselected, as shown in the right image in Figure 3-22. Notice the minus sign that appears below the cursor when holding down the Alt key, indicating the next selection will be subtracted from the current selection. Window selections can also be used in sub-object mode to select or deselect more than one sub-object.

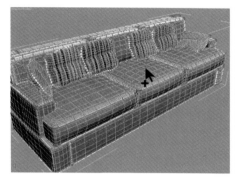 

Figure 3-22. Hold down Ctrl to add selections (left); hold down Alt to subtract selections (right)

Sub-objects that you select turn red in viewports. Once sub-objects are selected, they can be transformed just like any other object. Sub-objects can also be cloned like any other object. Holding down the Shift key while applying a transform (move, rotate, or scale) causes the selected sub-objects to be cloned. After applying the transform, the **Clone Part of Mesh** dialog box appears and prompts you to choose **Clone To Object** or **Clone To Element** (Figure 3-23). The **Clone To Object** option makes the cloned selection an entirely new object with a name of your choosing. **Clone To Element** causes the cloned selection to remain part of the existing object but become a new element within that object.

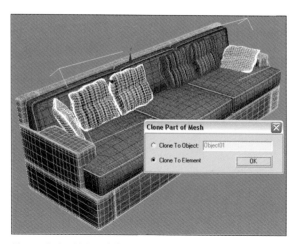

Figure 3-23. Using Shift to copy a sub-object selection

When working with editable mesh objects in the **Modify** panel, you are provided four rollouts: **Selection, Soft Selection, Edit Geometry,** and **Surface Properties.** Each rollout contains powerful features that take quite some time to master. The remainder of this chapter focuses on the most important features of these rollouts.

Editing mesh objects

This exercise demonstrates a few of the ways to edit mesh objects.

1. Continue from the previous exercise.

2. In the **Modify** panel, click the **Vertex** sub-object level in the **Selection** rollout, as shown in the left image of Figure 3-21. The **Vertex** icon will turn yellow.

3. In the **Front** view, select a few vertices using a selection window. The selected vertices turn red. You can now perform a transform on the selected vertices.

4. Right-click in the active viewport and select the **Face** sub-object level from the quad menu, as shown in the right image of Figure 3-21.

5. In the **Front** view, select a few of the faces in the top half of the sphere using a window selection.

6. Hold down the **Ctrl** key and select all of the faces in the bottom half of the sphere, as shown on the left in the following image:

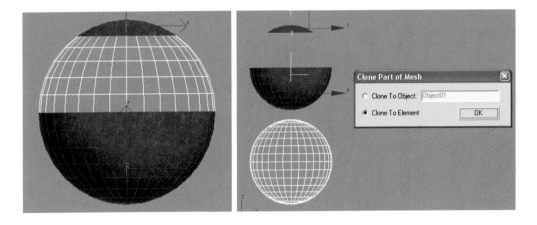

7. Hold down the **Shift** key, move the cursor over the y axis of the transform gizmo, and click and drag upward. A copy of the selection is made.

8. Move the copy above the original sphere and release the mouse. The **Clone Part of Mesh** dialog box appears.

9. Click **OK** and click the highlighted **Faces** icon in the **Selection** rollout. The **Edit Mesh** modifier is now closed.

The Selection rollout

The **Selection** rollout (shown in Figure 3-24) focuses on providing efficient methods for selecting sub-objects. Depending on the object you're working on, this can be a challenge at times. A good understanding of all the options in the **Selection** rollout can greatly facilitate the process of making a sub-object selection.

Figure 3-24. The Selection rollout

- By Vertex: This option allows you to click a vertex in order to select all edges, faces, polygons, or elements connected to the vertex. In Figure 3-25, all four polygons are selected just by clicking the one vertex connected to each of them.

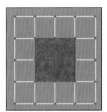

Figure 3-25. The By Vertex option enabled

- Ignore Backfacing: This option allows you to select only those sub-objects with normals facing toward your perspective in the active viewport. In the top image of Figure 3-26, for example, a window selection is made of a pool table in the Front view. From a perspective view, you can see that faces on the backside (relative to the Front view) are not selected. This option is tremendously helpful when you want to select the faces on just one side of a wall, as well as dozens of other situations.

- Ignore Visible Edges: This is a powerful option that really has little practical value in architectural visualizations. It allows you to select all polygons that lie within the same plane. Normally, when you click a single polygon, only that polygon is selected. This option ignores the edges of the polygon you select and selects all polygons that lie on the same plane (or close enough to the same plane, as determined by the planar threshold). I tried to but could not find a single situation in which this option would benefit the selection process.

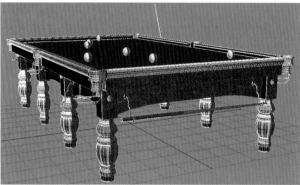

Figure 3-26. The Ignore Backfacing option enabled

- Show Normals: This option causes all face normals to be displayed, which can be a visual aid when trying to determine why materials, lighting, shading, or individual faces of a model appear flawed or missing altogether. A face normal determines which way a face is oriented, and greatly affects all of the aforementioned characteristics. For example, if you apply a material that is only one-sided (i.e., viewable from one side) to a sphere, and all of the face normals are oriented inward and away from your perspective, then you won't see the half of the sphere closest to you. All you would see would be the inside of the back half of the sphere. You won't need this option very often if you do good modeling, but when you do need it, you'll be very thankful you have it. The Scale option lets you change the length of the line that represents a normal. Figure 3-27 shows the faces of a T.V. frame selected with the Show Normals option enabled.

- Hide: It should be no surprise that this option simply hides selected sub-objects, while Unhide All makes them visible again.

- Named Selections: Once you select a group of sub-objects, you can assign a name to the selection by typing the name in the Named Selection Sets drop-down list on the Main toolbar. By clicking Copy and Paste under the Named Selections section of the Selection rollout, you can copy and paste your selection to other objects later.

Figure 3-27. The Show Normals option enabled

Using Selection rollout options

This exercise demonstrates use of a few of the **Selection** rollout options.

1. Reset 3ds Max.
2. In the Perspective view, create a cylinder with a radius of **25** and a height of **50**.
3. In the **Display Properties** rollout of the **Display** panel, enable **Vertex Ticks**. This will make the exercise easier to visualize.
4. In the **Modify** panel, add an **Edit Mesh** modifier and enter the **Face** sub-object level.
5. Enable the **By Vertex** option and select the center vertex on the top of the cylinder. All of the faces on the top of the cylinder are selected, as shown in the following image:

 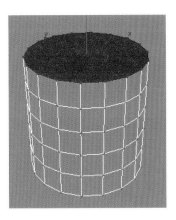

6. Enable the **Ignore Backfacing** option.

7. In the Front view, create a window selection around the entire cylinder to select all the faces. Click the **Arc Rotate SubObject** icon in the viewport navigation controls, and rotate the view in the Perspective view. You can see that because of the **Ignore Backfacing** option, none of the faces on the back of the cylinder were selected.

8. Enable the **Show Normals** option. The normals of all the selected faces appear.

The Soft Selection rollout

The **Soft Selection** feature, shown in Figure 3-28, is one of my favorites in 3ds Max. It's a great way to move subobjects, whether you're working on a piece of furniture or a large 3D terrain object. When you select a sub-object or a group of sub-objects and apply a transform without a soft selection applied, only those selected sub-objects are moved. When you enable **Soft Selection,** however, other sub-objects in the vicinity of those selected are also affected by the transformation of the selected sub-objects. The degree to which those other sub-objects are affected depends on their proximity to the selected sub-objects and the settings in the **Soft Selection** rollout. The purpose of this feature is to soften the effect of a transformation.

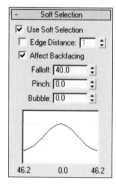

Figure 3-28. The Soft Selection rollout

Notice in the left image of Figure 3-29 that a group of vertices selected on the comforter laying on the bed is moved upward without soft selection enabled. There is a distinct cliff-like look to this transformation. In the image on the right, soft selection is enabled before the transformation. Notice that the vertices in the vicinity of those selected are highlighted to some degree, and the transformation appears more like a rolling hill than a cliff.

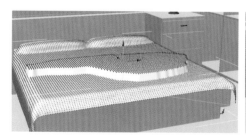 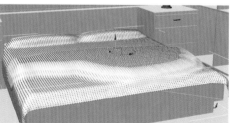

Figure 3-29. Soft selection enabled

As I mentioned, soft selection works great for terrain features, but architectural elements such as buildings, light poles, or tennis courts can't benefit much from soft selection because these elements must be precisely crafted and don't usually involve curved surfaces.

The following is a description of the relevant options available within the **Soft Selection** rollout:

- Use Soft Selection: This option simply enables the Soft Selection feature.

- Affect Backfacing: This option is enabled by default and causes a window selection to select not only those sub-objects in the foreground with normals facing your perspective, but also those sub-objects on the backside of the objects with normals facing away from your perspective. Disable this option when you want your window selection to only select those sub-objects on the side closest to your perspective.

- Soft Selection Curve: The Soft Selection Curve, as shown in the bottom of Figure 3-28, is a graphical representation of how the transformation of selected sub-objects affects transformation of surrounding sub-objects within a given range. The curve is controlled by three parameters: Falloff, Pinch, and Bubble.

- Falloff: This parameter defines the greatest distance from the selection at which sub-objects will still be affected. Any sub-object at a distance greater than this value will not be affected. The value entered in the Falloff field is displayed on the left and right ends of the Soft Selection Curve. Notice that the far left image in Figure 3-30 shows a single vertex selected and moved upward without soft selection enabled. The middle image shows the same transformation with the default Falloff value of 20, and the image on the right shows the same transformation with a Falloff value of 40.

Figure 3-30. The effects of using Falloff

- Pinch: This parameter controls how much the affected sub-objects will appear to be pinched at the point where selected sub-objects meet unselected sub-objects. The left image in Figure 3-31 shows the same vertex transformation as described previously, this time with a Pinch value of 1.0. Notice that the apex of the transformation is pinched, but the resulting falloff appears to have been diminished. This isn't the case, however—changing the Pinch value simply changes the shape of the Soft Selection Curve, which is a reflection of how much the surrounding sub-objects will be transformed. In this case, the pinch of the curve is achieved by allowing sub-objects to be affected only if they're very close to the selected sub-objects. Increasing the falloff at this point simply has the effect of reducing the steepness of the curve.

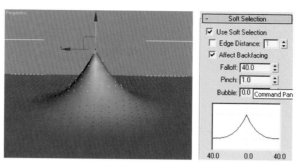

Figure 3-31. The effect of using Pinch

- Bubble: This parameter has the opposite effect of pinch in that it gives a bubble-like appearance to those sub-objects halfway between the selected sub-objects and the sub-objects at the limit of the falloff. Figure 3-32 shows the effect of a Falloff value of 40.0, a Pinch value of 0.0, and a Bubble value of 1.0.

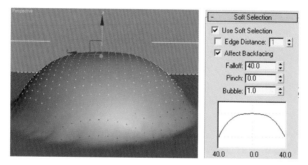

Figure 3-32. The effect of using Bubble

- Edge Distance: This option is explained last because an understanding of the previous Soft Selection parameters is necessary. The Edge Distance value sets a limit on the number of edges away from the selection that will be affected by the Falloff, Pinch, and Bubble values. When enabled, it doesn't matter how high your falloff distance is set. By default, only sub-objects within one edge of the selected sub-objects will be affected. Changing this value to 2 will allow sub-objects two edges away from the selection to be affected, and so on.

Using soft selections

This exercise demonstrates the use of soft selections when applying transforms.

1. Reset 3ds Max.

2. In the **Perspective** view, create a plane with a length and width of **100**, and set the number of length and width segments to **40**.

3. Right-click in the **Perspective** view and use the quad menu to convert the plane to an editable mesh.

4. In the **Selection** rollout, click the **Vertex** sub-object level.

5. Open the Soft Selection rollout, as shown in the right image of Figure 3-32, and select **Use Soft Selection**.

6. Click a vertex near the center of the mesh.

7. Click and drag the spinner to the right of the **Falloff** field. Drag upward to increase the **Falloff** value. Notice that the vertices in the mesh surrounding the selected vertex change colors as the falloff changes.

8. Select the move transform, place the cursor over the **z** axis of the transform gizmo, and click and drag the soft selection upward. Your view should look similar to the right-hand image in Figure 3-30.

The Edit Geometry rollout

To cover the features within the **Edit Geometry** rollout (Figure 3-33) to their full potential and capability, one would need an entire chapter. Much of this rollout, however, provides no benefit to those of us working in the field of architecture. Therefore, I will cover those features that you should concentrate your efforts on, and point out features that you can ignore. Many features of the **Edit Geometry** rollout are only available in certain sub-object modes. When not available, those features are grayed out and not selectable.

Some features within this rollout are available both in and out of sub-object mode, while others are available only in select sub-object modes. To eliminate redundancy, I will first discuss the important features available both in and out of sub-object mode, and then discuss those that are available only in certain sub-object modes.

Figure 3-33. The Edit Geometry rollout

Important features available anywhere

This section explains the important features available in and out of sub-object mode: **Attach, Explode, Remove Isolated Vertices, View,** and **Grid Align.**

Attach

You can use the **Attach** button to attach objects to the currently selected editable mesh object. Object types that can be attached include primitives, patches, compound objects, and any other object types that can be converted to an editable mesh. Many objects cannot be attached. These include lights, cameras, helpers, third-party plug-in objects (such as RPCs), and basically any object that cannot be collapsed to a mesh. Certain objects, such as particle systems, which can be collapsed to a mesh, shouldn't be collapsed because doing so removes any unique features the object holds, which in the case of particles is motion.

Objects that are attached to other objects are automatically converted to editable meshes and inherit the properties of the object to which they are attached. When you attach an object to another, and both objects have different materials applied, a dialog box appears giving you three options: **Match Material IDs to Material, Match Material to Material IDs,** and **Do Not Modify Material IDs or Material.** These options will be discussed in Part 3 of this book.

To attach an object to another, select a mesh object, such as the teapot in Figure 3-34 (which was first converted to a mesh object), click the **Attach** button (which turns yellow), move the cursor over the other object you want to attach (the cursor changes when it's over acceptable objects), and pick the object (such as the torus shown in Figure 3-34). To exit the Attach command, you must either right-click in the current viewport, hit Esc on the keyboard, or click the **Attach** button.

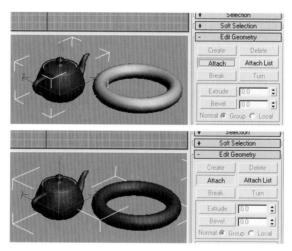

Figure 3-34. One object being attached to another

Instead of picking each individual object you want to attach, you can select from a list. To do so, click the **Attach List** button, which opens the **Attach List** dialog box shown in Figure 3-35. This dialog box looks similar to the **Select Objects** dialog box (the 3ds Max 9 predecessor to the Select From Scene dialog box) and it allows you to select objects in the same way. Only acceptable objects are listed in this dialog box.

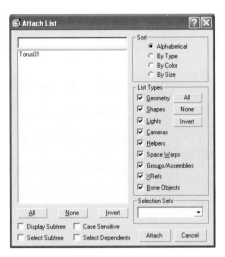

Figure 3-35. The Attach List dialog box

In sub-object mode, the **Attach List** button changes to the **Detach** button. This is because the only things that can be attached in sub-object mode are sub-objects, which aren't named. Additionally, the only thing that can be detached from an object is a sub-object.

Although any sub-object type can be detached, objects that are attached become new elements within the object they are attached to, and therefore can be selected in their entirety with one click of the mouse, using the Element sub-object mode.

One of the things that can bring even a fast computer to a halt when rendering is a scene with too many objects. Every time 3ds Max renders a scene, it must prepare all scene objects. Preparing objects involves several steps; and the more objects a scene contains, the more steps 3ds Max must repeat. If you have two objects and attach one to the other, 3ds Max only has to perform the steps once instead of twice.

So what constitutes too many objects? For a typical workstation, such as the typical quad-core with 4GB of RAM, I would never allow my scenes to contain more than 2,000 objects, and I usually try to keep it to a few hundred whenever possible. Before I was wise to this, I often rendered scenes with an extremely large number of objects, and preparing the objects took an excessive amount of time. The bottom line is, if you have two or more objects with the same material applied, and have no specific need to keep them as separate entities, then you should attach and collapse the objects. Besides the benefit of reduced rendering times, attaching objects makes finding and organizing objects much easier.

Attaching Objects

This exercise demonstrates the use of the **Attach** feature in the **Edit Geometry** rollout.

1. Reset 3ds Max.
2. Create two spheres in the Perspective view.
3. Select one of the spheres and convert to an editable mesh.
4. In the **Edit Geometry** rollout, select **Attach**.
5. Select the other sphere and right-click to end the Attach command.
6. Both spheres are now elements of the same object.
7. Save your work for use in the next exercise.

Explode

Occasionally, you may have the need to blow objects up. The **Explode** feature (shown in Figure 3-36) gives you this ability outside of sub-object mode, and within the Face, Polygon, and Element sub-object modes. This feature is like the opposite of **Attach,** allowing you to separate selected faces into individual objects or elements within the same object. The value to the right of the **Explode** button determines which faces are exploded. If the angle between the normals of selected faces exceeds the value shown, then those selected faces with the exceeding angles are exploded. If the **Objects** option is selected, then all exploded faces become individual objects. If **Elements** is selected, all exploded faces become elements within the object.

Figure 3-36. The Explode feature

Remove Isolated Vertices

This feature is not needed very often, but occasionally it can come in handy. It allows you to remove vertices within an object that are not part of any face, and thus serve no function or purpose. Vertices can become isolated as a result of certain modeling techniques, such as deleting vertices in vertex sub-object mode or performing Boolean operations.

The left image in Figure 3-37 shows a simple plane with **Vertex Ticks** turned on for ease of display. The middle image shows the same plane after select vertices have been deleted, leaving an isolated vertex on each of the four corners. By clicking **Remove Isolated Vertices,** the four vertices are deleted. With some features, such as **Boolean,** 3ds Max usually detects such an occurrence and asks you if you wish to remove the isolated vertices. It's also worth mentioning that, by default, 3ds Max will automatically remove any vertices that become isolated when you delete faces in sub-object mode. Nonetheless, when they exist, they can prevent you from applying certain modifiers. Some of my past coworkers swear that isolated vertices are the cause of occasional 3ds Max program crashes.

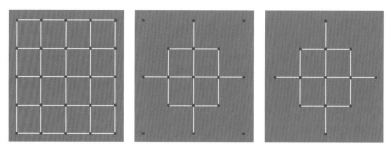

Figure 3-37. Removing isolated vertices

View Align and Grid Align

The **View Align** and **Grid Align** features allow you to move selected objects or sub-objects so that all the vertices that make up the objects or sub-objects you select lie in a plane perpendicular to the active viewport's perspective. In the top-left image of Figure 3-38, a group of vertices are selected, and in the perspective view to the right, those vertices are raised up a small amount. If at any time you want to bring all or some of the vertices back to a single plane (as shown in the bottom images), select the vertices you want to move (or any other sub-object type), right-click in the Top viewport (since it's the view you want to align to), and click the **View Align** icon. All selected vertices will become aligned in the same plane, and that plane will exist at the averaged location of all moved vertices.

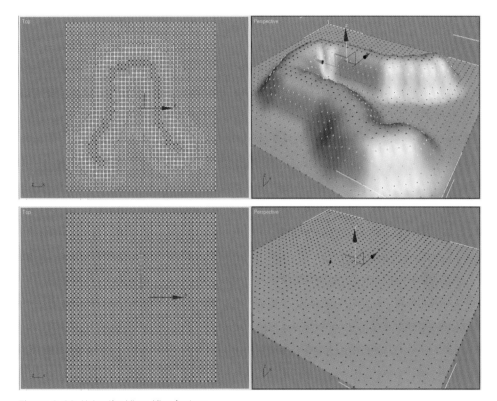

Figure 3-38. Using the View Align feature

Important features available only in sub-object modes

This section covers the important features available only in sub-object modes: **Detach, Delete,** and **Weld**.

Detach

This feature, available in all but the Edge sub-object mode, simply separates selected sub-objects from the rest of the main object. To detach sub-objects, make a sub-object selection, click the **Detach** button, and give the new object a name. When prompted to name the new object, you are given the options **Detach to Element** and **Detach as Clone**. The **Detach to Element** option makes the sub-object selection an element within the object. The **Detach as Clone** feature makes a copy of the detachment so that the original can be left intact and unchanged.

Detaching Objects

This exercise demonstrates the use of the **Detach** feature in the **Edit Geometry** rollout.

1. Continue from the previous exercise.
2. Click the **Element** sub-object level.
3. Select one of the sphere elements and click **Detach** in the **Edit Geometry** rollout.
4. Click **OK** to detach the selected sub-object as a new object in the scene.
5. Click the **Element** sub-object level to exit sub-object mode.

Delete

This feature deletes any sub-object selection. When you delete a vertex, any face using the deleted vertex will also be deleted.

Weld

This feature, available only in Vertex sub-object mode, works in the editing of meshes much like it does in the editing of splines. The **Weld** command simply welds all selected vertices that lie within the distance specified in the **Selected** field. In Figure 3-39, a simple plane is created with a width and length of 4 units, and containing 4 length and width segments (as shown in the top two images). Therefore, the distance between each vertex is exactly 1.0. The bottom-left image shows two vertices selected, which are then welded together, as shown in the bottom-center image. They are welded because the value entered into the **Selected** field is **1.01** (see Figure 3-39)—just greater than the distance of 1.0 between the vertices.

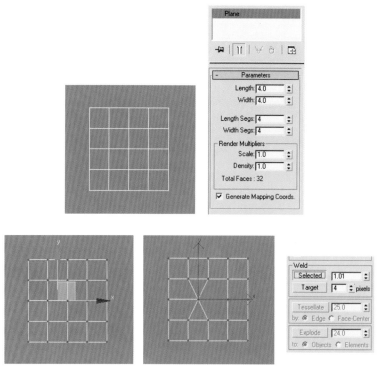

Figure 3-39. Welding vertices

Editing poly objects

The poly object is one of the most powerful and widely used features in 3ds Max, regardless of industry. This feature gives you far more modeling power than the edit mesh and it is much more widely used in the creation of everything from furniture to walls to 3D sites. Inside the modify panel of the edit poly object are several rollouts not found with the edit mesh. For the visualization user, there are three rollouts, shown in Figure 3-40, whose features stand out in terms of practicality. The **Edit Edges** rollout is only available within edge subobject mode, while the **Edit Polygons** rollout is only available within polygon subobject mode. The **Paint Deformation** rollout is available in any sub-object mode.

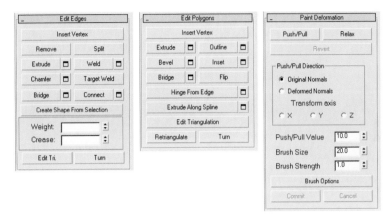

Figure 3-40. Three powerful rollouts of an edit poly object

The features in each of these rollouts are designed primarily to give the user greater flexibility and power in the modeling of an object. For example, while in Edge subobject mode, you can select edges, as shown in the left image of Figure 3-41, and using the Connect Edges option you can quickly generate edges to model a window opening.

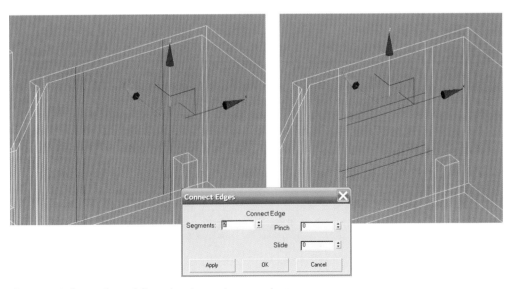

Figure 3-41. Connecting existing edges to creates new edges

If you then enter polygon subobject mode and select the two new polygons that were created, you can use the Bridge Polygons feature to connect the inside and outside surfaces of the wall, which automatically removes the two polygons and leaves an opening in which you can place a window, as shown in Figure 3-42. The Connect and Bridge features are not available with an edit mesh object and are just two examples of the many great features the edit poly has to offer.

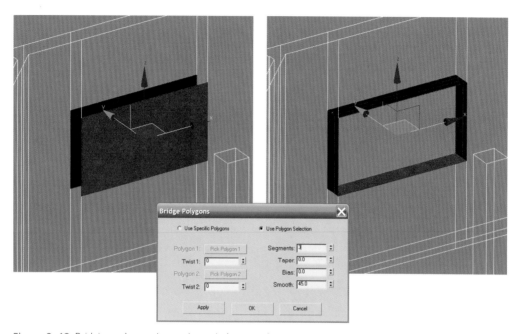

Figure 3-42. Bridging polygons to create a window opening

Within the Paint Deformation rollout is another great feature that, as the name implies, lets you paint deformations into any subobject type. In Figure 3-43, for example, I carved the name of my business into the terrain. By setting the Push/Pull value to 2'0", the Brush Size to 4'0", and dragging within a viewport, all subjects that the paint brush gizmo moves over will be pushed up 2'0" in elevation. This is a fantastic way to apply some relief to terrain, assuming you have enough vertices in the edit poly object to provide smooth deformations.

Figure 3-43. Using paint deformation to sculpt the name '3DAS' into the ground

In the follow on companion to this book, 3ds Max 2008 Architectural Visualization, Intermediate to Advanced, the edit poly object type is investigated in much greater detail and is implemented in the creation of many different object types in numerous different tutorials. If you want to know more about the edit poly object, that book should be a great help.

Summary

Hopefully, you now understand some of the basics behind some of the powerful modeling features widely used in the visualization industry and hopefully you understand how important it is to set up 3ds Max properly before beginning any project. It can be heartbreaking to fall victim to some of the perils that can come from not properly setting up the 3ds Max environment, such as losing hours of work or learning months later that you've been using the wrong graphics driver.

This chapter has covered the most important concepts in scene setup, as well as the important basic features of splines, shapes, and meshes. The concepts in this chapter will give you the foundations of efficient architectural modeling.

The Critical Compound Objects Types (Loft, Boolean, Pro Boolean, Terrain, and Scatter)

NOW THAT THE BASICS OF modeling have been covered, it's time to discuss some of the truly powerful modeling tools for architectural visualizations. Within the **Geometry** tab of the **Create** panel is a drop-down list (discussed in Chapter 1) that provides access to numerous object-creation tools for every different industry. Many of these groups of tools provide little or no help to visualizations, however, as they are geared more toward other industries. In fact, of the 11 groups listed, only 3 are discussed in this book. The first group, **Standard Primitives,** is obviously a must for all 3ds Max users. Another group, **Particle Systems,** is a must for anyone needing to show flowing water, snow, or other types of systems comprised of small particles. The third group of tools covered in this book, **Compound Objects,** provides five critical modeling tools for the visualization industry.

Compound objects, as the name implies, are object types created from two or more objects. Compound objects can be created from two splines, two primitives, or any number of object types. What makes compound objects so critical is that they each perform at least one specific task far better and faster than any other tool in 3ds Max. As I say throughout this book, there are usually numerous means to the same end. Sometimes, however, there is clearly a fastest means, and the compound objects discussed in this chapter constitute five such examples.

Creating Lofts

If somebody were to ask me what the most powerful and versatile feature of 3ds Max is for creating architectural visualizations, I would say without hesitation: the Loft feature. Whether you're creating walls, street curbs, rain gutters, or window sills, no other feature in 3ds Max can create the architectural features you will need as quickly and with as much flexibility as lofts can. In 3ds Max, there are so many ways to do the same thing, but when it comes to lofts, there's clearly a fastest way.

The term "loft" has many definitions, but the one that applies most closely here is "to propel into space." The Loft feature in 3ds Max requires two splines or shapes: one that defines a path, and one that defines the shape that gets "propelled into space" along the path.

To access the Loft command, select a shape or spline and click **Create ➤ Geometry ➤ Compound Objects ➤ Loft.** When you do, five rollouts appear, as shown in Figure 4-1. The remainder of this section explores the contents of these rollouts.

Figure 4-1. The Loft feature

The Creation Method rollout

This rollout simply gives you the option of lofting a shape along a path, with the loft being created at the shape's location or the path's location. Personally, I cannot think of a single architectural application for which the **Get Path** creation method would be more beneficial. Figure 4-2 shows the difference between the two options. The image on the left shows two rectangles, the larger representing the wall outline of a building and the smaller representing a typical wall section. The middle image shows a loft created at the path location, and the right image shows a loft created at the shape location. The difference should be clear.

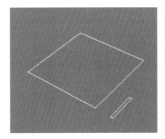

Figure 4-2. Creating lofts with Get Path (center) and Get Shape (right)

Lofts in visualizations should be created using the **Get Shape** option, in which the user creates the paths in the locations where the lofts will exist, and then creates the shapes off to the side in some arbitrary location. To create a loft using this method, select a single path (a shape or spline that represents the location of the loft), click **Get Shape,** and then select the shape. The path must be a continuous, unbroken shape or spline for the **Get Shape** option to be selectable.

The other option available in the **Creation Method** rollout allows the user to move or copy the shape or path during creation or keep the default method of instance. The instance method allows you to update the loft by updating either the path or shape after creation. The **Move** and **Copy** methods do not offer this flexibility of modification, and I therefore recommend always leaving the **Instance** option selected. As long as the object remains a loft, a direct link is maintained with the path and profile. This aspect of lofts is illustrated in a crude but easy-to-understand example in Figure 4-3, which depicts a loft used to represent the walls and fascia of a simple structure.

The top-left image in Figure 4-3 shows a path representing the perimeter walls of the structure and a small shape representing the wall section. The top-middle image shows the loft created from the two. In the top-right image, you can see that the height of the loft is increased, which was done by simply moving individual vertices of the shape. The loft changes its structure accordingly. In the bottom-left image, two vertices of the path are moved, and again the loft changes accordingly, as shown in the bottom-right image. This link that the loft maintains with the shape and path makes the loft a powerful and versatile tool.

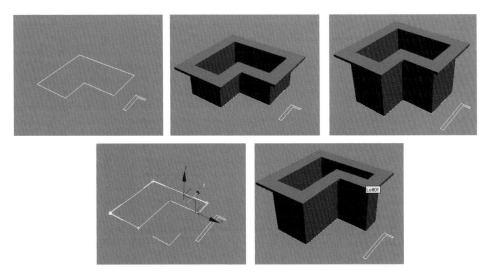

Figure 4-3. The power of instanced lofts

Creating a loft

This exercise demonstrates how to create a simple loft that represents the walls of a building using two shapes to represent a loft path and a loft shape.

1. Reset 3ds Max.

2. Change the units to **US Standard.**

3. In the Top view, create a rectangle with a length and width of **30**'. This shape will represent the loft path.

4. In the Top view, create a second rectangle, with a length of **10'** and a width of **8"**. This shape will represent the loft shape.

5. Select the smaller rectangle (representing the loft shape) and click the **Hierarchy** tab.

6. Click **Affect Pivot Only.**

7. Click the **Align** icon, and in the Top view, click the smaller rectangle. The **Align Selection** dialog box appears.

8. Under **Current Object,** select **Pivot Point,** and under **Target Object,** select **Minimum,** as shown in the following screenshot. Select the **X** and **Y** positions, and deselect the **Z** position. Click **OK** to end the command. This command moves the pivot point to one of the bottom corners of the shape.

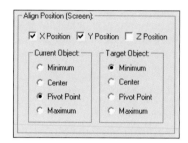

9. Select the large rectangle representing the loft path.

10. In the Command panel, click **Create ➤ Geometry ➤ Compound Objects ➤ Loft**.

11. Click **Get Shape.** The loft will be created, as shown in the following illustration:

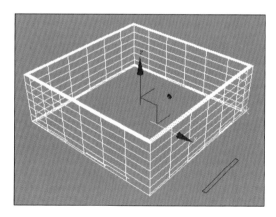

12. Select the small rectangle (representing the loft shape) and add the **Edit Spline** modifier.

13. Enter Vertex sub-object mode, and highlight the top two vertices of the loft shape.

14. In the Top view, move the selected vertices **2'** upward along the y axis. The loft representing the walls of a building should increase in height by the same 2'.

The Surface Parameters rollout

The next rollout, **Surface Parameters** (see Figure 4-4), contains several useful features that help the loft stand out as one of the most versatile and powerful modeling tools. Fortunately, most lofts will not require these settings to be adjusted. **Smoothing Length** and **Smoothing Width** should be left enabled because they remove any shading imperfections, which can otherwise be quite noticeable. **Apply Mapping** allows you to apply materials to a loft in a way no other tool can: along the length of a loft. If you want the image of tree bark, for example, to be repeated along the branch of a tree that twists and turns, this option makes that possible with minimal distortion to the map. Otherwise, you are left to create mapping with tools that would make this much more difficult and probably lead to significant distortion of the map. The **Length Repeat** and **Width Repeat** parameters control how often the maps are tiled in their respective directions.

Under the **Materials** section is an option you may find useful: **Generate Material IDs.** This option applies material IDs to a loft in the same way they're assigned to the loft's shape. For example, in Figure 4-4, a multi/sub-object material composed of two sub-materials is applied to the wall loft. Notice the bottom of the wall has a brick material applied, and the top is painted a light tan color. This is because the bottom segment of the shape is assigned a sub-material ID of 1 (brick) and the top segment of the shape is assigned a sub-material ID of 2 (paint); and those two materials are occupying the material 1 and material 2 slots within the multi-object material defined in the **Material Editor.**

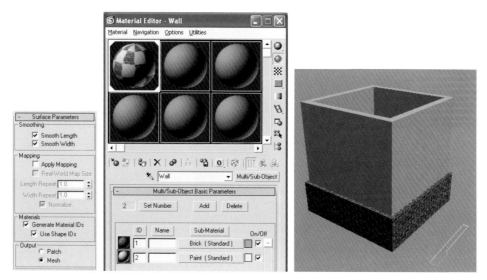

Figure 4-4. Generating material IDs for lofts

Once you select Use **Shape IDs** and apply a multi/sub-object material to the loft, the loft uses the material IDs of the shape to determine which parts of the loft get which sub-material. As a matter of practice, I do not use this feature much because there are usually better ways to apply materials to lofts, which will be discussed in Chapter 6. Nonetheless, it is a feature that many veteran users like and is worth some experimentation.

The **Output** section gives you the option to create the loft as a patch or a mesh. The default **Mesh** option should be kept because meshes allow for better editing, and your lofts will eventually be collapsed to a mesh anyway.

The Path Parameters rollout

The next rollout, **Path Parameters** (see Figure 4-5), allows you to apply multiple shapes along the same path. You can specify where in the path each shape begins its effect on the loft in one of three ways: percentage down the length of the path, distance down the length of the path, and the path steps (i.e., vertices) down the length, starting with vertex 1.

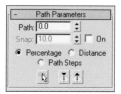

Figure 4-5. The Path Parameters rollout

The top-left image in Figure 4-6 shows a loft created with the circle shape, and the top-middle image shows the same loft modified by adding a star shape at 100% down the length of the path (i.e., the other end of the loft). To do this, type **100** in the **Path** field (as shown in the top-right image of Figure 4-6), click **Get Shape** again, and pick the star shape. Notice that 3ds Max transitions the loft from the circle shape to the star shape. The bottom-left image shows the same loft with the star shape being applied 50% down the length of the path.

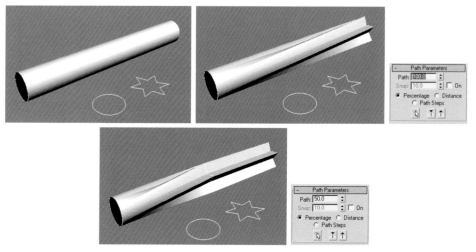

Figure 4-6. Lofting with multiple shapes, using percentage values

Another way to loft multiple shapes along the same path is using the loft's steps to determine the location of each shape's effect on the loft. The top-left image in Figure 4-7 shows the same loft in the previous example with two steps added along the loft (as shown in the **Path Steps** field of the top-right image). The bottom-left image shows the result of checking **Path Steps** (bottom-right image), entering **1** into the **Path** field, reexecuting the **Get Shape** command for step 1, and repeating this process for steps 2 and 3. In short, steps 0 and 3 (the ends of the loft) get the circular shape, while steps 1 and 2 (the middle of the loft) get the star shape.

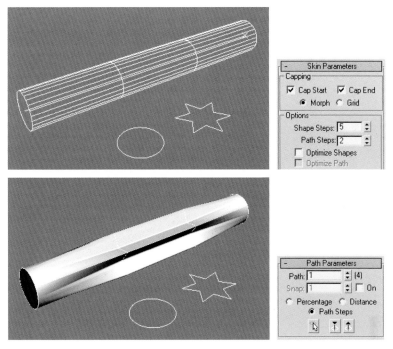

Figure 4-7. Lofting with multiple shapes using Path Steps

The final way to loft multiple shapes along the same loft is by using a specific distance to determine the location of each shape's effect on the loft. The loft in the preceding example is exactly 1 50 units long, and therefore, with the **Distance** option enabled, you can achieve the same result by reapplying the star shape to the loft at a distance of 50 and 100. In short, the distances of 0 and 150 units (the ends of the loft) get the circular shape, while the distances of 50 and 100 (the middle of the loft) get the star shape. The images in Figure 4-8 show the four distances for which the two shapes must be applied.

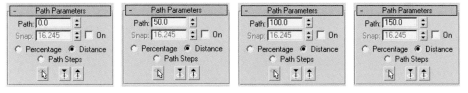

Figure 4-8. Lofting with multiple shapes using Distance

The Skin Parameters rollout

The next rollout, **Skin Parameters** (see Figure 4-9), begins with options to cap the start and end of the loft. A cap simply closes or fills in the ends of the loft with faces so that the loft doesn't appear hollow. The **Cap Start** and **Cap End** options are selected by default, along with the **Morph** option, and should not be changed unless there is a specific reason to justify doing otherwise. I have never found such a reason.

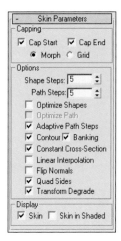

Figure 4-9. The Skin Parameters rollout

Under the **Options** section is the most critical portion of the loft rollouts, which was discussed briefly in the previous example. The **Shape Steps** parameter lets you increase or decrease the number of additional vertices added between the original vertices that make up the shape. The **Path Steps** parameter allows you to do the same thing for the path. Both have a default of 5, but they will almost always need to be based on the situation.

Figure 4-10 shows an example of modifying both the shape steps and path steps. The image on the left shows a small circle, which represents the shape, lofted along a larger circle that represents the path. The loft is created using all of the default values for each rollout, to include five path and shape steps. Notice in the middle image what happens when only **Shape Steps** is reduced to **0**, thus retaining only the original four vertices to define the look of the shape. The result is a loft with a diamond-shaped cross-section. In the image on the right, **Shape Steps** is put back to its default value of 5, and this time **Path Steps** is reduced to 0, leaving only the original four vertices to define the path. The result is a diamond-shaped path with a circular cross-section.

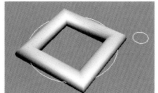

Figure 4-10. Using Shape Steps and Path Steps

The **Optimize Shapes** and **Optimize Path** options remove any unnecessary vertices in the shape or path, such as multiple vertices in a straight section of the shape. The **Adaptive Path Steps** option automatically places vertices in the location necessary to produce a smooth look to all curved sections of the shape. Figure 4-11 shows one example of these options, in which a loft representing a street curb is lofted with and without the **Optimize Path** option enabled. Notice that when enabled (as in the left image), all unnecessary steps are removed from the straight segments of the path.

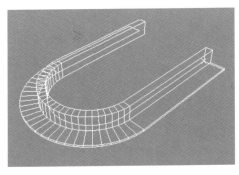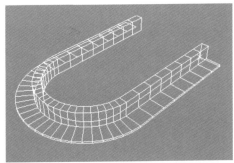

Figure 4-11. The Optimize Path option enabled (left) and disabled (right)

There are several other options in this rollout, but the only others you will likely have to modify within architectural projects are the **Banking** and **Flip Normals** options. I highly recommend turning off **Banking** unless you specifically need it to correctly model something like a roller coaster, for which you want the shape to be banked at curves in the path. Leaving **Banking** checked often causes slight but often noticeable imperfections in the modeling process where corners exist in the path. Additionally, you may encounter rare occasions when your loft appears to be inside out. This occurs when, for whatever reason, the program doesn't know which way the loft should be viewed. When this happens, try selecting the **Flip Normals** option to correct the problem.

Additionally, you may find it visually helpful to disable the **Transform Degrade** option so that you can see changes to the loft while you are applying transforms. Otherwise, you have to finish applying the transform before you get to see what the result is.

The last section within the **Skin Parameters** rollout, **Display,** needs no modification.

Modifying the shape steps and path steps of a loft

This exercise demonstrates how to modify the shape steps and path steps of a loft to provide an adequate number of vertices for smooth curves.

1. Reset 3ds Max.

2. Change the units to **US Standard.**

3. In the Top view, create a circle with a radius of **10'**, and a second circle with a radius of **2'**.

4. Select the larger circle.

5. In the Command panel, click **Create ➤ Geometry ➤ Compound Objects ➤ Loft ➤ Get Shape.**

6. Click the smaller circle. The loft is created with default settings, as shown in the left image in the following illustration.

7. In the Command panel, click the **Modify** tab.

8. Open the **Skin Parameters** rollout and change **Path Steps** to **0**. The loft becomes diamond-shaped because there are no longer any path steps, as shown in the middle image.

9. Change **Path Steps** back to its default value of **5,** and then change **Shape Steps** to **0**. The loft is now circular again but has a diamond-shaped cross-section, as shown in the right image.

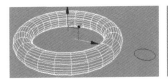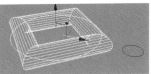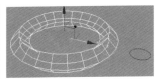

The Deformations rollout

The last rollout for lofts, **Deformations,** appears only within the **Modify** panel. It contains some powerful tools, but their practicality is very limited in architectural visualizations. I do not use them at all because I simply never have the need to deform lofts in these ways. In other fields of work, however, these tools can be invaluable. I will not cover deformations in this book.

Creating Booleans

With the release of a 3ds Max 8 Extension, Autodesk gave its loyal followers arguably the best new feature in several years when it integrated the **ProBoolean** plug-in into 3ds Max. The ProBoolean feature is an immensely powerful tool that serves as a solution to the many problems that users of the standard **Boolean** feature have faced. The standard Boolean feature has been around since the beginning of 3ds Max and it has been a feature that most users have either come to love or hate. I can't think of any feature so underrated and so unjustifiably criticized as the Boolean, especially since the release of the ProBoolean feature. Unfortunately, those who have expressed their displeasure with the use of the Boolean feature over the years have usually done so because they were not aware of what the Boolean could actually do or were not following some basic guidelines which make using the Boolean command failsafe. At the end of this section on Booleans, I will point out the guidelines that should be followed when using the Boolean feature.

Figure 4-12.
The Boolean feature

While the ProBoolean feature is a critical asset to our work and in fact a much more powerful and versatile tool than the standard Boolean, as of this latest release of 3ds Max, Autodesk has yet to fix a bug in ProBoolean that truly limits its usefulness to those of us in the visualization industry. Until this bug is fixed, I consider the standard Boolean a critical feature that anyone in the visualization should have in their modeling toolbox. In just a moment, I will explain what this bug is, but for now let's look closely look at the standard Boolean and what it's capable of.

A Boolean is an object created from the combination of two separate objects. How the objects combine to form a Boolean depends on the type of Boolean operation performed. Some examples include adding the geometry of one object to another, or using one object's volume to subtract from another object's volume. With Booleans, you can easily create window and door openings within a wall; you can create streets, parking symbols, and sidewalks out of a terrain surface; you can cut ornate designs out of simple primitives; and much more. One of the best things about Booleans is how simple they are to create. Now we'll focus on the procedures used to create each of the different types of Booleans.

To access the Boolean feature (shown in Figure 4-12), select **Create ➤ Compound Objects ➤ Boolean.** Each type of Boolean operation requires two objects; the first object is operand A and the second object is operand B. There are four rollouts that make up the Boolean feature. The first, **Name and Color,** requires no explanation, and the last rollout, **Display/Update,** is of little importance, and a rollout I have never found necessary. With the **Pick Boolean** rollout, the only feature you will probably ever use is the **Pick Operand** button, which actually executes the Boolean command. The point is, the Boolean feature is a very simple feature with only a few important options.

Union

The **Union** operation (Figure 4-13) combines two objects into one, regardless of whether they overlap. To perform a union, select an object (A), select **Boolean** ➤ **Union,** and then select a second object (B), which you'll add to A. Which object is A and which is B is irrelevant.

 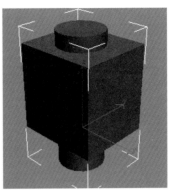

Figure 4-13. An example of a union

Subtraction

The **Subtraction** operation (see Figure 4-14) subtracts one object's volume from another. To perform the operation, select the object that you want to subtract from (A), and then select the second object whose volume you want subtract from the first (B). The result is that object B's volume is subtracted from object A. With the **Subtraction** operation, you have the option of subtracting B from A (default) or A from B. It makes no difference which method you use as long as you select the objects in the order required to achieve the result you need. This is one of countless examples in 3ds Max where there are more ways than one to accomplish a task.

 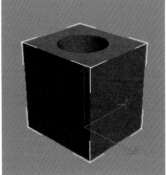

Figure 4-14. An example of a subtraction

Intersection

The **Intersection** operation (Figure 4-15) creates an object from only the overlapping part of two objects. As with the **Union** operation, which object is A and which is B is irrelevant. This operation has only rare use in architecture.

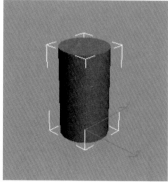

Figure 4-15. An example of an intersection

Creating a Boolean

This exercise demonstrates how to create the various Boolean types.

1. Reset 3ds Max.

2. In the Perspective view, create two equally sized spheres that overlap each other, as shown in the left image of the following illustration.

3. With one of the spheres selected, in the Command panel, click **Create ➤ Geometry ➤ Compound Objects ➤ Boolean ➤ Pick Operand B**. The Boolean is created with the default **Subtraction** method.

4. Click on the Intersection and Union options to see the result of these types of Boolean operations. Compare your results to the following illustration, which shows the two original spheres (left), and from left to right, an example of a union, an intersection, and a subtraction.

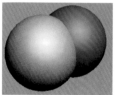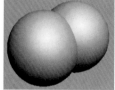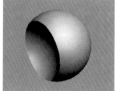

Cut

At the beginning of this section on Booleans, I mentioned that the ProBoolean feature contains what I consider a serious bug that drastically limits its usefulness in the visualization industry. This bug is simply the inability to split polygons on an object, which the **Cut** mode of the standard Boolean does quite nicely. It's the inability of the ProBoolean to perform this simple task that makes learning the Boolean feature not only worthwhile, but quite necessary in the visualization industry.

The Cut operation uses the volume of one object to split another object into two parts, or to change another object's structure by adding vertices. For example, the left image in Figure 4-16 shows an extruded star intersecting a plane. The middle image shows the result of using the **Refine** option, which creates new edges in the plane where it's intersected by the star. The third image shows the result of the **Split** operation, a personal favorite. This operation lets you perform a cookie-cutter type of action, in which the volume of an object that lies within the volume of an intersecting object is separated from the rest of itself.

What makes the Cut>Split feature so great is that once you complete the operation, you can add the Edit Mesh or Edit Poly modifier to the Boolean object, go to face or polygon subobject mode, and see the cut faces automatically selected. Because the cut faces or polygons are automatically selected, you can easily split the subobjects apart from the rest of the object by using the Detach command.

As we will see in the next section, the ProBoolean feature can also cut the volume of one object out of another, but when you add the Edit Mesh or Edit Poly modifier, those cut faces are not automatically selected. Because of this, you have to manually select all of the cut faces if you want to split them apart from the main object, which for even a moderately complex object can take an enormous amount of time to do.

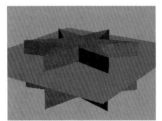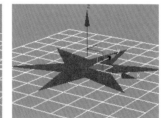

Figure 4-16. Example of the Cut operation

Suggestions for creating Booleans

As I stated at the beginning of this section, Booleans have received a great deal of criticism by users who have had poor results with their use because of not following some basic rules. They can certainly seem temperamental and uncooperative when conditions for their creation are not ideal, so when you create Booleans, here are a few things to keep in mind:

• Make sure that the objects you're subtracting from other volumes are closed surfaces. When I first started creating Booleans, I would import what I thought were closed splines from AutoCAD, extrude those splines to create a solid, and subtract those solids from my wall loft to create window and door openings. Many times the Boolean operation would be erratic or not work at all. For the longest time, I didn't realize that the problem was that during import, the start and end vertices of the splines didn't automatically weld. 3ds Max treated them as open surfaces, even though when extruded they appeared to be solids. The easy fix is to manually weld the vertices before extruding.

- Boolean operations do not always work well when some of the object faces are long and skinny. If an operation does not work right the first time, try adding more vertices to the mesh through object parameters, or with the **Subdivide** modifier. The ProBoolean is a lot more forgiving of these long and skinny faces, and except for very extreme cases, has little problem with this situation.

- Objects that have modifiers in their modifier stack can sometimes cause problems with the Boolean operation. One thing to try, and something I always do anyway when creating Boolean objects, is to collapse each object to a mesh prior to the operation. Collapsing after the operation is also a good practice in that it makes future Booleans work better and helps to reduce file size.

- Boolean operations can be erratic when face normals are not consistent. Make sure each object's face normals are unified and facing the proper direction. The **Normal** modifier can sometimes help accomplish this.

- Never perform a Boolean on linked objects. Booleans will not work on linked objects, and one of the operands will most likely disappear.

Creating ProBooleans

ProBoolean uses the same basic principles of subtraction, intersection, union, etc., but performs these operations with far fewer problems and with far greater functionality. To perform a ProBoolean operation, select an object, apply the ProBoolean command, click the **Start Picking** button, and simply pick the operands you want to use in the operation. Unlike the Boolean command, the ProBoolean command gives you the ability to continuously add more operands to the operation. Notice at the bottom of Figure 4-17 that three separate objects have been subtracted from the initial object. And unlike the Boolean command, with ProBoolean, you can leave the operation, work on another part of your scene, and come back later to continue adding other operands to the operation.

Just like the Boolean command, with ProBoolean you can change the type of operation you want to perform after the first operation has already been completed. For example, you can create a subtraction and immediately change it to a union without having to undo your work. To change an operation, simply select a new type from the **Operation** section and click the **Change Operation** button to complete the change. However, unlike the Boolean, when you create a ProBoolean operation you can still edit all of the original objects that make up the ProBoolean and you can apply transforms to those objects, causing the ProBoolean to update automatically.

Figure 4-17.
The ProBoolean

Creating a ProBoolean object

This exercise demonstrates how to create a ProBoolean object from several different objects and then change the operation after the object is created.

1. Reset 3ds Max.

2. In the Top view, create a box and a sphere so that the volume of each overlaps each other, similar to the image below.

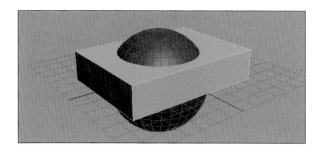

3. Select the box, and in the Command panel, click **Create ➤ Geometry ➤ Compound Objects ➤ ProBoolean**.

4. Click the **Start Picking** button.

5. Click on the sphere. The sphere is subtracted from the box because Subtraction is the default operation type.

6. Create a cylinder in the Top view so that its volume lies within the boundary of the Pro-Boolean object, as shown in the next image.

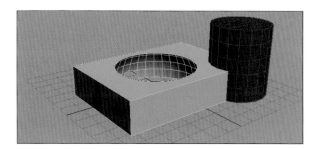

7. Select the ProBoolean object you created, go to the **Modify** panel and click **Start Picking** again.

8. Click on the cylinder. The cylinder is subtracted from the ProBoolean object.

9. In the **Operation** section of the **Parameters** rollout, change the operation type from Subtraction to **Intersection**. Notice that nothing changed. This is because you have to tell 3ds Max what object(s) you want specifically to be changed to an intersection.

10. At the bottom of the **Parameters** rollout, select the sphere object, as shown in the left image below, and click the **Change Operation** button. Notice that the ProBoolean object changes to show a volume that is the result of the intersection of the box and the sphere. The effect of the cylinder is not apparent anymore because the cylinder was outside the boundary of the new intersection object and had nothing to subtract from.

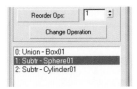 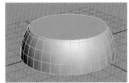

Notice that because the sphere is selected in the operand list, as shown in the previous image, the sphere is also listed in the modifier stack, as shown in the next image. Because of this, you can select the sphere in the modifier stack and change all of the parameters that the original sphere contains.

11. Click on the sphere in the modifier stack as shown in the next image. The Modify panel changes to show all of the parameters found with the initial sphere object.

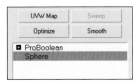

12. Increase the radius of the sphere slightly so that the resulting ProBoolean object becomes bound by the limits of the initial box operand and so that the affect of the column subtraction is apparent as well, as shown in the image below.

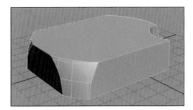

13. In the modifier stack, click on the plus symbol to the left of the ProBoolean name. This opens the operand stack.

14. Click on the word **Operands**. The word becomes highlighted in yellow indicating that you can now transform the operand.

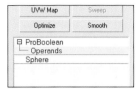

15. Click on the **Move** transform icon and use the transform gizmo to move the sphere around in a viewport. Notice that what you always see is the result of the intersection of the box and the sphere combined with the subtraction of the cylinder.

This previous exercise simply scratches the surface of the power and versatility of the Pro-Boolean object. There are still numerous functions and controls available with this feature and before leaving a discussion of the ProBoolean, I want to cover one more area of this command that can be invaluable to our work in the visualization industry.

If you were to use the standard Boolean command to subtract an object from a flat surface, such as an plane or an extrude line, as shown in the left image of Figure 4-18, you would be left with nothing but a void where the subtracted volume use to be, as shown in the middle image. With Pro-Booleans, the default subtraction method treats the surface as if were a solid, cutting into the surface and adding faces along the sides, as shown in the right image.

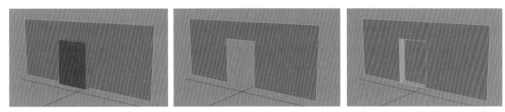

Figure 4-18. Variations of the ProBoolean subtraction operation

To completely cut out a void using ProBoolean, you have to use the **Cookie** option as shown in Figure 4-19. The **Imprint** option will cut the faces of one object with the boundary of another, just like the Cut>Split option in the standard Boolean command. However, as I mentioned earlier, with the ProBoolean method, i.e. the Subtraction>Imprint option, the cut faces are not automatically selected when you add the Edit Mesh or Edit Poly modifier and enter face or polygon subobject mode. The **Merge** option simply combines two objects, similar to the Union option, except the Merge option does not remove any faces in the process. I do not know of any practical visualization application for this option.

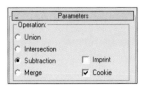

Figure 4-19. ProBoolean operation types

In the **Advanced** rollout of the ProBoolean command are numerous controls that allow you to control the re-triangulation of faces that occurs when a ProBoolean is created. These controls are certainly nice to have but they are not critical to the use of ProBoolean and are not covered in this book.

Creating terrain

The Terrain modeling tool is a great way to create terrain from elevation contour lines. Drawings containing elevation contour lines are usually created by surveyors or landscape architects with a program such as AutoCAD. Whether these lines are created in 3ds Max or imported from other programs, they must be closed to be used in the Terrain feature.

To create terrain, place the contour splines at varying elevations, select all the splines, and click the **Terrain** button in the **Compound Objects** drop-down menu. When you do, several rollouts appear with numerous options, as shown in Figure 4-20. You can add additional splines at any time by clicking the **Pick Operand** button in the **Pick Operand** rollout. All of the splines that make up the terrain object are listed as operands in the **Operands** list. The top three images in Figure 4-21 show several splines positioned at various elevations, and the bottom two images show the result of applying the Terrain command with different options found in the **Form** section of the **Parameters** rollout.

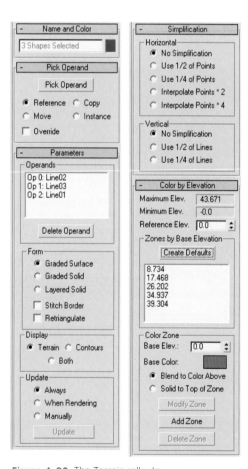

Figure 4-20. The Terrain rollouts

The **Form** section includes options for how the terrain is formed. The **Graded Surface** and **Graded Solid** options, both shown in the bottom-left image of Figure 4-21, will almost always be the most applicable to architectural visualizations because they depict natural terrain. Both options provide the same result, except that **Graded Solid** puts a bottom and a skirt on the surface, making the surface viewable from any direction. The **Layered Solid** option, shown in the bottom-right image of Figure 4-21, provides a tiered terrain, which may be beneficial in certain situations. The other options within the **Parameters** rollout do not need to be discussed for architectural work.

Figure 4-21. Creating terrain

The **Simplification** rollout contains some very important options to understand. If it is not necessary to have highly detailed or accurate terrain, you may want to try the **Use 1/2 of Points** or **Use 1/4 of Points** options. These options simply reduce the number of vertices used to model the terrain, which reduces the total number of polygons and the strain on your computer. If the number of polygons is not a factor, and you intend to have the best looking terrain you can, I recommend using the **Interpolate Points *4** option. This option provides the best terrain by interpolating the spaces in between the lines, thus providing smooth, realistic curves. Under the **Vertical** section, use the **No Simplification** option for best results, or the **Use 1/2 of Lines** or **Use 1/4 of Lines** options if you are trying to reduce polygons.

Although not a favorite of mine, you may want to try coloring your terrain with features in the **Color by Elevation** rollout. There are much better ways to apply materials to your terrain, which will be discussed in Chapter 6, but if you want a simple and quick method to give your terrain color, this may suffice. Simply click the **Create Defaults** button to apply default colors to default elevations. To make a change, highlight one of the elevation values that now appears in the elevations windows, and use the color swatch to change the color of each zone. You must click the **Modify Zone** button before the changes take effect.

Creating a terrain object

This exercise demonstrates how to create a terrain object using splines that represent contour lines.

1. Reset 3ds Max.

2. In the Top view, create a series of five circles that do not overlap, as shown in image 1 of the following illustration. These lines will represent contour lines.

3. Select each spline individually, and using the **Transform Type-In** dialog box or the transform gizmo, move each spline (except the outer spline) upward along the z axis. Move the smaller splines that are closer to the center farther upward (as shown in image 2), as they represent higher elevations.

4. Select all of the splines, and in the Command panel, click **Create ➤ Geometry ➤ Compound Objects ➤ Terrain.** A terrain object is created, as shown in image 3. Notice, however, that the terrain is jagged around the base. This is because there are not enough vertices to define the perimeter.

5. Select the bottom outer circle, enter **Segment** sub-object mode, and select the four segments that define the circle (as shown in image 4).

6. Scroll down to the bottom of the **Geometry** rollout under the **Edit Spline** modifier and type **10** in the **Divide** field.

7. Click **Divide.** The original four segments are divided into ten additional segments each, and the base of the terrain object is now smooth, as shown in image 5 and 6. You can repeat this process for each spline if necessary.

8. Undo steps 5 through 7 to return the terrain to its original form with the jagged bottom.

9. Select the terrain object and click the **Modify** tab in the **Command** panel.

10. In the **Simplification** rollout, click **Interpolate Points * 4.** This also increases the number of points used to define the elevation lines; however, unlike dividing the line segments as described in steps 5 through 7, this method does not provide the same flexibility for defining the number of additional vertices used.

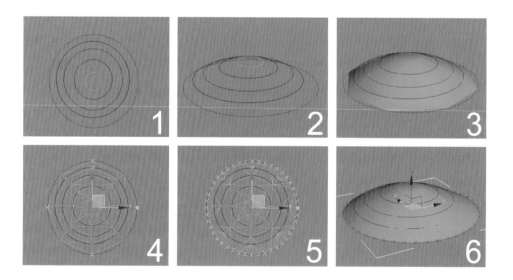

Creating scatter objects

The Scatter feature arranges copies of a selected object over the surface or within the volume of another object. The object that is scattered is the source object, and the object that the source is scattered on or within is known as the distribution object. In architectural visualizations, the Scatter feature's usefulness is limited primarily to the creation of vegetation. In this way, it's a great tool for scattering leaves around the branches of a tree or blades of grass around the surface of a lawn.

Figure 4-22 shows an example of the scatter routine by scattering a palm tree around the surface of a simple plane object. The top-left image shows the plane and a tree off to the side. To scatter the tree, select the source object (palm tree) and select **Create ➤ Compound Objects ➤ Scatter.** Complete the scatter routine by clicking the **Pick Distribution Object** button (first rollout) and then clicking the distribution object, which in this scene is the plane. The top-right image shows the result. By default, 3ds Max only places one object, and requires you to specify the number of duplicates desired. Also, notice that the plane appears to be a different color. This is because, by default, a copy of the distribution object is created with a new color and exists in the same space. The first thing to do is to turn off this distribution object. Scroll down to the **Display** rollout, open the rollout, and select **Hide Distribution Object,** as shown in Figure 4-22.

Figure 4-22. The Scatter feature

Within the **Scatter Objects rollout is a section called Objects, which contains the source and** distribution operands (palm tree and plane objects, respectively). In the **Source Object Parameters** section (see Figure 4-23), you can change the number of duplicates, but caution should be taken to ensure that you don't lock up your computer by entering too large a number for the particular object you want to scatter. Many operations in 3ds Max (such as this one) can consume a lot of RAM if you enter too large a value for the parameter. If you make too many duplicates of an object with a large number of polygons, the computer may run out of memory and crash. The right image in Figure 4-23 shows the result of increasing the **Duplicates** value to **20.**

Figure 4-23. Increasing the Duplicates value to 20

The remaining three options in this section do not require any modifications, but I will explain them in the event that a rare exception arises. **Base Scale** specifies how much the distribution object is scaled before being scattered, with 100% signifying no change in size. The **Vertex Chaos** value specifies how much randomness to apply to the positioning of vertices. This option can distort the appearance of the object being scattered, but can sometimes add a nice touch of realism in certain situations. The **Animation Offset** value specifies the number of frames that must go by before another duplicate is created.

Distribution object parameters

The first option in this section, **Perpendicular,** aligns each duplicate so that the duplicate's normal is aligned with the normal of the face it's closest to. Without **Perpendicular** enabled, all duplicates would remain oriented in the direction of the initial object. The left-hand image in Figure 4-24 has **Perpendicular** enabled, and the image on the right shows the same object with **Perpendicular** disabled.

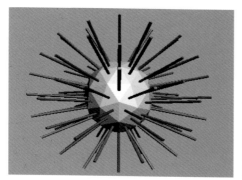 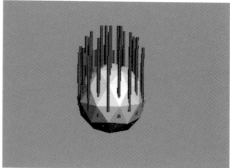

Figure 4-24. The Perpendicular option enabled (left) and disabled (right)

The **Use Selected Faces Only** option allows you to select specific faces on which to distribute the duplicates. The next variable, **Distribute Using**, determines how the duplicates are to be scattered over the distribution object.

The Transform rollout

The **Transform** rollout specifies the maximum amount of transformation randomly applied to each object. The duplicates can be randomly rotated, moved, or scaled about any or all three axes. The top-right image in Figure 4-25 shows the palm trees again, this time with a **Z Rotation** value of **90** applied. This means that all objects are randomly rotated around their z axis +/– 90 degrees. The bottom-right image has a **Z Scaling** value of 50% applied. This means that all objects are randomly scaled along the z axis between +/– 50% (i.e., some trees are 50% taller, some are 50% shorter, and some are anywhere in between). These two settings are particularly useful when scattering vegetation, which, as I stated before, is probably the most practical application of the Scatter command.

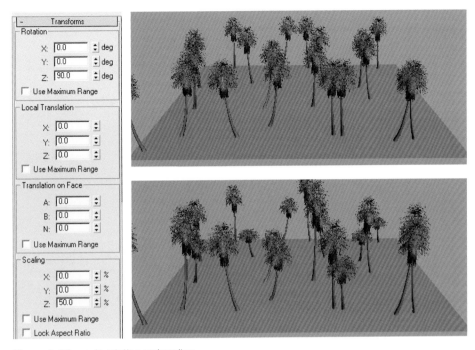

Figure 4-25. z axis rotation and scaling

Creating a scatter object

This exercise demonstrates how to create a scatter object, using a teapot as the object to be scattered and a plane as the distribution object.

1. Reset 3ds Max.

2. In the Top view, create a plane with a width and length of **100**, and a teapot with a radius of **10**, as shown in image 1 of the following illustration.

3. Select the teapot, and in the Command panel, click **Create ➤ Geometry ➤ Compound Objects ➤ Scatter.**

4. Click **Pick Distribution Object** and click the plane in any viewport. The scatter object is created with only one object (by default), as shown in image 2. Notice also that a duplicate plane object is created, which becomes the real distribution object. This object, however, is not desired and should be hidden from view.

5. In the **Display** rollout, enable the **Hide Distribution Object** option. The duplicate plane disappears.

6. Within the **Source Object Parameters** section of the **Scatter Objects** rollout, type **12** in the field next to **Duplicates,** and press Enter. There are now a total of 12 teapots that make up the scatter object, as shown in image 3. Notice, however, that all of the teapots are oriented along the same axis.

7. Within the **Rotation** section of the **Transforms** rollout, type **90** in the field next to **Z:**. This will randomly rotate each teapot around the z axis somewhere between 0 and 90 degrees, as shown in image 4.

8. Within the **Distribution Object Parameters** section of the **Scatter Objects** rollout, change the **Distribute Using** option from **Even** to **Area**. This changes how the objects are distributed about the distribution object, as shown in image 5. You should test the **Even, Area,** and **Volume** options to see which produces the best look.

9. Within the **Scale** section of the **Transforms** rollout, type **50** in the field next to **Z:**. This will randomly scale each teapot along the z axis somewhere between +/– 50%, as shown in image 6.

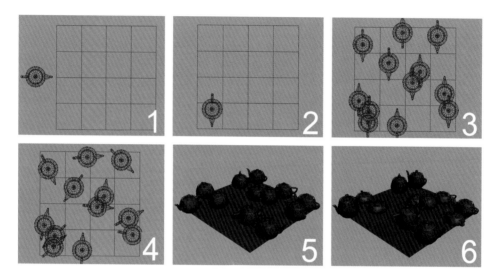

Summary

The five compound objects discussed in this chapter provide tremendous modeling power for 3ds Max users in the visualization industry. Whether you are trying to create terrain from an engineering drawing of contour lines, scatter leaves along the branches of a tree, or erect complex walls capable of easy modification, compound objects can do the job.

This chapter has covered four powerful modeling tools that begin the creation process of certain scene elements. More often than not, however, the compound objects you create in your scenes will still need further manipulation before they are complete. Whether your objects are created as compound objects or standard primitives, the next chapter discusses the critical modeling modifiers that will help you finish the modeling process for your scene.

CHAPTER 5

The Critical Modeling Modifiers

MODIFIERS ARE POWERFUL FEATURES IN Max that no 3ds Max user could do without. But with over 90 different modifiers for the typical object, you can quickly become overwhelmed trying to learn too many of them. Like most areas of Max, you should attempt to master just the important features that will allow you to work effectively and efficiently in your line of work. This chapter covers 19 of the most critical modifiers for those of us working on architectural visualizations. This list is by no means all you need to know or should strive to learn, as there are many other less utilized, but very effective, modifiers. However, this list consists of what I consider the critical, must-know modifiers, and for me, comprises the vast majority of the modifiers I use on a regular basis. They are listed in alphabetical order.

This chapter does not include a discussion of the **Edit Mesh** and **Edit Spline** modifiers, the two most frequently used modifiers for visualizations. These modifiers are discussed in detail in Chapter 3.

Bend	Mesh select	Smooth
Camera Correction	MultiRes	STL Check
Cap Holes	Noise	Subdivide
Displace	Optimize	Sweep
Extrude	Shell	TurboSmooth
FFD	Slice	Wave
Lathe		

The Bend modifier

A modifier that any veteran 3ds Max modeler will have to rely on from time to is the **Bend** modifier. This modifier does exactly what its name implies; it bends an object. Whether you're trying to create the bends in chandelier, a snow sled, or a simple faucet, this is a modifier you should definitely know how to use.

Figure 5-1. The Bend modifier used to create the bends in various objects

The very first thing that you need to understand about the **Bend** modifier is that you cannot bend an object without the necessary vertices in place to allow the bend to occur. In the left bench shown in Figure 5-2, there are clearly no vertices along the length of the wood slats that make up the seating area of the bench. If the **Bend** modifier is added to this bench, as shown in the middle bench, the wood slats do not bend because there are no vertices around which the bend can occur. In the middle image you can see the ends of the bench are bending, as is the bottom support bar (although not very well due to lack of vertices). In the right image, the bench appears to bend properly because there are enough vertices along its length to allow for a proper bend. To add vertices like this, try the **Subdivide** modifier, discussed later in this chapter.

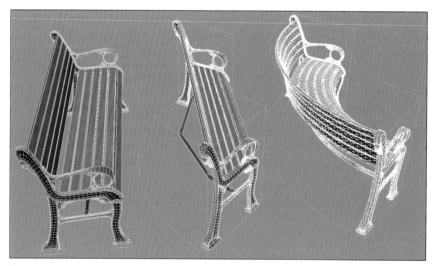

Figure 5-2. The Bend modifier used to bend a bench

Within the **Parameters** rollout of the **Bend** modifier, shown in Figure 5-3, are parameters that give you precise control over how the bend should occur. The **Angle** specifies the amount of bend while the **Direction** and **Bend Axis** combine together to specify the orientation of the bend. Some trial and error might be required when first using this modifier but by adding a +/- 90 degree bend and switching from one axis to another, you should be able to achieve the proper orientation of the bend. If not, change the **Direction** value to 90 and try each axis again. The right bench in Figure 5-2 used the parameters shown in Figure 5-3, and as you can see, a **Direction** value of -90 was needed to make the bench bend in the proper direction. Notice also the **Subdivide** modifier in the stack, mentioned earlier. This provided the extra vertices needed to make the bend.

Figure 5-3. The Bend modifier

As an additional note, like most modifiers, you can open the modifier and if you do, you'll see that you can transform its gizmo and its center. By doing this you can achieve even greater control over how the bend takes place.

At the bottom of the **Parameters** rollout is the **Limits** section. This is a more advanced area of the modifier that you might want to explore at some point, if you need to apply the bend only to a specific part of an object. An example of how this section might be used is in the movement of a garage door. If you animate a garage door so that it bends as it moves up, you will have to use the **Limit Effect** option so that the bend is only applied to part of the door at any time; the top of the door that is already hidden from view. If you do not use this option in this situation, you would see the entire garage door bend even when part of it is still vertical and in view.

The Camera Correction modifier

This next modifier does not even appear in the **Modify** panel's modifier list, but it's a modifier nonetheless. The **Camera Correction** modifier is one of the most widely used modifiers in the visualization industry and some companies rely on it for every camera placed in a scene.

This modifier simply applies a two-point perspective to a camera's view. By default, all camera views use a three-point perspective, which means that vertical lines appear to converge together with height. The degree to which they converge depends on the focal length of the lens used as well as the degree to which a camera tilts upward or downward, but in two-point perspective, vertical lines will always remain vertical regardless of the type of lens used and regardless of a camera's tilt.

In the example in Figure 5-4, the **Camera Correction** modifier is used to make all the vertical lines parallel, and provide what many veteran visualization artists would agree is a more natural and realistic image.

Figure 5-4. Using the Camera Correction modifier to change from 3-point perspective (left) to 2-point perspective (right)

As mentioned, this modifier is not available in the **Modifier List**. To add it, select the camera, and select the modifier from the viewport quad menu or from the **Cameras** section of the **Modifier** menu. Once you add the modifier, you can manually change the amount of correction, but you will usually find 3ds Max to provide the best guess for the proper 2-point perspective.

The Cap Holes modifier

Sometimes in the course of modeling or importing 3D models from other programs, faces can go missing. The **Cap Holes** modifier, shown in Figure 5-5, detects and fills these holes by creating faces along open edges. **Cap Holes** is also an option that is automatically enabled during the creation of a loft. If disabled, the loft would have openings at each end. Although this modifier is not needed as frequently as most others discussed in this chapter, when it is needed, it comes in very handy.

Figure 5-5. The Cap Holes modifier

Figure 5-6 shows an example of a plane with a hole that is easily filled using the **Cap Holes** modifier.

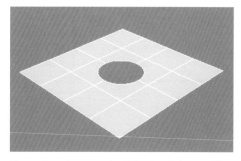
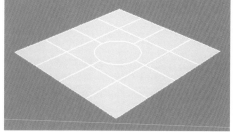

Figure 5-6. An example of the Cap Holes modifier

Using the Cap Holes modifier

This exercise demonstrates use of the **Cap Holes** modifier to fill in missing faces of a box.

1. Reset 3ds Max.

2. In the Perspective viewport, create a box of any size, with **4** length, width, and height segments, as shown in the left image of the following illustration.

3. Apply the **Edit Mesh** modifier (discussed in Chapter 3), enter **Face** sub-object mode, and delete a few faces from the box, as shown in the middle and right images.

4. Apply the **Cap Holes** modifier. All of the missing faces are filled in, and the box returns to its initial condition.

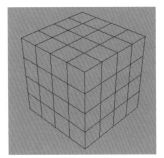 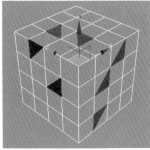 

The Displace modifier

The **Displace** modifier, shown in Figure 5-8, changes the geometry of an object through the use of a map or a bitmap image. When a map is applied to an object, the areas of the object on which darker parts of the map exist are recessed (pushed down) and areas of the object on which brighter areas of the map exist are elevated (pushed up).

Figure 5-7 shows an example of the **Displace** modifier in action. The image on the left is used to create an impression in a high-density plane, as shown in the image on the right. In order for the **Displace** modifier to work properly in this type of situation, you must create a high-density mesh to work with, because without enough vertices, the **Displace** modifier can't create detail.

Figure 5-7. An example of the Displace modifier in action

In the **Parameters** rollout is a section called **Displacement,** which contains a **Strength** value that directly controls the amount of displacement. In the **Image** section are buttons for loading and unloading bitmaps and maps. The **Blur** value controls the blur applied to the image, which in the case of the skater shown in Figure 5-7, can smooth out the rough edges. In the **Map** section, you can control the alignment of the bitmap or map; options include **Planar, Cylindrical,** and **Spherical.**

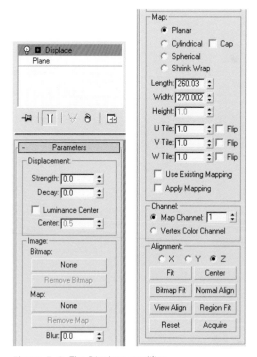

Figure 5-8. The Displace modifier

The images in Figure 5-9 show another example of the **Displace** modifier, this time in the creation of a volcano. The image on the left shows a high-density mesh prior to displacement. The middle image shows the map used for the displacement. The right image shows the result of the **Displace** modifier (with the map) applied to the plane object, using a **Strength** of **80**. If the **Strength** value were **40**, then the volcano would be half as tall.

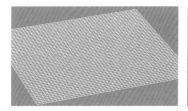 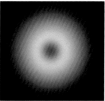 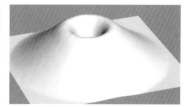

Figure 5-9. A volcano created with the Displace modifier

Using the Displace modifier

This exercise demonstrates use of the **Displace** modifier to model terrain.

1. Reset 3ds Max.

2. In the Perspective viewport, create a plane object with a width and length of **100** units, and with **30** length and width segments, as shown in the top-left image of the following illustration.

3. Apply the **Displace** modifier.

4. Within the **Image** section of the **Parameters** rollout, click the button that says **None** directly below **Map,** as shown in the top-middle image. The **Material/Map Browser** appears. (This tool won't be discussed until Chapter 6, but don't worry—for now you'll only have to do one simple thing with it.)

5. In the **Material/Map Browser,** select **Noise** from the list of map types, as shown in the top-right image. Select **OK** to close the **Material/Map Browser.**

6. Within the **Displacement** section of the **Parameters** rollout, type **20** in the **Strength** field (bottom-left image), and press **Enter.** The vertices that make up the plane object are now displaced along the z axis, as shown in the bottom-right image. The amount of displacement for each vertex depends on where the black and white portions of the noise map exist. (Maps will be covered in much greater detail in Chapters 7 and 8.)

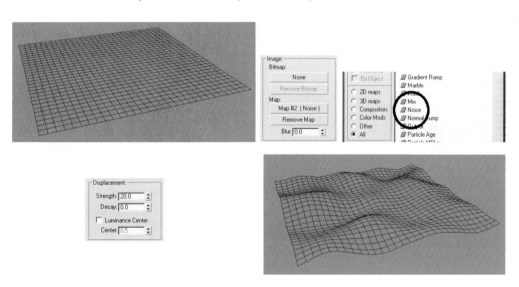

The Extrude modifier

The **Extrude** modifier, shown in Figure 5-10, is one of the simplest and most often used modifiers for visualizations. The modifier simply makes a copy of itself along the local Z axis a given distance away from the original, and connects the two splines or shapes to form a mesh. The **Amount** value is the extrusion distance, and the **Segments** value defines how many segments will be created evenly along the length of the extrusion. The **Capping** options, which are automatically enabled, create faces to cover the ends of the extrusion. Only closed splines or shapes that are extruded can be capped. Mapping coordinates and material IDs are also generated automatically. The **Smooth** option, which is also automatically enabled, smoothes the extrusion.

Figure 5-10. The Extrude modifier

Using the Extrude modifier

This exercise demonstrates use of the **Extrude** modifier by creating a tube from a circle.

1. Reset 3ds Max.

2. In the Perspective viewport, create a circle with a radius of **10**, as shown in the left image of the following illustration.

3. Apply the **Extrude** modifier with the default settings.

4. In the **Amount** field, type **10,** and in the **Segments** field, type **3**. This creates a column ten units tall, divided into three equal segments. These extra segments would be necessary if you later wanted to apply certain modifiers, such as the Bend modifier. Without the extra vertices, these types of modifiers will not work.

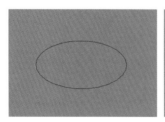 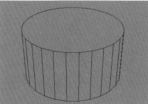 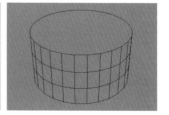

The FFD modifier

The **FFD** modifier is actually a group of five different modifiers (Figure 5-11) which all do basically the same thing; freely deform an object's geometry. FFD actually stands for Free-Form Deformation and this modifier uses a lattice of controls points which you can push and pull to 'free-form' your geometry as needed. By controlling the number, the initial positioning and the tension between the control points, you can craft your models quite nicely in a way that would be difficult to do with any other feature.

```
Edit Poly
Face Extrude
FFD 2x2x2
FFD 3x3x3
FFD 4x4x4
FFD(box)
FFD(cyl)
Flex
HSDS
```

Figure 5-11. The various FFD modifiers available

Figure 5-12 shows an example of where the **FFD** modifier can really shine. In this example, you can see that the pillow and bed sheet have a certain amount of thickness or fluff to them. The **FFD** modifier is a great tool to add this fluff at any point in the creation process. For example, one of the pillows in this scene is floating above the bed because I've decided it needs a little more thickness and I want to use the control points in the **FFD** modifier to add this thickness and bring the bottom of the pillow down so that it's resting on the bed.

Figure 5-12. A pillow with a FFD modifier applied

I chose the **FFD (box)** modifier rather than the **FFD (cyl)**, both shown in Figure 5-13, because the control points of the box version more closely fit the shape of the pillow than do the cylinder. Had the pillow been cylindrical then I would have applied the **FFD (cyl)** modifier.

Figure 5-13. A pillow with a FFD (box) modifier (left) and a FFD (cyl) modifier (right)

I could have chosen the **FFD 2x2x2**, the **FFD 3x3x3**, or the **FFD 4x4x4**, all shown in Figure 5-14, however, the only difference between the three is the resolution of the lattice, i.e. the number of control points that can be used to push and pull at the geometry. With more control points I have greater control over the shaping of the object, however with greater control comes greater work. If I can do all the forming I need with the control points of a **FFD 2x2x2**, then using a 3x3x3 or a 4x4x4 lattice just means I have to do more work moving more points than necessary.

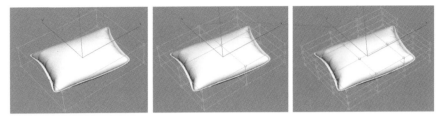

Figure 5-14. A pillow with the FFD 2x2x2 (left), the FFD 3x3x3 (middle), and the FFD 4x4x4 (right)

Regardless of how many control points I need for any given model, I will always use the **FFD (box)** or **FFD (cyl)** modifiers because unlike the other 3, with these 2 modifiers I can set the exact number of control points I want by clicking the **Set Number of Points** button, shown in Figure 5-15. Even for a simple and small object like a pillow, a 2x2x2 or 3x3x3 resolution doesn't provide much precision to control small areas of an object without affecting the entire object.

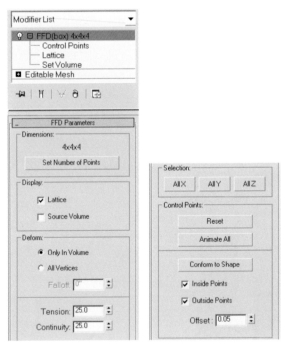

Figure 5-15. The FFD (box) modifier

Besides the ability to set lattice resolution at whatever you need, this particular modifier (along with the cyl version) gives you the added ability to select all of the control points along the same x, y, or z axis, using the **All X**, **All Y**, and **All Z** buttons. For example, if you select the **All X** option and click on the top left control point, all 4 of the control points along the same axis will become selected, as shown in the left image of Figure 5-16. If you select the **All X** and **All Y** options and click on the same control point, then all 16 of the control points in the same plane will become selected, as shown in the right image. This is extremely helpful and time saving when you need to select and move a large number of control points at once.

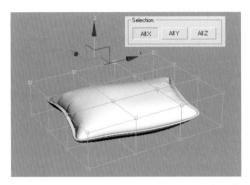 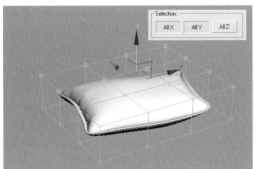

Figure 5-16. Selecting a control point using the All X and All Y options

Returning to the pillow floating above the bed, if I want to thicken the pillow and make it look fluffier, all I need to do is select the **All X** and **All Y** options, click on any control point on the bottom of the lattice and move it down until the pillow appears to rest on the bed, as shown in the left image of Figure 5-17. And just to make the pillow look a little different, I moved a few additional control points, as shown in the right image.

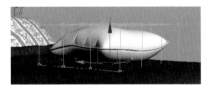 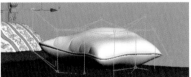

Figure 5-17. Moving control points to shape the form of a pillow

The FFD modifier is one of the best modeling tools for furniture creation, but it's quite useful in its ability to shape other objects as well. It was probably first conceived as a character modeling tool but it is versatile enough to be applied to other object types such as 3D terrain, vegetation, and water.

The Lathe modifier

This is a seldom-used but sometimes critically important modifier that enables you to create a 3D object by rotating a shape or spline along an axis. The **Lathe** modifier, shown in Figure 5-18, is named after the machine tool that spins a block of material while a cutting or forming tool is applied to the block, allowing it to be shaped into an object with symmetry about an axis of rotation. One of the most common uses of the **Lathe** modifier in architectural visualizations is in the creation of columns and balusters, as shown in Figure 5-19. Other possible uses include lamps, fountains, door knobs, and any other types of objects that have rotational symmetry along one axis.

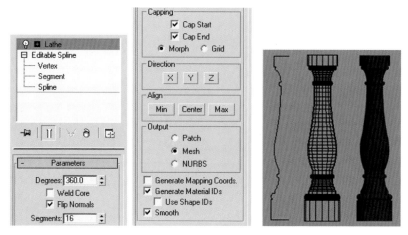

Figure 5-18. The Lathe modifier

When you first apply the **Lathe** modifier, Max rotates the shape 360 degrees using 16 segments during the course of the rotation. In most cases, 16 segments are sufficient to provide smooth curves about the axis of rotation; however, for close-ups, this value may need to be increased. Figure 5-19 shows balusters with a varying number of segments. The first baluster on the left contains the minimum required 3 segments, and the remaining balusters contain 4, 5, 8, and 16 segments, respectively. Although the first few examples contain far fewer segments than what is necessary for a smooth rotation, using 3, 4, or 5 segments provide a unique and often desirable look for balusters or columns.

Figure 5-19. The Lathe modifier with 3, 4, 5, 8, and 16 segments, from left to right

In the **Align** section of the **Lathe** modifier, you can align the axis of revolution to the minimum, center, or maximum extents of the shape. By default, the **Lathe** modifier rotates a shape about its pivot point, which for many shapes is its center. This is often not desirable and can result in very strange models. In the case of the balusters just discussed, the pivot point of the shape was located at the center of the shape, and when the **Lathe** modifier was applied, the result was the right image in Figure 5-20. The left image shows the result of aligning the axis of rotation to the minimum extent of the shape.

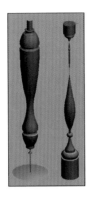

Figure 5-20. The Lathe modifier with a Min rotation (left) and a Cen rotation (right)

The Mesh Select modifier

If you would like to limit the affects of a modifier to select subobjects, the **Mesh Select** modifier is the best tool at your disposal. To use this modifier, simply add the modifier, click the + symbol to open the modifier, select a subobject level, highlight those subobjects that you want involved in the next modifier you add, and then add that modifier. In Figure 5-21, the **Mesh Select** modifier is added to an editable poly of a chair. The **Mesh Select** modifier was then opened, the faces making up the cushion were selected, and then the **Optimize** modifier was added. The result is an object that has some faces optimized and other faces untouched.

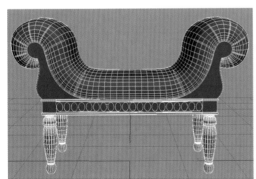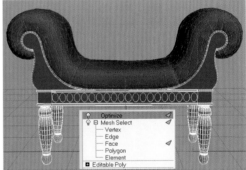

Figure 5-21. The MeshSelect modifier used to limit the affect of other modifiers to select subobjects

The Mesh Select modifier does not work with all modifiers but certainly enough to make it an invaluable tool.

The MultiRes modifier

The **Optimize** modifier is certainly a great tool for reducing an object's polygon count, but in many situations it can't compare to the power and versatility of the **MultiRes** modifier. The purpose of both modifiers is the same, to reduce an object's polygon count, but the **MultiRes** modifier will almost always produce a better looking object than the **Optimize** modifier. However, this doesn't mean the **MultiRes** modifier should always be used instead of the **Optimize** modifier.

Besides giving you what is usually a better and cleaner looking object, the **MultiRes** modifier also has the distinct advantage of allowing you to specify an exact vertex count that you want the object to have or a vertex count based on a percentage of the original vertex count. You can, for example, set the **Vert Percent**, shown in Figure 5-22 to 50 and the result will be an object whose vertex count (and face count) is 50% of the original count. With the **Optimize** modifier, you can never be sure of what the total count is going to be after implementing the modifier or after adjusting its parameters. You can only guess over and over again to achieve the count you want.

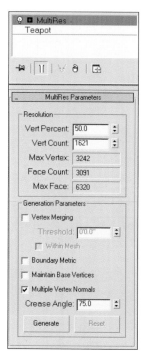

Figure 5-22. The MultiRes modifier

To implement the **MultiRes** modifier, add the modifier to a suitable object, click the **Generate** button at the bottom of the rollout, and enter a new value in the **Vert Percent** or **Vert Count** fields. Depending on the complexity of your object, 3ds Max may take a few moments to calculate the initial MultiRes object, but once generated, you can quickly and easily use the sliders to change the vertex percentage or vertex count on the fly. For complex objects, the **Optimize** modifier would take the same amount of time to apply each new change to its parameters, so this is yet another advantage of the **MultiRes** modifier.

Using the MultiRes modifier

This exercise demonstrates the use of the **MultiRes** modifier while comparing its polygon reducing capabilities with the **Optimize** modifier.

1. Reset 3ds Max.

2. In the Perspective view, create 2 teapots side-by-side with **10** segments each. The 2nd teapot must be a copy, not an instance.

3. Within the **Statistics** tab of the **Viewport Configuration** menu, select the **Total+Selection** option.

4. Press the keyboard shortcut **7** to enable the **Show Statistics** feature.

5. Add the **Optimize** modifier to the 1st teapot. Notice that the polygon count of the teapot is just over 3,000 and the teapot's appearance is quite ragged, as shown in the left teapot below.

6. Add the **MultiRes** modifier to the 2nd teapot.

7. Click the **Generate** button, and type **50** in the **Vert Percent** field. Notice that the polygon count of this 2nd teapot is almost identical to the polygon count of the 1st teapot, yet its appearance is far less ragged, as shown in the right teapot below.

Another advantage of this modifier is the ability to limit the affect of the modifier to certain parts of an object, such as the bowl in the blender object shown in Figure 5-23. To do this, click on the + symbol next to the **MultiRes** modifier, select **Vertex**, select the vertices that you don't want to be involved in the optimization, and within the modifier enable the **Maintain Base Vertices** option. Once you click **Generate** and enter a new value for **Vert Count** or **Vert Percent**, those selected vertices will remain intact, as shown in the blender on the right.

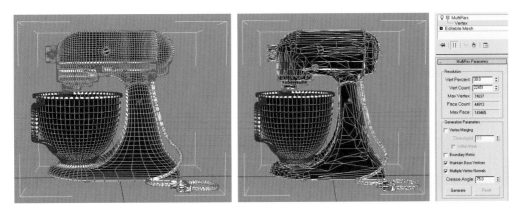

Figure 5-23. Applying the MultiRes modifier to select vertices of a mesh

A disadvantage of the **MultiRes** modifier is that for complex models, it can initially consume an enormous amount of RAM, take several moments to generate a new model, and cause your file size to balloon to a much larger size. For example, if you create a teapot with the maximum number of segments, i.e. 64, and apply the **MultiRes** modifier to this high polygon object, 3ds Max will consume a whopping 500MB of RAM to complete the computations. If you try this, you'll also see that there is no way to get this RAM back unless you save the file and reopen it. Once you do reopen the scene, you will have almost all of the RAM back that you had prior to using the **MultiRes** modifier and you will still be able to adjust the vertex count in real-time without having to wait on a new mesh to be generated. Unfortunately, when you save the file, you will also see that the file for the teapot without the **MultiRes** modifier is only about 10MB, but the file with the modifier is about 10 times that size, or about 100MB. 3ds Max needs to create this added space in the file in order for it to be able to show you changes to the vertex count in real-time. Once you are satisfied with your new model and the results of the modifier, you can return the object back to its normal file size by collapsing it back to an editable mesh or poly. In the case of the teapot, this returns the teapot back to approximately 10MB.

Yet another disadvantage of this modifier is that you can't easily go down in the modifier stack like you can with the Optimize modifier. Once you generate a **MultiRes** modifier, you will see that going down the modifier stack causes the following message to appear: "A modifier exists in the stack that depends on topology. Changing parameters may have undesirable effects."

For all of its advantages, the **MultiRes** modifier should be used sparingly and with caution. If you can live with its disadvantages, the benefit of a cleaner and better looking model might be hard to pass up.

The Noise modifier

Here's a handy modifier that gives you the power to create everything from moving water to wind blowing through trees. The **Noise** modifier, shown in Figure 5-24, randomly moves the vertices of an object along selected axes. The **Strength** value sets the amount of displacement in the direction of the selected axis. The **Seed** value is a variable that assigns a new orientation for each numerical value entered. Two objects with the same value will look identical—but changing the value of either to any other value will make the two objects look completely different. There is also a **Fractal** option, which in conjunction with the **Roughness** and **Iterations** settings, can give an object a more jagged appearance. **Roughness** defines the amount of variation, and **Iterations** defines the number of times the variation is made. More iterations means a more chaotic look and longer computation times. If you select the **Animate Noise** option, the vertices will move back and forth throughout the duration of frames specified. **Frequency** determines the speed of noise changes, and **Phase** determines where the noise wave starts and ends. As with any modifier, animating the **Phase** value is a simple and easy way to animate the effects of the modifier.

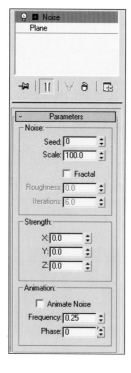

Figure 5-24. The Noise modifier

Figure 5-25 shows an example of the **Noise** modifier at work. The top-left image shows a high-density plane with a width and length of 150 units before the modifier is applied. The bottom-left image shows the same plane with the modifier applied and a **Z Strength** value of **50.** In the top-right image, the **Z Strength** value is doubled to **100.** In the bottom-right image, the **Fractal** option is enabled.

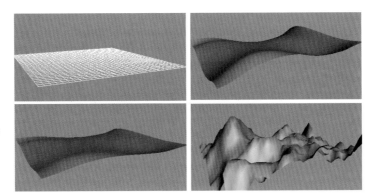

Figure 5-25. An example of the Noise modifier

Using the Noise modifier

This exercise demonstrates use of the **Noise** modifier to create relief in a mesh.

1. Reset 3ds Max.
2. In the Perspective viewport, create a plane with a length and width of **10**, and **4** length and width segments, as shown in the left image of the following illustration.
3. Apply the **Noise** modifier. There should be no change to the plane.
4. Within the **Noise** section of the **Parameters** rollout, change the **Scale** value to **10.**
5. Within the **Strength** section, change the **Z** value to **5.** The plane appears to take on a wavy appearance, as shown in the middle image.
6. Change the **Z** value to **10.** The displacement of the vertices doubles because the strength of the noise is doubled.

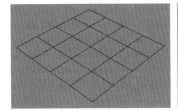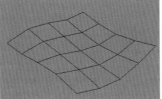

The Optimize modifier

The **Optimize** modifier, shown in Figure 5-26, is an extremely useful modifier that can help you reduce the total number of polygons in a model without significantly degrading its appearance. After you apply the modifier, you should analyze the last value in the rollout: **Before/After.** This tells you how many faces make up the object with and without the modifier applied. In most cases, you will probably find that the default settings are optimal for reducing faces without significantly degrading appearance. If after applying the modifier you decide that the impact is negligible, you can try adjusting some of the parameters within the modifier.

The **Face Thresh** parameter is the best parameter to experiment with. This value is the minimum angle that can exist between the normals of any two faces. If the angle between any adjacent normals is less than this value, Max removes as many faces as it can and creates new faces as necessary, while not allowing the angle between any adjacent normals to be less than the **Face Thresh** value. Figure 5-27 shows the model of a volcano to illustrate the benefits of using the **Optimize** modifier. The top-left image shows a high-density wireframe model comprised of 3,200 faces. Although this results in smooth curves and looks great when shaded, as shown in the top-right image, this is a large number of faces. If the viewer's perspective does not warrant such detail, you can use the **Optimize** modifier to reduce the overall number of faces. The bottom images in Figure 5-27 show the result of applying the **Optimize** modifier with all of the default values. The number of faces is reduced from 3,200 to 760 without any perceptible loss of detail (at least from this distance).

Figure 5-26. The Optimize modifier

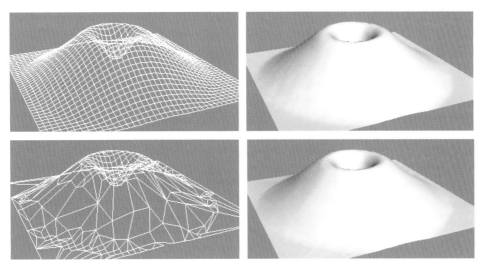

Figure 5-27. An example of the Optimize modifier in action

The Shell modifier

Depending on the way you build your architectural structures, the **Shell** modifier may be a tool you come to depend on or one you rarely use. I do not personally use it at all in my workflow, but know many that would say they couldn't live without it.

The **Shell** modifier duplicates and offsets all the faces of an object both inward and outward and then creates faces to connect the two sets of faces. It is most commonly used to turn an object that appears to be just a surface, into a solid. For example, the left image in Figure 5-28 is nothing more than an extruded unclosed spline that represents the outer perimeter of a building (since it's unclosed, no top or bottom was formed). When the **Shell** modifier is added to this object, the result is what appears to be a solid object with a thickness.

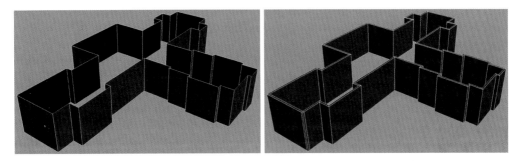

Figure 5-28. An extruded unclosed spline (left) and the same object with the Shell modifier (right)

Within the **Parameters** rollout of the modifier, Figure 5-29, is an **Inner Amount** and **Outer Amount**. These two values specify where the duplicate surfaces are going to be offset. For example, the shell in Figure 5-28 has an **Inner Amount** set to 8" and an **Outer Amount** set to 0". This means that a duplicate set of faces will be created and offset 8" inside the original faces and the original faces will be offset 0", which just means that they won't move. If you wanted the walls to grow 8" outward as well, then you would need to enter 8" as the **Outer Amount**. If you did, then the walls would be 16" thick.

There are several other more advanced options in this modifier but the only other one you will definitely need to use is the **Straighten Corners** option, which will ensure that your shell thickness remains constant throughout the entire object and set correctly to the thickness specified in your inner and outer amount values. Without this option, you can expect erratic results.

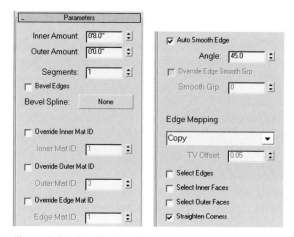

Figure 5-29. The Shell modifier

The Slice modifier

Here's another modifier that most users don't find a need for as much as other modifiers like the **Extrude** or **Optimize** modifiers, but when needed it certainly can be effective. The **Slice** modifier, shown in Figure 5-30, creates additional vertices in an object along a cutting plane that can be positioned and orientated in any way through the object. By adding this slice plane, you can use the new vertices, edges, or polygons to craft the object in many different ways and perhaps better, you can extract the edges of the new plane to create shapes that represent the perimeter of your object at some point of your choosing.

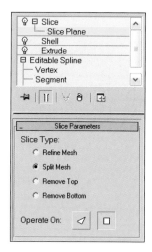

Figure 5-30. The Slice modifier

In the previous modifier discussion, I created an 8" thick set of walls using the **Shell** modifier. Now I want to add a slice plane to the walls and create a shape from the new edges. When you add the **Slice** modifier to an object, the slicing plane (shown as an orange gizmo) is positioned at the bottom of the object. To reposition it, open the modifier, click on **Slice Plane** and move the gizmo (now shown in yellow). You can rotate the gizmo as well if you want to create non-horizontal edges. Once you have the gizmo in place, as shown in Figure 5-31, add an **Edit Mesh** or **Edit Poly** modifier and go to a subobject level to manipulate the new subobjects.

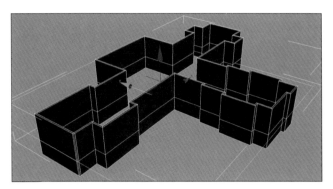

Figure 5-31. A new set of edges created from the slice plane of the Slice modifier

Of particular use is the ability to create a new shape from the new edges. So if you go to **Edge** subobject mode you will see that the new edges are automatically selected and you can click on the **Create Shape from Edges** button (remembering to use the **Linear** option) to create the new shape representing the perimeter of your object. This can be extremely useful if you need a shape with which to create a loft or sweep along the outside of your walls. You can also use it to create a shape from the perimeter of far more complex objects that would be difficult to create any other way.

The default **Slice Type** is the **Refine Mesh** option, which simply means that new vertices will be added along the slice plane but that no new elements within the object will be created. On the other hand, if you use the **Split Mesh** option, once you add the **Edit Mesh** or **Edit Poly** modifier and enter **Element** subobject mode, you would see that the slicing plane has sliced your object into two separate elements. This means that if you go to **Edge** subobject level and move the automatically selected edges upward, you will see a gap develop between the bottom and top halves of your object, as shown in Figure 5-32. The other options allow you to remove everything above or below your slicing plane.

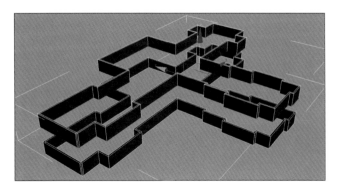

Figure 5-32. The results of the Split Mesh option and repositioning the sliced edges

The Smooth modifier

The **Smooth** modifier, shown in Figure 5-33, is a critical component in the creation of many architectural models. This modifier simply gives the surface of an object a smoother appearance; not by adding vertices, but by changing the way surfaces are shaded. Smoothing eliminates the appearance of facets by grouping faces into smoothing groups. Adjacent faces are grouped into the same smoothing group when the angle between their normals is not greater than the specified threshold. Adjacent faces that lie in the same smoothing group are shaded to appear to be part of the same smooth surface.

Figure 5-33. The Smooth modifier

All objects have smoothing automatically applied upon their creation. By default, when you apply the **Smooth** modifier to an object, Max assumes you wish to assign smoothing manually and disables the **Auto Smooth** feature in the modifier. So the initial result of applying the **Smooth** modifier is that the object will have no smoothing. The left image in Figure 5-34 shows a sphere with the **Smooth** modifier applied (and the **Auto Smooth** feature disabled). Notice that every face is visible because there is no smoothing applied. The right image shows the result of enabling the **Auto Smooth** option, in which the sphere receives its original smoothing again (assuming that angle between adjacent faces does not exceed the **Threshold** value). Once the **Smooth** modifier is applied, you can control precisely which faces receive smoothing by changing the **Threshold** value.

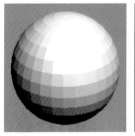

Figure 5-34. Smoothing a sphere

The images in Figure 5-35 show the effect of smoothing on a simple box. The image on the left shows a simple box without the **Smooth** modifier applied. When the **Smooth** modifier is first applied, the box remains the same; however, when the **Auto Smooth** feature is enabled and the threshold (the angle between the adjacent sides of the box) is increased to 90 or greater, Max places all the sides into the same smoothing group, resulting in the image on the right. Max applies the same smoothing group to all faces, assuming that you want the object to appear smooth even though it contains a 90-degree angle. The result, obviously, is a strange looking object.

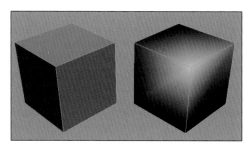

Figure 5-35. Smoothing a box

The STL Check modifier

This modifier checks an object to ensure it can be exported to the StereoLithography (STL) format. Exporting to STL format, or similar formats such as VRML, is something you are sure to be doing in the next few years with the explosion of a new technology known as 3D printing. 3D printing allows you to print your models directly to a 3D printer, with or without materials applied. In order to do this, the model must have good integrity. The STL format requires the object to have a closed surface (i.e., a surface with no holes or gaps). When you apply the modifier, all problems are listed in the **Status** section of the **Parameters** rollout. The modifier checks for such errors as open edges, multiple edges, double faces, and spikes. Spikes are faces that are connected at only one edge. You can select one or all of these options. Once found, the modifier can select the problem edges or faces.

The left image in Figure 5-36 shows a simple plane with selected faces missing. The right image shows same plane after applying the **STL Check** modifier. Notice the highlighted areas, which indicate problems with the model's integrity. For more information on 3D printing, check out the leading company on this new technology, EMS, at www.ems-north.com.

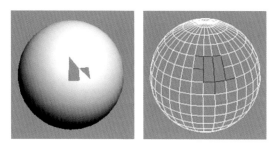

Figure 5-36. An example of the STL Check modifier

The Subdivide modifier

During the discussion of the **Bend** modifier, I mentioned that in order to properly bend an object, you have to ensure you have enough vertices in place to allow a proper bend to occur. Figure 5-2 showed a bench that used the **Subdivide** modifier to add these vertices so that the bench could be curved. Well the **Subdivide** modifier (Figure 5-37) is as easy as modifiers come and certainly one of the most critical to visualization users. It simply sets the maximum size for all the faces of an object and breaks down any face that exceeds this size into smaller faces.

Figure 5-37. The Subdivide modifier

There are only two reasons I can think of for why anyone would want to add more faces to an object. One would be to allow for smooth curves and bends in an object, as was just mentioned. The other reason would be to allow for more accurate compound object creation.

Examples of objects that you could utilize the **Subdivide** modifier to obtain proper bends and curves would be 3D terrain and pool water, both shown in Figure 5-38. In this example, the smooth water and 3D terrain would not be possible without enough faces. Flat surfaces like the pool patio don't need to be subdivided because those surfaces will not need to be bent or molded in some 3D type of mesh. Notice that the pool deck contains very large faces, some 50 feet long. Other examples of object types that could benefit from this modifier are furniture, appliances, curtains, and trees, just to name a few.

Figure 5-38. Using the Subdivide modifier to allow for waves in a pool and 3D terrain

Examples of compound objects that benefit from the use of the **Subdivide** modifier are the **Boolean**, **Scatter**, and **ShapeMerge**. Even if you only create 2D terrain, subdividing a mesh object before using the **Boolean>Cut>Split** feature is usually necessary to obtain accurate cuts in the mesh. This concept is discussed in Chapter 4, but essentially Booleans don't work well with long and skinny faces, like the ones shown in the pool deck of Figure 5-38. So if you wanted to cut out part of the pool deck to make a planter, you would need to first subdivide it before performing the **Boolean** operation. You can always use the **Optimize** or **MultiRes** modifier afterwards to remove the extra, unnecessary faces. This method of subdividing a mesh before using the **Boolean** command is actually performed behind the scenes by the **ProBoolean** feature, and is what enables it to make the accurate cuts. However, as discussed in Chapter 4, the **ProBoolean** is not as good as the **Boolean** feature for creating most site elements, because it does not allow you to automatically select the cut faces and detach them from the rest of the object.

Although not discussed in this book, the **ShapeMerge** is another example where subdividing a mesh would be beneficial to good clean cuts. However, **ShapeMerge** is not as reliable as the **Boolean>Cut>Split** and since it doesn't do anything unique, it is not discussed in this book.

Another example where subdividing an object would benefit a compound object is in the use of the **Scatter** command. One of the distribution methods of the **Scatter** command is **All Face Centers**, which places a copy of the scattered object at the center of each face. Well if your mesh is made up of long skinny faces, such as the pool deck in Figure 5-38, then placing a scattered object at the center of each face would yield strange results. However, if you first subdivide the distribution object prior to using the **Scatter** command with the **All Face Centers** option, then you would see an evenly distributed scatter with a density equal to the degree to which you subdivided the distribution object.

The Sweep modifier

The **Sweep** modifier is an extremely useful feature in 3ds Max that does much of what the **Loft** feature does, with one major advantage. Unlike the **Loft**, the **Sweep** modifier allows you to 'sweep' a shape along multiple, non-continuous splines. If for example you wanted to use the Loft feature to create curbs for the site shown in Figure 5-39, you would have to create dozens of individual lofts because the loft cannot accept non-continuous splines like this, even if they are all part of the same object. The **Sweep** modifier, however, can use an object like this made up of dozens of individual non-continuous splines, which makes this the best and fastest way to create this type of object. If you wanted to create the hundreds of individual parking stops for this site, creating them with lofts could take hours, but by attaching all of the parking stop lines together as one object, you can easily sweep all of them at once in just a few seconds.

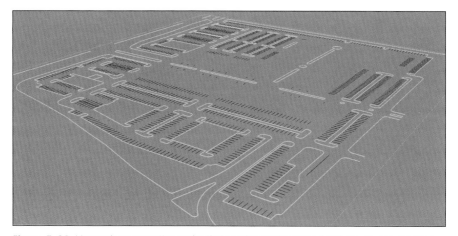

Figure 5-39. Linework representing curbs that can be easily created with the Sweep modifier

The **Sweep** modifier, shown in Figure 5-40, contains a **Section Type** rollout that allows you to select the shape that you need to sweep along a path and a **Sweep Parameters** rollout that contains parameters that allow you to adjust the alignment and positioning of the sweep.

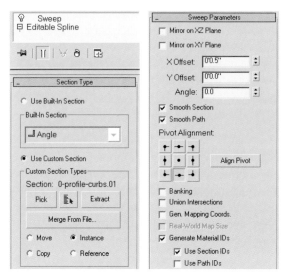

Figure 5-40. The Sweep modifier

When you add the **Sweep** modifier to a spline, the first thing you need to do is select a shape to sweep. Since the built-in sections that come with the program will almost never suffice, select the **Use Custom Section** option, followed by the **Pick** button, which allows you to click on the shape you want to sweep. Once you click on the shape in a viewport, you will undoubtedly have to adjust the alignment. By default, the alignment is set to the center of the sweep, so in the case of the curbs shown in Figure 5-41, the curbs will be half buried in the road, as shown in the left image. By clicking on the bottom-center pivot alignment button, the curbs are moved upward so that the bottom of the curbs are aligned to the splines, and hence the pavement, as shown in the right image. Also, you will often need to adjust the horizontal alignment of a sweep, and because the 9 pivot alignment buttons might not suffice, you can enter values in the **X Offset** and **Y Offset** fields to move the sweep object farther inside or outside of the original path splines.

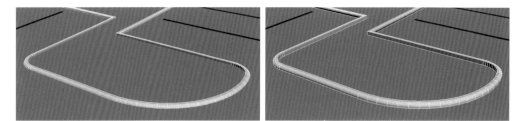

Figure 5-41. The Sweep modifier

Some of the best uses of the **Sweep** modifier in visualization include, among many other object types, roof ridges and valley caps, furniture, walls, trim, parking stops, and railings.

The TurboSmooth modifier

The **TurboSmooth** modifier, shown in Figure 5-42, is a fast and memory-efficient modifier that smoothes an object by adding vertices around corners and edges. The sharper the corner or edge, the greater the effect of this modifier. Although this modifier has less applicability in architectural modeling than other modifiers discussed thus far, it comes in handy when you want to smooth certain object types that appear too chiseled. These object types can include terrain, statues, fountains, or furniture, to name a few.

In the **Main** section of the rollout, you can specify how many iterations to run (i.e., how many times to apply the modifier action). This essentially makes the object smoother with each additional iteration. Since the **TurboSmooth** modifier can significantly slow down viewport refresh rates, you can specify one **Iteration** value for the viewport, and another for rendering. When you enable the **Render Iters** feature, the **Iterations** value determines the number of iterations shown in the viewport, and the **Render Iters** value determines the number of iterations for the rendering.

Figure 5-43 shows the previous volcano example with the original plane object containing far fewer initial vertices. Despite having a mesh with only a fraction of the vertices, applying the **TurboSmooth** modifier yields almost the same result as starting with a high-density mesh.

Figure **5-42**. The TurboSmooth modifier

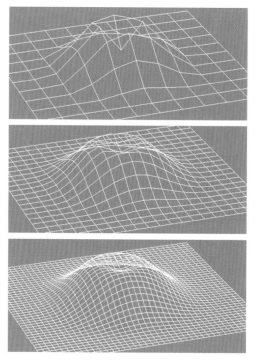

Figure 5-43. The TurboSmooth modifier in action, with zero, one, and two iterations, from top to bottom

Using the TurboSmooth modifier

This exercise demonstrates use of the **TurboSmooth** modifier to subdivide the polygons on a mesh.

1. Reset 3ds Max.

2. In the Perspective viewport, create a plane with a length and width of **10**, and four length and width segments, as shown in the left image of the following illustration.

3. Apply the **TurboSmooth** modifier to the plane, using the default settings. Notice that each polygon on the plane is divided into four equally sized polygons. Applying this modifier to an object representing jagged terrain would cause the terrain to be smoothed.

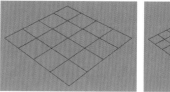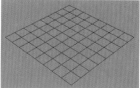

The Wave modifier

As the name implies, the **Wave** modifier is used primarily to create the appearance of waves in an object. In visualization, this feature isn't used much, but when you need to animate water, or when you need to animate things like flags, curtains, or grass blowing in the wind, the **Wave** modifier is one of the best tools available.

Figure 5-44 shows an example of the **Wave** modifier in action using a flat circular mesh object, which is the mesh that represented the spa water shown in Figure 5-38. As shown in the modifier stack, the object started out as a spline and the **Edit Mesh** modifier was added to produce the flat disc shown in image 1. The **Subdivide** modifier was then added to break the faces down into smaller sizes, as shown in image 2. Subdividing the mesh in this way is usually necessary to achieve a smooth look to the waves, as discussed earlier in this chapter.

In image 3, you can see the affect of a single **Wave** modifier using an amplitude of 2 inches and a wavelength of 2.5 feet. The amplitude was only 1 inch in the real project, but was made 2 inches here to help accentuate the affect of the modifier (subtle waves are often better than very noticeable ones). A second **Wave** modifier was then added to make the waves look less organized and hence, more realistic. When the second modifier was added, the gizmo had to be rotated 90 degrees so that the waves would be oriented in a different direction. Otherwise, the second modifier would have just magnified the affects of the first. To animate the waves created with the **Wave** modifier, simply animate the phase. If you are not familiar how to animate a parameter like this, refer to chapter 13 for a discussion on animation.

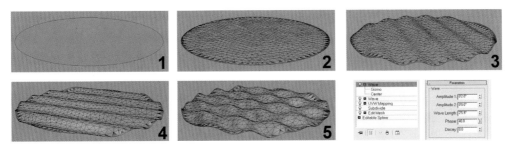

Figure 5-44. The Wave modifier in action

Using the Wave modifier

This exercise demonstrates how to create waves in water, as shown in Figure 5-44.

1. Reset 3ds Max.

2. Create a circle with a radius of **7** feet.

3. Add the **Edit Mesh** modifier. The object is now renderable, as shown in image 1 of Figure 5-44.

4. Add the **Subdivide** modifier with a size of **6** inches. The mesh is now of suitable density to create waves, as shown in image 2.

5. Add the **Wave** modifier using an amplitude of **1** inch and a **Wave Length** of **2'6"**.

6. In the modifier stack, right-click the **Wave** modifier you just added and select **Copy**.

7. Right-click in the same place and select paste. This creates a 2nd duplicate modifier which basically doubles the magnitude of the 1st.

8. Open the **Wave** modifier, select **Gizmo** and rotate the gizmo **90** either direction. The result is a more chaotic wave configuration.

9. If you want to try animating the waves, press the keyboard shortcut **N** to activate the **AutoKey** command, drag the Time Slider to the last frame, and type **2.5** in the **Phase** field for both wave modifiers.

10. Press **N** to close the **AutoKey** command.

11. Press the **Play** button to play the animation. You should see some gently rolling waves.

Summary

This chapter has covered a number of powerful modifiers for use in architectural visualizations. As I stated at the beginning of the chapter, this list is by no means all you should know. The use you find for some modifiers are limited only by your imagination. Many of the tips and tricks you come across in the 3D community involve innovative ways of using modifiers to perform a specific function in record time. With nearly 100 different modifiers available for some objects, just about anything that can be dreamed-up can be modeled. The only questions are "How will it be modeled?" and "How long will it take?"

PART 3

Materials

Creating maps is much like creating a recipe. Many times you don't know what you want for the end result, and you find yourself stumbling onto a great product. Other times you may know exactly what you want, but you don't know what ingredients or quantities to use. In either case, it will probably require a good amount of trial and error.

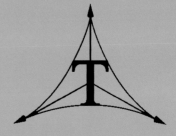

CHAPTER 6

Material Basics

THE WORD "MATERIAL," AS GENERALLY defined in dictionaries, is simply the substance out of which a thing is or can be made. In 3ds Max, the meaning is not much different— it is a characteristic that defines the appearance of an object. Within each material are numerous properties that determine the appearance. Thanks to the power of the **Material Editor** in 3ds Max, we can realistically simulate any material on Earth by controlling all the visual properties a material possesses.

This chapter focuses almost entirely on the **Material Editor** and, more specifically, those features that you would incorporate with your work on visualizations. In the next two chapters, I'll cover the critical map channels and map types, and discuss UVW mapping in great detail. But for now, a good understanding of the **Material Editor** interface is crucial to working efficiently with materials.

The Material Editor

The **Material Editor** is an immense interface with which materials are defined and applied. It can be accessed by selecting **Rendering ➤ Material Editor,** by clicking on the **Material Editor** icon on the **Main** toolbar, or by pressing **M**. Just like all features in 3ds Max, the **Material Editor** contains far more power and functionality than is typically needed for architectural visualizations. Likewise, there are some features that are significantly more critical to know than others. As usual, I will place greater emphasis on those features that are critical in the creation of architectural visualizations.

Sample slots

The sample slots in 3ds Max are the windows in which materials are displayed on sample objects both before and after they are applied to objects in your scene. The sample slots can display either a map or material. Select the slot in which you want to work by simply clicking anywhere inside the slot. Only 1 slot can be selected at a time, and the selected (or active) slot is indicated by a white border, as shown in Figure 6-1. 24 slots are available, but by default, 6 slots are displayed in a 2 X 3 grid. To access the remaining 18, use the slider below the slots.

Figure 6-1. Material Editor sample slots

Clicking the **Options** icon (shown in the following image) opens the **Material Editor Options** dialog box, which gives you the option to change the slot layout to a 5 × 3 or 6 × 4 array, as shown in Figure 6-2. Right-clicking inside a sample slot also brings up a menu that allows you to change the layout.

The **Material Editor Options** dialog box contains many other options that can change the appearance of the sample slots—but personally, I like the slots the way they appear by default, and will leave these options for you to explore.

Figure 6-2. Available sample slot layouts

Changing the sample slot background

The **Background** icon provides an important feature that allows you to change the background of the slots. Sometimes the default gray background is not conducive to displaying transparent materials such as glass. In these instances, you can click the **Background** icon (shown in the following image) to change the background to a multicolored checkered image (or any other image you want).

Changing the sample slot object type

You also have the option to change the object type displayed in the sample slots from the default sphere to a box, cylinder, or any other object type you want. To do so, click and hold the **Sample Type** flyout icon (shown in the following image) and select the object type.

To create a custom object, create a .max file with the lone object in it and make sure that the object can fit inside a 100-unit cube. Click the **Options** icon, which opens the **Material Editor Options** dialog box, and under **Custom Sample Object,** click the **File Name** button to find the file that contains the object you want to load (see Figure 6-3).

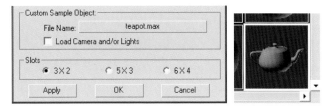

Figure 6-3. Choosing a custom sample slot object type

Magnifying a sample slot

You will probably find it difficult at times to see the details of your materials within the sample slots, especially if you use the 6 X 4 layout. To see a larger display of a sample slot, double-click the sample slot and resize it to your liking by clicking and dragging on any corner (see Figure 6-4). You should leave the **Auto** option enabled so that any changes made to your material are updated in the sample slot.

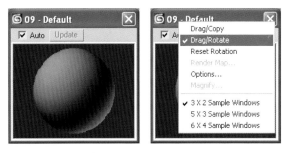

Figure 6-4. Magnifying a sample slot

If you want to see the sample object from a different perspective, you can rotate the view just like in a viewport. To do so, right-click inside the sample slot, select **Drag/Rotate,** and drag on the object. Holding down Shift constrains the rotation around a single axis. Reset the view by selecting **Reset Rotation** from the **Material** menu.

Working with sample slots

This exercise demonstrates some of the ways you can work with sample slots.

1. Reset 3ds Max.

2. Press **M** to open the **Material Editor.**

3. Click the **Options** icon (shown in the following image). The **Material Editor Options** dialog box opens.

4. In the **Slots** section, select the **6 × 4** option (see the following illustration) and select **OK**. The sample slot layout changes from the default 3 × 2 to a 6 × 4 layout.

5. In the **Blinn Basic Parameters** rollout, type **75** in the **Opacity** field, as shown in the following illustration. This makes the material slightly transparent.

6. Click the **Background** icon (shown in the following images). The background of the sample slot changes to a checkerboard display, making the transparent material easier to work with.

7. Click and hold the **Sample Type** icon. A flyout menu appears with three possible sample types (shown in the following image).

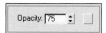

8. Move the cursor over the box type and release the mouse button. The object in the active sample slot changes to a box.

9. Double-click the active material sample slot. The sample slot is made into a larger separate window.

10. Place the cursor over any corner of the window. Sizing arrows appear.

11. Click and drag to resize the window.

12. Right-click inside the resized sample slot and select **Drag/Rotate.**

13. Click and drag inside the sample slot to rotate the view of the box sample type.

14. Right-click inside the sample slot again and select **Drag/Copy** to return the click/drag option to its default setting.

15. Click the **X** button in the top-right corner of the resized sample slot to close the sample slot.

Naming materials

The importance of a good naming convention for your materials cannot be overemphasized. Just like the objects in your scene, the materials you use should be named in a manner that allows you to find them quickly and easily, and immediately recognize which objects in your scene those materials are applied to. It would be very time-consuming to find the material you're looking for if it looks like other materials and is named something like "23-Default," especially if the material is not loaded in a sample slot and you have to search for it in the **Material/Map Browser.**

The best way that works for me is to give each material the same name as the object it is applied to in the scene. As an example, in my scenes, I would name an object that represents sidewalks **Site-Sidewalks,** and use this same name for the material that is applied to the sidewalk object (see Figure 6-5). If I want to apply this same material to the object that represents the curbs, I will change the name of the material to **Site-Sidewalks/Curbs.** This way, I know immediately upon looking at the material name what object or objects this material is applied to.

Figure 6-5. The Material drop-down list and the Material Editor's title bar

All materials are given a default name, which is listed in the **Material** drop-down list, located below the sample slots (as shown in the left image of Figure 6-5). In this case, the name has been changed to **Site-Sidewalks.** Notice that this name also appears in the **Material Editor's** title bar. You can rename a material by typing a new name in the drop-down list.

Creating new materials

To create a new material, drag a material from one sample slot to another, and change the name of the new copy.

You can also create a copy of a material by clicking the **Make Material Copy** icon (below). If you apply the new copy to your scene without changing the name, a dialog box appears stating that a material with the same name already exists in the scene. You are then given the option to replace or rename the material.

Assigning materials to objects

Once you load a material into a sample slot, you can assign it to an object in your scene. There are two main methods to do so.

One way is to simply drag and drop the material from the sample slot directly onto an object in a viewport. This method does not usually work too well if there are several objects near the cursor at the point of release inside the viewport, because 3ds Max won't know to which object you want it to apply. If you pause the cursor momentarily over the object, you will see the object's name appear next to the cursor, indicating the object to which you're about to apply the material.

A more reliable way to assign materials, the **Assign Material to Selection** icon (shown in the following image), requires you to select the object or objects you want to apply the material to, and then select the icon.

Whenever the material of a selected object is shown in a sample slot, the sample slot will display small white triangles in each of its corners, as shown in the right image in Figure 6-6. This indicates that the material is applied to the selected object and that the material is "hot." "Hot" materials are connected to the objects in the scene; and changing the material in the **Material Editor** causes the scene to be updated automatically. Usually, this is what you want anyway, but on occasion, you may want to work on a copy of a material without affecting the scene in any way. To "cool" an object in this way, simply make a copy of the material without changing the name or reassigning the material from the new sample slot copy. Any changes you make will no longer affect your scene.

Figure 6-6. A cool material (left) and a hot material (right)

Whenever you apply a material to an object in your scene, the material is added to the scene library, regardless of whether the material is displayed in a sample slot. A library is simply a collection of materials stored within a file, whether that be a .max scene file or a standard .mat material library file, which will be discussed in greater detail later. In this case, when a material is applied to an object, that material becomes part of the scene library; but once all objects that hold that material are deleted, the material is removed from the scene library.

By clicking the **Put Material to Scene** icon (shown in the following image), however, you can put a material in the scene library without having to worry about it being removed.

Creating, naming, and assigning new materials

This exercise demonstrates how to create, name, and assign new materials within the **Material Editor.**

1. Reset 3ds Max.
2. Press M to open the **Material Editor,** if it's not already open.

3. Click inside the **Material** drop-down list, and change the name to **Building-Walls,** as shown in the following illustration.

4. Click and hold inside the active sample slot of the material you just renamed, drag the sample slot to an adjacent slot, and release the mouse button. The material is duplicated inside the sample slot you copied to.

5. Change the name of the material copy to **Building-Doors.** You've just created a new material, but you haven't assigned it to an object yet.

6. Create a simple box in any viewport.

7. Inside the **Material Editor,** click the **Assign Material to Selection** icon (shown in the following image). The material named **Building-Doors** is now assigned to the box you just created.

8. Click the **Make Material Copy** icon (shown in the following image) and, inside the **Material** drop-down list, change the material name to **Building-Windows.** This creates and names a new material without deleting an already existing material. Had you just changed the name without using the **Make Material Copy** command, the material named **Building-Doors** would no longer exist.

9. Click and hold the material named **Building-Walls,** and drag the material onto the box in any viewport. Notice the corners of the material sample slot have white triangles. This indicates that the selected object contains this material.

10. Deselect the box object in the scene. Notice now that the white triangles in the sample slot have changed to gray triangles, indicating that this material is on an object in the scene, but not on an object that is currently selected.

11. Save your work for use in the next exercise.

Loading materials in the sample slots

At times, you may want to create a new material from an existing material in your scene that is not loaded in a sample slot, or create a new material from one found in another 3ds Max scene. There are two main methods to load materials into sample slots.

The first way to load a material is by using the **Pick Material from Object** icon (shown in the following image). Simply select the sample slot you want to load the material into, click he **Pick Material from Object** icon, and click the object in your scene that contains the material you want to load.

The second method is by clicking the **Get Material** icon (shown in the following image), which opens the **Material/Map Browser**. Once you find the material you're looking for, you can load it into the sample slot by double-clicking the material or dragging and dropping the material into the sample slot. (The **Material/Map Browser** will be covered later in this chapter.)

Removing materials and maps

Click the **Reset Material/Maps to Default Settings** icon (shown in the following image) to reset the material or map to its default settings. The two reasons you may want to do this is to free up a used sample slot, or to remove an unwanted material or map from an object.

When you click this icon without the active material being assigned to an object in your scene, the message box in Figure 6-7 appears. If you select **Yes,** the sample slot is returned to its initial state, and you can start the material creation process from scratch.

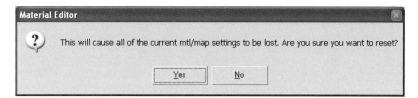

Figure 6-7. Resetting the material/map settings of an unassigned material

When you click the **Reset Material/Maps to Default Settings** icon with the active material already assigned to an object in your scene, a different dialog box appears, cautioning you that the material you want to reset is currently assigned to at least one object in the scene (shown in Figure 6-8). If you select the default option, **Affect only mtl/map in the editor slot,** the material remains unchanged, and the sample slot is simply reset to its initial state. Essentially, this erases the sample slot but not the material applied to the object.

If you select the other option, **Affect mtl/map in both the scene and in the editor slot,** the material is reset to its default settings, not just the sample slot. The material will remain with the same name and will still be applied to the same object(s)—but because the material settings are reset, this option achieves basically the same thing as deleting the material from the scene.

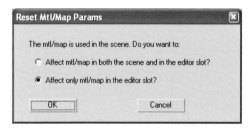

Figure 6-8. Resetting the material/map settings of an assigned material

Loading and removing materials and maps

This exercise demonstrates how to load and remove materials and maps within the **Material Editor.**

1. Continue from the last exercise.
2. Press **M** to open the **Material Editor,** if it's not already open.
3. Click a new sample slot without an assigned material.
4. Click the **Pick Material from Object** icon (shown in the following image).

5. Move the cursor, which is now displayed as an eyedropper, over the box in any viewport. The eyedropper changes from appearing empty to appearing full when placed over an object with a material assigned.
6. Click the box in any viewport. The material assigned to the box is now loaded into the active sample slot. This material should be named **Building-Walls.**
7. For visual purposes, change the color of this material by clicking the color swatch next to **Diffuse** in the **Blinn Basic Parameters** rollout, as shown in the following illustration:

8. The **Color Selector** dialog box opens, as shown in the following image. Move the cursor over the color selector, click to select a color, and click **Close.**

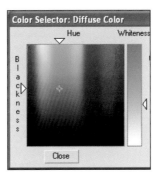

9. Click the **Reset Material/Maps to Default Settings** icon (shown in the following image), select the default option **(Affect only mtl/map in the editor slot),** and select **OK** to close the command. Notice that the box stills contains the material, but the material in the sample slot is no longer that material.

10. Reload the material on the box back into the active sample slot using the **Pick Material from Object icon**.

11. Click the **Reset Material/Maps to Default Settings** icon again, this time selecting the other option, **Affect mtl/map both in the scene and in the editor slot**. Select **OK** to close the command. Notice this time the material name doesn't change but the material returns to its default settings and the box receives those new settings.

Selecting objects by material

The **Material Editor** features a great tool that allows you to select objects in your scene that have the selected material applied to them. When you click the **Select by Material** icon (shown in the following image), the **Select Objects** dialog box opens with all the objects selected that have the selected material applied. Click the **Select** icon to select these objects.

Showing maps in a viewport

When a viewport is in shaded mode, you can display the maps contained within materials by clicking the **Show Map in Viewport** icon (shown in the following image). This feature allows you to easily distinguish one object from another within the viewports and quickly determine which objects have what materials applied.

The quality of the maps displayed and the speed at which the viewports can refresh the views depends heavily on the quality of the graphics card. Figure 6-9 shows an example of the **Show Map in Viewport** feature. The cushions of both chairs contain the same material, but the cushion on the right has the **Show Map in Viewport** feature enabled, whereas the cushion on the left does not. In a scene with many different architectural elements and many different materials, having this option enabled can be a great visual help.

Figure 6-9. Example of the Show Map in Viewport feature disabled (left) and enabled (right)

Material Editor icons

Table 6-1 provides a quick reference for each of the icons that surround the **Material Editor** sample slots. Some of these icons have just been discussed, and others will be discussed in the next chapter.

Table 6-1. Material Editor icons

Icon	Name	Description
Site-Sidewalks ▼	**Material drop-down list**	Displays the name of the material, which can be changed by typing a new one in this field. The drop-down list lists the names of the sub-materials that make up the material.
Standard	**Material Type** button	Displays the current material or map type. Opens the **Material/Map Browser** and allows you to assign a new material or map type.
	Pick Material from Object	Selects a material from an object in the scene and iconloads it into the selected sample slot.
	Get Material icon	Opens the **Material/Map Browser.**
	Put Material to Scene icon	Updates any materials in the scene that havechanged.
	Assign Material to Selection	Places the selected material on the selected icon object.
	Reset Map/Mtl to Default	Resets all map and material settings to their original **Settings** icon configurations.
	Make Material Copy icon	Makes a copy of the selected material in a different sample slot.
	Make Unique icon	Makes the selected instanced material a completely new and unconnected material.
	Put to Library icon	Opens a dialog box that allows you to rename the material and save it to the current library.
	Material Effects Channel	Assigns a material effect ID to the material. The ID icon can tell 3ds Max what video post or rendering effects are assigned to what materials.

Continued

Table 6-1. Material Editor icons (Continued)

Icon	Name	Description
	**Show Map in Viewport** icon	Shows the material's map on an object in a shaded viewport.
	**Show End Result** icon	Toggles between showing a sub-material or submap and showing the end result of the material or map.
	**Go to Parent** icon	Moves up one level within the current material.
	**Go Forward to Sibling** icon	Moves to the next map channel with a map loaded.
	**Sample Type** icon	Changes the sample type object from one solid type to another. The default type is a sphere; other options include a cylinder, cube, and a custom object that you select.
	**Backlight** icon	Toggles the backlighting in the selected sample slot on and off.
	**Background** icon	Toggles a multicolored checkered background behind the selected material on and off. This is a visual aid for viewing certain materials, such as transparent ones.
	**Sample UV Tiling** icon	Changes the UV tiling for the map in the sample slot. The default is 1×1; other options include 2×2, 3×3, and 4×4. These settings change only the display in the sample slot and have no effect on the material.
	**Video Color Check** icon	Checks the selected material to see if it contains any colors not supported by the NTSC and PAL formats.
	**Make, Play, Save Preview**	Lets you make, play, and save an animated material icon preview.
	**Options** icon	Opens a dialog box that includes options defining the number of sample slots, sample slot light intensity, custom slot backgrounds, and much more.
	**Select by Material** icon	Lets you select all objects in your scene that use the current material by opening the **Select Objects** dialog box with those objects selected.
	**Material Map Navigator**	Opens the **Material/Map Navigator** dialog box, icon which displays all the sub-materials and utilized maps of the current material.

The Material/Map Browser

The **Material/Map Browser,** shown in Figure 6-10, is an interface that lets you browse for materials in the current scene you are working in, in the library of another scene, or in a library stored in a special Max-created file with the .mat extension. In addition to loading materials from a library, you can use the **Material/Map Browser** to create or update material libraries yourself.

The **Material/Map Browser** opens when you click the **Get Material** icon, the **Material Type** icon, or a map icon. If you are currently browsing a library, the material library name is shown across the top of the browser. Directly below, on the right-hand side, is the material name, followed by icons that provide different viewing options. To the right of these are icons that let you clear and delete materials from a library, as well as update the current scene you're working in with the materials from a library. These icons are only available when a library is open. Below these icons is a window that displays the materials and maps in the currently open library. Materials have a blue sphere to the left of the material name, while maps have a green parallelogram. If materials or maps have the **Show Map in Viewport** option enabled, these icons will be displayed in red.

At the top-left of the browser is a text field in which you can type the material name to search and select the material you're looking for. Below this are radio buttons that allow you to change the location in which to browse for materials.

If you want to search for materials in a separate library file saved on your computer, click the **Mtl Library** button. Doing so activates the **File** section on the bottom-left of the browser, in which you can open, merge, or save libraries through an explorer window.

Other options for browsing include searching the **Material Editor's** 24 sample slots, or searching within the scene in which you are working. The option I use most often is the **Selected** option. Along with the **Pick Object From Material** icon (which looks like an eyedropper), I use this option to load a material from an object I've selected in my scene.

To load a selected material from the **Material/Map Browser** into the selected sample slot, you can either drag and drop the material name or double-click it.

Figure 6-10. The Material/Map Browser

Material libraries

Material libraries provide a great way to manage, load, and save materials and maps for current or future use. When I'm working in architectural scenes that can often contain several dozens of materials, I don't like to waste time recreating the same materials over and over again, or searching through old project files to find the scene that contains the materials that I used before. Instead, with a couple of clicks of the mouse, I can have all of my typical materials available for viewing and loading into the **Material Editor** sample slots.

To create a library of your favorite materials, you can edit an existing library or create a new one from scratch, as shown in Figure 6-11. In either case, you will need to open the **Material/Map Browser** and click the **Save As** button to save the library to a certain location with a certain name.

If you start with an already created library, you should delete the materials you don't want and add the materials in your scene that you do want. To add the materials you want, highlight the sample slot with the desired material and click the **Put to Library** icon.

If you are starting a new library from scratch, you should merge all the objects from the various scenes that contain the desired materials and click the **Scene** option under the **Browse From** section of the **Material/Map Browser**. When you click the **Scene** radio button, all of the materials loaded in your scene will appear in the **Material List** window on the right side of the browser. If you want, you can delete individual materials from the scene library, and then save the scene library as a completely separate material library elsewhere on your computer.

Figure 6-11. The temp.mat material library

Creating and editing material libraries

This exercise demonstrates how to use the **Material/Map Browser** to create and edit material libraries.

1. Reset 3ds Max.

2. Press **M** to open the **Material Editor**.

3. Click the **Get Material** icon (shown in the following image) to open the **Material/Map Browser**.

4. Under the **Browse From** section of the **Material/Map Browser,** select **Mtl Library**.

5. In the **File** section, select **Open**. This opens the **Open Material Library** window to the **Autodesk\3dsMax2008\matlibs** directory. This directory contains a number of existing libraries that shipped with Max.

6. Select the **Wood.mat** file, and select **Open** to open this library. The contents of this library are now shown in the **Material/Map Browser.**

7. Double-click the material labeled **Wood_Bark.** The material is now loaded into the active sample slot. You can also drag and drop the material into the sample slot.

8. Inside the **Material/Map Browser,** highlight the material labeled **Wood_Driftwood.**

9. Click the **Delete from Library** icon (shown in the following image). The material is now deleted from the Wood.mat library. Next, you'll save this library under a new name.

10. Under the **File** section, click **Save As,** and name the library **Wood_New.** You've just created a new library that contains one fewer material than the library named Wood.mat.

The Material/Map Navigator

The **Material/Map Navigator** icon (shown in the following image) opens the **Material/Map Navigator** (Figure 6-12), a feature in the **Material Editor** that displays the entire material hierarchy of the selected sample slot.

This feature is handy when you want to explore the layers of just the selected sample slot and not have to sift through dozens of materials in the **Material/Map Browser.** In the browser, all materials and maps are displayed, unlike the navigator, which displays only the contents of the selected sample slot.

Figure 6-12. The Material/Map Navigator

Material Editor rollouts

While the **Material Editor** sample slots and the icons that surround them manage materials and their display, they don't affect the actual appearance of the materials (with the exception of the **Material Type** button). A material is fashioned by the tools and features found in the rollouts below the sample slots. Although these rollouts can appear quite complicated and intimidating, they are in fact quite easy to conquer.

The **Material Editor** contains seven initial rollouts for the standard material (Figure 6-13), most of which will require little or no use for foundation-level readers in the visualization industry. The standard material type is the default type, and provides a single, uniform color distribution based on the settings of the **Ambient, Diffuse,** and **Specular** color swatches. Other material types will be discussed in the next chapter, but for right now, you'll explore the rollouts for the most commonly used material type, the standard material.

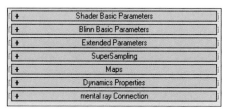

Figure 6-13. The seven standard rollouts

The Shader Basic Parameters rollout

The first rollout, **Shader Basic Parameters** (Figure 6-14), specifies the shading type, which will be explained in greater detail in the next chapter. To the right of the shader type are four options: **Wire, 2-Sided, Face Map,** and **Faceted.**

Figure 6-14. The Shader Basic Parameters rollout

The Wire option

The **Wire** option makes a model appear as a wireframe object, with the wires running along the edges of the individual polygons of the model. This option is a great way to create fences, window mullions, and a few other architectural features, because it requires only a fraction of the number of faces required to model the same looking object. The left image in Figure 6-15 shows the sample slot of a material with the **Wire** option enabled. In the right-hand image, a simple plane with four length and width segments is used to simulate a small wire fence by applying a material with the **Wire** option enabled. The number of faces needed to produce the object is only 32, but modeling the same object requires 356 faces. This disparity is multiplied when you create larger models. A fence that runs 100 yards could easily require tens of thousands of faces, yet the simple plane with a material applied that uses the **Wire** option would only require about a tenth of the number of faces.

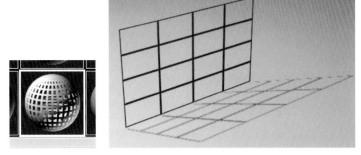

Figure 6-15. An example of a material with the Wire option enabled

Using the Wire option to create a fence

This exercise demonstrates one of the many uses of the **Wire** option in visualizations.

1. Reset 3ds Max.

2. In the Front viewport, create a plane with a width of **100** units, a length of **20** units, **20** width segments, and **4** length segments.

3. Click the **Zoom Extents** icon to maximize the view of the plane.

4. Press **M** to open the **Material Editor.**

5. In the **Shader Basic Parameters** rollout, enable the **Wire** option and **click the Assign Material to Selection icon. The plane now looks like a** wire fence with the wires running along the edges of each polygon.

6. Click the **Quick Render** icon (shown in the following image) to see the results of applying the **Wire** option to the material.

7. Open the **Extended Parameters** rollout, and in the **Wire** section, increase the **Size** to **2.**

8. Render the object again with the new wire size. The viewport will not show changes to the wire size, so you must render the object to see the effects of the change.

9. Save your work for use in the next exercise.

The 2-Sided option

The **2-Sided** option is a great feature that can be beneficial to you in many situations. It simply makes the faces of an object viewable from both sides, regardless of which side the face normals are oriented toward. This option comes in handy when, for whatever reason, some of the face normals of an object are oriented in the wrong direction and your usual remedies are not fixing the problem. As shown in the left image in Figure 6-16, some of the faces of the wall are oriented inward. Although a simple **Unify Normals** routine will fix this particular situation, it may not help for more complex models. In those situations, making the material two-sided will fix the problem, as shown in Figure 6-16's right-hand image.

Figure 6-16. A one-sided object (left) and a two-sided object (right)

Another situation in which this feature works great is when you want to give the appearance of increasing the number of faces in your scene without having to do so, and without increasing the strain on your computer. Modeling blades of grass, for example, can be quite a demand on your computer since you need so many faces for even the smallest of areas. Both images in Figure 6-17 show an object that contains the same number of faces, yet the image on the right appears to contain twice as many blades of grass as the left image because the object in the right image uses a two-sided version of the same material.

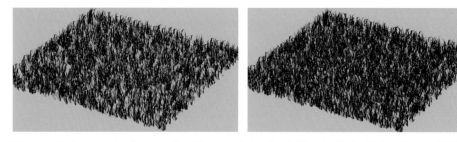

Figure 6-17. An example of grass without the 2-Sided option (left) and with the 2-Sided option (right)

The other two options in the **Shader Basic Parameters** rollout, **Face Map** and **Faceted,** are simply unnecessary in architectural visualizations. **Face Map** applies maps to each polygon of an object, and **Faceted** ignores smoothing between faces. Neither of these options will benefit your work. It should be noted that if you use Direct3D drivers, there is a high probability that the **2-Sided** option will not work.

Enabling the 2-Sided feature

This exercise demonstrates the use of the **2-Sided** option in visualizations.

1. Continue from the previous exercise.

2. In the Perspective viewport, rotate the view so that you can see the backside of the plane object. Notice that you cannot see the plane from the backside because the material is one-sided.

3. Press **M** to open the **Material Editor,** if it's not already open.

4. In the **Shader Basic Parameters** rollout, enable the **2-Sided** option. Notice the plane is now visible from the backside.

The Blinn Basic Parameters rollout

Within the **Blinn Basic Parameters** rollout (shown in Figure 6-18) is a drop-down list that contains all of the available shading options (for the standard material, 3ds Max gives you eight). Shaders are mathematical algorithms that determine the way light illuminates a surface. The default shader is the Blinn shader, which works well for most materials you will want to represent, especially exterior scenes in which you're not close enough to the objects to see the benefit of using other shaders. For now, I would suggest sticking with the Blinn shader even in cases in which other shaders would be better. This is mainly because the use of other shaders requires knowledge of a much larger number of settings, many of which can be confusing if you don't have an advanced level of understanding about 3ds Max.

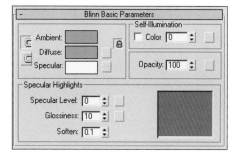

Figure 6-18. The Blinn Basic Parameters rollout

The Ambient, Diffuse, and Specular Color swatches

The next section of this rollout contains three color swatches that control the ambient, diffuse, and specular components of an object's illumination. To the left of the color swatches are two small squares that you can click to lock the ambient and diffuse colors so that they stay the same. By default, 3ds Max has locked the **Ambient** and **Diffuse** swatches. Except for situations when you want to take advantage of advanced lighting techniques such as radiosity, it is not necessary to unlock these two components. The two small squares to the right of the **Diffuse** and **Specular** color swatches are shortcut buttons for adding maps in lieu of or in conjunction with the diffuse or specular portions (also referred to as channels) of an illuminated surface. When a map is loaded, the buttons show an uppercase **M,** and when the loaded map is inactive, a lowercase **m** is displayed.

Just as the **Ambient** and **Diffuse** color swatches are locked by default, so too are their channels, as indicated by the lock symbol to the right of the color swatches. This lock should be left in place because disabling it would only be needed when advanced lighting and material techniques are used.

The Specular Highlights section

Below the color swatches is the **Specular Highlights** section. The **Specular Level** option controls the intensity of the specular highlights, and the **Glossiness** option controls the size of the highlights. The **Soften** value spreads the highlight across the area controlled by the **Glossiness** value, but its impact is all but negligible. The graph on the right-hand side of the **Specular Highlights** shows a representation of the **Specular Level** and **Glossiness** values across an object's surface, measured from the center point of the greatest specular highlight. The greater the **Specular Level** value, the greater the intensity of the highlight. The greater the **Glossiness** value, the smaller the area of specular highlight. The spinners to the right of the input fields provide a quick and easy way to change these values, and the graph provides a great way to see how the values affect the overall surface. Although the **Specular Level** value can go as high as 999, in creating architectural visualizations I have never needed a **Specular Level** greater than 100, which represents maximum specular reflection. Figure 6-19 shows several different sample slots with their corresponding **Specular Level** and **Glossiness** values.

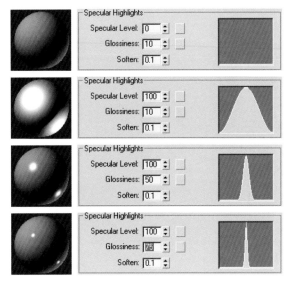

Figure 6-19. Various specular highlights

The Self-Illumination section

In the **Self-Illumination** section of this rollout, you can specify how much illumination a material creates for itself, and how much effect shadows and highlights have.

By changing the value in the field to the right of the word **Color,** you can control how much diffuse color illumination an object receives. A value of **0** results in no self-illumination, whereas a value of **100** results in the entire surface of the object receiving the same diffuse color illumination and no shadows or highlights. The three left-hand images in Figure 6-20 illustrate the range from 100 to 0.

If you click the **Color** option, the value field and spinners are replaced with a swatch that allows you to set the amount of glow a material creates for itself. A color setting of pure black results in no glow, whereas a setting of pure white results in the object appearing completely white over the entire surface and receiving no shadows or highlights. Any color in this swatch other than pure white results in a mix of the selected color and some degree of highlights and shadows. The three right-hand images in Figure 6-20 illustrate this.

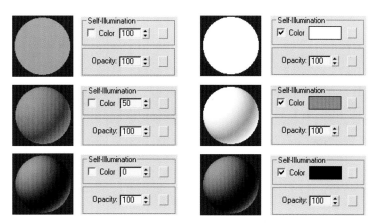

Figure 6-20. Various Illumination settings

Using the Blinn Basic Parameters rollout

This exercise demonstrates the characteristics of the **Blinn Basic Parameters** rollout.

1. Reset 3ds Max.

2. In the Perspective viewport, create a sphere of any size, and click the **Zoom Extents** icon to maximize the view of the sphere.

3. Press **M** to open the **Material Editor,** if it's not already opened.

4. In the first sample slot, change the name of the material to **Test.** You'll use this material to test the characteristics of the **Blinn Basic Parameters** rollout.

5. Apply the material (in its default state) to the sphere.

6. Click on the **Background** icon (looks like a checkerboard) to change the background. This will make the material easier to see when we make it transparent.

7. Click the color swatch next to **Diffuse,** and select a greenish color. Notice the sphere in the viewport changes to this color, as shown in image 1 of the following illustration.

8. In the **Specular Highlights** section, increase the **Specular Level** to **100.** Notice the intensity of the specular highlights increases dramatically, as shown in image 2.

9. Increase the **Glossiness** to **50.** This reduces the size of the specular area, as shown in image 3.

10. Next, decrease the **Opacity** to **50.** The sphere now becomes 50% transparent, as shown in image 4.

11. Increase the **Self-Illumination** value to **100.** Notice the sphere receives no shadows, as shown in image 5.

12. Lastly, enable the **Color** option under **Self-Illumination,** click the color swatch that appears next to it, and select a gray value halfway between pure black and pure white. Notice the sphere is now partially glowing, as shown in image 6.

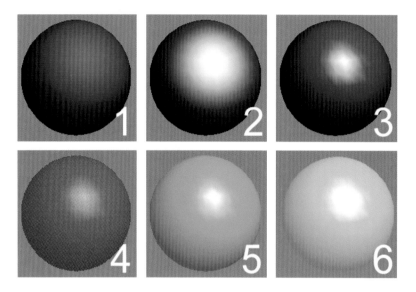

The Extended Parameters rollout

The **Extended Parameters** rollout (see Figure 6-21) contains three sections: **Advanced Transparency, Reflection Dimming,** and **Wire.** Reflection dimming produces very subtle changes to reflections that exist in shadows. Because it is an advanced feature, it will not e covered in this book.

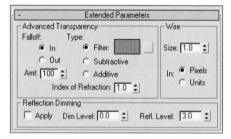

Figure 6-21. The Extended Parameters rollout

The Advanced Transparency section

The **Advanced Transparency** section can be used to add transparency to illuminated objects, such as a light bulb. Figure 6-22 illustrates the effect of various **Amount** and **Falloff** settings in conjunction with increased self-illumination and specular highlights (both within the **Blinn Basic Parameters** rollout).

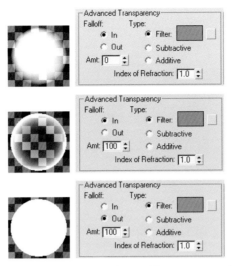

Figure 6-22. Various Advanced Transparency settings

The Wire section

The **Wire** section's only function is to control materials with the **Wire** option enabled. As discussed earlier, the **Wire** option is a handy feature for simulating fences and window mullions at a fraction of the processing power required for their 3D counterparts. The **Size** value controls the thickness of the wire, and the **In** setting determines whether the size is expressed in units or screen pixels. Figure 6-23 shows examples of wire **Size** settings of **1.0, 2.0,** and **3.0.**

Figure 6-23. Various wire size settings

The SuperSampling rollout

The only purpose of the **SuperSampling** rollout (shown in Figure 6-24) is to improve the quality of renderings and animations by decreasing the effect of aliasing. Aliasing is a term to describe imperfections in the rendering process caused by color changes that are too drastic, and that occur over too small an area of screen space to be adequately depicted by the pixels that define that space. In a single still image, aliasing is certainly noticeable and can reduce realism; and if the same scene is set in motion, it can produce a very distracting effect and ruin the animation. Two examples of this are flickering and texture crawling.

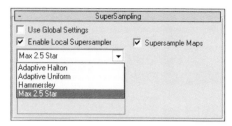

Figure 6-24. The SuperSampling rollout

Flickering occurs during animations when materials (such as the grass in Figure 6-25) have a speckled appearance with drastic changes in color occurring over a small number of pixels. In these cases, the computer cannot accurately determine which color to assign a given pixel, because the edge of two colors exists in the middle of a pixel. In the top image of each of the following sets (Figures 6-25 and 6-26), supersampling is disabled, and the contrast in adjacent pixels is harsher than in the bottom images, in which supersampling is enabled. When scenes with these textures are animated, the difference between the two can be dramatic.

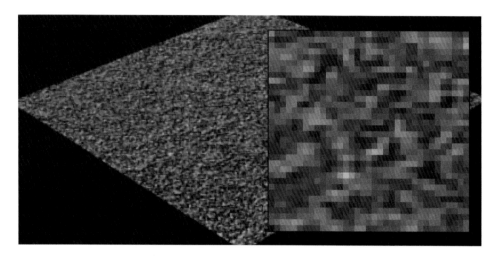

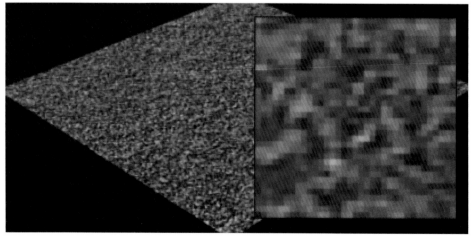

Figure 6-25. Supersampling disabled (top) and enabled (bottom)

Texture crawling occurs in animation in areas along the edges of lines and polygons. This undesirable effect happens because there are not enough pixels available on a typical monitor to properly display mathematically smooth lines and polygon edges. When a 3D scene is transposed onto a monitor's pixel grid, or raster, each pixel is colored according to whether or not it is covered by an object in the scene. Aliasing occurs because the raster system does not properly handle the case in which a pixel is only partially covered. Partially covered pixels occur along the edges of objects and are referred to as edge pixels or fragment pixels. The mishandling of fragment pixels results in harsh, jagged color transitions between an object's edge and the background. Examples of materials in which texture crawling is prevalent are bricks in a wall, pavers in a walkway, and fascia on a roof. In the top image in Figure 6-26, anti-aliasing is disabled and the edges are much more jagged than in the bottom image, in which antialiasing is enabled. In animations, these edges appear to crawl whether they are the edges of an object or the edges within a material applied to an object.

Figure 6-26. Anti-aliasing disabled (top) and enabled (bottom)

Anti-aliasing techniques attempt to smooth jagged edges by properly handling fragment pixels (i.e., adjusting the pixel color according to the amount of pixel coverage). 3ds Max incorporates anti-aliasing filters in the rendering process by default, and although they greatly improve render-ings and animations, in some scenes the standard filters aren't enough. Supersampling is an additional anti-aliasing process that samples the colors around a pixel and uses that information to determine the final color of the pixel. Supersampling can be initiated for specific materials or for the entire scene.

This rollout, shown in Figure 6-24, initiates supersampling specifically for the selected material. Four supersampling methods are available with 3ds Max, but each one slows the rendering process to some degree. My advice for supersampling is to not enable it until you see that you need it, and then to test each of the four methods on a small sample sequence with the problematic material isolated.

If you decide that you must use supersampling for an entire scene, go to the **Renderer** tab of the **Render Scene** dialog box and enable **Global SuperSampling.**

Another entirely different way to perform supersampling, which I like to use myself, is to render the scene at a higher resolution than what the final output is actually going to be, and then scale down to that final output. This is, in effect, a way of supersampling for yourself.

The Maps rollout

This rollout is the heart of material creation and is covered in great detail in the next chapter.

The Dynamic Properties rollout

This rollout is used in animations involving collisions and is not commonly needed in architectural visualizations.

The Mental Ray Connection rollout

This rollout is used for mental ray materials, which are not covered in this book.

Summary

This chapter has covered the essential features of the **Material Editor** in great detail. The **Material Editor** itself is a fairly simple interface, especially when you only focus on those features that would be of use to those of us in the visualization field. What makes the **Material Editor** seem so complex is not the number of features that make up the interface, but rather the degree to which you can make individual materials complex. You can create great looking materials in very little time, or even use existing material libraries—but either way, the time you spend navigating the **Material Editor** can be made minor. On the other hand, you can add tremendous complexity to your work by incorporating the seemingly endless features that affect your individual materials. Nonetheless, the **Material Editor** is just the first step in working with materials. You cannot create a great visualization without incorporating the process known as mapping. The next two chapters cover the critical map channels and map types, and UVW mapping. After reading these chapters, you should know everything you need to create great-looking materials.

CHAPTER 7

The Critical Map Channels

As MENTIONED IN THE PREVIOUS chapter, the **Maps** rollout is the heart of material creation. In this rollout, maps are applied to specific areas of a material, known as channels. A standard material contains each of the twelve map channels listed in Figure 7-1. Some of these channels can have a tremendous impact on architectural visualizations, while others have less importance. This chapter focuses on the critical map channels and how to use them to create realistic materials for use in visualizations.

Beginning with this chapter and continuing throughout the rest of this book, you will need select files to complete the tutorials. These files, along with the instructions of how to load them into 3ds Max, can be downloaded from the book's web page at **www.3dats.com\books**. You will also need to remember to add the appropriate folders to the **External Files** list within the **Configure Paths** dialog box.

Maps			
	Amount	Map	
☐ Ambient Color . . .	100 ↕	None	⊟
☐ Diffuse Color	100 ↕	None	
☐ Specular Color .	100 ↕	None	
☐ Specular Level .	100 ↕	None	
☐ Glossiness	100 ↕	None	
☐ Self-Illumination .	100 ↕	None	
☐ Opacity	100 ↕	None	
☐ Filter Color	100 ↕	None	
☐ Bump	30 ↕	None	
☐ Reflection	100 ↕	None	
☐ Refraction	100 ↕	None	
☐ Displacement . .	100 ↕	None	

Figure 7-1. The Maps rollout

The Maps rollout

The **Maps** rollout (shown in Figure 7-1) consists of four columns. The second column from the left indicates the name of the channel. The first column on the left is the enable/disable switch for the map that is loaded into that channel. When a map is loaded into a channel, its name appears in place of the channel button labeled **None** adjacent to the name of the channel. The column labeled **Amount** (third from left) specifies the percentage of the map that will be displayed, if one is loaded and enabled. With an amount of **100**, only the map will be displayed in the corresponding channel. With an amount of **50**, 50% of what is displayed for the channel will come from the map and 50% will come from the settings in the **Basic Parameters** rollouts. With an amount of **0**, the loaded map will not have any effect on the material. If the switch in the first column is set to disable the map, then the map will have no effect on the material, regardless of the value in the **Amount** column.

Now, let's take a look at those critical map channels at work. The examples in this chapter will make this interface very clear.

The Diffuse Color channel

The Diffuse Color channel—probably the most frequently used map channel—allows you to replace the diffuse color specified in the **Blinn Basic Parameters** rollout with a map. Since the diffuse color is usually the main component of an object's appearance, placing a map in the Diffuse Color channel will make the material appear just like the map. The Diffuse Color channel can completely replace the diffuse color if the amount is set to 100. Alternatively, it can exist in conjunction with the diffuse color by any percentage specified in the **Amount** field. Figure 7-2 shows maps applied to the Diffuse Color channel in varying amounts.

Figure 7-2. The Diffuse map mixed with the Diffuse Color using an Amount value of 100, 75, 50 and 25, from left to right

Using the Diffuse Color channel

This exercise demonstrates use of the Diffuse Color channel by loading into it a simple bitmap.

1. Reset 3ds Max.

2. Press **M** to open the **Material Editor.**

3. Click any sample slot, open the **Maps** rollout, and click the channel button labeled **None** to the right of the words **Diffuse Color**, as shown in the following illustration. The **Material/Map Browser** opens.

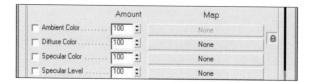

4. Double-click the word **Bitmap** in the **Material/Map Browser,** as shown in the following illustration.

5. Go to the directory **3dsMax2008\Images\3DATS**, select the file **Tile01.jpg**, and select **Open**. The image is now loaded in the Diffuse Color channel.

6. Click the **Go to Parent** button (shown in the following image) to return to the **Maps** rollout.

7. Click the **Diffuse Color map** shortcut button, shown in the following illustration (located to the right of the Diffuse color swatch). Notice the shortcut now has a capitalized **M** on it, indicating an active map is loaded into the Diffuse Color channel. A lowercase **m** would indicate that a map is loaded but has been deactivated. Since a map is already loaded, clicking this shortcut takes you directly to the **Bitmap Parameters** rollout, from which you can change the map. If a map is not loaded, clicking this shortcut takes you to the **Material/Map Browser.**

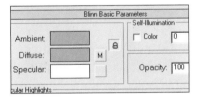

8. In the **Bitmap Parameters** rollout, click the channel button next to the word **Bitmap,** as shown in the following illustration. This opens a file explorer window from which you can load a new map.

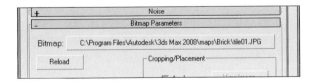

9. Press **Esc** to cancel this process, and click the **Go to Parent** button to return to the **Maps** rollout again.

10. In the Perspective viewport, create a box width a length, width, and height of **100**.

11. Apply the material you just created to the box.

12. Click the **Show Map in Viewport** option. The image of the tile can now be seen in a shaded viewport.

13. In the **Maps** rollout, disable the map loaded in the Diffuse Color channel by clicking the check box next to the words **Diffuse Color,** as shown in the following illustration:

The Opacity channel

The Opacity channel enables you to produce materials that are visible in certain parts and transparent in other parts. The left image in Figure 7-3 shows an image of a plant that can be applied to the Diffuse Color channel. The middle image shows a black-and-white version that can be applied to the Opacity channel. The image in the Opacity channel tells Max which parts of the Diffuse Color map to show and which parts to make transparent. Pure white areas of the Opacity map will allow the corresponding areas of the Diffuse Color map to be visible, while pure black areas cause the corresponding areas of the Diffuse Color map to be transparent. In the example below, the opacity map (middle image) allows the plant to be cut out of the photograph and displayed without the background, as shown in the image on the right.

 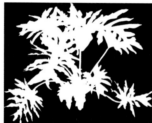 

Figure 7-3. Using the Opacity channel to mask portions of a photograph

In addition to using a black-and-white image for the Opacity map, such as a .jpg or .bmp, you can use the alpha channel of a .tga file to serve as the Opacity map. The result of using a .tga file for both the Diffuse Color and Opacity channels is the same as using two separate images; but when using a .tga file, you must tell 3ds Max to use the alpha channel in the Opacity channel. To use a .tga file, load the file in both the Diffuse Color channel and the Opacity channel. In the Opacity channel, go to the **Bitmap Parameters** rollout, and under the **Mono Channel Output** section, click the **Alpha** option, as shown in Figure 7-4. Then exit the Opacity channel, and in the **Blinn Basic Parameters** rollout, change all three color swatches to pure black, and set the **Specular Level** and **Glossiness** values to **0.** Not changing the color swatches to pure black can cause a white edge to appear around the cut out image and not reducing the specular highlights can cause highlights to appear when they shouldn't. In the sample slot, you should see the image with the background cut out.

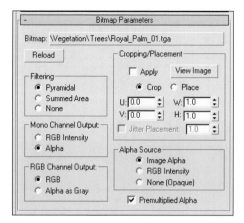

Figure 7-4. A .tga file used in the Diffuse Color
and Opacity channels

Some examples of things that Opacity maps can benefit in architectural visualizations include
vegetation, people, street signs, lampposts, animals, cars, and boats.

Using the Opacity channel

This exercise demonstrates use of the Opacity channel by loading an image into the Diffuse Color
channel and copying it into the Opacity channel.

1. Reset 3ds Max.

2. Open the **Material Editor.**

3. Click any sample slot, open the **Maps** rollout, and click the channel button labeled **None** to the
   right of the words **Diffuse Color,** as shown in the following illustration:

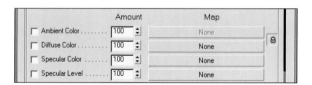

4. Double-click the word **Bitmap** in the **Material/Map Browser,** as shown in the following illustration:

5. Go to the directory **3dsMax2008\Images\3DATS,** select the file **Tree01.tga**, and click **Open.** The image is now loaded in the Diffuse Color channel.

6. Change the sample slot object type from the default sphere to a cube to better see the resulting appearance of the material. Notice the entire image appears on each side of the cube. You will now load the alpha channel embedded in this .tga file to show only the tree and to mask everything else in the image.

7. Click the **Go to Parent** button to return to the **Maps** rollout.

8. Click and hold on the map loaded in the Diffuse Color channel, as shown in the following illustration. Drag and release on top of the **Opacity** channel button.

9. You will be prompted to either make an instance of, copy, or swap the map loaded into the Diffuse Color channel, as shown in the right image of the preceding illustration. Select **Copy,** and click **OK.**

10. Click the **Opacity** channel button into which you just loaded the map. The **Bitmap Parameters** rollout opens.

11. Scroll down within the **Bitmap Parameters** rollout to the section labeled **Mono Channel Output,** and click the **Alpha** option, as shown in the following illustration. This tells 3ds Max to load the alpha map embedded in the .tga file into the Opacity channel. Notice now in the sample slot that only the tree is shown on the sides of the cube, while the rest of the image is cut out.

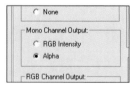

12. Within the **Cropping/Placement** section of the **Bitmap Parameters** rollout, click the **View Image** button, as shown in the following illustration. The .tga image is displayed.

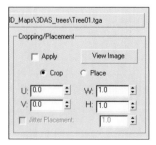

13. Click the **Display Alpha Channel** icon (the first icon to the right of the red, green, and blue channel buttons). This shows the alpha map (shown on the right in the following image) embedded in the .tga file, and why portions of the image are hidden. Any portion of the alpha map shown in black will hide the corresponding portion of the overall image. You can adjust an image's alpha map in programs like Adobe Photoshop by working with its channels within the program.

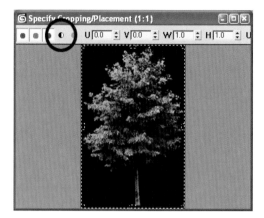
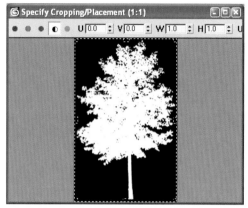

14. Now, to see the results of this new material in action, try applying the material to a simple plane object.

The Bump channel

The Bump channel is a powerful feature in 3ds Max that can give materials a realistic 3D appearance. The Bump channel uses the brighter areas of an image to make the material appear raised, while darker areas of the image make the material appear to be recessed. The ideal bump map is a purely grayscale image; however, a full color image will also work. The Bump channel amount can range from 0 to 999, although values over 300 usually result in so much relief that the material doesn't look realistic. The left image in Figure 7-5 shows a box object simulating stucco. The only map applied to the material is the black-and-white image to the right of the box, which was applied to the Bump channel with an **Amount** value of **50.**

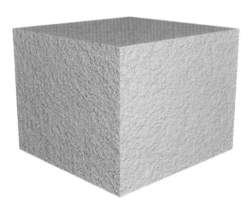

Figure 7-5. Applying a grayscale image to the Bump channel to produce a textured appearance

Bump maps can be used in a wide variety of material types, including walls, grass, water, concrete, tile, wood, and many others. Bump maps are also very handy when you want to produce objects with engravings or impressions.

Using the Bump channel

This exercise demonstrates use of the Bump channel by loading into it the grayscale image shown on the right in Figure 7-5.

1. Reset 3ds Max.
2. Open the **Material Editor**.
3. Click any sample slot, open the **Maps** rollout, and click the channel button labeled **None** to the right of the word **Bump.**
4. Go to the directory **3dsMax2008\Images\3DATS**, select the file **Stucco01.jpg**, and click **Open.** The image is now loaded in the Bump channel.
5. In the Perspective viewport, create a box with a length, width, and height of **100**.
6. Apply the material to the box.
7. Click the **Quick Render** icon to see the result of applying the map to the Bump channel of this material. Notice that the box appears to be made of stucco, as shown in the images in the following illustration.
8. In the **Maps** rollout of the stucco material you just created, increase the effect of the map in the Bump channel by increasing the **Amount** from the default value of **30** to **100**. The image on the right in the following illustration shows the result of increasing the Bump channel **Amount** to **100.**

9. Render the box again to see the effect of increasing the Bump channel **Amount.**

The Reflection channel

Reflections can add a tremendous amount of realism to any scene. Depending on the lighting in your scenes, reflections might be found on such objects as windows, water, or even polished teapots (as shown in Figure 7-6). If not used wisely and in moderation, however, reflections can impose a heavy burden on your processor and slow your rendering speed to a crawl.

Figure 7-6. Using an image to simulate an artificial reflection

The easiest and least processor-needy way to use reflections is to load a map into the Reflections channel. This makes the material appear to reflect objects in your scene. For example, in Figure 7-6, the image of the lake was loaded into the Reflection channel of a material applied to the teapot. This was the only change made to the material to make it appear this way.

The reflection amount can range from 0 to 100, where 0 results in no reflection and 100 results in a near mirror-like reflection, depending on the other rollouts and map channel settings. Figure 7-7 shows reflection amounts ranging from 100 to 25.

Figure 7-7. Reflection amounts of 100, 75, 50, and 25, from left to right

More realistic but processor-hungry ways of producing reflections include using the Flat Mirror and Raytrace maps, as shown in Figure 7-8.

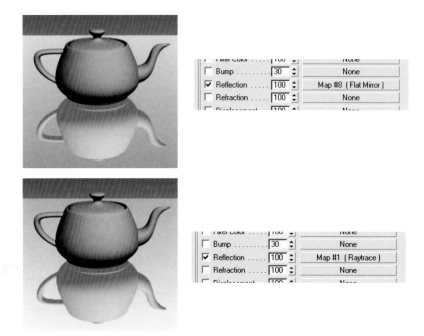

Figure 7-8. Reflections using a Flat Mirror map (top) and a Raytrace map (bottom)

To create Flat Mirror **reflections,** simply add the Flat Mirror map type to the Reflection channel. Flat Mirror maps render much quicker than Raytrace maps; however, more caution must be taken in their use. Notice that in the **Note** section of the **Flat Mirror Parameters** rollout, it states, **Unless 'Apply Faces with ID' is checked, this material must be applied as a sub-material to a set of coplanar faces.** This means that if you choose to use the Flat Mirror map, you must ensure that the material is applied only to objects that lie in the same plane. Not doing so can result in the material causing erratic reflections or no reflections at all. Figure 7-9 illustrates this with the same material applied to two reflective objects. On the left side of the image is a simple flat plane object, which creates proper reflections. On the right side is a curved mesh whose reflections are incorrect because not all the faces in the object are coplanar.

Figure 7-9. Flat mirror reflections on coplanar faces (left) and non-coplanar faces (right)

Raytrace maps provide the most powerful and realistic reflections of all the standard map types. To create Raytrace map reflections, simply add the Raytrace map type to the **Reflection** channel. The Raytrace map contains four rollouts (shown in the left image of Figure 7-10) with numerous settings that can take a long time to master. Although only advanced users will find it necessary to adjust many of these settings, there are a few important settings that anyone using raytracing should understand.

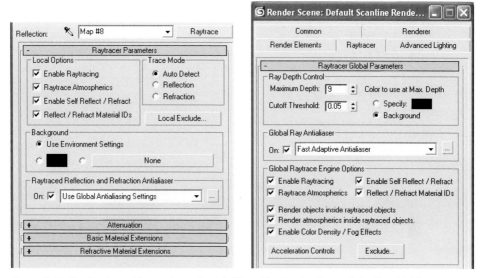

Figure 7-10. The Raytracer Parameters rollout (left) and the Render Scene dialog box (right)

In the **Local Options** settings, enable **Raytrace Atmospherics** if you want to include atmospheric effects such as fog or volume light. Atmospheric effects (covered in Chapter 18) can significantly increase your rendering times, and when included in reflections, this effect is multiplied. If it is not necessary to include atmospherics, you should disable this option.

At the bottom of the **Raytracer Parameters** rollout is a setting that controls anti-aliasing for the material. This option is disabled until it is enabled globally in the **Render Scene** dialog box. By default, all reflections lack anti-aliasing because in most cases it is not necessary; also, enabling this option can significantly increase rendering times. When you're close enough to objects using raytraced materials that you can see the impact of not using anti-aliasing, you may decide to enable this option. Before you can enable this option for a specific material, however, you must enable the **Global Ray Antialiaser** option found in the **Raytracer** tab of the **Render Scene** dialog box (see the right image of Figure 7-10). When you do, the **Raytrace Reflection and Refraction Antialiaser** option will be selectable for specific materials. The button to the right of this setting is a shortcut that will take you to the **Render Scene** dialog box. If you decide to use this option, make sure you create a material specifically for those objects that you want to use anti-aliasing for, and have the option disabled for all other ray-traced materials.

The last option that bears covering is the **Local Exclude** option found in the **Raytracer Parameters** rollout. Use this feature to exclude objects that you don't want to be reflected. For some complex objects that would significantly burden the computer if they included reflections, you might want to exclude reflections if doing so would not be noticeable.

Using the Reflection channel

This exercise demonstrates use of the Reflection channel by loading into it a Raytrace map.

1. Reset 3ds Max.
2. Open the **Material Editor**.
3. Click any sample slot, open the **Maps** rollout, and click the channel button labeled **None** to the right of the word **Reflection.**
4. Load a Raytrace map into the Reflection channel.
5. In the Perspective viewport, create a plane of any size and a teapot centered on the plane, as shown in the left image of the following illustration.
6. Select the plane and apply the raytrace material.
7. Render the scene to see the results of the raytrace material. The plane now reflects the teapot, as shown in the right image.

The Displacement channel

The next critical map channel that you should have in your arsenal is the Displacement channel. Unlike the Bump map, the Displacement map actually displaces the geometry of a surface according to light and dark areas of a map or image loaded into the Displacement channel. Use of this channel is similar to using the **Displace** modifier. In order to use this map type for mesh objects, the **Displacement Approx.** modifier must be applied.

Figure 7-11 illustrates an example of how displacement mapping can be used to simulate terrain or water. To apply the Displacement map as shown in this example, create a plane object with just one length and width segment. Load a Noise map (described in more detail in the next chapter) into the Displacement channel with an amount of 100, and apply the map to the plane object. Last, apply a **Displacement Approx.** modifier to the object. The result will look like the plane object shown in Figure 7-11. To achieve smoother curves in the object, start with a plane object with more length and width segments, or change the **Subdivision Presets** from the default **Medium** setting to **High.** You can explore other settings in the modifier to achieve higher-quality displacements, but caution should be taken in these settings, as they can easily result in meshes with an astronomical number of faces.

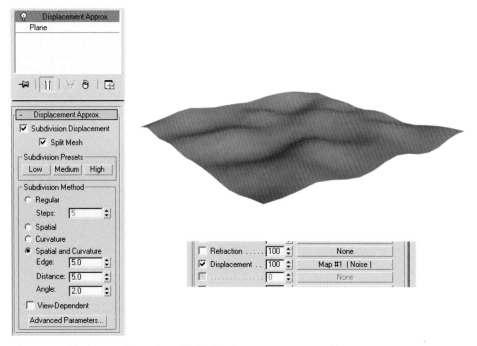

Figure 7-11. Displacement mapping with the Displacement Approx. modifier

Using the Displacement channel

This exercise demonstrates use of the Displacement channel by loading into it a Noise map to simulate mountainous terrain.

1. Reset 3ds Max.

2. Create a plane with a length and width of **100**, and **1** length and width segment.

3. Open the **Material Editor**.

4. Load a Noise map into the Displacement channel.

5. Apply the material to the plane.

6. Select the plane and add a **Displace Approx.** modifier. In the viewport, you will see no change to the plane.

7. Render the scene to see the result of the material and modifier applied to the plane, as shown in the following illustration:

8. Double the default **Amount** value of the displacement to **200,** and render the scene again. Notice the displacement in the plane is twice as great, as shown in the following illustration:

9. Return to the modifier stack for the plane and select the base object in the stack (i.e., the plane).

10. Change the number of length and width segments to **10**, leave the modifier stack, and render the scene again. Notice the terrain is much smoother, as shown in the following illustration, because there are many more vertices to define the curves:

The Refraction channel

Refraction is the bending of light as it passes through one medium into another. Like reflections, refractions can significantly improve the quality and realism of your scenes; but also like reflections, this improvement comes at a price. Refractions are also a more advanced feature that should only be used when all of the other channels discussed in this chapter are understood.

You can create refractions using a bitmap or a procedural map. The most important variable controlling refraction is the index of refraction (IOR), found in the **Extended Parameters** rollout of the standard material (Figure 7-12). The IOR simply controls how much the material refracts transmitted light. At an IOR of 1.0 (the IOR of a vacuum) objects do not distort. At 1.5 (the IOR of glass), objects will distort a large amount. Table 7-1 shows some typical objects and their IOR values.

Table 7-1. Some typical objects and their IOR values

Object	Value IOR
Vacuum	1.0
Air	1.0003
Water	1.333
Glass	1.5 to 1.7

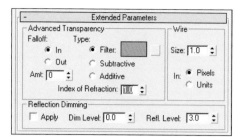

Figure 7-12. The Index of Refraction setting, found in the Extended Parameters rollout

To create refractions using a Thin Wall Refraction map type, load the Thin Wall refraction into the Refraction channel, click the Go to Parent icon, and in the Extended Parameters rollout, change the Index of Refraction value. Try some of the values shown in Table 7-1. The Reflect/Refract map type can be used as a procedural map to create automatic refractions. However, for more accurate refractions of an object in a refractive medium (such as an object in water), you should use the Thin Wall Refraction material. Figure 7-13 shows an object refracted at various values.

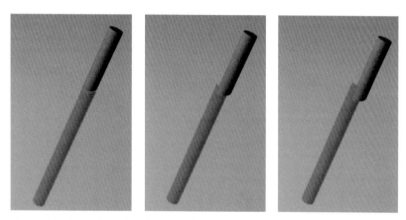

Figure 7-13. IOR values of 1.0, 1.5, and 2.0, from left to right

Summary

This chapter has delved into the heart of material creation for the standard material: the **Maps** roll-out. Although there are numerous types of materials, the standard material is the most commonly used, and for foundation level users, the one that should be concentrated on. Within this chapter, you applied the Bitmap map type to the most critical map channels: those channels that will afford you the widest range of material creation for visualizations. There are many other channels, which you can use to add even greater depth and realism to your scenes, but the uses for those channels are not as extensive as the ones covered in this chapter. Additionally, the skills needed to utilize those channels are far greater than the skills needed to learn the critical channels covered in this chapter.

For the sake of simplicity, this chapter focused primarily on the Bitmap map type. The next chapter describes the other critical map types that can be applied to the map channels you've just learned about. After learning these map types, you will begin to see that there isn't much in the way of materials that you can't create.

CHAPTER 8

The Critical Map Types

THE NUMBER OF USES FOR maps in the various map channels of a material is about as limitless as your imagination. They can be applied to objects as simply as you would apply wallpaper to a wall, or they can be used in complex ways to control very specifically the parameters of other maps. Just as in other areas of 3ds Max, there are usually numerous ways to accomplish the same thing when creating materials; likewise, when creating materials, there are many features that, while great for other industries, serve little purpose in architectural visualizations. I will not cover these features. Instead, I will explain the map types that are critical for the visualization industry, and show you how to get the most out of them to create stunning materials that will help bring your work to life.

The Bitmap map

The Bitmap map type (shown in Figure 8-1) is the most commonly used map type in architectural visualizations and, fortunately, one of the easiest. When you load this map type into a map channel, five rollouts appear. With the exception of the **Bitmap Parameters** rollout, each of these rollouts appears with many of the other map types.

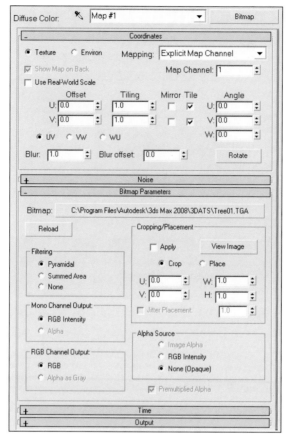

Figure 8-1. The Bitmap Parameters rollout

The Coordinates rollout

The **Coordinates** rollout, shown in Figure 8-2, controls how a map is positioned and oriented on an object, and how it is repeated (tiled) over the object's surface. Before this rollout can be adequately explained, you must understand UVW coordinates. UVW coordinates are the material version of the XYZ coordinates. Just as an object's position in 3D space is defined in XYZ coordinates, a material's position on an object is defined in UVW coordinates. These coordinates are required for every object to which a map is applied. The difference in the letters used is simply to avoid confusion between transformation coordinates.

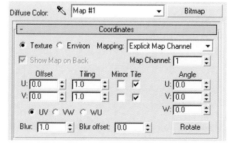

Figure 8-2. A bitmap applied to a simple box with default coordinate values

The first option I want to point out is the option to create the map as a texture or environment map. Environment maps are images applied to the background of a viewport. I highly discourage anyone from using them, because they're always fixed, regardless of how the view changes; and they're usually not realistic. I recommend leaving this option on **Texture,** as shown in Figure 8-2.

Offset and tiling

Below this option are the **Offset** and **Tiling** parameters, which control where the center of the image falls on an object's surface, and how many times the image will be copied over the length of an object's surface. To see how these parameters really work, lets look at an example.

The images in Figure 8-3 show a material with a bitmap image of a leaf applied to a box. In the top-left image, the **Tiling** value is kept at its default value of **1.0.** Because of this, the leaf appears only once on each side of the box, rather than being repeated. The **Offset** value is also kept at its default value of **0.0,** which causes the leaf to be centered on each side of the box, rather than being offset from the center.

In the top-right image, the **Tiling** value is changed to **2.0,** which causes 3ds Max to try to place the same image of the leaf twice on each side of the box. To do so, 3ds Max must reduce the image to half its original size. However, since the image is scaled down from its center, it's cut in half along each edge of the box. To change the position of the tiled leaf images, you must use the **Offset** feature.

The bottom-right image shows the effect of a **U Offset** value of **0.25,** for which the image is moved 25% along the u axis. This offset causes the two images of the leaf to be centered and fit perfectly within each side of the box, but only along the u axis of each side. The bottom-right image shows the effect of a **V Offset** value of **0.25,** for which the image is moved 25% along the v axis. This offset causes the two images of the leaf to be centered and fit perfectly within each side of the box along the v axis.

Figure 8-3. Examples of the Tiling and Offset features

Angle

To the right of this **Tile** option are three parameters that allow you to rotate the bitmap along the u, v, or w axes. You will probably never need to change the **U** and **V** values; however, you may often find it necessary to change the **W** value to something like **45.0,** which essentially turns the bitmap 45 degrees about the w axis, as shown in Figure 8-4.

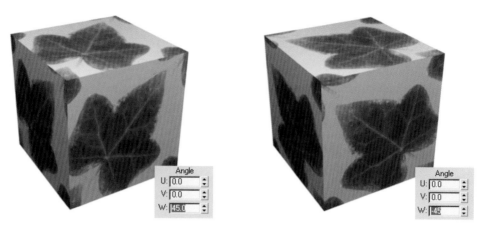

Figure 8-4. Rotating a bitmap +/– 45 degrees along the w axis

Blur and blur offset

If you find that a particular material in your scene is producing an undesirable amount of aliasing, despite whatever anti-aliasing filters you might be using, you might want to try increasing the **Blur** value, located in the bottom-left of the rollout. Rather than using other methods, such as super-sampling, which can significantly increase your rendering times, increasing the **Blur** value can reduce jagged edges without affecting rendering times. Try increasing the default value of **1.0** to **1.5, 2.0,** or **2.5,** until the aliasing effect is removed. Figure 8-5 shows examples of different **Blur** settings.

Figure 8-5. Blur settings of 1.0 (default setting), 2.0, and 3.0, from left to right

You can also increase the blur offset of an individual material to simulate objects in a scene that are out of focus due to their distance from the camera. Unlike **Blur,** which applies a greater blur to objects the farther away they are from the view, **Blur offset** applies the same blur amount regardless of distance.

The last parameter worth mentioning in the **Coordinates** rollout, **Map Channel,** will be left until the next chapter, because its use is tied directly to the discussion of UVW Mapping.

Using the Coordinates rollout of a Bitmap map

This exercise demonstrates some of the key features within the **Coordinates** rollout of a Bitmap map.

1. Reset 3ds Max.

2. Create a box with a length, width, and height of **100**.

3. Open the **Material Editor.**

4. In the Diffuse Color channel of any material, load a Bitmap map using the image **Tile01.jpg** in the **3dsMax2008\Images\3DATS** folder.

5. Apply the material to the box. The result should look like image 1 in the example figure at the end of this exercise.

6. Go to the **Coordinates** rollout of the material you just created and change the **Tiling** amount to **2.0,** as shown in the following illustration. The result should look like image 2 in the example figure.

7. Change the **W** angle value to **45.0,** as shown in the following illustration. This rotates the map 45 degrees along the w axis of the material. The result should look like image 3 in the example figure.

8. Disable the **Tile** option, as shown in the following illustration. This prevents the map from being copied across the surface of the box. The result should look like image 4 in the example figure.

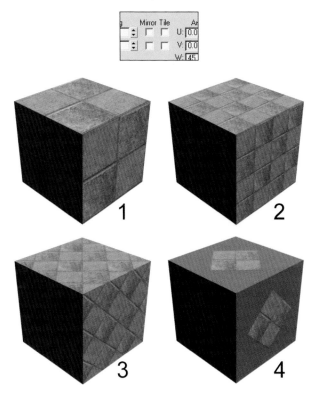

The Noise rollout

The **Noise** rollout (see Figure 8-6) is a personal favorite of mine because it does something that nothing else in 3ds Max seems to be able to do: it can make certain map types appear to not lose their resolution, regardless of how close the maps are to the camera.

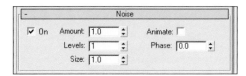

Figure 8-6. The Noise rollout

Figure 8-7 shows the result of the camera coming close to the street and grass objects in a scene. In the top-left image, the maps appear normal, but in the top-right image, the maps appear pixilated because the resolution of the maps is not high enough to support such close views. The bottom image shows the same map with noise enabled. Notice the **Amount** is set to the maximum possible value of **100.0** and the **Size** is set to the minimum possible value of **0.001**. The grass texture is no longer pixilated, regardless of how close you get. Furthermore, the grass will never appear bland, regardless of how far away it is.

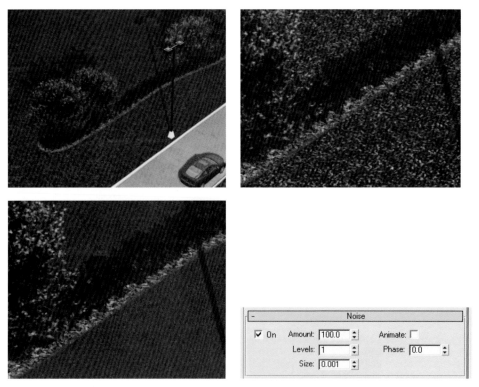

Figure 8-7. Using the Noise settings to reduce pixilation

These settings can also reduce the need for tiling a bitmap. The top image in Figure 8-8 shows a street texture that appears to be tiled, even though it's seamless. The bottom image shows the same Bitmap map with noise applied, using the same settings as the last example. Notice the tiled effect is no longer visible, yet there is still a decided texture.

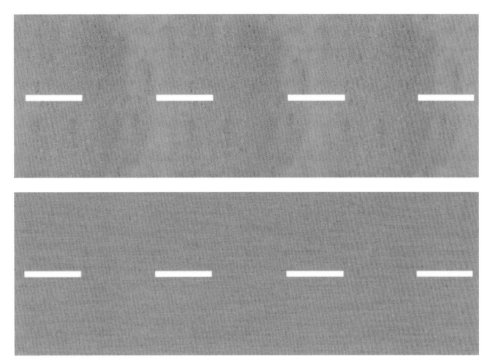

Figure 8-8. Using the Noise setting to reduce the tiled effect of bitmaps

Though the need should be rare, you can even animate the noise by enabling the **Animate** option and changing the **Phase** value over time.

The Time rollout

This rollout is used to control the playing of video clips that are applied as maps. For example, if you want to show a TV playing in your interior scene, you can set the **Start Frame** to a particular frame in your animation so that the TV turns on at a certain point along the animation. Other options include **Playback Rate,** which changes the playing speed of the video clip, and **End Condition,** which can make the video play over and over again.

The Output rollout

The **Output** rollout contains several parameters, but none that I find particularly useful in architectural visualizations. The parameters can be used to control the final output of a map's saturation, contrast, brightness, highlights, midtones, and more—but each of these should need no adjusting. If a material needs adjustments in any of these areas, the chances are that either the scene has poor lighting or the material is poorly constructed and should be adjusted with other parameters.

The Gradient map

The Gradient map produces a change from one color or map to another. It can be used in practical ways with just about every map channel, or in conjunction with another map type. It uses two or three colors or maps to produce a gradient in a linear or radial direction. Its only unique rollout is the **Gradient Parameters** rollout, which contains three color swatches and map icons for loading maps into its color channels. Color #1, or its representative map, is placed at one end of the gradient,

Color #3 is placed at the other end, and the position of Color #2 is determined by the **Color 2 Position** parameter, located below the color swatches. A **Color 2 Position** value of **0.5** places Color #2 halfway between #1 and #3, a value of **0.9** places Color #2 near Color #1, and a value of **0.1** places it near Color #3.

The Gradient map will probably not be one of your more frequently used maps, but it can come in handy in certain situations. One common use is in background images representing the sky, for which you can specify two or three colors at some point in the sky, and have 3ds Max interpolate all of the colors in between, as shown in Figure 8-9. The gradient is applied to the Diffuse Color channel of a material, which is applied to a cylindrical object representing the sky.

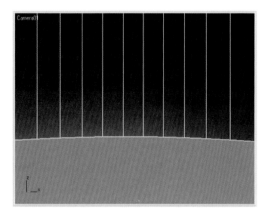 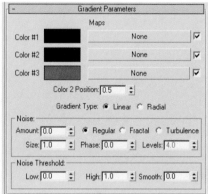

Figure 8-9. Applying a gradient to the Diffuse Color channel

Another way I like to use Gradient maps is to represent the mulched areas around trees, as shown in Figure 8-10. The image on the left shows the boundary between grass and mulch as a harsh abrupt change, which is not as realistic as the image on the right, in which a radial gradient is applied to the Opacity channel of the mulch material. When used in this method, the areas of the Opacity channel that receive pure black are transparent, and the areas that receive pure white are completely opaque. This causes the simple square-shaped mesh to disappear around the edges, giving it an apparent round shape that fades into the grass object. Note, however, that the mulch object must be moved slightly above the grass object so that the two objects don't occupy the same space. You can do the same thing by using the Gradient map in the Diffuse Color channel, with Color #1 being the same as the surrounding grass, and Colors #2 and #3 being the mulch.

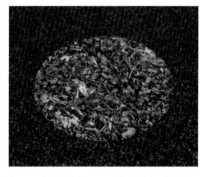 

Figure 8-10. Using a gradient to soften the edge between grass and mulch

These are just two examples in which the Gradient map can come in handy to represent architectural elements. Your imagination can help you use this map type to benefit many other elements.

The Gradient Ramp map

The Gradient Ramp map (shown in Figure 8-11) is a more powerful and versatile version of the Gradient map. The Gradient Ramp map produces any number of changes from one color or map to another, and a variety of controls make this map type useful in many different situations.

The Gradient Ramp map contains only one unique rollout: **Gradient Ramp Parameters.** Along the top of the rollout is the Gradient bar, which presents a linear representation of the color changes from the start point on the left to the end point on the right. By default, three flags that control color or maps appear along the bottom edge of the Gradient bar. When one of the flags is selected, the flag turns green and its RGB value appears above the Gradient bar, along with its position on the gradient. The position is represented as a percentage, with 0% and 100% representing the left and right edges of the bar, respectively. The Gradient bar can contain an unlimited number of flags, and therefore an unlimited number of colors or maps.

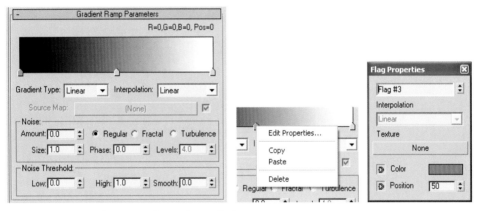

Figure 8-11. The Gradient Ramp Parameters rollout

To change the color of a flag or add a map to it, right-click the flag and select **Edit Properties** (as in the middle image of Figure 8-11). A dialog box appears with a field at the top displaying the flag name, as shown in the right image. You can change the flag name and switch to a different flag using the spinner. Load a map by clicking the **Texture** icon, or change the color by clicking the color swatch. Change the flag's position by typing a new value, using the spinner, or closing the dialog box and dragging the flag along the Gradient bar. Create a new flag by simply clicking anywhere in the Gradient bar.

Below the Gradient bar are two drop-down lists that allow you to specify the shape of the gradient, as well as the interpolation, which controls the transition from one flag to another. Below these drop-down lists are controls for adding noise to the final output. With all of these features, the Gradient map can produce an enormous variety of looks to a map. Like some other map types, the number of ways you can use the Gradient Ramp map is limitless.

Using the Gradient Ramp map

This exercise demonstrates use of the Gradient Ramp map.

1. Reset 3ds Max.

2. Create a box with a length, width, and height of **100**.

3. Open the **Material Editor.**

4. In the Diffuse Color channel of any material, load a Gradient Ramp map.

5. Apply the material to the box. The result should look like image 1 in the four-box example illustration at the end of this exercise.

6. In the **Gradient Ramp Parameters** rollout, right-click the flag at the bottom-left corner of the Gradient bar and select **Edit Properties,** as shown in the following illustration. The flag will turn green when selected.

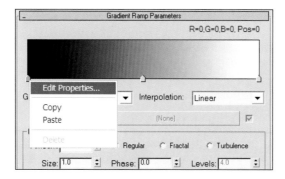

7. Click the color swatch in the **Flag Properties** dialog box that appears, and select the color red from the color selector, as shown in the following illustration. Close the color selector and the **Flag Properties** dialog box.

8. Render the scene again. The result should look like image 2 in the following example illustration.

9. Right-click the flag at the bottom-right corner of the Gradient bar, and select a green color for this flag using the same process as in steps 6 and 7.

10. Render the scene again; the result should look like image 3 in the example illustration.

11. Click, hold, and drag the middle flag under the Gradient bar to a location near the right flag, as shown in the following illustration. This simply changes the location at which the three colors merge.

12. Render the scene again; the result should look like image 4 in the following illustration.

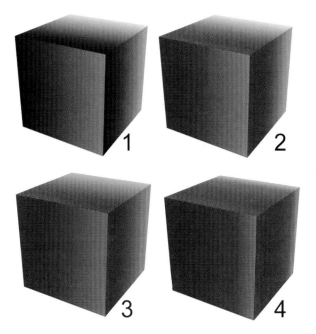

The Mix map

The Mix map, shown in Figure 8-12, combines two colors or maps in specified amounts to produce a blended result. This map type contains only one unique rollout: **Mix Parameters**. At the top of the rollout are two color swatches and map icons. Use the color swatches to choose two different colors to mix, and use their adjacent map icons to load maps in place of the colors. Below the color swatches is a **Mix Amount** parameter and its adjacent map icon.

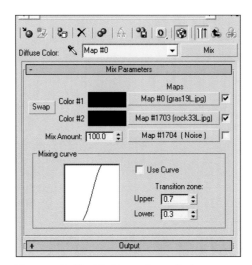

Figure 8-12. The Mix Parameters rollout

The **Mix Amount** controls how much of each color or map is used in the blend. A **Mix Amount** of **0.0** results in 100% of Color #1 being shown and 0% of Color #2 being shown. A **Mix Amount** of **100.0** produces the opposite result. A **Mix Amount** of **50.0** results in 50% of each color or map being displayed. Figure 8-13 illustrates how two bitmaps can be mixed together with a range of mix amounts. Color #2 (grass image 2) is mixed with Color #1 (grass image 1) using a mix amounts of 0, 25, 50, 75, and 100.

Figure 8-13. Two separate grass images mixed with amounts of 0, 25, 50, 75, and 100, from left to right

The **Mix Amount** map icon can be used to produce a randomized blend between both colors or maps, in which Color #1 is displayed in random locations and Color #2 is displayed in all other locations. Figure 8-14 shows a material with a Mix map applied to the Diffuse Color channel. If you make Color #1 red and Color #2 yellow, and load a Noise map into the **Mix Amount** slot, the result is a material with a randomized mixture of both colors. Changing the **Size** value within the **Noise Parameters** rollout changes the size of the red and yellow parts. To have more of Color #1, use more black in both color slots in the **Noise Parameters** rollout. To have more of Color #2, use more white.

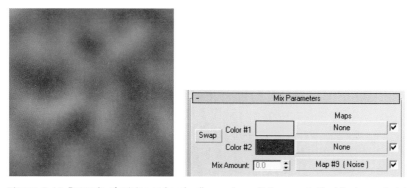

Figure 8-14. Example of mixing red and yellow, using a Noise map in the Mix Amount slot

The Noise map

The Noise map is a map type that is probably most useful in controlling the appearance of other map types, as just explained in the discussion of the Mix map type. By loading a Noise map into the Bump channel, for example, you can randomly apply bumps to an object in a noise pattern.

The Noise map contains three rollouts. The **Coordinates** rollout for noise is built much like the **Coordinates** rollout for other map types (explained previously), and adjusting this rollout is usually not necessary. The only unique rollout for this map type is the **Noise Parameters** rollout. Along the top of the rollout are the **Noise Type** options of **Regular, Fractal,** and **Turbulence.** Which option you select depends on the look you're trying to achieve. **Fractal** is a favorite of mine when I'm trying to depict aged surfaces, such as rusted metal. Figure 8-15 displays an example of each.

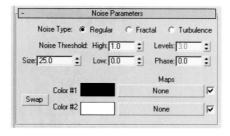

Figure 8-15. An example of mixing red and yellow with a Noise map, using (from left to right) Regular, Fractal, and Turbulence noise types.

In the middle of the rollout is the **Size** parameter. Smaller values make the mixture appear grainier, while larger values make the mixture appear more marbleized. The images in Figure 8-15 use the default **Size** of **25.0,** but because the scale of the map is dependent on object size, you will almost always have to experiment with various size values to achieve the correct scale. By animating the **Phase** value, you can make the material appear to move like a fluid.

The two color swatches provide a way to control the characteristics of the parent material. When applying a Noise map to the Bump channel, for example, the two colors indicate which part of the object shows elevated areas and which part shows recessed areas. Pure white areas of a noise map will cause the object to show elevated areas while pure black areas will cause the object to show recessed areas.

The Noise map has many applications. One of my favorites is using it in the Bump channel of a material simulating water. By adding the Noise map, some areas of the water material appear to be elevated and other areas appear to be recessed. The effect is a water material that appears to have rolling waves.

Using the Noise map

This exercise demonstrates use of the Noise map in the Bump channel to create some relief to terrain.

1. Reset 3ds Max.
2. Create a plane with a length and width of **100**.
3. Open the **Material Editor.**
4. In the Bump channel of any material, load a Noise map.
5. Apply the material to the plane and render the scene. The plane appears to have some relief, as shown in the left image of the following illustration.
6. In the **Noise Parameters** rollout, reduce the **Size** value from the default value of **25.0** to a new value of **10.0.** The scale of the relief is reduced accordingly, as shown in the right image of the following illustration:

The Smoke map

The Smoke map is very similar to the Noise map, both in its features and its application. The **Smoke Parameters** rollout works in nearly the same way as in the **Noise Parameters** rollout, and like the Noise map, the Smoke map is great for producing random areas of opacity, bump, and diffuse color. Figure 8-16 shows one example of the Smoke map using the default settings. It should be noted that, as with other maps, the final appearance of an image like the one in Figure 8-16 depends not only on some of the map settings, but also the size of the object to which the material is applied. For example, using the default **Size** value of **40.0** will not work for an object that is only 1 unit long and 1 unit wide.

 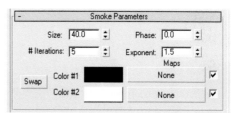

Figure 8-16. A Smoke map applied to the Diffuse Color channel

The Waves map

The Waves map is a nice feature that does a pretty good job simulating the wave action of water. By adjusting the parameters of this rollout, you can simulate everything from calm water with very little wave action to large, choppy waves moving at high speed. To achieve the exact result you're looking for, you'll probably have the best luck changing each parameter to extreme values so that you can see their individual effects on the result. To illustrate the effect of each setting, Figure 8-17 shows several different images and the settings used for each. The default black color is replaced with a dark blue color to better simulate water. It is important to note that in this case, the material is applied to a simple plane with a width and length of 100 units. Using different sized objects will require these settings to be scaled appropriately.

The **Amplitude** controls the apparent height of the waves by setting the contrast between the two different wave colors. Lighter areas represent the ridges, or higher parts in the waves, and darker areas represent the troughs, or lower parts in the waves.

The **Wave Radius** controls the curvature of the waves, with small numbers simulating small ripples that originate nearby, and large numbers simulating waves originating from a great distance.

The **Wave Len Max** value controls the thickness of Color #1, which since set to white by default, controls the wave thickness.

The **Wave Len Min** value controls the thickness of Color #2, which since set to black by default, controls the trough thickness.

The **Num Wave Sets** value specifies how many wave sets are used in the pattern. Wave sets are groups of radially symmetrical waves that originate from randomly selected points. To simulate a stone dropped in water, you would have one origin for the ripples, so **Num Wave Sets** would be set to 1. Setting this value to a higher number, such as 5, could simulate water in a swimming pool, with wave action originating from no specific location.

You can load maps into the color channels; however, achieving realism while doing so can be more difficult than just using colors.

Finally, by animating the **Phase** value, you can simulate wave movement.

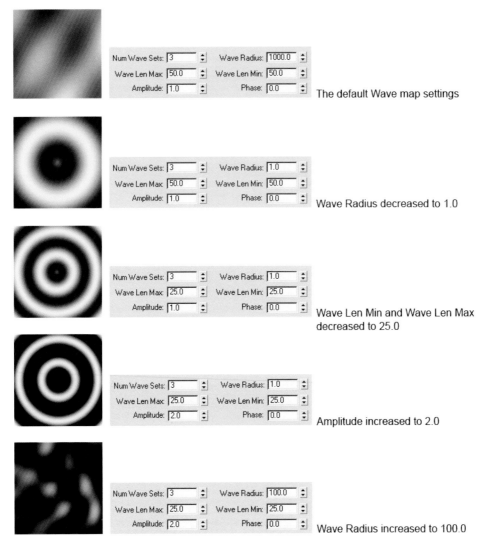

Num Wave Sets: 3   Wave Radius: 1000.0
Wave Len Max: 50.0   Wave Len Min: 50.0
Amplitude: 1.0   Phase: 0.0   The default Wave map settings

Num Wave Sets: 3   Wave Radius: 1.0
Wave Len Max: 50.0   Wave Len Min: 50.0
Amplitude: 1.0   Phase: 0.0   Wave Radius decreased to 1.0

Num Wave Sets: 3   Wave Radius: 1.0
Wave Len Max: 25.0   Wave Len Min: 25.0
Amplitude: 1.0   Phase: 0.0   Wave Len Min and Wave Len Max
decreased to 25.0

Num Wave Sets: 3   Wave Radius: 1.0
Wave Len Max: 25.0   Wave Len Min: 25.0
Amplitude: 2.0   Phase: 0.0   Amplitude increased to 2.0

Num Wave Sets: 3   Wave Radius: 100.0
Wave Len Max: 25.0   Wave Len Min: 25.0
Amplitude: 2.0   Phase: 0.0   Wave Radius increased to 100.0

Figure 8-17. A Wave map applied to a 100-square-unit plane object

The Falloff map

Here's another one of those 3ds Max features that's so useful and so large in application, an entire chapter could be devoted to its use. Like other map types, the uses of the Falloff map are limited only by one's imagination, and with a little imagination one can produce some amazing materials. In short, the Falloff map creates a gradient of two colors or maps in specific intensity and in a specific direction. It uses an object's face normals and viewing direction to determine where to place the colors. Faces perpendicular to the viewing direction receive the **Front** color (black by default) and faces parallel to the viewing direction receive the **Side** color (white by default). All other faces are shaded somewhere between the two colors, depending on the angle.

This gradient can benefit any map channel by accentuating certain map characteristics and toning down others. It can be used to ease the transition from one map characteristic to another, or to accelerate it. It functions as a little bit of many different map types, including Mix, Gradient, and Composite.

The Falloff map type contains only one unique rollout: **Falloff Parameters** (shown in Figure 8-18). In the first section of this rollout, **Front:Side,** you define the two colors that are used with the map and how the falloff is applied. To the right of the color swatches are amount fields (not labeled) that dictate what percentage of the diffuse color is defined by the color swatches and what percentage is defined by a map. **Falloff Type** and **Falloff Direction** determine how the two colors or maps are applied. Because the number of combinations is too enormous to cover, I will just cover a few. To see the true potential of this map type, one must explore the variables.

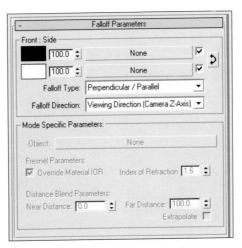

Figure 8-18. The Falloff Parameters rollout

The default settings include black-and-white color swatches, a **Perpendicular / Parallel Falloff Type,** and a **Viewing Direction (Camera Z-Axis) Falloff Direction.** What this means is that the color black will be placed everywhere the face normals are parallel to the viewing direction, and white will be placed everywhere the normals are perpendicular. You can change the placement of the two colors and the direction they fall off by changing the **Falloff Type** and **Falloff Direction** values. For example, if you change the **Falloff Direction** to **Camera X-Axis,** the white appears on the front and back of an object and falls off to the black areas on the sides. The easiest way to see the effects of the Falloff map is to apply it to the Diffuse Color or Opacity channel of a material.

Figure 8-19 shows how adding a Falloff map to the Diffuse Color channel affects a material. The image on the left shows the default settings of the Falloff map when the material is applied to a simple cylinder. Since the Front color is black, the faces that are parallel to the view receive black, and the faces perpendicular to the view receive the Side color (white). The image on the right shows the effects of swapping the two colors.

Figure 8-19. The effect of adding a Falloff map to the Diffuse Color channel

Figure 8-20 shows how adding a Falloff map to the Opacity channel affects a material. The image on the left shows the default settings of the Falloff map when the material is again applied to a simple cylinder. Notice in the image on the left that the front of the cylinder is transparent. This is because the front of the cylinder receives the black color—and in the Opacity channel, black means transparent and white means opaque. The image on the right shows the result of swapping the colors.

Figure 8-20. The effect of adding a Falloff map to the Opacity channel

Figure 8-21 shows another good example of the Falloff map at work. In this example, the Falloff map is applied again to the Opacity channel, and the only setting that is changed from the default value is the Falloff Type. By changing the Falloff Type to Distance Blend, you can make a material become transparent as it gets farther from the viewing direction. The top image shows a road with a length of 1,000 units and no Falloff map applied. Below this is an image of the same road and material with a Distance Blend Falloff Type applied to the Opacity channel. Notice at the bottom of the Falloff Parameters that the Near Distance value is 0.0, and the Far Distance value is 1000.0. This means that the material begins to become transparent at a distance of 0 and becomes completely transparent at a distance of 1,000 units from the view. In the bottom image, the Near Distance is set to 500.0 so that the road begins its transparency at 500 units away.

No Falloff map applied

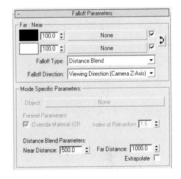

Figure 8-21. The effect of adding a Distance Blend falloff type to the Opacity channel

Using the Falloff map

This exercise demonstrates use of the Falloff map in the Opacity channel to give some unique looks to materials.

1. Reset 3ds Max.

2. In the Perspective viewport, create a teapot of any size.

3. Open the **Material Editor.**

4. In the Opacity channel of any material, load a Falloff map.

5. Apply the material to the teapot and render the scene with the default settings. The rendered image looks like an x-ray of the teapot (as shown in the left image of the illustration at the end of this exercise).

6. In the **Falloff Parameters** rollout, click the **Swap Colors/Maps** button to the right of the color swatches, as shown in the following illustration.

7. Render the scene again. The teapot now has a different but equally unique look (shown in the right image of the following illustration). Try experimenting with all the variables discussed in this chapter.

Summary

Creating maps is much like creating a recipe. Many times you don't know what you want for the end result, and you find yourself stumbling onto a great product. Other times you may know exactly what you want, but you don't know what ingredients or quantities to use. In either case, it will probably require a good amount of trial and error. There is simply no limit to the number and types of materials you can create, even with just the map types covered in this chapter. There is also no limit to the complexity with which materials can be created. One thing to keep in mind, however, is that simple is sometimes better. Great materials don't have to mean complex materials. Furthermore, you should utilize an existing material whenever possible rather than recreating one. Good use of material libraries can go a long way to increasing efficiency and productivity.

The final process in working with materials is UVW mapping. In the next chapter, you will learn how to precisely control the location and orientation of a map on an object and how to shape it to the specific type of object you apply it to. After learning this process, you will know everything you need to know to create and apply powerful and life-breathing materials to your scenes.

CHAPTER 9

UVW Mapping

THE LAST STEP IN THE PROCESS of applying materials in 3ds Max is UVW mapping. UVW coordinates were covered briefly in Chapter 8, but now it's time to discuss the process of mapping in greater detail. UVW mapping is the process by which materials are positioned, scaled, and oriented on objects in a scene. The UVW coordinate system is the same as the XYZ coordinate system, but uses the next three sequential letters to differentiate mapping from modeling. The u, v, and w directions correspond to the x, y, and z directions, respectively.

In 3ds Max, there are two types of maps: 2D and 3D. Since 2D maps are by definition two-dimensional, they require specific instructions, known as mapping, on how to be applied to a three-dimensional object. You control how 2D maps are applied to objects by controlling their mapping. 3D maps, also referred to as procedural maps, use mathematical calculations to determine how materials are placed on objects. Because of this, 3D maps do not require the same instructions 2D maps do (i.e., they do not require mapping). This chapter focuses on how to control the mapping of 2D maps.

Generating mapping coordinates

Whether a material contains an image or a 2D map, the material will require mapping to be applied properly to an object. Most primitive objects you create in 3ds Max will generate their own mapping coordinates, as will shapes when you apply certain modifiers, such as **Extrude.** What this means is that when mapping coordinates are created for an object, 3ds Max makes its best guess as to how the map is supposed to be applied to the object. Unfortunately, this best guess is rarely going to suffice, and you will almost always want to tweak the way a map is applied to an object. The left image in Figure 9-1 is an image of a brick wall, which is applied to the wall in the images to the right. The wall in the middle image had mapping coordinates generated automatically, which stretched the brick wall image throughout the entire length of the wall. However, this may not be the desired look. If you want, for example, the brick wall image to repeat so that you can make the bricks appear smaller and more realistic, as shown in the image on the right, you can apply a **UVW Map** modifier.

Figure 9-1. A brick wall image used with two different mappings

The UVW Map modifier

The **UVW Map** modifier (shown in Figure 9-2) is the primary tool to control the mapping of an individual object. Two identical objects with the same material applied can look completely different if they receive different **UVW Map** modifiers

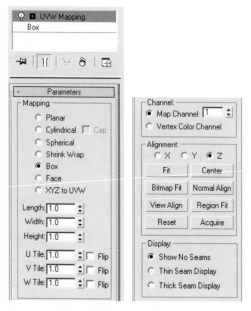

Figure 9-2. The UVW Map modifier

The modifier contains only one rollout: **Parameters.** At the top of this rollout are options for seven different mapping coordinates. Each one employs a unique method for placing the map on an object. Figure 9-3 illustrates a few of the more practical coordinate types.

Planar: The first image on the left shows a box with planar coordinates. Only the top side of the box receives the map properly because the map is applied in only one plane (hence the term "planar"). Notice that the other sides contain streaks that begin at the edge of the image that's applied on the top side. I rarely use this map coordinate because in most cases the box method will produce better results.

Cylindrical: The map is wrapped around the cylinder without any distortion; however, the top receives improper mapping. If the top and bottom of the cylinder were detached from the rest of the object, you could apply planar or box coordinates to finish the mapping. As an example, this would be the optimal coordinate type for mapping the trunk of a tree.

Spherical: The map is wrapped around a sphere. Although there is some distortion of the map across the surface of the sphere, this is the best coordinate type for a sphere. As an example, this would be the optimal coordinate type for mapping a spherical sky.

Box: This is the most practical coordinate type, comprising the vast majority of all mapping I perform. For objects shaped any other way than spherical and cylindrical, this will probably be the coordinate type that yields the best results.

Figure 9-3. The planar, cylindrical, spherical, and box coordinate types, from left to right

Working with the UVW gizmo

3ds Max allows you to use a modifier gizmo in much the same way you use a transform gizmo. The modifier gizmo is shaped to resemble the way the map is applied to or wrapped around an object. Figure 9-4 displays each of the gizmos for the map coordinate types displayed in Figure 9-3. With the modifier gizmo, you can further control the location and orientation of the map.

Figure 9-4. UVW Map gizmos

Sizing and tiling

The size of the gizmo controls the size of the map as it is applied to the object. When the UVW map is first applied to the object, its size is scaled to the length, width, and height extents of the object. If the object is a box with a height, width, and length of 100 units, then the gizmo will have a length, width, and height of 100 units, as shown in Figure 9-5.

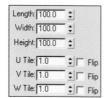

Figure 9-5. Gizmo size and tiling options

To make the gizmo half this size, enter a value of **50.0** for each dimension, or tile the map twice over the same distance. Entering a value of **2.0** in each of the **UVW Tile** fields will produce the same result as reducing the gizmo size from 100 units in each dimension to 50 units.

To apply a map with correct scale, you must first determine the dimensions of the image being mapped. As an example, if you are trying to apply the image of the brick wall shown in Figure 9-6 to an object representing a wall, you should determine what size of brick wall the image represents in real life. In this case, the image of the brick wall is three bricks long and six bricks tall. Knowing that a standard brick is 8 inches long and 2.66 inches tall, you can conclude that the image shows a brick wall that is 2'0" long and 1'4" tall. Therefore, if you want your object to be mapped to an accurate scale, you should use the box mapping option with a **Length** and **Width** of 2'0.0" and a **Height** of 1'4.0", as shown in Figure 9-6.

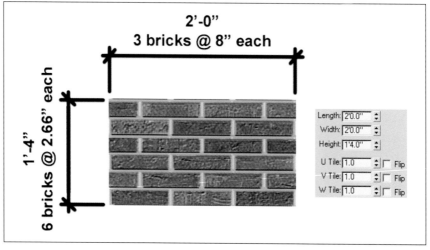

Figure 9-6. A simple map with UVW mapping information

Alignment

When you first apply the **UVW Map** modifier, the gizmo is centered on the object and sized to the extents of the object. These two characteristics are set by default whenever the **UVW Map** modifier is applied, and are represented by two separate options: **Fit** and **Center**. These options, along with several others, can be found in the **Alignment** section of the **Parameters** rollout, as shown in Figure 9-2. After manipulating the UVW gizmo, you may find the need to return the gizmo to its original state, in which case you can select the **Reset** option or even reapply the **Fit** option. You may need only to adjust the gizmo so that it becomes centered on the object, in which case **Center** is the option you want.

The only other option I use regularly, and the one I find most useful, is the **Acquire** option. **Acquire** allows you to copy the UVW map parameters from one object and apply them to another, which can save a great deal of time when creating mapping coordinates for a large number of objects.

To use the **Acquire** option, select the object you want to copy the mapping to, apply the **UVW Map** modifier to the object, select **Acquire,** and select the object to which you want to copy the mapping. The **Acquire UVW Mapping** dialog box will appear, as shown in Figure 9-7, prompting you to select either **Acquire Absolute** or **Acquire Relative.** For most architectural elements you apply mapping to, the option you select won't matter. Most objects will have a map that is tiled over and over again throughout the surface area of the object, and the exact starting location of the mapping is almost always insignificant. This is especially the case when you deal with seamless maps, which are maps that show no easily discernible border when tiled over and over again.

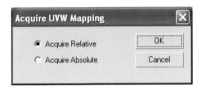

Figure 9-7. The Acquire UVW Mapping dialog box

The **Acquire Relative** option places the map on the object in the same location as the object from which the mapping is borrowed. The **Acquire Absolute** option places the map on the object as if it were being tiled from the borrowed object.

Working with the UVW Map gizmo

This exercise demonstrates how to use the UVW Map gizmo to accurately map an image onto an object.

1. Reset 3ds Max.

2. Change the units to architectural units.

3. Create a box with a length of **20'0"**, a width of **8"**, and a height of **6'0"**.

4. Open the **Material Editor,** and in the Diffuse Color channel of any material, load a bitmap using the image **Rockwall01.jpg** in the **3dsmax2008\3DATS** folder, as shown in the following illustration:

5. Apply the material to the box and select the **Show Map in Viewport** option. In the Perspective viewport, the result should look like the top-left image in the following illustration. Notice how unnatural the image is when stretched to fit the length of the wall to which it's applied (or squashed when looking at the width). The rockwall would look even more unnatural if there were other objects in the scene to provide scale and to show how overly large the individual rocks are.

6. Apply the **UVW Map** modifier using the **Box** option. The resulting image shouldn't change at all since the box you created had mapping automatically generated (which naturally was the Box mapping type). In the UVW Map modifier, the length, width, and height should be automatically set to the size of the box (as shown in the top right image) since mapping automatically fits to the extent of the object it's applied to.

7. Make a guess at how large the portion of the rock wall you see in the image would be in real life. (In order to place the image correctly on your object, you will have to tell 3ds Max how big or small to make the image in your scene.) If your object is 100 yards long, and you stretched this image over it, the image would look unrealistic in your scene because it clearly represents a much smaller wall. For the purpose of this exercise, let's assume that the rock wall in the image (at least the part you can see) is 5'0" long and 4'0" tall in real life.

8. In the **UVW Map** modifier, set the **Length** and **Width** to **5'0"** and the **Height** to **4'0"**.

9. The wall object in the Perspective viewport should look like the bottom-left image of the following illustration:

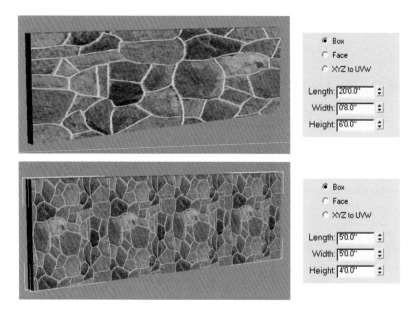

Map channels and multi/sub-objects

If you ever decide to apply a multi/sub-object material to an object, and require each sub-material to have its own UVW map (i.e., not require each sub-material to be mapped by the same UVW coordinate values), you must use map channels. Let's say you create a box and want to apply the left image in Figure 9-8 to each side of the box, and the middle image to the top of the box, as shown in the right image of Figure 9-8.

Figure 9-8. Two different maps of a multi/sub-object material applied to the same object (using map channels)

The first thing you will have to do is create a multi/sub-object material with both of these sub-materials. Since multi/sub-objects have not yet been discussed, the method to do so will be explained here. If you want to follow along with the following demonstration, you can use the two images shown in Figure 9-8. They are named **Wallpaper01.jpg** and **Wallpaper02.jpg** and can be found in the **3dsMax2008\Images\3DATS** folder.

To create a multi/sub-object material, click a new material slot, click the **Material Type** icon, and select the multi/sub-object. Click the empty sub-material map slot for material ID 1 (see Figure 9-9), and assign the left image in Figure 9-8 (Wallpaper01.jpg) to the Diffuse Color channel. Assign the middle image (Wallpaper02.jpg) to the Diffuse Color channel of material ID 2.

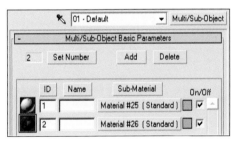

Figure 9-9. A multi/sub-object material with two sub-materials

Select the box in one of the viewports and add the **Edit Mesh** modifier. Go to the **Polygon** sub-object level, and select all of the side polygons in one of the viewports. Go to the **Surface Properties** rollout, and assign the side polygons to material ID 1, as shown in Figure 9-10. Select the top polygon and assign it to material ID 2.

Figure 9-10. Assigning material IDs to sub-objects

Apply the material to the box and enable the Show Map in Viewport option. Your result should look like Figure 9-11. You have just applied a multi/sub-object material to an object.

Figure 9-11. A multi/sub-object box

But how do you tile the image on the top of the box two times in each direction, as shown in Figure 9-12? You could always tile the image in the **Material Editor,** but that would affect all the objects in your scene with this material. If you only want to affect this one object, you must use the **UVW Map** modifier. The problem is then that the **UVW Map** modifier affects all the sub-materials on a single object. To apply the **UVW Map** modifier to only one sub-material, you must use map channels. By assigning a unique map channel to each sub-object material, you can limit specific **UVW Map** modifiers to specific sub-object materials.

Figure 9-12. An example of changing the map channel in the Material Editor

Let's see how it works. Go back to the **Coordinates** rollout of the map applied to the Diffuse Color channel of material ID 2. Change the **Map Channel** value to **2**, as shown in Figure 9-13.

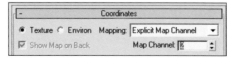

Figure 9-13. Changing the Map Channel value in the Material Editor

Render the image now, and you should get the **Missing Map Coordinates** error message. This is because the box doesn't have a UVW map applied to material ID 2. You must apply a second **UVW Map** modifier to the box and change its **Map Channel** value to **2**, as shown in Figure 9-14.

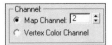

Figure 9-14. Changing the Map Channel value
in the UVW Map modifier

Now, you can finally tile the image on the top of the box by changing the **U Tile** and **V Tile** values
to **2.0,** as shown in Figure 9-15, to achieve the desired result.

Figure 9-15. Changing the U and V Tile
values in the UVW Map modifier

Working with map channels

This exercise demonstrates how to use map channels to apply multiple **UVW Map** modifiers to a
single object with a multi/sub-object material.

1. Reset 3ds Max.

2. In the Perspective viewport, create a box with a length of **10'0"**, a width of **8"**, a height of **8'0"**,
   and **2** height segments. This box will represent a wall that will receive a multi/sub-object
   material.

3. Add an **Edit Mesh** modifier to the box, enter Face sub-object mode, and highlight the faces in
   the top half of the wall, as shown in the left image of the following illustration:

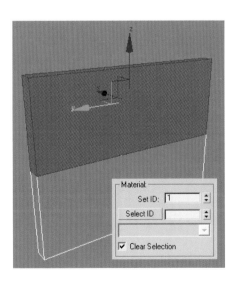 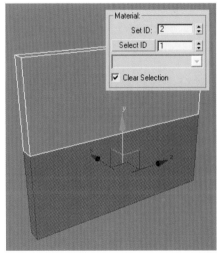

4. Scroll down to the bottom of the **Edit Mesh** modifier, and in the **Material** section of the **Surface
   Properties** rollout, enter a value of **1** in the **Set ID** field. This assigns a material ID of 1 to the
   highlighted faces.

5. Highlight the faces in the bottom half of the wall and assign a material ID of 2 to these faces,
   as shown in the right image of the preceding illustration.

6. Open the **Material Editor,** and in any material, select the **Material Type** button.

7. Select **Multi/Sub-Object** and select **OK** to close the **Material/Map Browser.** This changes the material type from **Standard** to **Multi/Sub-Object** and opens the **Replace Material** dialog box.

8. Select **Discard old material,** and select **OK** to close.

9. In the **Multi/Sub-Object Basic Parameters** rollout, select **Set Number,** as shown in the following illustration:

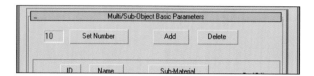

10. Change the **Number of Materials** value to **2** and click **OK** to close. This changes the number of sub-materials to 2.

11. Click the **Material Type** button for material 1. This reopens the standard rollouts that you would see for any standard material.

12. In the Bump channel, load a bitmap using the **Siding01.jpg** image in the **3dsMax2008\Images\ 3DATS** folder, as shown in the following illustration, and enable the Show Map in Viewport option. Increase the Bump **Amount** to **300** to accentuate the effect of the Bump map. This will create the appearance of 3D siding on the material.

13. Change the diffuse color of material 1 to something other than the default gray.

14. Click the **Go to Parent** icon twice to return to the root of the multi/sub-object.

15. Click the **Material Type** button for material 2.

16. In the Diffuse Color channel, load a bitmap using the image **Brick01.jpg.**

17. Enable the **Show Map in Viewport** option and apply the material to the box representing the wall in your scene.

18. Apply the **UVW Map** modifier to the wall, change the mapping type to **Box,** and render the scene. The wall should look like image 1 in the illustration at the end of this exercise.

19. Change the length, width, and height of the UVW mapping to **5'0",** and render the scene again. The wall should now look like image 2. Notice that the brick portion looks OK, but the siding portion has improper UVW mapping.

20. Add a second **UVW Map** modifier to the wall, as shown in the following illustration, and change the mapping type to Box. Change the length, width, and height of the UVW mapping to **4"** (inches); and render the scene again. Now the siding portion of the wall looks OK and the brick portion has poor mapping, as shown in image 3.

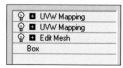

21. In the **Modifier Stack**, select the first UVW map (the bottom one), and in the **Channel** section of the **Parameters** rollout, change the **Map Channel** to **2**. This makes the first UVW map apply only to sub-maps in channel 2. Now you must tell 3ds Max which sub-map will be in channel 2.

22. Return to the Diffuse Color channel of the brick material, and in the **Coordinates** rollout, change the Map Channel to **2**. This assigns the brick sub-material to channel 2 and makes the UVW map assigned to channel 2 apply only to the brick sub-material.

23. Render the scene a final time, and it should look like image 4 in the following illustration. Now both materials of the wall have proper mapping because they each have their own UVW map applied to their individual map channels.

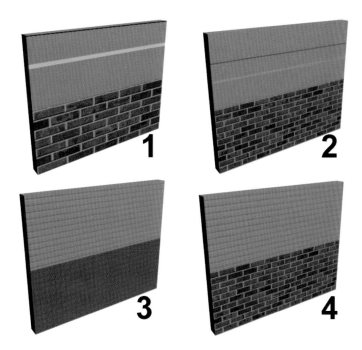

Summary

This chapter has focused on the last step in the material application process: UVW mapping. UVW mapping controls the position, scale, and orientation of maps on objects in a scene. Although there are several different mapping tools in 3ds Max for the various different industries, the **UVW Map** modifier is the main tool that controls mapping for architectural scenes.

Also covered were map channels, which allow you to apply multiple **UVW Map** modifiers to a single object that uses a multi/sub-object material. Although I'm not a huge fan of the multi/sub-object material, I find there are times when it becomes useful, and knowing how to apply different **UVW Map** modifiers to each of the different sub-maps of a single object is important. Doing so would not be possible without assigning each sub-map an individual map channel and applying a separate **UVW Map** modifier to each map channel.

There are many other powerful material features that can add a great deal of depth to your scenes, but at this point, the foundations of materials have been covered and it's time to move on to the next major step in the 3D creation process: lighting!

PART 4

Lighting

Whether aware of it or not, a viewer will usually grade the quality of an architectural visualization by the quality of the lighting. Lighting is without a doubt one area in scene creation that will make or break a visualization. If any additional time can be spent improving the quality of your work, lighting should be the first area you consider.

CHAPTER 10

Basic Lighting

IF YOU ASK ANY VETERAN 3ds Max user what the most important element of a good 3D scene is, you'll always get the same answer—lighting. Good lighting can make a scene with bad modeling or materials look good. Likewise, poor lighting can make a scene with good modeling and materials look bad. Lighting can have a dramatic effect on the composition of your scene. It can convey a specific mood or inspire the viewer to feel a particular way. In fact, many competitions in the 3D world are won or lost by the application of lighting.

This chapter deals with the principles and procedures of standard lights, which are lights that are not based on real-world light properties. Although standard lights do not incorporate the properties of real-world lights, it is possible to set up standard lights in your scenes so well that they simulate real-world lights and give your scenes a photorealistic look.

Chapter 11 covers photometric lights, which are lights that simulate real-world properties. With photometric lighting, you can see what your interior scene looks like illuminated by a single 100-watt lightbulb, multiple 4-foot cove fluorescent lights, or any number of real-world light types. The last chapter on lighting, Chapter 12, provides an introduction to global illumination, which is a system that uses physically based lighting to accurately depict the way light bounces off objects, and cumulatively affects the lighting and shading of surrounding objects. By the end of these three chapters on lighting, you will have the ability to light your scenes in a photorealistic manner.

Standard lights vs. photometric lights

3ds Max provides two types of lights, which can be accessed through the drop-down list of the **Lights** section in the **Create** panel (Figure 10-1): standard lights and photometric lights.

Figure 10-1. The two light types: standard and photometric

Standard lights are not physically based, and therefore do not exhibit real-world lighting proper-ties. With standard lights, you can control attenuation, which is a term used to describe how light fades as it moves away from its source. You can specify with great precision where a light begins and ends its attenuation, or whether or not a light attenuates at all. In addition, standard lights use a multiplier value of 1.0 to represent a fully bright light, and a color swatch to determine the light's color.

Photometric lights, on the other hand, are physically based, and therefore exhibit real-world lighting properties. Attenuation and color in photometric lights are automatically calculated and are based on the type of real-world light source used. Because photometric lights are physically based, a scene must be built at the proper scale for the lighting to be accurate. In the real world, a single 100-watt light-bulb could light a small 10-by-10-foot room, but if that room was built out of scale and was as big as a stadium, that same light might be unnoticeable.

Which type of light you decide to use in your 3D scenes depends on several different things. If you can successfully use standard lights to accurately create the realism your project calls for, then standard lights might be the best option. However, if you are trying to simulate very accurately what a scene looks like with a particular type of real-world light, then photometric lights are the way to go. If you want to maintain precise control over the attenuation of a light to achieve a unique effect, then you need to use standard lights. If you want to incorporate some advanced lighting procedures such as global illumination, then again photometric lights will be the best option. Whatever your project calls for, 3ds Max provides the power and versatility to meet any type of lighting need.

The standard light source types

There are three standard light source types in 3ds Max: **direct lights, omni lights,** and **spotlights,** as shown in Figure 10-2. Each source type has unique characteristics and is suited for different uses. Depending on the scene type, any one of these source types may be best suited to serve as the primary light source.

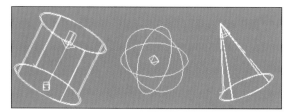

Figure 10-2. The standard light source types: direct (left), omni (center), and spotlight (right)

There is an additional source type known as **skylight,** indicated in Figure 10-1; however, skylight is designed for use specifically with Light Tracer, which is not covered in this book. Light Tracer is a global illumination system that offers good rendering results but is little used in a production environment because of its long rendering times.

Figure 10-1 also shows the availability of two other standard light source types: **mR Area Omni** and **mR Area Spot**. These two types are for use with the mental ray renderer, which is not covered in this book. These two types are likewise not covered.

Omni lights

Omni lights cast light in all directions from a single point. They are probably most widely used in all types of lamps, from street lamps to desk lamps; but under the right controls, they can even be used to effectively simulate sunlight. Placed far enough away from the objects in a scene, an omni light's rays can appear to be parallel, as shown in the left image of Figure 10-3. In this way, it can simulate sunlight, which strikes the Earth with parallel rays, since the Sun is so far away from Earth. However, since the light of an omni light source emanates from a singe infinitely small point, an omni light placed close to the objects in a scene will casts shadows in all directions, as shown in the right image.

Figure 10-3. An omni light creating parallel shadows (left) and non-parallel shadows (right)

Spotlights

Spotlights cast light in a specific direction from a single point, as shown in Figure 10-4. They are probably the most versatile of the three light source types. They can be used in numerous ways, from the headlights of a car to the track lights found on the ceiling of a residence; from the light shaped by a lamp shade to the spotlight that illuminates a tree from below at night.

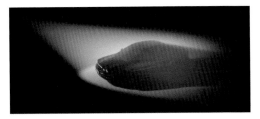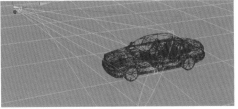

Figure 10-4. The spotlight

Direct lights

Direct lights cast parallel light rays in a single direction, and are therefore most widely used in simulating sunlight. Likewise, the shadows cast by direct lights are always parallel; they will not spread, regardless of how close the lights are to the objects. Unlike omni lights and spotlights, direct lights do not emanate from a single point, but rather from a flat circular area defined by the user, as shown in Figure 10-5.

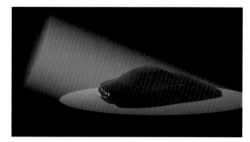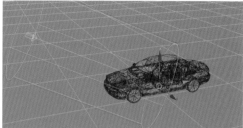

Figure 10-5. The direct light

Creating lights

Before you place your first light in a scene, 3ds Max places two default lights to provide light to any objects that you create. Otherwise, you wouldn't see anything you create until placing your first light. One default light is positioned above and to the left, and another is placed below and to the left. As soon as you create your first light, 3ds Max removes these two default lights. If you delete all your lights from a scene, the two default lights return.

There are three ways to create, position, and orient lights in 3ds Max. Omni lights require a single click of the mouse in a viewport to create and place. They do not require any other steps to be oriented because omni lights cast light in all directions. **Free** and **target lights,** which can be used for spotlights or direct lights, require a specific orientation because their light is cast in a specific direction. Both types are identical except for one major characteristic. Free lights have only one component: the light; whereas target lights have two components: the light and the target. Target lights are always oriented to face the target, and because the target can move independently from the light, the target can be animated. The left image in Figure 10-6 shows a target spotlight and the right image shows a free spotlight. Notice that both images are the same except for the small box (target) near the center of the left image. Target lights always face their targets, so moving this target changes the direction that the light faces. To change the direction of a stationary free light, you can apply the rotate transform or use one of the viewport navigation control icons listed in Table 10-1.

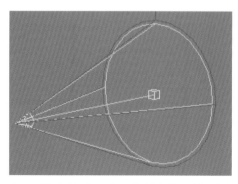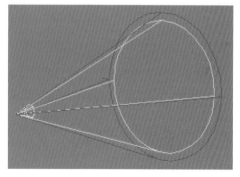

Figure 10-6. The target spotlight (left) and the free spotlight (right)

Free lights and target lights are both light types that can be used in the creation of spotlights and direct lights. The creation process for free lights is the same whether you want to create a spotlight or a direct light. Likewise, the creation process for target lights is the same regardless of which light type you want to create.

To create a free light using the Command panel, click **Create** ➤ **Lights** ➤ **Free Spot or Free Direct, and** click once in any viewport. The light will face the direction of the view unless the viewport is displaying a User, Perspective, Camera, or Target Light view, in which case the light will face in the negative z direction.

To create a target light, click **Target Spot** or **Target Direct,** click and hold inside a viewport, and drag the mouse to position the target. Release the mouse button to place the target.

Sometimes, you might find it helpful to see a view of your scene from the perspective of one of your lights. Once a light is created, you can easily switch a viewport to the view through the light's perspective by right-clicking the viewport name, selecting **Views** from the menu, and selecting the light's name from the next menu. Seeing the view from a light is only possible with a direct light or spotlight.

Creating lights

This exercise demonstrates how to create free and target lights.

1. Reset 3ds Max.

2. In Perspective view, create a teapot of any size.

3. Within the **Create** panel, click the **Lights** icon. The **Object Type** rollout appears with eight buttons available.

4. Click the **Free Spot** button.

5. In Front view, click, hold, and drag to create the light, and move it into a position centered on the teapot. Release the mouse button to place the light.

6. Right-click within the active view to end the light-creation command.

7. Using the move and rotate transforms, position and orient the light so that it's above and away from the teapot, and pointing down at it. Notice the highlights move around on the teapot as the light is moved.

8. Right-click the Perspective view name, select **Views** from the menu, and select **Fspot01** from the next menu.

9. In any other view, apply a couple of transforms to the free spotlight to see their effects on the newly created light view.

10. Press **Delete** to delete the light. Notice that the light view changes back to Perspective view.

11. In the Command panel, click the **Target Spot** button.

12. In the Top view, click, hold, and drag to create the light, and move the light target into a position centered on the teapot. Release the mouse button to place the light target.

13. Right-click the Perspective view name, select **Views** from the menu, and select **Spot01** from the next menu.

14. In any other view, apply a couple of transforms to the target spotlight and the target to see their effects on the newly created light view.

Viewport navigation controls

When you create a light view, the viewport navigation controls in the bottom-right corner of the screen change to account for the source of the new view. Table 10-1 shows each of the new icons available when a light view is active.

Table 10-1. Light view icons in the viewport navigation controls

Icon	Name	Description
	Dolly Light	Moves the light along the axis in which the light is pointing
	Dolly Target	Moves the target along the axis in which the light is pointing
	Dolly Light+Target	Moves light and target along the axis in which the camera is pointing
	Light Hotspot	Changes the light's **Hotspot/Beam** diameter value (discussed later in this chapter)
	Light Falloff	Changes the light's **Falloff/Field** diameter value (discussed later in this chapter)
	Roll Light	Spins the light along its local z axis
	Orbit Light	Rotates the light around the target
	Pan Light	Rotates the target around the light

Some additional notes about the viewport navigation controls are as follows:

- By holding down the mouse scroll wheel, you can execute the Truck Light command without having to click the icon. The Truck Light command works just like the pan command and can even be accessed through the same viewport navigation icon.
- By holding down the Shift key, you can constrain light movement to a single axis.
- By holding down the Ctrl key, you can magnify the effects of the viewport navigation controls.

Light placement

In addition to the ability to place lights using transforms and viewport navigation controls, 3ds Max gives you the opportunity to place lights precisely using two other helpful features: Align Camera and Place Highlight.

Align Camera

The Align Camera feature aligns a camera, or in this case a light, to the normal of a specific face on a specific object. This allows you to precisely position and orient an existing light so that it is directly in front of and facing a particular object.

To use this feature, select a light as shown in the top-left image of Figure 10-7. Click and hold the **Align** icon in the **Main** toolbar, and select the **Align Camera** icon from the flyout. Click and hold on top of any face inside the active viewport. A blue normal arrow will appear on the face that your mouse is over, as shown in the top-right image. Once you let go, the selected light will move directly in front of and aligned with the normal of the face you choose, as shown in the bottom-left image. The image on the bottom-right shows the new view from the selected light.

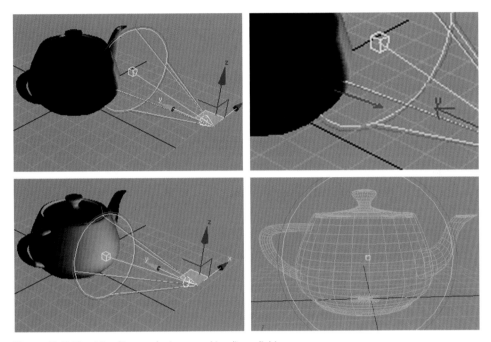

Figure 10-7. The Align Camera feature used to align a light

Place Highlight

Another tool that you can use to position lights in your scene is the Place Highlight command. This feature is similar to the Align Camera feature, except that Place Highlight moves the selected light to a position that causes a highlight to appear in the current viewport. This does not align the light to a face normal as does the Align Camera feature; it simply moves the light so that it provides the maximum possible highlight in the area of the object that you move your cursor over. Also, instead of showing you just a blue arrow to align the camera with, the Place Highlight command displays the light in its new position as you move your cursor from one face to another.

The icon for the Place Highlight command is located directly above the **Align Camera** icon within the **Align** flyout. To use this command, click the **Place Highlight** icon and click and hold the left mouse button on top of any face inside the active viewport. A blue normal arrow will appear on the face that your mouse is over, and the light will move into position. If you move the cursor over other faces, the light will follow along and update its position. To finish the command, release the left mouse button and the light will remain in position, aligned with the normal of the last face your mouse was over.

Positioning lights

This exercise demonstrates how to use the Align Camera and Place Highlight features to position lights effectively within your scenes.

1. Reset 3ds Max.

2. Create a sphere of any size within the Perspective view.

3. Create a free spotlight anywhere in your scene.

4. Click and hold the **Align** icon to reveal the flyout icons, and click the **Align Camera** icon.

5. Click and hold the left mouse button on top of any face of the sphere inside the active viewport. A blue normal arrow will appear on the face that your mouse is over. Release the mouse button and the light will move into position.

6. Click and hold the **Align** icon again to reveal the flyout icons, and click the **Place Highlight** icon.

7. Click and hold the left mouse button on top of any face of the sphere inside the active viewport. A blue normal arrow will appear on the face that your mouse is over, and the selected light will align itself with this normal and be positioned in the location that maximizes the highlight. Release the mouse button and the light will move into position.

Light parameters

When an omni light is created, five new rollouts appear (as shown in Figure 10-8), with the last one specifically geared toward the type of shadows used. When a spotlight or direct light is created, the same rollouts appear, as well as an additional rollout geared toward the type of light source used. This section of the chapter covers each of these parameters, highlighting those parameters that should receive special attention.

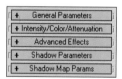

Figure 10-8. The common standard light rollouts

When you switch to the **Modify** panel, three additional rollouts appear; one for atmospheric effects, which is covered in Chapter 18, and two for mental ray, which is not covered in this book.

The General Parameters rollout

When a light is created, it is automatically turned on. At the top of the **General Parameters** rollout (shown in the left image of Figure 10-9) is an option to turn the light off, which can be used at any time. This same option can be found in the **Object Properties** menu or in the quad menu of the light. A light that is turned off will show as black in the viewports.

To the right of the **On/Off** option is a drop-down list that can be used to change a light from one source type to another. If a spotlight or directional light is used, an option to enable or disable a target becomes selectable, along with the distance in scene units from the light to the target. This distance has no effect on the lighting in your scene; it serves only as a guide.

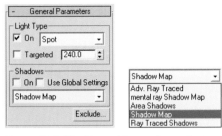

Figure 10-9. The General Parameters rollout

In the **Shadows** section is an option to enable shadows for the selected light, which is disabled by default. Another option allows you to use global settings to determine the characteristics of the light. This is a great option when you want to maintain consistent settings across several lights without having to instance the lights. This option applies the same settings to all the lights, so that changing a setting for one changes the same settings for all the lights that have this option enabled.

The **Exclude** button at the bottom of the rollout gives you the ability to exclude select objects from a light's effect. When you click this button, the **Exclude/Include** dialog box appears, as shown on the left in Figure 10-10. By default, objects are included in a light's effect—however, you can also selectively keep objects from being illuminated by the light, or you can keep them from casting shadows caused by the light, or both. In Figure 10-10, the popcorn maker is excluded from the shadow casting caused by the light, and the result is that the object doesn't cast shadows. It doesn't cast shadows on other objects like the floor, and it also doesn't cast shadows on itself.

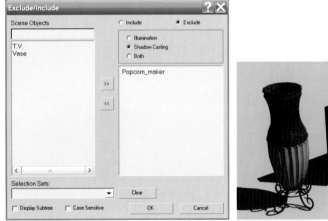

Figure 10-10. Excluding an object from shadow casting

Also in the **Shadows** section of the rollout is one of the most important settings involving lights. The shadow type drop-down list, shown in the right image of Figure 10-9, provides all the available shadow types that can be used with the selected light. Knowing which shadow type to use for any given light is critically important. The different shadow types provide a wide range in quality, use, appearance, rendering time, and RAM used.

Shadow map

Shadow map is the default shadow type. It is not a true shadow, but rather a faked shadow created by mapping an image onto the objects behind the object casting the shadow. The resolution of the applied map, which is set in the **Shadow Map Params** rollout, determines how accurate the shadows are. Because it is a faked shadow and not as accurate as other shadow types, the shadow map produces soft shadows rather than crisp, hard shadows. For spot lights and omni lights, these edges become more erratic and degraded as the light is moved farther away from the object casting shadows, or as the resolution of the map is decreased. Direct lights do not have this problem because the rays of light are parallel, and like the sun in real life, the distance of a directional light to the objects in a scene has no bearing on the shadow map quality. The left image in Figure 10-11 shows a television casting decent shadows with an omni light positioned very close by. In the right image, the light is moved far away from the television, resulting in poor shadows. Later in the chapter, you will learn how to correct for this degraded quality.

Figure 10-11. A shadow map with a light source close by (left) and far away (right)

The greatest advantage of this shadow type is that it is often faster than any other type. Some disadvantages are that this shadow type uses a large amount of RAM and it's the only shadow type that is not capable of respecting transparency. An object with transparency applied, such as glass, will cast the same shadow as a fully opaque object, as shown in the left image of Figure 10-12. The right image is possible with all other shadow types.

Figure 10-12. Transparent objects not supported by shadow maps (left) and supported by other shadow types (right)

Using shadow map lights and the various light source types

This exercise demonstrates some of the characteristics of shadow map lights and the three different light source types.

1. Reset 3ds Max.

2. In the Perspective view, create a plane with a length and width of **10'**.

3. In the Perspective view, create a teapot with a radius of **1'** and center the teapot on the plane.

4. Click the **Zoom Extents Selected** icon.

5. In the Command panel, select **Create ➤ Geometry ➤ Lights ➤ Omni.**

6. In the Top view, click near the bottom-right corner of the plane to place the light.

7. Raise the light **10'** above the plane. This places the light in a good location to cast a shadow that can be easily seen.

8. Right-click inside the Perspective view (to make it active) and click the **Quick Render** button in the **Main** toolbar. The teapot renders without any shadows.

9. Click the **Modify** tab, and in the **General Parameters** rollout, enable the **Shadows On** option. This enables shadows with the default shadow map type.

10. Click the **Quick Render** button again. Now the teapot casts shadows; however, notice how poor the shadows appear to be.

11. Move the light to about twice the distance from the teapot, and render the Perspective view. Notice that the shadows are now even lower quality. Later in the chapter, you'll use the available shadow parameters to improve the quality of the shadows.

12. Use the **Undo** icon to return the light to its original location.

13. In the **General Parameters** rollout, click the **Light Type** drop-down list and select **Spot.** Notice that the omni light changes to a spotlight with a cone pointing in the negative z direction.

14. In the **Main** toolbar, click and hold the **Align** flyout and select the **Place Highlight** icon.

15. Click and hold on the teapot and move the cursor around the surface of the teapot. Release the mouse button when you are happy with the placement of the highlight. Notice that the light is moved into a position where it places a highlight on the teapot in the location you selected.

16. Render the scene again. The spotlight is now casting light on the teapot.

17. Click the **Light Type** drop-down list and change the light type to **Directional.**

18. Render the scene again.

19. Keep this scene open or save it for use in the next tutorial.

Area shadows

This shadow type can be applied to any light type and is often used to simulate shadows cast by large light sources, such as stadium lights or long rows of track ceiling lights. It produces area shadows using a virtual light of a specific size and shape defined by the user. In the **Area Shadows** rollout that appears when this shadow type is used, you specify the size, shape, and quality of the shadow, as well as how the shadow is dispersed. The areas shadow type produces soft edges that become softer as the light is moved farther away from the objects casting shadows. When used properly, this shadow type can produce a unique and very realistic look; however, it often takes a great deal of time and experimentation with the many settings to produce the desired look. Figure 10-13 shows an example of the unique shadow effects capable with area shadows.

Figure 10-13. An example of area shadows

Some advantages of this type of shadow are that it supports transparency and opacity mapping, and uses very little RAM. A major disadvantage, however, is that it can take a very long time to render— even more so with higher-quality settings.

Raytraced shadows

As the name implies, raytraced shadows are generated by tracing a sample of rays as they leave a light source and interact with the object casting the shadow. Raytraced shadows are much more accurate and usually more realistic than shadow maps or area shadows, and always produce a hard edge. When used improperly, however, the hard edge that comes with raytraced shadows can produce an unrealistic look. Since raytraced shadows are not generated using a map, you do not have to adjust resolution as you do for shadow maps and area maps. Figure 10-14 shows an example of the hard edges that result from using raytraced shadows.

Figure 10-14. An example of raytraced shadows

Some advantages of raytraced shadows are that they support transparency and opacity maps, and they are extremely accurate. The two biggest disadvantages are that raytraced shadows can significantly increase render times and they do not allow for soft shadows.

Advanced raytraced shadows

Advanced raytraced shadows are a personal favorite of mine for many scene types, especially those with an extremely large polygon count, or for long animations with a short production deadline. They combine the best characteristics of all the available shadow types. Like raytraced shadows, they are very accurate and physically realistic, meaning that they take into account an object's physical and material attributes. They support transparency and opacity maps, and unlike raytraced maps, can be modified to produce soft edges. They also use a small amount of RAM and are usually much faster to render than raytraced shadows. They can even be used to produce a look similar to area shadows if you use some of the antialiasing options found in the **Adv. Ray Traced Params** rollout. Advanced raytraced shadows can be made to look similar, and sometimes indiscernible from raytraced shadows, or they can be made unique by incorporating softer shadows, as shown in Figure 10-15.

Figure 10-15. An example of advanced raytraced shadows producing similar results to raytraced shadows, but with the ability to produce softer shadow edges

Using area, raytraced, and advanced raytraced shadows

This exercise demonstrates some of the differences between the different shadow types.

1. Continue from the last tutorial or go to the **3dsMax2008\Scenes\3DATS** directory and open the file **Ch10-01.max**.

2. Select the directional light.

3. Click the **Modify** icon.

4. In the **General Parameters** rollout, click the **Shadow Type** drop-down list and change the shadow type from **Shadow Map** to **Area Shadows.**

5. Render the Perspective view. Notice the soft-and-speckled appearance to the shadows.

6. Repeat step 4 using the **Ray Traced Shadows** and **Adv. Ray Traced Shadows** options.

7. Keep this scene open, or save it for use in the next tutorial.

The Intensity/Color/Attenuation rollout

This rollout provides direct control over a light's intensity, color, and attenuation (see Figure 10-16).

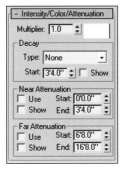

Figure 10-16. The Intensity/Color/Attenuation rollout

Intensity

The intensity of a light is a measure of the light's strength, or ability to illuminate a scene. It is directly controlled by the **Multiplier** setting, which by default is set to **1.0**. Doubling this value doubles the intensity of the light, as shown in Figure 10-17.

Figure 10-17: A Multiplier setting of 1.0, 0.5, and 2.0, respectively

Color

You can change the color a light produces using the color swatch in this rollout, much like adding a colored filter to a light. The color of the light in your scene can have a dramatic impact on the mood that your scene inspires. Adjusting the color slightly can also add a great deal of realism. For example, bright sunlight has a yellow hue to it, so adding a small amount of yellow light to a scene can make a daytime exterior rendering look more realistic. For a scene that occurs during a sunset or sunrise, you might try changing the color of your light to incorporate a small amount of red or orange.

Decay

In this section of the rollout, you can specify the rate at which the intensity of your light decays, or diminishes, with distance. In the real world, light decays the farther away it gets from its source. It does so at a specific rate, which is equal to the inverse square of the distance. In the **Type** drop-down list are options for setting decay at the real-world setting of **Inverse Square,** at a more subtle setting of **Inverse,** or at the default setting of **None.** If you are trying to simulate sunlight, you shouldn't allow your light to decay because the light that strikes the earth is constant over the small amount of area that your scenes occupy. On most other light sources, decay is a good option to use, although you will probably find that setting a light to **Inverse Decay** will cause too much decay and not allow your scene to be illuminated enough. This is because in the real world, there is so much more ambient light and radiosity. For most lights, I have found the **Inverse** setting to produce a more realistic look.

You can also specify a start distance for the decay of light. By setting a value of 120 units, or 10', your light won't start decaying until a distance of 10 feet from the light. By enabling the **Show** option, you can see this distance pictorially in the viewport.

Attenuation

Attenuation is another term to describe the diminishing of light with distance, and in 3ds Max, attenuation settings give you another way to control the intensity of light with distance.

The **Near Attenuation Start** value specifies the distance at which the light begins to produce illumination. The **End** value specifies the distance at which light reaches full brightness after fading in from zero illumination at the **Start** distance.

The **Far Attenuation Start** value specifies the distance at which light begins to fade out from full illumination, and the **End** value specifies the distance at which the light is completely diminished.

Figure 10-18 shows an example of near and far attenuation. In this example, a direct light is set up to cast light in the direction of five teapots that are lined up in a row. As the settings in the rollout indicate, **Near Attenuation** and **Far Attenuation** have been enabled. The **Near Attenuation Start** value is set to **20.0,** which means the light doesn't begin until 20 units away from the source. The top-left image shows that the pink teapot on the far right is positioned before the **Near Attenuation Start** distance and is therefore not illuminated at all. The **Near Attenuation End** value is set to **40.0,** which means that the light reaches full intensity at 40 units from the source. The yellow teapot is positioned between the **Near Attenuation Start** and **Near Attenuation End** distances, and is therefore only partially illuminated. The **Far** Attenuation Start value is set to 60.0, which means that the light begins to diminish at 60 units from the source. The blue teapot is positioned between the Near Attenuation End and Far Attenuation Start distances, and is therefore fully illuminated. The Far Attenuation End value is set to 80.0, which means that the light is completely diminished at a distance of 80 units from the source. The green teapot is positioned between the **Far Attenuation Start** and **Far Attenuation End** distances, which means it is partially illuminated. The red teapot is positioned after the **Far Attenuation End** distance, and is therefore not illuminated at all.

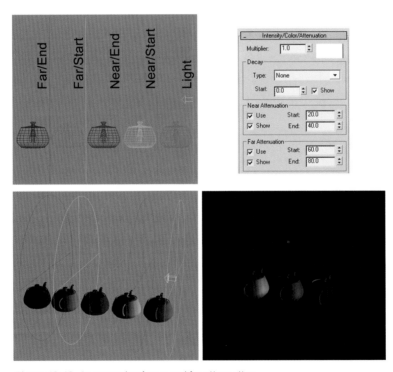

Figure 10-18. An example of near and far attenuation

To enable **Near Attenuation** or **Far Attenuation,** enable the **Use** option for either one. You can enable the **Show** option to graphically see in the viewports where the attenuation distances lie in relation to other objects in your scene.

Working with intensity, color, and attenuation settings

This exercise demonstrates the effect of changing the intensity, color, and attenuation settings of a light.

1. Continue from the last tutorial or go to the **3dsMax2008\Scenes\3DATS** directory and open the file **Ch10-02.max**.

2. Select the directional light.

3. Render the Perspective view.

4. Click the **Modify** tab, if it's not already active.

5. Open the **Intensity/Color/Attenuation** rollout and change the intensity from **1.0** to **2.0**. Notice the shaded view reflects the change of the light's intensity.

6. Render the Perspective view again. Notice the light is twice as intense.

7. Click the color swatch next to the **Intensity** setting and select any color from the color selector. Notice the shaded view reflects the change again. Close the color selector.

8. Render the Perspective view again. Notice the objects in the scene take on the color of the light.

9. In the **Far Attenuation** section, enable the **Use** option for far attenuation.

10. Right-click the slider arrows next to the **End** field of **Far Attenuation**. Notice both the **Start** and **End** settings are changed to **0**.

11. Render the Perspective view. There is nothing visible because the light is set to diminish completely at a distance of 0' from the light.

12. Increase the **Start** setting of **Far Attenuation** until the visual guide in the viewport passes the teapot.

13. Render the Perspective view again, and you should be able to see the teapot again. If not, increase the **Start** value until the guide is clearly past the teapot's position.

14. Keep this scene open or save it for use in the next tutorial.

The Advanced Effects rollout

In the **Affect Surfaces** section of this rollout (Figure 10-19) are a couple of options that allow you to adjust the contrast and soften the edge between diffuse and ambient areas of the surface. I have never found a use for these features and have always left them at their default value of 0.0.

Figure 10-19. The Advanced Effects rollout

In the **Projector Map** section of this rollout is an extremely useful feature for architectural visualizations. With the Projector Map feature, you can use a light as a projector to project the image of a map or animation onto the surface of objects in your scene, as shown in Figure 10-20.

The projector feature works the same way as a projector you would find in a movie theater, in which an image or animation is placed in front of a light and is projected onto a surface.

To load a map into a light, simply click the button labeled **None** and select a map type from the Material / Map Browser. Doing so will enable the Project Map feature automatically so that you don't have to enable the **Map** option. Once you load a map, you can drag and drop it into a material sample slot in the **Material Editor.** When you drag and drop a map to or from the **Material Editor,** you are asked if you would like to make a copy or instance of the map. You should always choose the Instance option so that changes you make to the map in the **Material Editor** cause the projector map to change as well. You can also drag and drop an image directly from the **Asset Browser** or a map from the Material / Map Browser.

Figure 10-20. Using a projector light to simulate a real-life projector

Another practical example of the use of a projector map is in the simulation of shadows. The left two images of Figure 10-21 show a scene with a simple plane that is mapped with the image of a tree. Since the tree is just an image and not a 3D object, the shadow cast by the tree would just be the shadow of the plane. To remedy this, the **Cast Shadows** option is disabled for the plane (tree), and the black-and-white image of the tree canopy (far-right image) is loaded into the projector map slot of the light, which is positioned just above the image of the tree. The multiplier of the projector light is then changed to −0.5, which causes light to be taken out of the area defined by the white portion of the tree canopy image. Negative multiplier values cause light to be removed from the objects hit by the light. The more negative the value, the darker the shadows.

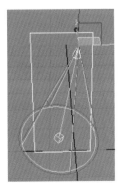

Figure 10-21. Using a projector map to simulate the shadow of a tree

The Shadow Parameters rollout

The **Shadow Parameters** rollout, shown in Figure 10-22, provides settings that control the look of shadows.

Figure 10-22. The Shadow Parameters rollout

You can use the color swatch to change the color of the shadows or simply change the strength of the shadows. The left image in Figure 10-23 shows a table casting a shadow created with the default shadow parameters. In the middle image, the color swatch is set to a gray color, which lightens the shadows significantly. The right image shows even lighter shadows created with a pure white color.

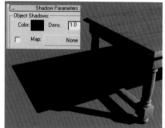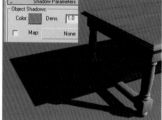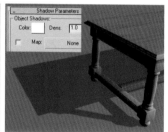

Figure 10-23: Using the Color swatch to change shadow strength

The **Dens.** field to the right of the color swatch changes the density of the shadow, which is simply another way to lighten or darken shadows. Changing the density from its default value of 1.0 to 0.5 will cause the shadows to be half as dark.

The strength, or darkness, of shadows is a very important setting for the main shadow casting light in your scene. Very dark shadows imply a bright, sunny day; however, if other elements in your scene don't support a bright sunny day, then your scene's realism will suffer.

Below the **Dens.** field is a button you can use to load a map into the shadow of an object. In Figure 10-24, the image of a tile floor is loaded into the shadow of the table, producing a strange but unique effect. Notice the table casts a shadow on itself, making part of the table appear to be made out of the same tile. The practicality of this feature may be limited, but it's a good one to keep in your bag of tricks.

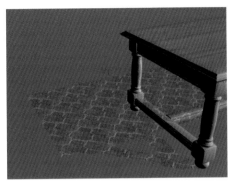 

Figure 10-24. Loading a map into the shadow of a table

The **Light Affects Shadow Color** feature blends the light's color with the shadow color, which usually produces results that can be achieved by changing the other shadow parameters discussed.

The **Atmospheric Shadows** section of the **Shadow Parameters** rollout deals with atmospheric effects, which are covered in Chapter 18.

Changing the color and strength of shadows

This exercise demonstrates how to change the color and strength of shadows using the settings in the **Shadow Parameters** rollout.

1. Continue from the last tutorial or go to the **3dsMax2008\Scenes\3DATS** directory and open the file **Ch10-03.max**.
2. Select the directional light.
3. Render the Perspective view.
4. In the **Command** panel, click the **Modify** icon.
5. Open the **Shadow Parameters** rollout.
6. In the **Object Shadows** section, click the color swatch, select any color from the color selector, and click **Close**.
7. Render the Perspective view. Notice that the shadow takes on the color you selected.
8. Use the **Undo** icon to return the color to black.
9. Change the **Dens.** setting to **0.5**.
10. Render the Perspective view. Notice that the shadow is now only as half as strong as it was.
11. Use the **Undo** icon to return the shadow to full strength.
12. Keep this scene open or save it for use in the next tutorial.

Rollouts for specific shadow types

The following sections will describe the various rollouts for using the different shadow types.

The Shadow Map Params rollout

The **Shadow Map Params** rollout, shown in Figure 10-25, appears whenever the selected light uses shadow maps. A shadow map is simply an image of a shadow mapped onto objects that receive shadows. The size or resolution of the mapped image, in pixels, is a major factor in the accuracy and look of the shadow.

Figure 10-25. The Shadow Map Params rollout

The top image in Figure 10-26 shows a column with a shadow created with a shadow map. 3ds Max computes this shadow by creating a mapped image of the object from the perspective of the light. The **Size** value in the **Shadow Map Params** rollout specifies how many pixels squared the image will be. A larger **Size** value results in greater resolution and accuracy of the mapped image. The bottom three images show the effect of increasing the **Size** value. As the **Size** increases, the number of pixels used to make up the shadow increases, thereby allowing more accurate shadow edges.

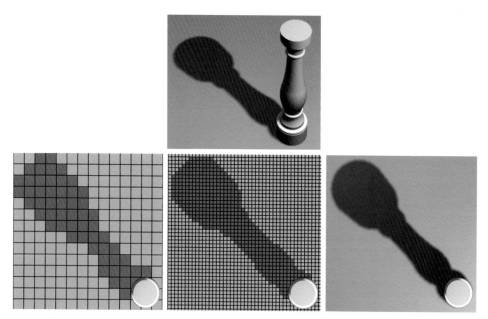

Figure 10-26. The effect of increasing the shadow map size

It is important to note that when using shadow maps, the quality of the shadows depends directly on not only the size of the shadow map, but the distance of the light to the objects receiving the shadows. Moving your light farther away from the objects in your scene will cause the shadow map to be less accurate.

Although shadow maps are not my favorite shadow types, when I do use them I always set the **Size** value to at least **2000**. This usually produces good results and a fairly clean-edged shadow, even when the light is at a reasonable distance. You could use higher values, but shadow maps consume a large amount of RAM. At some point, you will be using too much RAM, and you may even run out. If your light fails to produce any shadows at all, you will know that you've set the **Size** value too high.

Also within the **Shadow Map Params** rollout is a setting for map bias, which moves the shadow toward or away from shadow-casting objects. The **Bias** setting is used to prevent shadow-bleeding and to correct problems when objects cast shadows on themselves. These problems are usually minimal or insignificant, and this setting can usually be left at its default value of **1.0**.

Sample Range specifies how much area within the shadow is sampled, or averaged. This directly affects how soft the shadow's edge is. The left image of Figure 10-27 shows the column's shadow with the **Sample Range** set to its default value of **4.0**. In the middle image, the **Sample Range** is reduced to its minimum value of **0.1** to emphasize the effect of the setting. The right image shows the effect of doubling the **Sample Range** value to **8.0**. The **Sample Range** can be a very critical setting when you are trying to soften the edge of your shadows, which become harder when you increase the shadow map's **Size** value. As a side note, notice in the middle image that there are a few places where the column casts a shadow on itself, and the result is poor. However, this is only noticeable because the **Sample Range** is set to its minimum value. When the **Sample Range** is set to a reasonable value, the effect is unnoticeable.

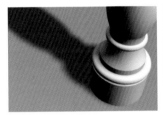  

Figure 10-27. Sample ranges of 4.0, the default value (left); 0.1, the minimum value (middle); and 8.0 (right)

Absolute Map Bias is not an option you should ever have to worry about, and it will not be covered in this book.

Use the **2 Sided Shadows** option whenever you are trying to correct problems in your shadows that exist due to certain faces on your objects not casting shadows. This occurs when the normal of a face is oriented away from the light and not visible from the light's perspective. The example in Figure 10-28 shows the typical teapot in its default state, in which light passes through the area surrounding the lid without detecting a surface. Because of this, shadows are not cast and the effect is very noticeable. To correct this problem, enable the **2 Sided Shadows** option, and shadows will be cast for faces that are oriented away from the light, as shown in the right image.

Figure 10-28. The 2 Sided Shadows option disabled (left) and enabled (right)

Changing the quality of a shadow map

This exercise demonstrates how to change the resolution of a map to improve a shadow's quality.

1. Continue from the last tutorial or go to the **3dsMax2008\Scenes\3DATS** directory and open the file **Ch10-04.max**.

2. Select the directional light.

3. Go to the Modify panel, and in the **General Parameters** rollout, click the drop-down list and change the shadow type to **Shadow Map** (if not already set).

4. Render the Perspective view.

5. Open the **Shadow Map Params** rollout.

6. Change the **Size** to **100** and render the Perspective view. Notice that the shadows have blurred significantly.

7. Change the **Size** to **1000** and render the Perspective view. Notice that the shadows become much sharper.

8. Keep this scene open or save it for use in the next tutorial.

The Area Shadows rollout

The **Area Shadows** rollout, shown in Figure 10-29, includes a **Basic Options** section to change the shape of the light and enable the **2 Sided Shadows** option. Below this is a section that controls antialiasing options, which primarily affect the edge of the shadow. By experimenting with these options, particularly **Sample Spread** and **Jitter Amount,** you can achieve some fascinating results. Area shadows are not as practical as other shadow types, but they can produce unique results that may come in handy some day. If you decide to use area shadows to achieve a particular effect or look, try to keep the **Shadow Integrity** and **Shadow Quality** settings as low as possible to reduce excessive rendering times. The **Area Light Dimensions** section controls the length, width, and height of the light source.

Figure 10-29. The Area Shadows rollout

The Ray Traced Shadow Params rollout

The **Ray Traced Shadow Params** rollout, shown in Figure 10-30, is a small rollout with just a few settings. The **Ray Bias** and **2 Sided Shadows** options work the same for raytraced shadows as they do for shadow maps.

Figure 10-30. The Ray Traced Shadow Params rollout

   The only unique setting is **Max Quadtree Depth.** The definition and concept of a quadtree can be difficult to grasp. Suffice to say that when using raytraced shadows, you should keep the **Max Quadtree Depth** value set to at least **7**. Increasing the value up to a maximum of **10** may reduce rendering times at the cost of memory, but it may be worth a try.
   Whenever possible, avoid using omni lights with raytraced shadows for reasons directly related to quadtrees. Omni lights used with raytraced shadows will require more memory and could take significantly longer to render than raytraced shadows used with spotlights or directional lights.

The Adv. Ray Traced Params rollout

The **Adv. Ray Traced Params** rollout, shown in Figure 10-31, contains only one unique option not already discussed with other shadow types. The mode option, set to **2-Pass Antialias** by default, should be kept at this setting, as it provides the best results at a negligible increase in rendering time.
   The **Antialiasing Options** section of the rollout is identical to the same section that appears with area shadows. Again, these settings affect the edge of the shadows and allow you to produce a wide array of shadow affects. By experimenting with the shadow spread and the jitter amount, you can make some very unique and unusual shadow types that might come in handy for some future project.

Figure 10-31. The Adv. Ray Traced Params rollout

The Optimizations rollout

The **Transparent Shadows On** option in the **Optimizations** rollout (shown in Figure 10-32) gives you the ability to use opacity maps with advanced raytraced shadows.

Figure 10-32. The Optimizations rollout

If you do not enable this option, objects with transparent areas derived from opacity maps will not render correctly. The left image in Figure 10-33 has the **On** option enabled, and the right image has it disabled.

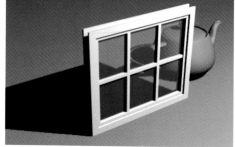

Figure 10-33. The Transparent Shadow On option enabled (left) and disabled (right)

The remainder of this rollout contains several settings that are best left at their default values.

The Spotlight and Directional Parameters rollouts

The **Spotlight Parameters** and **Directional Parameters** rollouts, shown in Figure 10-34, are identical rollouts that perform the same function. They control the shape and size of hotspots and falloff areas of a light.

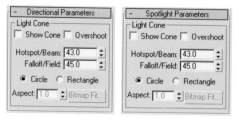

Figure 10-34. The identical Directional and Spotlight Parameters rollouts

The first option enables the **Show Cone** feature, which causes the cone to be visible when the light is not selected. Without this option enabled, a light's cone disappears when the light is deselected.

The next option, **Overshoot,** causes the light to cast light in all directions; however, projections and shadows will only occur within its cone. I recommend not using this feature.

The **Hotspot/Beam** parameter controls the size of a light's hotspot in units. In conjunction with the **Falloff/Field** parameter, it controls the look of hotspots and falloff areas. The actual size used may be irrelevant, depending on the distance of the light to the objects being illuminated. The hotspot area of an illuminated object receives a light's full intensity and the falloff area receives a diminished amount of the light. Proper use of these two parameters is usually crucial to the realism of the lights in your scene.

The left image in Figure 10-35 shows a surface illuminated by a light with a **Falloff/Field** setting almost identical to the **Hotspot/Beam** setting. In the right image, the **Hotspot/Beam** value is reduced to the lowest possible value. Notice the transition from hotspot to falloff in each image. In the left image, there is virtually no falloff because the hotspot size is almost the same as the falloff size. Note that the **Falloff/Field** setting cannot be set lower than the **Hotspot/Beam** setting.

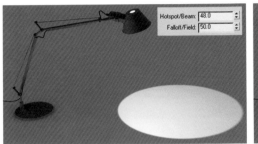

Figure 10-35. A high Hotspot/Beam value (left) and a low Hotspot/Beam value (right)

Changing the quality of a shadow map

This exercise demonstrates how to change the resolution of a map to improve a shadow's quality.

1. Continue from the last tutorial or go to the **3dsMax2008\Scenes\3DATS** directory and open the file **Ch10-05.max**.

2. Select the directional light.

3. Render the Perspective view.

4. Go to the **Modify** panel and open the **Directional Parameters** rollout.

5. Right-click the slider arrows next to the **Falloff/Field** parameter to reduce the value to **0.5**. Notice the scene becomes dark in the view.

6. Render the Perspective view. Notice the scene is completely dark.

7. Click a few times on the upward **Hotspot/Beam** arrow until the entire teapot is illuminated in the viewport.

8. Render the Perspective view. Notice the teapot is now illuminated.

9. Click several times on the upward **Falloff/Field** arrow until the entire plane is illuminated in the viewport.

10. Render the Perspective view. Notice the scene is much more illuminated now.

Viewport Shadows

Since the first release of 3ds Max, users have pleaded for the ability to see viewport shadows. Autodesk finally came through on this request with the release of 3ds Max 2008 and we can now see viewport shadows, like the one shown in Figure 10-36.

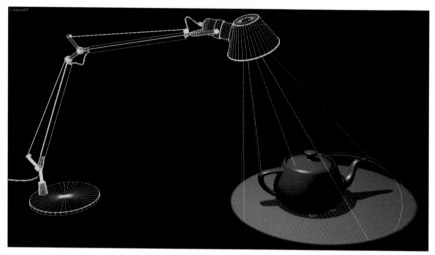

Figure 10-36. The new viewport shadows feature

Within the Viewport Configuration dialog box is a new tab called **Lighting and Shadows**, shown in Figure 10-37. In order to see viewport shadows the **Good** or **Best** option needs to be select.

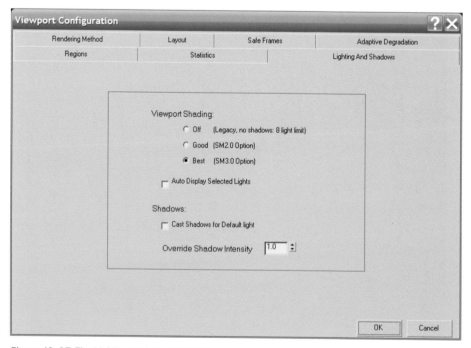

Figure 10-37. The Lighting and Shadows dialog box

This tab allows you to enable viewport shadows, but except for the default lighting, this alone won't actually allow shadows to be displayed for any of the lights in a scene. You have to enable viewport shadows for each individual light that you create. The easiest way to do this is to select a light, right-click inside the active viewport, and within the quad menu select **Viewport Shadows**, as shown in Figure 10-38.

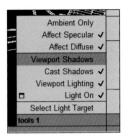

Figure 10-38. The viewport shadows option within the quad menu of an individual light

Being able to see shadows in viewports will save a tremendous amount of time if you're conducting a shadow study or working on scenes where shadow placements are critical. With past releases, you would have to conduct a rendering to see exactly where shadows fall.

Summary

This chapter has covered a large amount of information concerning the most critical component of a 3D scene—lighting. Lighting is part science and part art. If an architect gives two 3ds Max users the same set of architectural drawings and asks for an architectural visualization, the modeling by both users should look nearly identical. The materials applied to the scene should also be similar based on the guidance and input given by the architect. The lighting, however, may vary drastically based on the types of lights used and the artistic skills of the user.

This chapter focused on the basics of lighting, and the discussion was limited to standard lights. Chapter 11 will cover photometric lights and briefly explore their integration with advanced lighting features. Chapter 12 will focus closely on one of the most ubiquitous procedures of advanced lighting—global illumination. Although global illumination is considered an advanced lighting feature, my coverage will be limited to the critical components of this feature, and the discussion will be understandable at the foundations level.

By the end of these three chapters on lighting, you will have the foundation skills required to produce photorealistic visualizations.

CHAPTER 11

Photometric Lighting

STANDARD LIGHTS GIVE YOU THE ability to create great lighting for architectural scenes with minimal effort. With photometric lights, however, you can take your visualizations to a new level. Photometric lights are based on real-world light characteristics and enable you to create physically accurate lighting. You can simulate everything from the common 100W light bulb to the sun.

Photometric lights achieve the best results when used in combination with global illumination, which is covered in the next chapter. As a foundation for discussion on global illumination, this chapter covers each of the five types of photometric lights and two lighting systems which allow you to simulate sunlight. With a good understanding of the concepts in this chapter, the advantages of the realism that photometric lighting has to offer will be clear.

Exposure control

Before beginning a discussion on photometric lighting, we need to discuss a feature in 3ds Max that is critical to its use—exposure control. Exposure control corrects the output level and color range of a rendering to better match what your eyes would see in real life. Exposure control can improve the lighting of any scene, even when standard lights are used. When photometric lighting is used, exposure control becomes more critical. When you use attenuation in a scene, which is automatic with photometric lights, your lights tend to have a high dynamic range, because some parts of your scene with a light close by may be brightly lit, while other parts may be dimly lit.

The exposure control settings, shown in Figure 11-1, are found in the **Environment and Effects** dialog box, which you can access through the **Rendering** menu or open by pressing the keyboard shortcut "**8**." The **Exposure Control** rollout is located in the **Environment** tab, and when a selection is made from the drop-down list, an additional rollout appears directly below, providing settings for the exposure control selection.

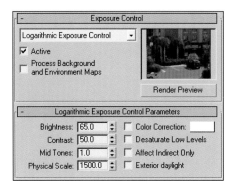

Figure 11-1. The exposure control settings

Types of exposure control

There are four types of exposure control in 3ds Max: Automatic, Linear, Logarithmic, and Pseudo. Deciding which one to use will probably take some experimentation, but some general guidelines are as follows:

- **Automatic:** This type of exposure control is good for still images or images where subtle effects are used. Effects are covered in Chapter 18.

- **Linear:** This type is best used for scenes with a low dynamic range, for example, dark or nighttime scenes where the range of brightness is very low from one area of the scene to another.

- **Logarithmic:** This type is best used for scenes with a high dynamic range, for example, exterior scenes where the range of brightness is very high from one area of the scene to another. This type also works best for scenes where a standard light is the primary light source in your scene. In addition, the logarithmic exposure control should be used for animations, because the automatic and linear options can cause flickering.

- **Pseudo:** This exposure control type is simply a tool that displays illumination levels in your scene using colors. When you render your scene with this type of exposure control, an additional render window opens that displays your scene with a rainbow of colors and a scale at the bottom signifying the illumination levels for each color. This feature serves nicely for performing advanced light studies in your scenes.

Exposure control parameters

The **Exposure Control Parameters** rollout changes depending on the type of exposure control selected. The Pseudo exposure control contains a completely unique rollout; however, the other three types contain exactly the same settings, though Logarithmic contains two additional options: **Affect Indirect Only** and **Exterior daylight** (as shown in Figure 11-1). The **Affect Indirect Only** option should be used when standard lights are the primary lights, and the Exterior daylight option should be used when the IES Sun, IES Sky, or Daylight systems are used. The remainder of this chapter focuses on an explanation of these features.

If any adjustments to the settings in the **Exposure Control Parameters** rollout are warranted, they will be small. For example, if you're using logarithmic exposure control and you need to change the default brightness level of 65 to 80 or higher, you probably have more fundamental problems with your lighting that should be corrected elsewhere. Large adjustments can harm the realism of your scene more than no adjustments at all. The **Render Preview** button lets you create a small preview of your scene with the selected exposure control without having to render the scene.

Photometric light types

There are five types of photometric lights, as shown in Figure 11-2: **Point, Linear, Area, IES Sun,** and **IES Sky.** The controls for point, linear, and area lights are similar in many ways to the controls for standard lights. IES Sun and IES Sky, however, are very unique lights with very difficult controls that will be discussed later in this chapter. **IES** stands for Illuminating Engineering Society, which is recognized as the technical authority on illumination.

Figure 11-2. The photometric light types

Point, linear, and area lights

As their names imply, the point, linear, and area lights emit light from different geometries. A point light emits light from a single point in space, a linear light from a line of definable length, and an area light from a definable area. Unique icons distinguish one type from another, as shown in Figure 11-3.

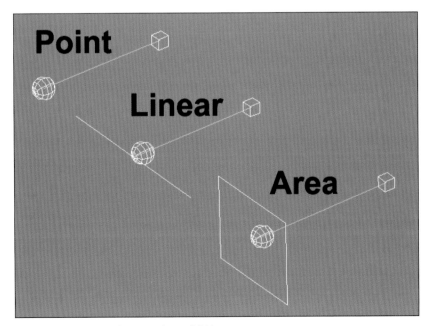

Figure 11-3. The point, linear, and area light types

When either a linear or area light is created, a unique rollout is used for each. The **Linear Light Parameters** rollout specifies the length of the line that will emit light, and the **Area Light Parameters** rollout specifies the area that will emit light. Both rollouts are shown in Figure 11-4.

Figure 11-4. The Linear and Area Light Parameters rollouts, respectively

All other rollouts for the point, linear, and area light types are the same as the rollouts available with standard lights, with the exception of one: the **Intensity/Color/Distribution** rollout, described next.

Intensity/Color/Attenuation rollout

This rollout, shown in Figure 11-5, is similar in function to the **Intensity/Color/Attenuation** rollout used with standard lights; however, attenuation is calculated automatically with photometric lights, so the attenuation settings are replaced with a distribution setting.

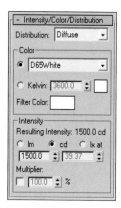

Figure 11-5. The Intensity/Color/Distribution rollout

Distribution

The Distribution drop-down list allows you to specify light distribution in four different ways: Isotropic, Spotlight, Diffuse, or Web. The type of distribution available will vary among the different light types.

An **isotropic** distribution casts light equally in all directions. This distribution is available only with a point light type.

A photometric **spotlight** casts a focused beam of light similar to the spotlight of a standard light. However, a photometric spotlight diminishes the light to 50% at the hotspot/beam angle. Standard light is at 100% at the hotspot/beam angle. With both standard and photometric lights, the intensity falls off to zero by the time the light reaches the falloff/field angle. The hotspot/beam and falloff/field angles are set in the **Spotlight Parameters** rollout, as shown in Figure 11-6.

Figure 11-6. The Spotlight Parameters rollout

A **diffuse** distribution emits light from a virtual surface, with more intense light leaving the surface at perpendicular (90 degree) angles and less intense light leaving the surface at angles parallel to the virtual surface. This distribution is available only with area and linear light types.

A **web** distribution casts light according to a 3D definition specified in an external file. These files are often available from lighting manufacturers and from the Internet. When a web distribution is selected, one more unique rollout appears—the **Web Parameters** rollout, as shown in Figure 11-7. This distribution is available with each of the three light types.

Figure 11-7. The Web Parameters rollout

Color

In the Color section of the rollout, you can set the color of your photometric light in one of two ways. You can use the drop-down list to select the color based on the real-world color characteristics of a particular type of light, as shown in the left image of Figure 11-8, or you can enable the Kelvin option and use the temperature setting to specify particular color, as shown in the right image.

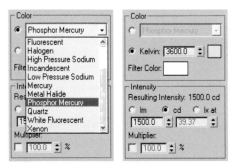

Figure 11-8. Specifying a light's color with a light type (left) and with a temperature setting (right)

When you select a light type from the drop-down list, the color swatch next to the Kelvin parameter is updated to reflect the light you select. For example, the typical incandescent light will have a very faint beige color and a phosphor mercury light will have a light green color.

When you select the Kelvin option, the color swatch also updates to reflect the change in color.

You can also adjust the color of the light by using the **Filter Color** swatch directly below the Kelvin temperature setting. Adjusting a color with this swatch simulates the effect of using a colored filter in front of the light.

Intensity

The intensity settings specify the strength or brightness of the light in physically based quantities. There are three different real-world units used to specify the intensity of a light: lm (lumens), cd (candela), and lx (lux).

- The **lumen** value is a measure of the overall output of a light and is usually listed on a package of light bulbs right next to the watts used.

- **Candela** is a measure of light energy per unit of time emitted by a point source in a particular direction; you should just remember it as another way to measure intensity of a light.

- The **lux** value specifies intensity at a particular distance away from the light source.

The **Multiplier** setting simply multiplies the intensity of the photometric light the same way it does for standard lights.

Creating photometric lights

This exercise demonstrates how to create photometric lights and modify their characteristics.

1. Reset 3ds Max.

2. In the Perspective view, create a plane with a width and length of **20'**.

3. In the **Name and Color** rollout, click the color swatch and select a pure white color for the plane. Using white allows you to see the light's color better.

4. In the Top view, create a teapot with a radius of **2'** and center the teapot on the plane.

5. In the Command panel, click **Create ➤ Lights,** and from the drop-down list, select **Photometric.**

6. Click the **Target Point** button. In the Top view, click and hold near the bottom-right corner of the plane to create the light, and drag the cursor to the center of the teapot. Release the mouse button to set the light's target near the teapot.

7. Without moving the target, move the light **5'** above the plane and render the Perspective view. Notice that the illumination is barely perceptible, if at all, because you are using a photometric light without any exposure control. The light automatically creates an inverse squared attenuation, and it is too far away from the teapot to illuminate it without exposure control.

8. Press the keyboard shortcut "**8**" to open the **Environment and Effects** dialog box.

9. In the **Exposure Control** rollout, click the drop-down list and select **Logarithmic Exposure Control.**

10. Render the Perspective view. Notice that the scene is brighter now.

11. In the Top view, move the light toward the center of the scene until it's directly above the teapot and render the Perspective view again. Notice that the teapot is much brighter now, because the light is closer. Also, the light is white, because the default color is set to a D65White light.

12. Go to the **Modify** panel, click the **Multiplier** option, and change the multiplier value to **200%**. This makes the light twice as intense.

13. Click the **Color** drop-down list and change the light to a **Phosphor Mercury** type. Notice the green hue shown in the view.

14. Click the **Distribution** drop-down list, select **Spotlight,** and render the Perspective view. Notice that the light falls off to zero intensity when it reaches the falloff/field angle.

Preset Lights

One of my favorite features in 3ds Max is the set of available **Preset Lights**—a group of preset photo-metric lights that load specific light settings based on their real-world characteristics. For example, when you load the typical 100W light bulb, the settings in the **Intensity/Color/Distribution** rollout auto-matically change to the settings required to reproduce the real-world characteristics of a 100W light bulb, as shown in Figure 11-9.

Figure 11-9. The real-world settings of a preset 100W light bulb

To create a preset light, click the **Create** menu and select **Lights** ➤ **Photometric Lights** ➤ **Presets**; then select the type of light you want to create, as shown in Figure 11-10.

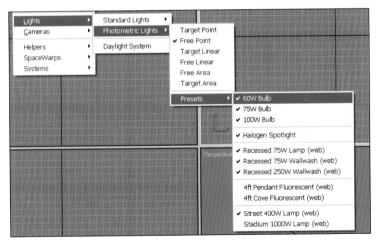

Figure 11-10. The available preset lights

Fortunately, 3ds Max has provided us with some of the most common light types found in the real world. If you want to create others not included in this list, determine the intensity value for the light you want to create using one of the three unit types mentioned. Then select the light type from the drop-down list in the **Color** section of the rollout. You can also make adjustments to the preset lights in order to create new lights.

IES Sun

IES Sun is a physically based light that simulates the bright light of the sun. It consists of a single light and target. When you create an IES Sun, five rollouts appear (not including the two mental ray rollouts that we will disregard). Four of the five rollouts are nearly identical to rollouts that appear for other light types. The most unique rollout, **Sun Parameters** (Figure 11-11), gives you control over the intensity of sunlight, the types of shadows it casts, and the objects to exclude from its affect.

By default, 3ds Max creates the IES Sun with an intensity of 80,000 lx. Notice, that no distance is associated with this unit of measure, as in other photometric light types, because the intensity that reaches the objects in your scene will be the specified value regardless of how far away the light is placed from the objects in your scene. In other words, objects in your scene are illuminated the same regardless of how high above your scene you place the IES Sun. Because of this, there is no attenuation for this light.

As with other light types, I recommend using advanced raytraced shadows with many of your scenes, depending on your exact needs. In the **Sun Parameters** rollout, you can specify the types of shadows to be used with the sunlight.

Notice the **Shadow Parameters** rollout is very similar to the same rollout with other light types. The only thing missing is the color swatch that allows you to change the color of the shadows and the feature that allows you to assign a map to the shadows. Instead of the color swatch, use the **Density** setting to directly specify how dark you want your shadows to be.

Figure 11-11. The Sun Parameters and Shadow Parameters rollouts

IES Sky

IES Sky is a physically based light that simulates the atmospheric effects of skylight. Skylight is the ambient, indirect light that results from the scattering of sunlight through the atmosphere.

The **IES Sky Parameters** rollout (Figure 11-12) is very simplistic, consisting partly of a multiplier, a color swatch, and a switch for the light and shadows. It also contains a setting for the cloud coverage that impacts how much light is scattered through the sky. In the **Render** section is the setting **Rays per Sample**. This is the number of rays 3ds Max uses to calculate skylight as it reaches a given point in space. Increasing this value can improve your renderings but also increases rendering times. When used in animations, flickering can result when this value is too low. Make sure you increase the default value to about 30 to prevent flickering.

Remember that the IES Sky will work correctly only when the sky object is pointing in the negative direction of the Z axis, or downward when viewed from the Top view.

Figure 11-12. The IES Sky Parameters rollout

Creating sunlight and skylight photometric lights

This exercise demonstrates how to use the sunlight and skylight features to simulate real-world direct and indirect illumination from the sun.

1. In the **3dsMax2008\Scenes\3DATS** folder, open the file **Ch11-01.max**.

2. In the **Command** panel, select **Create ➤ Lights,** and from the drop-down list, select **Photometric.**

3. Click the **IES Sun** button and in the **Sun Parameters** rollout change the shadow type to **Adv. Ray Traced** and enable the **Shadows** option.

4. In the Top view, click and hold near the top-left corner of the plane to create the light, and drag the cursor to the center of the building. Release the mouse button to set the light's target near the building, as shown in the following left image.

5. In the Front view, move the IES Sun approximately 45 degrees up, as shown in the following right image.

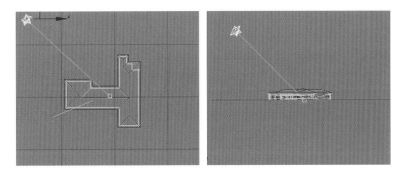

6. Render the Camera view. Notice that portions of the building in the direct path of the sunlight are completely white and all other portions are completely back, as shown in the following illustration. To improve the lighting in this scene, add exposure control.

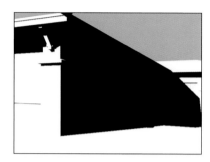

7. Press the keyboard shortcut "**8**" to open the **Environment and Effects** dialog box.

8. In the **Exposure Control** rollout, click the drop-down list and select **Logarithmic Exposure Control.**

9. In the **Logarithmic Exposure Control Parameters** rollout, enable **Exterior daylight.**

10. In the **Exposure Control** rollout, click **Render Preview.** You see a small sample of what the rendered image will look like.

11. Render the Camera view. Notice that the scene looks better, but there is still no illumination in areas not in the direct path of the sunlight, as shown in the following illustration. The next step is to create the effect of bounced atmospheric light.

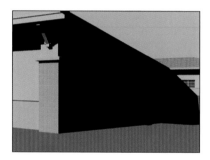

12. In the Command panel, with **Photometric** still selected as the light type, click the **IES Sky** button.

13. Place the IES Sky in the same location and in the same manner as you placed the IES Sun. Remember to elevate the IES Sky approximately 45 degrees into the sky.

14. Render the Camera view. Notice now that there is an appearance of indirect illumination in areas that were previously dark. In the next chapter, you'll learn methods to improve lighting even more in scenes such as this using global illumination.

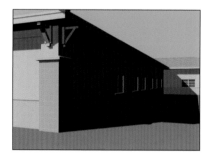

Daylight

The combination of direct sunlight and indirect skylight is a system that 3ds Max refers to as Daylight. Although you can create daylight manually by creating the IES Sun and IES Sky lights separately, you can use the Daylight feature in 3ds Max to do the work for you. The Daylight system uses a light that simulates the sun and mimics its movement over the earth at a specific location. With the Daylight system you can simulate sunlight in Paris at 4:02 p.m. on January 14 or in Rome at 9:31 a.m. on October 14. You can also animate the sunlight to see the sun's movement at a specific location and use the system to perform shadow studies for proposed or existing structures.

The Daylight feature is located in the **Systems** section of the **Create** panel, as shown in Figure 11-13.

Figure 11-13. The Sunlight and Daylight features

When you click the **Daylight** button, the **Control Parameters** rollout appears, as shown in Figure 11-14. The rollout provides controls for specifying a location on earth, a time of day, and a year for the position of the sun. The Orbital Scale has no effect on the quality or accuracy of the light; it simply moves the sun higher up above the objects in your scene. The **North Direction** setting specifies the direction of north in your scene, as assigned by a compass rose that is created when the daylight is created, as shown in Figure 11-15. By default, north is 0 and points in the positive direction of the Y axis. East is 90 degrees and points in the positive direction of the x axis. You must correctly specify north in your scene to accurately depict the position and movement of the sun. Changing the direction of north will cause the compass rose to update, and rotating the compass rose will cause the North Direction parameter to update.

Figure 11-14. The Control Parameters rollout

To create daylight, click the **Daylight** button in the Systems section of the **Create** panel. Click and drag inside the Top or Perspective view to place the compass rose. Release the mouse button when the compass rose is to your liking, remembering that the size of the compass rose has no bearing on the affect of the light. After releasing the mouse button, drag the mouse again to elevate the sun upward along the positive direction of the z axis.

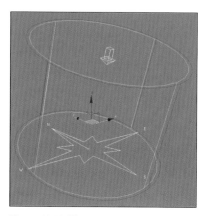

Figure 11-15. The compass rose and directional light of the Daylight feature

Once a daylight system is created, the system is modified primarily in two different places. Since the **Control Parameter** rollout, shown in Figure 11-14, deals with the movement of the sun over time, the rollout is accessed through the **Motion** panel once the system is created. The remaining rollouts are accessed through the **Modify** panel.

Standard lights vs. IES Sun and IES Sky

The first rollout in the **Modify** panel is the **Daylight Parameters** rollout, shown in Figure 11-16. In this rollout, you specify which type of light serves as the sunlight and which type of light serves as the skylight. By default, 3ds Max creates a standard directional light for the daylight system; however, you can use the IES Sun in its place to take advantage of its photometric qualities. Using the daylight system even with a standard directional light is beneficial, because you can simulate the correct position of the sun. By changing the light type to IES Sun, you can also achieve photometric quality and add a great deal of realism to your scene. To change the type of light used, click the **Sunlight** drop-down list and select IES Sun, as shown in Figure 11-16.

The same concept applies when using the light type that simulates skylight. By changing the **Skylight** setting to IES Sky, you can take advantage of the photometric quality of the IES Sky. As mentioned in the last chapter, the Skylight object is designed to work directly with the Light Tracer global illumination rendering solution. Since Light Tracer is rarely used in a production environment because of its lengthy rendering times, the Skylight is also rarely used. For that reason, this book does not cover the Light Tracer and Skylight features. When you do change the skylight to IES Sky, the **IES Sky Parameters** rollout appears along with the other rollouts in the **Modify** panel.

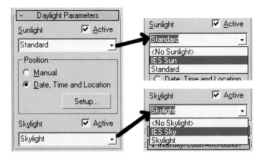

Figure 11-16. The Daylight Parameters rollout

The **Position** section of the rollout contains the **Manual** control that allows you to adjust the location of the light in your scene rather than setting the location based on date, time, and location settings. You can also adjust the intensity value of the sunlight in manual mode. The **Setup** button is a shortcut button that takes you to the **Motion** panel where you can modify the date, time, and location settings.

It is important to remember that the IES Sun and IES Sky lights are photometric lights, and to gain the most out of their use when using the scanline renderer, you need to use the advanced lighting feature radiosity along with exposure control, both of which are discussed in the next chapter. Light Tracer can be used in lieu of radiosity to achieve good results; however, I do not recommend Light Tracer in a production environment.

Sunlight

The Sunlight feature is found next to the Daylight feature in the **Systems** section of the **Create** panel. The Sunlight feature in 3ds Max is the same as the Daylight feature, except it lacks the added benefit of skylight and the option to utilize the IES Sun. When you create a sunlight system, a free directional light is created with raytraced shadows. The light is the same as the lights created through the **Lights** section of **Create** panel, except that this light is tied directly to the feature that simulates the position and motion of the sun. After creating the sunlight system, you can access this feature through the **Motion** panel. This feature exists primarily as a legacy tool, for when you load older files that were created before the Daylight system was developed.

Summary

Photometric lighting enhances any architectural scene and provides several benefits over standard lighting. With photometric lights, you can produce stunning realism and physically accurate lighting with minimal effort. This chapter covered each of the photometric light types and the two systems that are used to simulate sunlight. By combining the concepts covered in this chapter with the concepts covered in the next chapter, you can take your lighting to an even higher level.

Whether aware of it or not, a viewer will usually grade the quality of an architectural visualization by the quality of the lighting. Lighting is without a doubt one area in scene creation that will make or break a visualization. If any additional time can be spent improving the quality of your work, lighting should be the first area you consider.

CHAPTER 12

Global Illumination

AS ANY VETERAN 3DS MAX user will tell you, lighting is the most critical element in any visualization. No other phase of scene creation depends so heavily on experience and requires as much artistic talent. When used correctly, good lighting can make even the poorest designs look beautiful. Likewise, incorrect lighting can ruin a quality design and negate great work in all other phases of scene creation.

The previous two chapters dealt with lighting techniques for local illumination, which only takes into account the light that takes a direct path from the light source (also known as direct illumination). While local illumination provides fairly good results in a relatively short amount of time, it can never achieve the quality and realism that global illumination can provide. **Global illumination** is a lighting process that takes into account not only the light taking a direct path from the light source, but also the light that has bounced from other surrounding surfaces (also known as indirect illumination).

This chapter describes the process of using global illumination in your scenes to achieve photorealistic quality. True global illumination requires the use of photometric lights. Combined with the features discussed in the previous chapter on photometric lights, this chapter will describe how to achieve true global illumination with lights that you should be familiar with.

Principles of global illumination

Creating convincing lighting in 3ds Max is a complicated process, which reflects the complex nature of light behavior in the real world. To understand how 3ds Max calculates global illumination, you must first understand how light behaves in the real world and why the world appears to us the way it does. Why are our surroundings still illuminated when the sun is below the horizon? Why is the sky blue or a sunset red? Why is absolute darkness a rarity? The best examples are all around you. Let's start answering these questions by looking at Figure 12-1. In the left image, the scene receives only direct illumination, which causes the areas in shadow to be black. In contrast, the image on the right shows both direct and indirect illumination, and the areas of shadow are slightly illuminated. The shadows in the image on the right are not as dark, because light is bouncing all around the scene from one surface to another, eventually striking almost every part of every surface. If this were an outdoor scene, light would not only be bouncing from object to object, it could also be bouncing off particles in the air that redirect it in all directions.

Figure 12-1. Direct illumination (left) and global illumination (right)

Shaders

In 3ds Max, lighting is calculated with algorithms known as shaders. These algorithms predict the intensity and color of light being reflected off the surface of objects in a scene. Shaders also control the shape, size, and overall appearance of specular highlights of objects. By doing so, they help define for the viewer what kind of material makes up an object. In fact, no other material characteristic will give viewers a better indication of what kind of material they are looking at than specular highlights. For example, on smooth surfaces, the specular highlights are smaller and more pronounced, as shown in the far left pool table ball in Figure 12-2. On rougher surfaces, the specular highlights are spread out over a greater area and are not as pronounced, as shown on the middle left ball. Very rough surfaces can still show highlights but with a more speckled and noisy appearance, as shown in the middle right ball. By controlling the shape of a specular highlight, you can also give materials a very unique appearance and provide an even better indication of surface qualities, as shown in the far left ball.

Figure 12-2. Various types of specular highlights

3ds Max contains numerous shaders that enable you to simulate just about any type of surface material; however, using a wide variety of shaders and their many settings can be very confusing and is not necessary for inexperienced 3ds Max users. Once you have a solid foundation of global illumination, you should try experimenting with other shader types beside the default Blinn shader. The Blinn shader is used as the default shader because it has very soft and round highlights. This quality gives you the flexibility to simulate a wide range of materials rather than restricting you to just those materials that have harder and less round highlights.

Radiosity

Radiosity is a term used to describe the effect of light bouncing around in a scene. When light bounces from one object to another, it not only illuminates other objects, it transmits reflected color. This color bleeding effect is perhaps the single most critical component in making visualizations appear photorealistic. Notice that in several of the rendered images in this book's colored gallery, a great deal of color reflects from one object to adjacent objects. These subtle effects of color reflection are critical to the overall believability and realism of the rendering. While radiosity can dramatically effect the realism of a scene, its use can have an equally dramatic effect on the time needed to render.

To calculate radiosity, 3ds Max creates an invisible duplicate of a scene and breaks down each duplicate into a mesh of small polygons with a size of your choosing, as shown in Figure 12-3. As we will discuss further in this chapter, the size of the invisible polygons is critical to the accuracy of global illumination and equally critical to the time needed to calculate radiosity. When 3ds Max determines that light strikes one of these invisible polygons, it calculates where that reflected light goes next and with what intensity, color, and diffusion it strikes the next surface. This information is stored in the vertices of the polygon that the light strikes and contributes to the overall illumination of the polygon. The cumulative effect of all the bounced light in a scene, after attenuation eventually stops the bouncing process, is the **radiosity solution.** Calculating a radiosity solution can take hours, depending on the quality you specify for the solution and the size of the invisible polygons. Fortunately, however, the radiosity solution only needs to be created once for any given scene, and is valid until light settings are changed or scene objects are manipulated in any way. In other words, you can create an animation of any length while only calculating the radiosity once. This process is sometimes referred to as "baked light".

Figure 12-3. Subdividing the meshes of a scene

To use radiosity in a scene, click the keyboard shortcut **F10** to open the **Render Scene** dialog box, click the drop-down list in the **Select Advanced Lighting** rollout and select **Radiosity** (as shown in Figure 12-4). A number of rollouts will appear giving you precise control over radiosity calculation.

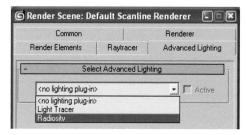

Figure 12-4. Enabling advanced lighting in 3ds Max

Radiosity Processing Parameters rollout

Within the **Radiosity Processing Parameters** rollout are numerous basic parameters that require your attention for any job.

Initial Quality

As its name implies, this value sets the overall quality of the radiosity process. The default of 85% is sufficient for calculating **Radiosity** during the final production rendering but is much higher than necessary for test renders. When experimenting with **Radiosity,** try using **Initial Quality** values as low as 30%. These values will suffice for test renders and are calculated in a fraction of the time needed to calculate the default value of 85%. Values as low as 50% can also produce great results for production renders.

Figure 12-5. Basic radiosity parameters

During the initial quality stage of the rendering process, the lights in your scene shoot virtual rays containing a certain energy value (dictated by the light settings). This energy is distributed over the individual faces of each object in the scene and is stored in the vertices of each face. But because of the arrangement, size, and orientation of the faces in an object, adjacent faces may have widely varying energy values. This variation can lead to unrealistic illumination and cause the quality of your radiosity solution to suffer dramatically, as shown in the left image of Figure 12-6. In this example, a single photometric point light illuminates a set of china and radiosity provides global illumination. In the left image, however, the illumination is extremely poor because of the wide variation in light energy stored in the vertices of each face. To remedy this variation, 3ds Max needs to gather energy information from each face and redistribute it as necessary to reduce variation. When this is done, the rendering can be greatly improved, as shown in the right image of Figure 12-6. This process, which is also the next key setting that should be adjusted, is termed **Refine Iterations** (discussed in the next section of this chapter).

Figure 12-6. Radiosity imperfections in the illumination of an object (left) and imperfections removed (right)

Enabling Radiosity

This exercise demonstrates how to quickly enable **radiosity** with the default parameters.

1. Open the file **Ch12-Radiosity01.max**, found in the **3dsMax2008\Scenes\3DATS** folder.

2. Render the **Camera** view. Notice that light does not reach some parts of the room and china, as shown in the left image in the following illustration. This is because no light is bouncing around.

3. Press the keyboard shortcut **F10** to open the **Render Scene** dialog box.

4. Click the **Advanced Lighting** tab.

5. In the **Select Advanced Lighting** rollout, click the drop-down list and select **Radiosity.**

6. In the **Initial Quality** field, enter a value of **50**. This will provide sufficient quality for most renderings, and will significantly reduce the solution calculation.

7. In the **Radiosity Processing Parameters** rollout, click the **Start** button. This starts the radiosity calculation process.

8. In the **Interactive Tools** section of this rollout, click on the **Display Radiosity in Viewport** option to disable this feature. Notice that the Camera view no longer shows the bounced light contribution.

9. Render the **Camera** view. Now the areas of the room that were completely dark before are illuminated by the bounced light; however, some areas are illuminated poorly and exhibit a large amount of noise, such as the china. Notice also that the purple and blue color of the walls is being reflected onto the china, but because of the imperfections of the global illumination solution, this translates to a large amount of noise, as shown in the right image in the following illustration. In the next exercise, we will remove these imperfections in the lighting.

10. Click on the **Display Radiosity in Viewport** option again to reenable this feature.

11. Save this scene for use in the next exercise.

Refine Iterations

Refining the radiosity solution using the **Refine Iterations** feature will almost always be part of any scene utilizing radiosity. 3ds Max offers three ways to refine iterations. You can refine iterations globally, that is refine all objects; you can refine only objects selected at the time of rendering; or you can specify a refine iteration value for each individual object through its **Object Properties** dialog box (as shown at the bottom of the Figure 12-7). The first two methods, **Refine Iterations (All Objects)** and **Refine Iterations (Selected Objects)** are found in the **Radiosity Processing Parameters** rollout (Figure 12-5). In very large scenes, you may find it impractical to refine iterations globally, because doing so causes the radiosity solution to take too long to calculate. Therefore, you can leave certain objects out of the refining process if they don't visually benefit from refinement and don't degrade the visual quality of surrounding objects. A good **Refine Iterations (Selected Objects)** setting for test renders is 3, while a good setting for production renders is 10.

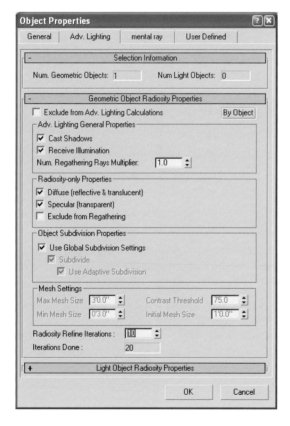

Figure 12-7. Advanced lighting settings for individual objects through the Object Properties dialog box

Figure 12-8 shows how using the **Refine Iterations** feature can improve the illumination of a scene. The image on the left shows the scene without the use of **Refine Iterations**. The image on the right shows how using **Refine Iterations** can remove the imperfections in light energy distribution.

Figure 12-8. Using Refine Iterations to correct the distribution of light energy in a scene

Light filtering

The last section of the **Radiosity Processing Parameters** rollout is the **Interactive Tools** section. Within this section, you can filter both direct and indirect light to further reduce the noise caused by uneven light energy distribution. This feature takes effect after the radiosity solution is calculated and, therefore, does not require recalculating the solution. Filtering the light with these features, especially **Indirect Light Filtering,** can supplement the process of refining iterations or sometimes even replace it.

Smoothing out the appearance of noise caused by uneven light energy distribution is almost always needed. Instead of using the **Refine Iterations** feature, which can add an enormous amount of time to your solution calculation, you might be able to get away with just increasing the **Indirect Light Filtering** setting to 10 or higher. The time needed to process indirect light filtering for the china shown in the left image of Figure 12-9 was less than a second. The time needed to use **Refine Iterations** could be several minutes depending on the speed of your computer, yet this process does not produce significantly better results in most areas, as shown in the left image. Though this will not always be the case with your scenes and refine iterations will often be necessary, experimenting here might save you some valuable time.

Figure 12-9. Using Indirect Light Filtering alone (left) and Refine Iterations alone (right)

The same section of the **Radiosity Processing Parameters** rollout contains an option to disable or enable radiosity in your viewports, and a button that takes you to the **Environment and Effects** dialog box, where you can adjust the exposure control settings of your scene.

Radiosity Meshing Parameters rollout

The **Radiosity Meshing Parameters** rollout includes settings that let you set the size of the polygons for the invisible mesh objects used to calculate and store the radiosity solution. Breaking the invisible mesh scene into very small polygons using these settings is critical for storing accurate light energy data in the vertices of the polygons.

By selecting the **Enabled** option in this rollout, as shown in the top of Figure 12-10, 3ds Max divides the mesh objects into polygons with maximum and minimum sizes as specified in the **Mesh Settings** section of the rollout. Reducing the **Maximum Mesh Size** value improves radiosity but increases the time needed to calculate a solution. The **Use Adaptive Subdivision** option is great for letting 3ds Max determine the size each polygon should be relative to the others. This option, enabled by default, reduces the size of the polygons that lie in areas of widely varying light energy values, areas that need more precise data stored in the vertices of the polygons. You only have to specify maximum and minimum mesh sizes, and 3ds Max determines what size, between these two values, each polygon should be. This option is similar to the **Optimize** modifier. If you do not enable the **Use Adaptive Subdivision** option, then you will be able to specify only the **Maximum Mesh Size** value, and every polygon in the invisible mesh that would otherwise be larger, will be reduced to the same maximum size.

When experimenting with radiosity, always enable global subdivisions and the **Use Adaptive Subdivision** option. Try a range of values for **Maximum Mesh Size** and **Minimum Mesh Size** to see how large your polygons can be before radiosity is degraded to an unacceptable level. With more experience, you can always disable both of these options or manually override them inside the **Object Properties** dialog box of any object, but these options are great for beginners.

Figure 12-10. The Radiosity Meshing Parameters rollout

To make the process of subdividing your scene more flexible, 3ds Max gives you the ability to override global settings and specify unique settings for individual objects that need different subdivision settings than the rest of the scene. This would be a great option for high polygon objects far away from a camera's perspective or high polygon objects that simply do not need so many polygons to store such accurate light information. To override the global subdivision settings in the

Render Scene dialog box for individual objects, select the object(s), open the **Object Properties** dialog box, click the **Advanced Lighting** tab, and disable the **Use Global Subdivision Settings** option, as shown in Figure 12-11. Click **OK** to complete the command.

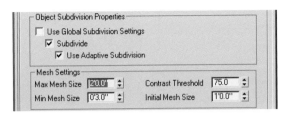

Figure 12-11. Using different subdivision settings for individual objects

If you understand the concepts discussed thus far in the chapter and want to experiment with more advanced **Radiosity** settings to fine-tune your results, try using the features in the **Light Painting** and **Rendering Parameters** rollouts.

Improving the radiosity solution

This exercise demonstrates how to improve the quality of the radiosity solution by using refine iterations, light filtering, and mesh subdivision.

1. Continue from the previous exercise or open the file **Ch12-Radiosity02.max** found in **3dsMax2008\Scenes\3DATS** folder.

2. Press the keyboard shortcut **F10** to open the **Render Scene** dialog box.

3. Click the **Advanced Lighting** tab.

4. In the **Radiosity Processing Parameters** rollout, type **10** in the **Refine Iterations (All Objects)** field.

5. Click the **Continue** button at the top of the rollout. This initiates the processing of refining the radiosity solution.

6. Render the **Camera** view. Now the imperfections in the reflected light, shown in the previous rendering (left image below) are removed, and the result is a less noisy GI solution (right image below).

7. Click the **Radiosity Meshing Parameters** rollout.

8. In the **Global Subdivision Settings** section, click the **Enabled** option. This tells 3ds Max to sub-divide the invisible mesh to obtain and store more accurate light energy.

9. Disable the **Use Adaptive Subdivision** option.

10. Scroll back to the **Radiosity Processing Parameters** rollout and click the **Reset All** button. This removes the radiosity solution which was invalidated when these last few settings were modified.

11. Click the **Start** button to recalculate a new radiosity solution. Notice that, when finished, the Camera view shows that the scene objects are subdivided so that no face is larger than the **3'0"** specified in the **Maximum Mesh Size** field, as shown in the left image of the following illustration. 3ds Max evenly subdivides faces that require further division, so that each is the same size. Light energy is stored in the vertices of these faces, so as the faces are reduced in size, the radiosity becomes more accurate.

12. Render the **Camera** view. Notice that the rendering has improved significantly with mesh subdivision, as shown in the right image of the following illustration.

13. In the **Radiosity Meshing Parameters** rollout, enable the **Use Adaptive Subdivision** option.

14. Scroll back to the **Radiosity Processing Parameters** rollout and click the **Reset All** button to remove the **Radiosity** solution again.

15. Click the **Start** button to calculate a new radiosity solution. Notice that the Camera view now shows that the scene objects are not subdivided evenly to a certain maximum size in areas like the floor and walls, as they were before. Instead, objects are subdivided into small faces in some areas and larger faces in others, as shown in the left image of the following illustration. Areas with smaller faces tend to be those where adjacent surfaces interact or where the edges of shadows lie.

16. Render the **Camera** view. Notice that the overall illumination of the scene has improved a little, particularly along the baseboards in shadow and the areas in shadow underneath the teacup plates.

17. In the **Radiosity Processing Parameters** rollout, type **3** in the **Indirect Light Filtering** field.

18. Render the **Camera** view. The noise from the previous rendering, shown in the left image below, has been blurred even more now by the indirect light filtering. Use of this feature is most apparent in areas with smaller mesh faces, such as the surfaces on the china. In this area, increasing the **Indirect Light Filtering** value to 3 softened the variations between the blue and purple reflections coming from the walls, as shown in the right image below.

Considerations when using radiosity

When using radiosity, especially in conjunction with photometric lights, you must always ensure the geometry is to the correct scale. For example, you can not expect a single 100W light bulb to illuminate all the objects in a room the size of a stadium. Likewise, radiosity calculations won't be accurate if the objects that are broken up (through use of global subdivisions) are not to scale.

Another thing to consider with radiosity is the effect of geometry through which light can leak, or escape. If you calculate the radiosity solution within a small room, for example, and faces are missing from one of your walls, light might be allowed to escape through the opening. If allowed to do so, the escaping light can adversely affect objects outside the room or increase the time needed to calculate a solution (because the light is escaping into infinity and still being analyzed).

While preparing a radiosity calculation, you may realize that certain objects in your scene have little impact on the overall radiosity in your rendering or that including them in the calculation unreasonably increases your solution calculation time. If this is the case, consider excluding these objects from the radiosity calculation process. Doing so can save a tremendous amount of time in calculating a radiosity solution, especially when objects of a high face-count are excluded. Take trees for example, which often contain tens of thousands of faces. If you can verify that high-polygon trees in your scene do not need to benefit from radiosity, you can reduce the solution calculation time by excluding them from it. To exclude an object from advanced lighting calculations, right-click the object, click Object Properties in the quad menu, click the Advanced Lighting tab, and then click the Exclude from Adv. Lighting Calculations option, as shown in Figure 12-12. Click OK to complete the command. Try excluding objects with a high face-count that don't reflect a significant amount of light or that don't receive a significant amount of reflected light.

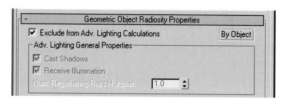

Figure 12-12. Excluding individual objects from advanced lighting calculations

Finally, because almost any adjustments to lights or objects in your scene will invalidate a radiosity solution, take care not to spend large amounts of time calculating a high-quality solution unless you are certain that your scene is finalized. When a solution is calculated, the solution is stored and saved with the file when the file is saved. Radiosity solutions can turn the smallest of scenes into a several-hundred-megabyte file, increasing load and save times for your files and complicating processes such as network rendering.

Summary

We have just discussed what is arguably the most complex area of 3ds Max and the most important element of photo-realistic scenes—global illumination. Global illumination is all about realistic light reflections and is the pinnacle of architectural renderings. Although a difficult tool to master, radiosity provides a great means to achieving global illumination. The key to mastery is effectively balancing the mesh size and the refine iterations, not only to eliminate inaccurate light energy distribution, but also to achieve the feel you want in the render.

Even if you move onto to other render engines that provide a superior lighting solution, such as mental ray or V-Ray, both of which are discussed in the intermediate/advanced version of this book, radiosity is a great feature that allows you to bake light into your scene, so that you can see fairly accurate GI in your viewports from any perspective. This allows you to show clients a decent preview from any perspective without making them wait on a new rendering for each new view.

The most important thing to remember when using global illumination is to keep your render times short during test renders and to render as often as possible when experimenting. You will learn through trial and error how the numerous values affect the overall outcome. Realistic global illumination does not come easy, and often requires many experiments with seemingly endless variables. Whole books are written on the subject, and this chapter barely scratches the surface, intending to give you a starting point from which to expand your knowledge. The possibilities from here are boundless.

PART 5

Cameras and Animation

Compared to other industries, the number and type of animated objects in an architectural scene is relatively small, but, for objects that do require animation in our line of work (such as cameras), the need for precision and is just as great as it is in other industries. Knowing how to work with controllers is critical to great animation.

CHAPTER 13

Camera Basics

CAMERAS IN 3DS MAX ALLOW you to view a scene from a particular perspective, using all the controls you would expect to find in real-world cameras, as well as many other controls that are not available in the real world. Cameras can capture individual still images or animated sequences. Multiple cameras give you the ability to record the same scene from multiple perspectives and play the role of film director. Compared to other features in 3ds Max, the complexity of cameras is rather minor and the number of parameters involved is relatively small. Just like other features, however, the elements that you do control and the procedures you implement in the use of cameras require just as much skill and experience to master.

In the field of architectural visualization, the use of cameras is not always as simple and straightforward as an outside observer might think. Although the need for special effects, smoke and mirrors, and high-speed and erratic camera movement is not as great as it is in other industries, cameras used for architectural visualizations require just as much precision in their positioning and movement to achieve impressive and cost-effective presentations. Prior to beginning any work on a project, the modeler should have a good understanding of exactly what needs to be seen through the cameras when all elements have been added to the scene. Not having this understanding can result in the modeler spending far too much time creating models or adding too much detail that will not be seen or that will be out of the camera's point of view. Likewise, there will often be areas in your scenes that you must hide from the camera's view because of lack of detail. When you watch a TV show and hear someone say that it's "filmed before a live studio audience," you know that the cameras used on the set can only pan so far to either side before revealing technicians, set equipment, and the studio audience. Cameras in a studiohave to be carefully positioned and oriented to capture all of the action, and constrained just as carefully to prevent showing too much. Equal care must be taken in the use of cameras in a visualization that maximizes cost efficiency and scene quality.

Finally, the user has the option to distort reality somewhat by making a scene appear bigger and better than it will actually be when the real structures are built. Using a wider-than-normal field of view on a camera, for example, can make a small room appear slightly bigger. Ultimately, it is through the lens of the camera that outside observers will view your presentation—thus, a good understanding of all the tools available for cameras and their use is critical in producing powerful presentations.

3ds Max provides many different ways to control the behavior of cameras. In Chapter 14, we'll cover the basics of camera animation, and in Chapter 15, you'll learn more advanced ways of controlling cameras through the use of the **Curve Editor** and controllers. For the remainder of this chapter, however, we'll focus on camera viewport navigation, camera placement, and the important camera parameters found in the rollouts of the **Modify** panel.

Camera types

There are two standard camera types in 3ds Max, both accessible through the **Camera** icon in the **Create** panel: **free cameras** and **target cameras.**

Both camera types are identical except for one major characteristic. Free cameras have only one component: the camera; whereas target cameras have two components: the camera and the target. Target cameras are always oriented to face the target, and because the target can move independently from the camera, the target can be animated. The left image in Figure 13-1 shows a target camera and the right image shows a free camera. Notice that both images are the same except for the small box (target) near the center of the left image. Target cameras always face their targets, so moving this target changes the direction that the camera faces. To change the direction of a stationary free camera, you can apply a rotate transform or use one of the viewport navigation control icons listed in Table 13-1. As a note, you can change the camera type from target to free and back again as needed.

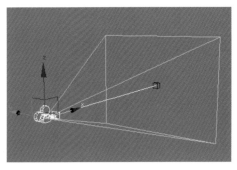 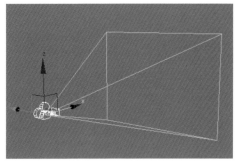

Figure 13-1. The target camera (left) and the free camera (right)

Creating Cameras

To create a free camera using the Command panel, click **Create ➤ Cameras ➤ Free,** and click once in any viewport. The camera will face the direction of the view unless the viewport is displaying a User, Perspective, Camera, or Target Light view, in which case the camera will face in the negative z direction.

One way to create a target camera is to click **Target,** click and hold inside a viewport, and drag the mouse to position the target. Release the mouse button to place the target.

An even easier way to create a camera is by using the Create Camera from View command. This command creates a target camera (only) that matches the view of the active viewport and turns that viewport's display into a Camera view. To use this command, create the view you want in the active viewport and press Ctrl+C. If you already have a camera, and you want to move it to match the view in your active viewport, select the camera and then press Ctrl+C.

Once a camera is created, you can easily switch a viewport to the camera view by pressing C. If more than one camera exists, you will be asked which camera you want to switch views to.

Creating cameras

This exercise demonstrates how to create the two types of cameras.

1. Reset 3ds Max and create a few primitives in the Perspective viewport.

2. Within the **Create** panel, click the **Cameras** icon. The **Object Type** rollout appears with two types of camera available.

3. Click the **Free** button.

4. In the Front viewport, click, hold, and drag anywhere to create the camera and simultaneously move it into position. Release the mouse button to place the camera.

5. Right-click twice within the Perspective viewport; once to activate the viewport and one more time to end the camera-creation command.

6. Press **C** to change the Perspective view into the Camera view.

7. In any other viewport, apply a couple of transforms to the free camera to see their effect on the newly created Camera view.

8. Press **Delete** to delete the camera. Notice that the Camera view changes back to the Perspective view.

9. In the Command panel, click the **Target** button.

10. In the Top viewport, click, hold, and drag to create the camera and move the camera target into position. Release the mouse button to place the camera target.

11. Right-click the Perspective viewport, and then press **C** to change the Perspective view into the Camera view again.

12. In any other viewport, apply a couple of transforms to the target camera and the target to see their effect on the newly created camera view.

13. Delete the camera.

14. Activate the Perspective viewport and press **Ctrl+C** to create a camera from the view shown in the Perspective viewport.

Viewport navigation controls

When you create a Camera view, the viewport navigation controls in the bottom-right corner of the screen change to account for the source of the new view. Table 13-1 shows each of the new icons available when a camera view is active. The one icon you will probably want to steer clear of is **Roll Camera,** because it will cause your view to be tilted to one side or the other.

Table 13-1. Viewport navigation controls for the camera views

Icon	Name	Description
	Dolly Camera	Moves the camera along the axis in which the camera is pointing
	Dolly Target	Moves the target along the axis in which the camera is pointing
	Dolly Camera+Target	Moves camera and target along the axis in which the camera is pointing
	Perspective	Moves the camera closer to target, hence changing the FOV
	Roll Camera	Spins the camera along its local Z axis
	Orbit Camera	Rotates the camera around the target
	Pan Camera	Rotates the target around the camera

Some additional notes about the viewport navigation controls are as follows:

- By holding down the mouse scroll button, you can execute the Truck Camera command without having to click the icon.
- By holding down the Shift key, you can constrain camera movement to a single axis.
- By holding down the Ctrl key, you can magnify the effects of the viewport navigation controls.
- By holding down the Alt key, you can achieve finer control when using the viewport navigation tools.

Camera placement

In addition to offering transforms and viewport navigation controls, 3ds Max gives you the opportunity to place cameras precisely using two other helpful features: **Align Camera** and **Place Highlight.**

Align Camera

Not to be confused with the Align command (which can be used at any time to precisely place any object), the Align Camera feature aligns a camera to the normal of a specific face on a specific object. This allows you to precisely position and orient an existing camera so that it is directly in front of and facing a particular object.

To use this feature (shown in the top-left image of Figure 13-2), select a camera, click and hold the **Align** icon in the **Main** toolbar, and select the **Align Camera** icon from the flyout. Click and hold on top of any face inside the active viewport. A blue normal arrow will appear on the face that your mouse is over, as shown in the top-right image. Once you let go, the selected camera will move directly in front of and align itself with the normal of the face you choose, as shown in the bottom-left image. The image on the bottom-right shows the new view from the selected camera.

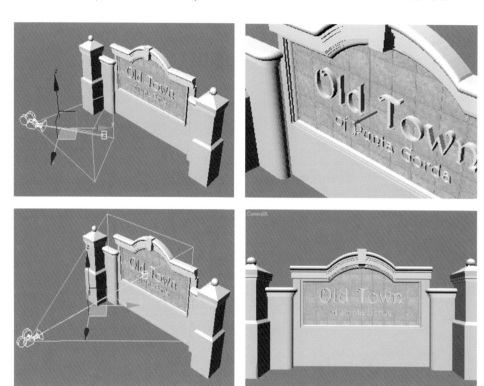

Figure 13-2. The Align Camera feature

Place Highlight

Another tool that you can use to align a camera to a specific face on a specific object is the Place Highlight command. This command works the same way as the Align Camera command, with one minor exception. Rather than showing you just a blue arrow to align the camera with, the Place Highlight command displays the camera in its new position as you move your cursor from one face to another.

The icon for the Place Highlight command is located directly above the **Align Camera** icon within the **Align** flyout icon. To use this command, click the **Place Highlight** icon and click and hold on top of any face inside the active viewport. A blue normal arrow will appear on the face that your mouse is over, and the camera will move into position. If you move the cursor over other faces, the camera will follow along and update its position. To finish the command, release the mouse button and the camera will remain in position, aligned with the normal of the last face your mouse was over.

Positioning cameras

This exercise demonstrates how to use the Align Camera and Place Highlight features to position cameras effectively within your scenes.

1. Reset 3ds Max.

2. Create a sphere of any size within the Perspective viewport.

3. Create a free camera anywhere in your scene.

4. Click and hold the **Align** icon to reveal the flyout icons and click the **Align Camera** icon.

5. Click and hold on top of any face of the sphere inside the active viewport. A blue normal arrow will appear on the face that your mouse is over. Release the mouse button and the camera will move into position.

6. Click and hold the **Align** icon again to reveal the flyout icons, and click the **Place Highlight** icon.

7. Click and hold on top of any face of the sphere inside the active viewport. A blue normal arrow will appear on the face that your mouse is over, and the selected camera will align itself with this normal. Release the mouse button and the camera will move into position.

Basic camera parameters

Cameras contain two unique rollouts: **Parameters** and **Depth of Field Parameters** (shown in Figure 13-3).

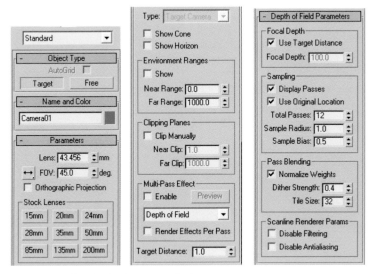

Figure 13-3. The standard camera rollouts

I'll discuss the most important of these features shortly.

Lens length and field of view

The first important parameter in the **Parameters** rollout, **Lens**, is linked directly to the next important parameter found directly below it, **FOV** (field of view). The **Lens** value is the focal length of the camera in millimeters, and controls the FOV seen through the camera. Changing either parameter causes the other parameter to change.

The **Lens** value in 3ds Max corresponds to the same FOV found on a camera in the real world. For example, using a standard 50mm lens will result in a FOV of 39.6 degrees in both 3ds Max and the real world. This and many other standard lens values can be found in the **Stock Lenses** section of this rollout. It is important to note that the typical camera that uses 35mm film does not use a 35mm lens. The typical everyday camera you buy in a store will use 35mm film, but will have a 50mm lens. A lens of 50mm provides the same type of image that your eyes perceive; anything else will distort the image to some degree.

By default, 3ds Max starts the first camera with a FOV of 45, which corresponds to a **Lens** value of 43.456mm. Although this is not a standard lens length, it is close to the standard 50mm and is perfectly suitable for most work. Personally, I use a 50mm or 35mm lens for almost every scene, depending on which one shows or hides the foreground the way I want. Occasionally, when rendering a scene such as a small room in which space is minimal, I use a wider-angle 28mm lens to make the room appear slightly bigger and more spacious. Any lens smaller than 28mm will produce unrealistic and distorted views and should only be used if a specific and necessary effect is desired.

The next options I find particularly useful are the **Show Cone** and **Show Horizon** options. When a camera is selected, light blue lines are displayed emanating from the camera. These lines represent the cone and show the boundaries of the camera's view. When the camera is not selected, the cone disappears unless the **Show Cone** option is enabled. Enabling the **Show Cone** option is particularly useful when using the Top view, moving objects around in a scene, and when you're trying to see when the objects come in and out of the camera's view.

The **Show Horizon** option displays a black line in Camera view to represent the horizon, as shown in Figure 13-4. Knowing where the horizon is when viewing your scene through a camera can be critical in the placement of distant objects. This option also helps you determine how far out you should place your terrain and where it should meet the sky. The closer your artificial horizon is to the true horizon, the more realistic your image will be. The horizon line can also show you if your camera is tilted to one side or another.

Figure 13-4. The Show Horizon option enabled

Using Lens length and FOV settings

This exercise demonstrates some of the important **Lens** length and **FOV** settings.

1. Reset 3ds Max and create a few primitives in the Perspective view.

2. In the Front view, create a free camera.

3. Activate the Left view, and then press **C** to change the view into a Camera view.

4. At the top of the **Parameters** rollout, click and drag on the slider arrows to the right of lens. Notice that the grid inside the Camera view and the cone inside the Perspective view change accordingly.

5. Click some of the various stock lenses to see their corresponding fields of view.

6. Click inside any viewport to deselect the camera. Notice that the camera cone is no longer visible.

7. Select the camera again and enable the **Show Cone** option (located below the **Stock Lenses** section).

8. Click inside any viewport to deselect the camera again. Notice that this time the camera cone is still visible.

9. Select the camera again and enable the **Show Horizon** option (located below the **Show Cone** option). This provides an artificial horizon as a display aid.

Environment ranges

In the next section of the **Parameters** rollout, **Environment Ranges,** you specify the distance from the camera for which environment effects, such as fog, are to be used. More detail regarding environment ranges will be covered in Chapter 18. For now, let's move on to the next set of parameters.

Clipping planes

The next important feature in the **Parameters** rollout is **Clipping Planes.** This feature lets you tell 3ds Max the distance at which you want the camera to begin viewing objects and the distance at which you want it to stop viewing objects. By default, cameras are not set to clip their views. To get a camera to clip its view, you must enable the **Clip Manually** option, as shown in Figure 13-5. With units set to US Standard, the default values for the Near Clip and Far Clip are 1.0" and 83'4" (1,000 units), respectively. This means that nothing within a distance of 1" from the camera will be seen, and likewise, nothing farther away than 83'4" will be seen.

Figure 13-5. The Clipping Planes section, with the Clip Manually option enabled

The Clipping Planes feature comes in handy in a number of situations. One is when you want to show a cut-away section of a building, as the image in Figure 13-6. The top two images show a simple building elevation and floor plan with the camera used to view the elevation. The bottom two images show the same elevation and floor plan with Clipping Planes enabled. In the bottom-right image, the near clip plane cuts through the building and the far clip plane lies on the outside. The result is a building section view, as shown in the bottom-left image.

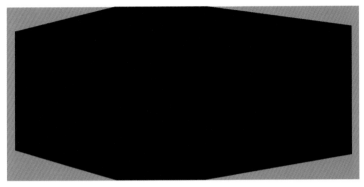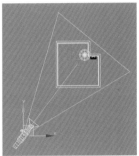

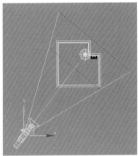

Figure 13-6. The Clipping Planes feature enabled to produce a building section

Another situation in which the Clipping Planes feature is useful is when you want to make an interior scene appear larger than it really is, as shown in Figure 13-7.

In the top-left image, you can see that the camera is placed just inside the walls of the room, and in fact, as close to the walls as possible in this corner of the room. The image on the top-right shows the resulting view from that location.

In the bottom-left image, you can see that the camera is placed outside the room, but with Clipping Planes enabled, you can hide the walls that block the view of the room. Notice that the near clip is placed just inside the walls. The bottom-right image shows the view from outside the room while using the Clipping Planes option. This result is an image that portrays a much more spacious room.

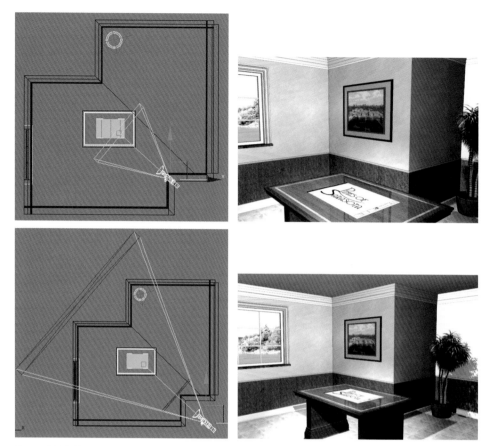

Figure 13-7. Clipping Planes enabled to make a room appear more spacious

Using clipping planes

This exercise demonstrates how to use clipping planes to hide the foreground of your scene. Though simplistic in nature, this same procedure can be used to hide objects that block the camera's view, as in the example in Figure 13-7.

1. Reset 3ds Max.

2. In the Perspective viewport, create a box of any size and click the **Zoom Extents All** icon. The view should look like the left image in the following illustration.

3. Press **Ctrl+C** to create a camera from the Perspective view.

4. Go to the **Modify** panel, and in the **Clipping Planes** section of the **Parameters** rollout, enable the **Clipping Manually** option.

5. To the right of the **Near Clip** value, click, hold, and drag the slider arrows upward until the front of the box is clipped, as shown in the right image of the following illustration.

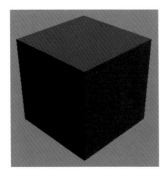 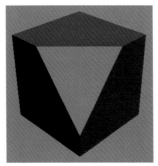

Summary

This chapter has covered the basics of viewport navigation, camera placement, and some of the important camera features found in the rollouts of the **Modify** panel. 3ds Max gives you an enormous amount of tools to control camera behavior—but as you saw in this chapter, a large portion of those tools are either just a different means to the same end, or they don't apply as well to visualizations as they do to other industries. Nevertheless, the features covered in this chapter are critical in everyday work, and along with the features covered in the next two chapters, you'll have many of the important tools needed to control camera behavior for your exact needs.

In Chapter 14, you'll learn the basics of camera animation, and in Chapter 15 you'll learn more advanced ways of controlling cameras through the use of the **Curve Editor** and controllers.

Animation Basics

IF SOMEONE WERE TO ASK me in what field I work, I would say, "3D computer animation." I could rightfully say, "3D computer renderings" or "3D computer stills," but it just wouldn't have the same pizzazz. Likewise, if you show people outside the 3D world your portfolio, they may be quite impressed with great stills, but if you show them quality animation, they will probably be left scratching their heads in amazement. We have reached the point where it is time to breathe life into what has been, until now, stillness.

Animations offer something unique that stills simply can't provide—a true sense of being immersed within a scene. They walk you through a project as if taking your hand and saying, "Look here, see that, watch this."

While an animation can give you much more, the final product comes at a hefty price. With a single still image, touching up blemishes or making enhancements to improve the overall appearance is easy. With an animation, you do not have the same kind of flexibility. Many post-production tools in 3ds Max and third-party programs allow you to improve the final look of an animation; however, the raw animation must have a certain level of quality to make the scene believable and free of glaring defects. In fact, faking 3D is not too difficult for individual objects or even an entire scene when the viewer is limited to a single perspective. However, when you take the viewer for a stroll into, out of, or through a project, it's quite clear just how three-dimensional a scene is. Of course, that clarity creates the problem of rendering up to 30 frames for each second of animation.

This chapter covers the basics of animation as they apply to architectural visualizations. In other industries, such as films and games, animation is an immense subject area that would require extensive coverage of nearly all the 3ds Max features. Fortunately for us, the animation requirements for an architectural visualization are relatively small. You will need to learn how to move cameras throughout your project and animate the elements in your scene that the viewer would expect to see in motion, such as people, cars, and water. But we won't need to cover the intricacies of complicated motion like you would if you were trying to perform character animation. In the next chapter, you will learn how to use the **Curve Editor** to provide greater control of your animated objects. With these two chapters, you will have all of the tools needed to animate an architectural visualization.

Basic animation interfaces

Before we create a simple animation sequence, we should discuss the basic animation interfaces. 3ds Max contains several powerful interfaces that give you more than enough control over your animations. The **Motion** panel and **Curve Editor,** covered in the next chapter, are two powerful interfaces that enable you to perform complex animation. For now, let's stick to those basic animation interfaces, so that we're prepared to dive into a discussion on key framing, which is arguably the most important concept of animation. After covering key framing, we will move on to the next chapter's discussion of the **Curve Editor.**

Time Configuration dialog box

The first and most basic interface that should be mentioned is the **Time Configuration** dialog box, shown in Figure 14-1. This dialog box controls the number of frames in your scene and the rate at which they are played back.

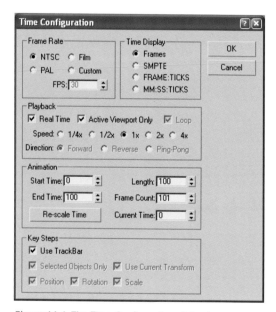

Figure 14-1. The Time Configuration dialog box

The **Frame Rate** section specifies the number of frames played per second for any animation you create. This rate can be designated as **NTSC** (National Television Standards Committee), **PAL** (Phase Alternating Line), or **Film** standard, or you can specify your own frames per second (fps) rate. The standard rate used in visualizations is the NTSC rate of 30 FPS, but if you are short on rendering time, because the project deadline is looming, you can get away with using the standard **Film** rate of 24 fps. This will shave 20% off your rendering time.

The **Time Display** section specifies how time is displayed in the time slider and throughout the other interfaces. I recommend leaving this setting on **Frames** as it provides the simplest and most straightforward display.

The **Playback** section controls only the viewport playback rate. The **Real Time** setting allows you to play back animations at the rate specified in the **Frame Rate** section regardless of your graphics card's limitations. When a scene becomes so large that your graphics card can't refresh the display fast enough to keep up with the animation playback rate, this option allows 3ds Max to skip displaying as many frames as necessary to keep the animation playing smoothly in real time. If you need to see each frame displayed, regardless of how choppy the animation is, disable this option.

The last important section in this dialog box, **Animation,** defines a length of time known as the active time segment. The **active time segment** is the number of frames that are accessible through the time slider. By default, the time slider is set to a length of 100 frames, with the starting frame being 0; however, the time slider may only dictate a small segment of the overall animation in a scene, hence, the term active time segment. You can have 1,000 frames in your animation, but by setting your **Start Time** to **0** and **End Time** to **200,** the active time segment will only be 200 frames. The rest of your animation will still exist but will not be accessible through the time slider.

Each scene may require a unique length, but you shouldn't need to change the start time. Although designating the first frame as 0 may seem strange, remember that frame 0 captures the scene before time starts. Therefore, by the time one second has passed, 31 frames have been played, not 30.

It is important to note that when you want to change the number of frames in your scene, you should always determine whether you need to rescale time. Clicking the **Re-scale Time** button opens the **Re-scale Time** dialog box with which you can change the number of frames and rescale time in the process. Rescaling time is sometimes necessary when your scene contains keyframes, which is a feature in animation that we'll discuss in the next few pages of this chapter. As an introduction to the concepts of keyframes and rescaling time, imagine that you have a 100-frame scene in which to rotate an object 360 degrees. If you change the scene length to 200 frames without rescaling time, the object will still turn during the first 100 frames but stop at frame 100. If you rescale time as you change the number of frames, the object will turn 360 degrees during the entire 200 frames.

Configuring time

This exercise demonstrates how to configure a 3ds Max scene for a certain number of frames and how to change the frame rate, so animations play at a desired speed.

1. Reset 3ds Max.

2. Click the **Time Configuration** icon to the left of the viewport navigation controls.

3. In the **Frame Rate** section, select **Custom** and change the **FPS** (frames per second) to **15,** and press Enter. This changes the playback speed of animations from 30 to 15, which is a typical web video speed.

4. In the **Animation** section, change the **End Time** value to **900,** and click **OK.** This changes the animation length from the default 100 frames to 900 frames, which at 15 fps corresponds to an animation length of 60 seconds.

Now that we have covered the details of time configuration, let's look at the time slider and the animation playback controls.

Time slider

The time slider (Figure 14-2) is a feature positioned immediately below the viewports showing the active time segment, as defined within the **Time Configuration** dialog box.

Figure 14-2. The time slider and track bar

The time slider moves above the track bar from the first frame on the left to the last frame on the right, and displays its current frame location and the total frame count on the slider itself. As just mentioned, you can change the number of frames displayed in the track bar in the **Time Configuration** dialog box.

You can click the arrows to the left and right of the time slider to move forward or back one frame at a time. You can also move the slider to a specific frame by either clicking the empty area to the left or right of the slider arrows at the frame you want to move to or by clicking and dragging the slider to the desired frame.

Animation playback controls

To the immediate left of the viewport navigation controls are the animation playback controls, as shown in Figure 14-3.

The **Play** button, located in the middle of the controls, plays animations at the frame rate specified in the **Time Configuration** dialog box. Clicking again pauses the animation. This button is actually a fly-out, and by holding down the **Play** flyout, you can access the **Play Selected** button, which is a handy feature that plays only those objects currently selected. When you use this feature, selected objects play, and all other objects are hidden from view. This is helpful when you want to focus on select objects or when your scene is so large that the graphics card can't keep up with the frame rate and display all your animated objects in real time.

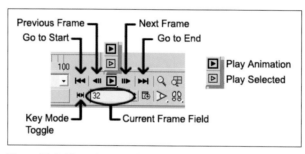

Figure 14-3. The animation playback controls

The arrows in the playback control area also move the time slider forward or back one frame at a time, or to the start or end frame, as shown in Figure 14-3. The greater-than sign (>) and less-than sign (<) keyboard shortcuts are a very handy way to move through time as well. One additional way to move the slider is to type a frame number in the current frame field.

At the bottom left of the time controls is the **Key Mode** toggle, which lets you change the **Next Frame** and **Previous Frame** buttons to the **Next Key** and **Previous Key** buttons. This toggle will be discussed further in the next section.

Keyframing

Before the advent of computers, animations were handdrawn one painstaking frame at a time. Since this was such a laborious process, a firm's junior animators would draw the majority of the individual frames while the senior animators concentrated on certain key frames, hence the term **keyframing.** The senior animator drew frames that showed key changes in action while the junior animator drew all the frames in between.

The process of keyframing is as important today as it has ever been. In computer animation, the animator dictates what a scene looks like at certain key frames, and the program fills in all of the frames in between with the necessary changes. Figure 14-4 shows a candle moving from left to right as it undergoes a massive squash transform during a simple eight-frame sequence. For display purposes, a feature known as ghosting, which will be discussed in the next chapter, is enabled to make the candle's condition at each frame visible. A keyframe is created at frame 0 where the candle is in its normal condition, and a second keyframe is created at frame 7 where the candle is given its new position and the squash transform. Given the candle's condition at frame 0 and frame 7, 3ds Max knows what condition it must be in at each frame in between to provide a smooth and continuous transition.

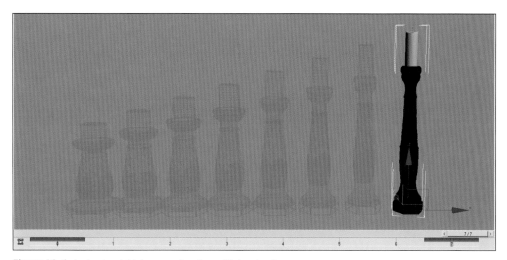

Figure 14-4. A simple eight-frame animation with two keyframes

Creating keyframes

Regardless of the type of action you need to animate in your scene, a keyframe is required at the start and end of the action to record the complete condition of the object at these frames and allow 3ds Max to figure out how to transition the object from one state to the other. There are numerous ways to assign keys in 3ds Max. Regardless of which method you use, keys are assigned to objects at particular frames; they are not assigned to frames, thereby affecting each object in the scene at those frames.

When a key is created at a particular frame, a key indicator will be displayed in the track bar at that frame, as shown in Figure 14-5. This indicator will display one, two, or three different colors for the three transform types depending on which transforms the object has received: red for position, green for rotation, and blue for scale. These color assignments are a great aid when working with keys in the **Curve Editor**, particularly manipulating the individual components of a key, which will be covered in the next chapter. For now, however, let's focus on how to create keys.

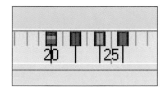

Figure 14-5. A key at frame 20 for all three transforms and keys for each individual transform at frames 22, 24, and 26

3ds Max provides several different methods of creating a keyframe. In each method, the object you want to assign a key to must first be selected.

One way to assign a key is to right-click the time slider, which brings up the **Create Key** dialog box shown in Figure 14-6. The default settings create a key for the position, rotation, and scale states at the current frame. Click **OK** to accept these settings and create a key.

Figure 14-6: The Create Key dialog box

Another way to create a key is to click the **Auto Key** button (which turns red), move the slider to another frame, and transform the object. The **Auto Key** button, shown in Figure 14-7, automatically creates a key at the first frame in the scene and a key at the frame the transform was applied. If another key existed at an earlier frame in the scene before the **Auto Key** was used, a key will only be created where the transform was applied.

 Figure 14-7. Auto and Set Key buttons

Similar to **Auto Key** is the **Set Key** feature which, when clicked, allows you to quickly create a key by clicking the larger button to the left displaying a key. The **Set Key** feature is used in conjunction with the **Set Key Filters**, a tool that determines which tracks will receive a key, while the **Auto Key** feature on the other hand creates a key for only those transforms that are applied. Note that the **Set Key** feature is not recommended unless you have a specific need that it addresses, as it seems to be bug-prone.

Keys can also be created in the **Motion** panel, the **Track View - Curve Editor**, and **Track View - Dope Sheet**, but for now, we will focus on the **Create Key** and **Auto Key** methods. Without understanding key creation using these methods, using the **Motion Panel** and **Track View** will be difficult.

Creating basic motion

Now that we've covered the basic animation interfaces and the concept of keyframing, let's move on to some basic examples of motion. The following example may seem simplistic, but it incorporates a great range of the procedures you will use in your own scenes.

The top image in Figure 14-8 shows a car with a trajectory path that includes two turns during a short 30-frame sequence. In the top image, the car starts at point A, makes a turn at points B and C, and comes to a stop at point D. How do you get an object to make such movements? As our previous discussion shows, keyframes need to be assigned to an object whenever you want the object to make an animated change in condition, whether that change is in trajectory, size, or shape.

The car has been assigned a key at frame 0 (point A), 10 (point B), 20 (point C), and at its final position at frame 30 (point D). If a key is created at frames 0 and 30 only, as shown in the bottom image, the car moves only in a straight line from point A to point D. Likewise, if you delete the keys at points B and C, the trajectory would change from the one shown in the top image to the one shown in the bottom. Now let's re-create this motion in a short tutorial.

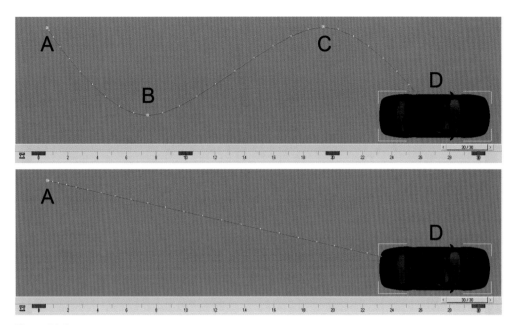

Figure 14-8. Changing the trajectory of a car

Creating basic motion

This exercise demonstrates how to create the motion shown in the top image of Figure 14-8, in which the car makes two distinct turns between its start and end points.

1. Reset 3ds Max.

2. Click the **Time Configuration** icon to the left of the viewport navigation controls. The **Time Configuration** dialog box opens.

3. In the **Animation** section, change the **End Time** to **30,** and click **OK** to close the dialog box. There is no need to rescale time, because there are no keys yet.

4. Make the Top viewport active, and click the **Maximize Viewport** toggle to maximize.

5. Create a teapot of any size, zoom away and pan the view to position the teapot at the left end of the screen, as shown by point A in Figure 14-8.

6. Right-click in the Top viewport and select **Properties** from the quad menus.

7. In the **Display Properties** section, enable the **Trajectory** option, and click **OK** to close the dialog box.

8. Click the **Auto Key** button. The button turns red.

9. Move the time slider to frame **10**.

10. Move the teapot to the right, one-third across the screen and slightly down. If necessary, pan and zoom to make room on the screen. This creates a key at frame 0 and another key at frame 10.

11. Move the time slider to frame **20**.

12. Move the teapot farther to the right the same distance as in the first move and move it slightly up. This creates a key at frame 20.

13. Move the time slider to frame **30**.

14. Move the teapot once more to the right the same distance as in the first two moves and move it slightly down. This creates a key at frame 30. The trajectory should look similar to that shown in the top image of Figure 14-8.

15. Click the **Play** button. The teapot should move swiftly along the trajectory path.

16. Right-click the red key shown directly above frame 10.

17. Move the cursor over the **Delete Key** flyout and select **All** from the list. The key at frame 10 is deleted, and the trajectory of the teapot changes drastically.

18. Click the **Undo** icon to restore the key at frame 10.

19. Save this scene. It will be used in the next chapter.

Summary

This chapter covered three of the most basic animation interfaces in 3ds Max: the **Time Configuration** dialog box, the time slider, and the animation playback controls. The principles of keyframing were also discussed to show how to change the action of an object. Having completed this last tutorial, you should now have a good foundation in the basic concepts of animation.

In the next chapter, we will further analyze the animation of the teapot and use this example to illustrate the concepts of controllers and constraints. We will also cover the use of the **Motion** panel and the **Curve Editor,** the two main interfaces with which to work with constraints and controllers. After this next chapter, you will know everything needed to perform almost any type of animation in an architectural visualization.

CHAPTER 15

Animation Controllers

3DS MAX GIVES YOU THE ability to create animations by making transforms and other changes to objects manually and using keyframes to record the changes. Not having to make changes to objects for every single frame of animation certainly makes life as an animator much easier than it used to be in the days when each frame was hand drawn. But 3ds Max contains far more power than we explored in the last chapter. One of the main concepts we covered, keyframing, is arguably the most important feature of computer animation; however, using features known as controllers and constraints in conjunction with your keyframes makes your potential as an animator almost limitless.

Controllers allow you to dictate long periods of complex and detailed action with just a few clicks of the mouse. For example, with controllers you can make a camera follow a long and complicated spline that represents the path of motion through a building, and specify with precise detail how the camera behaves at each step along the way. You can make a car follow the contour of a mountain road, slowing down the car during the turns and speeding it up during the straight sections of the road.

Numerous interfaces allow you to assign and edit controllers, but two interfaces stand out as the primary tools for working with controllers: the **Motion** panel and the **Curve Editor**. In this chapter, we will cover both of these and see just how easy it can be to work with controllers. After completing this chapter, you will have a great foundation for computer animation with 3ds Max.

Controllers

All animation in 3ds Max is dictated by special algorithms known as **controllers.** As the animator, obviously you dictate where an object goes and its condition at each keyframe. However, 3ds Max assigns default controllers to dictate how an object behaves between keyframes, at least until you make changes.

In the example used in the last tutorial of the previous chapter, a car moved from point A, to point B, to point C, and finally to point D, as shown in the top image of Figure 15-1. Notice that there are pronounced curves through points B and C, making the car's movements smooth as it moves from one point to another. These curves were created automatically as the default means of inter-polating the car from one keyframe to another. The curves were created by a type of controller known as the **Bezier control,** perhaps the most versatile controller available in 3ds Max.

But what if you want the car to move in a straight line from one point to another, without the curves, as shown in the bottom image of Figure 15-1? All you have to do is change the type of con-troller assigned to the car from **Bezier** to **Linear.** The way to do this will be discussed later in this chapter during the introduction to the **Motion** panel.

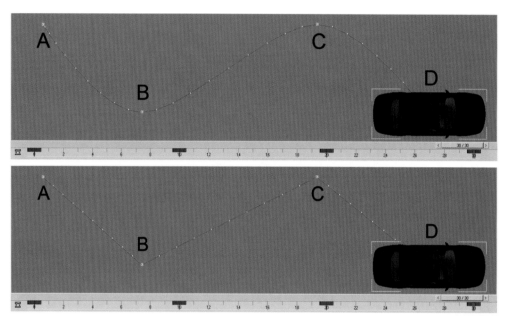

Figure 15-1. Animation using the Bezier controller (top) and Linear controller (bottom)

There are a few dozen different types of controllers that let you control your animations in just about any way imaginable. As an example, with the **Motion Capture Controller** you can use an external device such as a mouse to capture the motion you want a car to follow. Using the **Audio Controller,** you can use the amplitude from a music file to dictate how you want a radio to vibrate from the heavy bass coming from its speakers. You can assign random motion to the waves of water using the **Noise Controller.** The possibilities are as limitless as your imagination, and to completely cover every different type of controller and all of their possible uses would take volumes. But once again, in the world of architectural visualizations, it's not necessary to learn every possible feature. We are going to focus on a few key controllers that will give you the power to create great animations and the knowledge to experiment with the many other controllers.

Constraints

A **constraint** in 3ds Max is a type of controller tool that helps you automate action. Constraints are used to control one object's transformations through the use of another object. In the case of a car driving along a mountain road, the car is constrained by another object—the road. In the case of a camera walk-through, the camera is constrained to a specific path defined by a spline.

There are seven types of constraints in Max.

- The **Path Constraint** constrains the movement of an object to a path.
- The **Surface Constraint** constrains the movement of an object to the surface of another object.
- The **Position Constraint** constrains the movement of an object to the movement of another object.
- The **Attachment Constraint** constrains the movement of an object to the faces on another object.
- The **LookAt Constraint** constrains the orientation of an object, so that it always looks at another object.
- The **Orientation Constraint** constrains the rotation of an object so that it follows the rotation of another object.
- The **Link Constraint** constrains an object so that it's linked from one object to another.

Each of these seven constraints performs a unique function; together they give you the ability to constrain an object in just about any way you can imagine. Again, in the world of architectural visualizations, we need to focus on only a couple of these constraints. Although you may find an occasional use for each of the available seven, the two constraints that we are going to cover are the **Path** and **Surface Constraints.**

You can use two main methods to assign a constraint to an object. You can access constraints through the **Animation** menu, as shown in Figure 15-2, or through the **Motion** panel. In either case, constraints are only available when the object you want to constrain is selected. To assign a constraint through the **Animation** menu, select the object you want to constrain, select the type of constraint to use, and click on another object to which you want to constrain the first object.

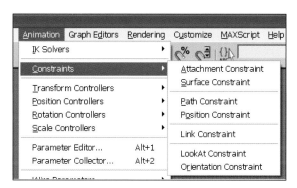

Figure 15-2. Assigning constraints through the Animation menu

Assigning a constraint through the Animation menu

This exercise demonstrates how to assign a path constraint using the **Animation** menu.

1. Reset 3ds Max.
2. In the Top viewport create a rectangle of any size, and inside the rectangle create a small teapot that is about one-quarter of the rectangle's size, as shown in the left image of the following illustration.

3. With the teapot selected, click the **Animation** menu, and select **Constraints ➤ Path Constraint**.

4. Click the rectangle in any viewport. Notice that the teapot is moved to one corner of the rectangle.

5. Click the **Play** button. The teapot moves around the rectangle during the course of the active time segment, as shown in the right image.

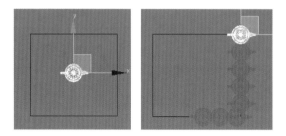

Motion panel

Now that controllers and constraints have been introduced, let's discuss one of the key interfaces used in conjunction with controllers and constraints—the **Motion** panel. The **Motion** panel, shown in Figure 15-3, is not only an interface through which you can assign controllers or constraints, it allows you to edit or manipulate those assignments, as well as create and edit keys.

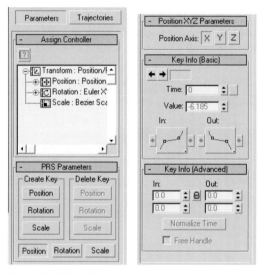

Figure 15-3. The Motion panel

The **Motion** panel is made up of two main areas: **Parameters** and **Trajectories.** The **Parameters** area lets you assign and edit controllers for the three transform types: position, rotation, and scale. Within this area you can also create, edit, and delete keys. In the **Trajectories** area, you can view and edit an object's trajectory. Both areas are invaluable in the controlling of animated objects.

Parameters

While the Parameters area of the Motion panel may look somewhat complicated and intimidating, it is really quite simple and not very large. The Motion panel interface itself is very straightforward, although some of the controllers and constraints that you can access through the Motion panel can be quite challenging to learn and use.

The first two rollouts, **Assign Controller** and **PRS Parameters,** are standard rollouts that appear for all controllers, while the additional rollouts change, depending on which controllers are assigned to an object.

Assign Controller rollout

As its name implies, the first rollout of the **Parameters** area, **Assign Controller,** allows you to assign or change controllers for an object. All objects are assigned default controllers upon their creation, but until an object is animated, the controllers are not activated and serve no purpose. The type of controller assigned depends on the type of transform or parameter that's being animated.

The **Motion** panel allows you to assign and edit controllers for transforms only. Later in the chapter, we'll discuss the **Curve Editor,** which gives the ability to assign or edit controllers for any object track type.

As Figure 15-4 shows, the default controllers assigned to position, rotation, and scale are **Position XYZ, Euler XYZ,** and **Bezier Scale,** respectively.

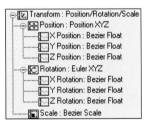

Figure 15-4. The Transform controllers

The **Position XYZ** and **Euler XYZ** controllers are both controllers that break down the X, Y, and Z components of an object's animation into three separate tracks: one each for X, Y, and Z. This compartmentalization allows each component to receive its own individual controller. By default, 3ds Max assigns the **Position XYZ** controller to each object's position transform track and the **Euler XYZ** controller for each object's rotation track. The **Bezier** Scale controller is assigned to the **Scale** transform.

So what does all of this mean? As I mentioned at the beginning of the discussion on controllers, the Bezier controller is perhaps the most versatile controller available in 3ds Max. It is also the default controller for many parameters, because 3ds Max assumes that whenever you want action, you want it to be smooth, rather than rough and abrupt. The Bezier controller provides a smooth interpolation between keyframes, so an object's animation is smooth. For example, if you animate a car leaving a four-way intersection from a complete stop, you shouldn't make the car instantly start moving at high speed in the first frame after it starts its movement. The car should gradually accelerate to its cruising speed. Likewise, when the car is coming to a four-way intersection, you should not take the car from its cruising speed to a complete stop in one frame. That would look unrealistic. If you want to animate a tree blowing in the wind, the tree's limbs should move smoothly back and forth, accelerating and decelerating with every movement. It would look unrealistic for a tree branch to be moving swiftly in one direction and in just one frame change direction and move swiftly in the opposite direction.

If, for some reason, you decide that you do want your car to go from 0 to 60 in one frame, you only need to assign a different controller—in this case the **Linear** controller, which provides linear (constant and straight) animation from one keyframe to another.

With that said, let's discuss how to assign or change a controller.

Assigning and changing controllers

To assign or change a controller, select an object, go to the Motion panel and open the Assign Controller rollout. In the Assign Controller window, highlight one of the three transforms types or one of the individual XYZ tracks within a transform. When you make a selection, the Assign Controller icon (shown to the right) becomes selectable. Click the Assign Controller icon, select a controller type from the menu that appears and click OK to complete the command. This will assign a new controller to the selected transform type or to the individual track you selected within the transform. You can highlight multiple XYZ tracks within a transform that has separate track assignments.

Changing controllers

This exercise demonstrates how to assign a new controller to an object.

1. Open the scene created in the last tutorial of Chapter 14, or open the file named **Ch15-01.max** from the **3dsMax2008\Scenes\3DATS** folder.

2. Select the teapot object.

3. Click the **Motion** panel tab.

4. Open the **Assign Controller** rollout.

5. In the **Assign Controller** window, highlight the **Position** transform, as shown in the left image of the illustration following step 7.

6. Click the **Assign Controller** icon.

7. Select **Linear Position** from the **Assign Controller** menu, as shown in the right image of the following illustration. Click **OK** to close.

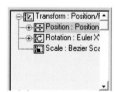

The teapot's X, Y, and Z movements are now controlled by the **Linear Position** controller, which causes the teapot to move in a straight line from one point to another, as shown in the following illustration. Notice also that the keyframe points indicated by the white dots along the trajectory are all evenly spaced. When the **Bezier Position** controller was assigned to the individual tracks of the **Position** controller, the keyframe points were not evenly spaced.

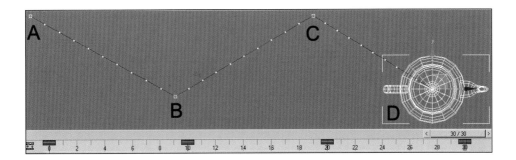

PRS Parameters rollout

The **PRS** (position, rotation, scale) **Parameters** rollout, shown in Figure 15-5, allows you to create or delete position, rotation, and scale keys without having to use the **Set Key** or **Auto Key** features. You can create or delete a key for only one of the three transforms at a time, depending on which transform button you click. The **Position, Rotation,** and **Scale** buttons across the bottom of the rollout determine which transform has its contents displayed in the **Key Info** rollout. To edit the rotation keys for an object, for example, click the **Rotation** button.

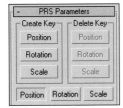

Figure 15-5. The PRS Parameters rollout

Position XYZ Parameters rollout

The **Position XYZ Parameters** rollout (Figure 15-6) appears by default when the **Position** button is highlighted in the **PRS Parameters** rollout, as shown in Figure 15-5, because the **Position XYZ** controller is the default controller assigned to an object's position transform when it is created. If the controller changes, this rollout will no longer be shown. Likewise, if you click the **Rotation** or **Scale** buttons in the **PRS Parameters** rollout, the **Position XYZ Parameters** rollout will disappear.

Figure 15-6. The Position XYZ Parameters rollout

Euler Parameters rollout

The **Euler Parameters** rollout, shown in Figure 15-7, appears by default when the **Rotation** button is highlighted in the **PRS Parameters** rollout, because the Euler controller is the default controller assigned to an object's rotation transform when it is first created. If you change controllers for the rotation transform, the **Euler Parameters** rollout will no longer be displayed.

Figure 15-7. The Euler Parameters rollout

Key Info (Basic) rollout

Each key stores information for each of the three axes, X, Y, and Z. When the **Position XYZ** or Euler controllers are being used, the **Key Info (Basic)** rollout, shown in Figure 15-8, will display information for only one key at a time and one axis at a time, depending on which **axis** is highlighted in the **Position XYZ** or **Euler Parameters** rollouts.

Figure 15-8. The Key Info (Basic) rollout for the Position XYZ and Euler controllers

As mentioned earlier, the **Bezier Float** controller is used by the individual tracks of the Position XYZ and Euler controllers. If the Bezier controller is assigned to an entire transform, rather than just the X, Y, or Z tracks of a transform, the **Key Info (Basic)** rollout changes to display X, Y, and Z parameters, as shown in Figure 15-9. Notice that the entire rollout is inaccessible until a key is created and the current frame is positioned on a keyframe.

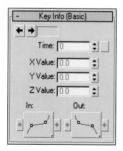

Figure 15-9. The Key Info (Basic) rollout for the Bezier controller

Once a key is created and the time slider is positioned on a key, the **Key Info (Basic)** rollout allows you to change several things related to the key.

The arrows at the top of the rollout allow you to quickly move from one keyframe to another, as long as more than one keyframe exists.

The **Time** field changes the time, or frame, at which the key is positioned. Since only one of the transforms is edited at a time, using this parameter moves only one transform key.

The **X, Y,** and **Z** values control the actual value of each of the X, Y, and Z components of an object's position, rotation, or scale, depending on which transform is being edited. For example, if a teapot is positioned at the world origin and the **Position** button is selected in the **PRS Parameters** rollout, the

X, Y, and **Z** values will display a value of **0.** If the teapot is moved to the coordinates 10, 5, 20, then the **X, Y,** and **Z** values will display values of **10, 5,** and **20,** respectively. Likewise, you can move the teapot along a particular axis by typing in the new position values directly into the fields or by using the slider arrows to the right of the fields.

The **In** and **Out** buttons, known as the **Key Tangent** flyouts, control the interpolation methods used by the selected key. Going back to the example discussed earlier in the chapter where a car accelerates or decelerates, the **In** and **Out** tangents control exactly how, or even if, that car accelerates or decelerates. If you click and hold either tangent flyout, a series of additional interpolation tangents is displayed, as shown in Figure 15-10. Selecting a different tangent changes the interpolation method and how the car moves from one keyframe to another. The next tutorial demonstrates the effect of some of the available interpolation methods.

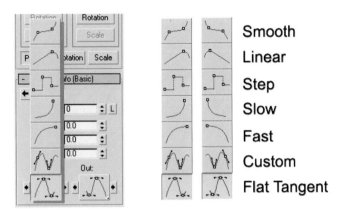

Figure 15-10. The standard interpolation methods for keys

Working with keys in the Motion panel

This exercise demonstrates how to create and edit keys in the **Motion** panel. To demonstrate these features, we will race three teapots to see how changing their assigned keys determines which teapot wins the race.

1. Reset 3ds Max.

2. In the far left side of the Top viewport, create a teapot of any size. Pan and zoom as necessary, so that the teapot takes up approximately one-fifth of the viewport's width.

3. Click the **Auto Key** button, move the time slider to frame **100,** and move the teapot to the far right side of the Top viewport.

4. Click the **Auto Key** button again to close the feature.

5. Move the time slider back to frame **0.**

6. Make two clones of the teapot using the **Copy** feature (not **Instance** or **Reference),** and position the three teapots side by side on the left-hand side of the Top viewport, as shown in the following illustration.

7. Click the **Play** button. Notice that each teapot finishes at the same time, because their motion is dictated by the same controllers and the same keys.

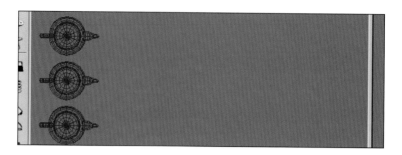

8. Click the **Stop** button.

9. Move the time slider back to frame **0.**

10. Click the middle teapot, and click the **Motion** panel tab.

11. Click and hold the **Out** tangent button and select the **Fast** tangent, as shown in the following illustration. The tangent buttons are only selectable on when the time slider is on a keyframe. Therefore make sure that you moved the time slider back to frame **0** (step 9).

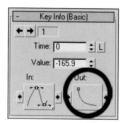

12. Click the **Play** button again. Now the middle teapot gets *out* to a *fast* start and takes a considerable early lead, as shown in the following illustration, but the other two teapots catch up with it at the finish. Notice the use of the words "out" and "fast" in the previous sentence. The teapot starts out quickly, because the **Out** tangent key at frame **0** was changed from **Flat** to **Fast**. Changing the **In** tangent at frame **0** would have no effect, because there is no frame before frame 0 and thus no way for the key to affect the speed that the teapot comes **in** to the keyframe. Also, notice the downward curve of the **Fast** icon. If you were to roll a ball down a hill shaped like this, the ball would start out rapidly but gradually slow down after coming out of the curve.

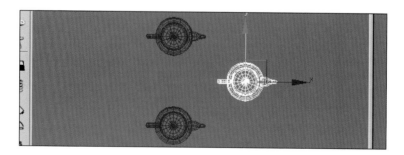

13. Click the **Stop** button and move the time slider to frame **100.**

14. Click the bottom teapot.

15. In the **Motion** panel, click and hold the **In** tangent button, and select the **Fast** tangent again as shown in the following illustration. The Fast tangent here is a mirrored version of the tangent you applied in step 11.

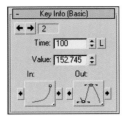

16. Click the **Play** button again. Notice now that the bottom teapot starts slowly, but comes *in* (to the finish) very rapidly and by frame **100** catches up with the other two teapots.

17. Click the **Stop** button and move the time slider to frame **0.**

18. Click the top teapot.

19. Click and hold the **Out** tangent button, and select the **Linear** tangent, as shown in the following illustration.

20. Click the **Play** button. Notice the constant speed of the top teapot throughout the entire **100** frames. You changed the **Out** tangent to linear so the teapot's speed was linear, or constant, during the first half of the animation. But how do you make one teapot finish before the others? Simple.

21. Click the **Stop** button.

22. Click the middle teapot.

23. Click and drag the key at frame **100** to frame **80,** as shown in the following illustration. When you click a key, it turns white.

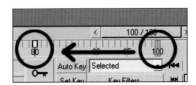

24. Click the **Play** button. Now the middle teapot gets to the finish line at frame **80** instead of frame **100,** clearly beating the competition.

Trajectories

The **Trajectories** area of the **Motion** panel, shown in the left image of Figure 15-11, displays an object's trajectory (path of travel) and allows you to edit the trajectory wherever keys exist. When you click the **Trajectories** button, the trajectory of the selected object appears as a red line with small squares at keyframe locations and small dots at every frame location, as shown in the image on the right.

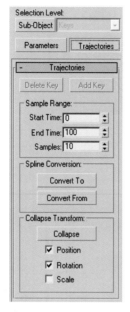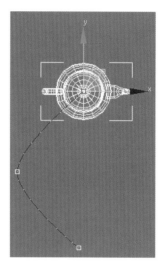

Figure 15-11. The Trajectories area of the Motion panel

To change the trajectory of an object that's already animated, select the object and click the **Trajectories** button. Then click the **Sub-Object** button above the **Trajectories** button, and, in any viewport, click one of the white squares and move it to a new location.

When the trajectory of an object is visible, you can add keys to any point on the trajectory by simply clicking the **Add Key** button at the top of the **Trajectories** rollout and clicking the trajectory at the point you want to add a key. Once a key is added, you can move it around as you like. You can just as easily delete a key by selecting it in a viewport and clicking the **Delete Key** button.

In the **Spline Conversion** section of the rollout you can create a spline from the trajectory of your object. Simply select your animated object, and click the **Convert To** button. When you do, a spline will appear that duplicates your object's trajectory. Conversely, you can quickly animate an object and assign a trajectory to it by selecting the object, clicking the **Convert From** button, and clicking the spline that you want the trajectory to simulate.

Curve Editor

The **Curve Editor,** shown in Figure 15-12, is a scene management tool that gives you great control over the creation and editing of keyframes. It uses curves on a graph to express animation, thereby allowing you to visualize the interpolation of your animations. With the **Curve Editor** you can assign controllers to your keys and manage animated parameters of an object, among numerous other things. This book introduces some of the best features the **Curve Editor** has to offer and shows you where further experimentation and exploration can take you.

The **Curve Editor** is one of two modes that make up a feature known as **Track View.** The other mode, the **Dope Sheet,** displays keyframes on a graph in a spreadsheet-like format, but is not covered in this book.

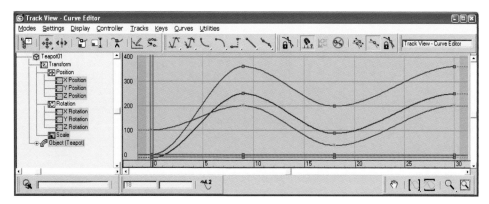

Figure 15-12. The Curve Editor

The **Curve Editor** is an extremely useful tool in editing animation. Although there are far too many features to cover in this chapter, one feature stands out for users in the architectural visualization industry—editing controllers. Although you can edit controllers in numerous other interfaces, such as the **Motion** panel or through the **Track Bar,** the **Curve Editor** gives you far more power and versatility to perform the editing and allows you to visualize the changes through the use of graphical displays. Earlier in the chapter we discussed the various interpolation methods used for keys, such as **Linear, Fast,** and **Smooth,** as shown in Figure 15-10. With the **Curve Editor,** these interpolation methods are graphically represented and can be easily edited to suit your needs.

The **Curve Editor** interface consists of a menu bar and toolbar across the top, a Controller window on the left that displays all scene objects and elements, and a Key window on the right that displays an object's animation graphically. Whenever you create an object, a material, a light, or any other type of scene element, it appears in the Controller window on the left, along with the parameters of the element. Whenever you select one or more objects in your scene, all keyframes for the selected objects are displayed in the Key window on the right.

To see these interfaces in action, let's complete two tutorials: one for editing controllers and one for editing animated parameters. After completing these tutorials, you should have a good understanding of the power of the **Curve Editor** and the skills for its basic use.

Editing controllers with the Curve Editor

This exercise demonstrates how to perform basic editing of controllers with the **Curve Editor.**

1. Reset 3ds Max.

2. Right-click inside the active viewport, select **Curve Editor** from the quad menu, and move the **Curve Editor** so that the Top viewport is completely visible.

3. Place the cursor over the open area of the controller window until the cursor changes into a hand symbol, as shown in the following illustration. Click and drag in the controller window, so that you can see word **Objects** in the bottom of the controller window. There are presently no objects in your scene, so no objects are displayed here.

4. In the far left side of the Top viewport, create a teapot of any size. Pan and zoom as necessary, so that the teapot takes up approximately one-fifth of the viewport's width. Notice that the teapot now appears under the **Objects** group in the controller window.

5. Pan up or down inside the controller window, so that you can see the X, Y, and Z position components of the teapot, as shown in the following illustration.

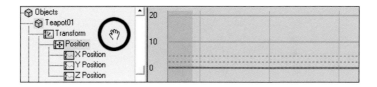

6. Click the **Auto Key** button and move the time slider to frame **100**.

7. On the main toolbar click **Select** and **Move,** then place the cursor over the X axis of the transform gizmo and drag the teapot to the far right side of the Top viewport along the X axis only. Notice that the X, Y, and Z components of the teapot's position transform are highlighted in the Controller window. Notice also that the teapot's position interpolation is now depicted graphically in the Key window, as shown in the following illustration.

8. Click the **Auto Key** button again to close the feature.

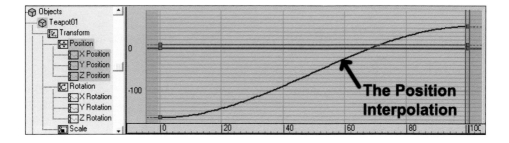

9. Click the **Play** button. Notice that the teapot starts off slowly, gradually accelerates to a cruising speed, and decelerates as it comes to frame **100**. Click the **Stop** button.

10. Right-click on top of the first key for the position interpolation, represented by a small gray square, as shown in the following illustration. This opens the Key Controller dialog box.

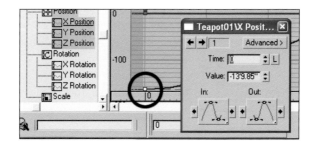

11. Click and hold the **In** tangent button and select the Linear tangent (second from top, showing the straight-line segment as in the following illustration). Notice that the interpolation curve did not change at all, because, as mentioned earlier, the **In** tangent only affects the frame coming into keyframe, and there are no frames before this first key.

12. Click and hold the **Out** tangent button and select the **Linear** tangent. Notice now that the left-hand side of the interpolation curve changes to a straight line, as shown in the following image.

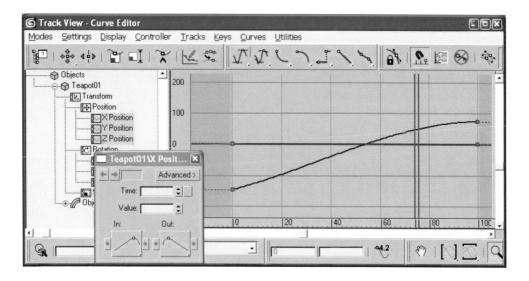

13. Right-click the last key, click and hold the **In** tangent button, and select the **Linear** tangent. Notice that the right-hand side of the interpolation curve changes to a straight line.

14. Click the **Play** button, and notice that the teapot moves at a constant, or linear, speed during the entire 100 frames. Click the **Stop** button.

15. Click the **Add Keys** button in the toolbar, as shown in the following image. This changes Move Key mode to Add Key mode.

16. Click near the middle of the position interpolation to create a key, as shown in the following illustration. This creates a key with the default **Flat** tangent. Also notice just to the right of the arrows in the top left corner of the Key Controller dialog box that this key becomes key **2**. The key that used to be key **2** is now key **3**.

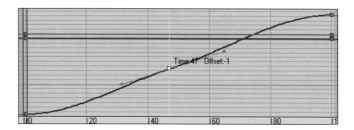

17. In the **Time** field of the Key Controller dialog box, type **50,** as shown in the following illustration. This moves the key to frame **50.**

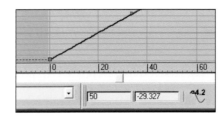

18. The Key window of the **Curve Editor** contains two vertical blue lines that represent the frame the time slider is on. Carefully place the cursor over these lines until left and right arrows appear. Click and drag the two lines so that they surround the key that you just created, as shown in the following illustration.

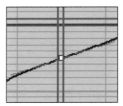

19. Right-click on top of the key you just moved to frame **50** (currently surrounded by the two vertical blue lines). This opens the Key Controller dialog box.

20. Move the Key Controller dialog box off to the side, so that you can see the key you created.

21. In the Key Controller dialog box, shown in the following image on the left, click and drag down the slider arrows to the right of the **Value** field until the interpolation is similar to the image on the right. This value represents the teapot's location along the X axis.

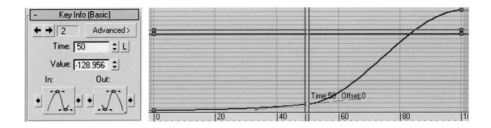

22. Click the **Play** button and let the animation play several times. Notice that the teapot starts off slowly but accelerates quickly near frame **50.** Click the **Stop** button.

23. Click and hold the **Move Keys** flyout in the **Curve Editor** toolbar and select the **Move Keys Vertical** icon, as shown in the following illustration.

24. Click and drag key **2** back to its original position, like the one shown in the following illustration. The **Move Keys Vertical** was used, so that the key only moves vertically and stays at frame **50**.

25. Click the **Display** menu at the top of the **Curve Editor** and select **All Tangents**. This turns on the tangent grips for all keys, rather than just the selected key.

26. Click either tangent grip (the light blue square) of key 2 and drag the grip, so that the interpolation looks like that shown in the following illustration.

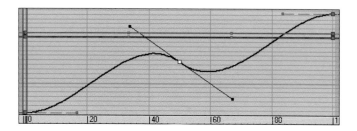

27. Click the **Play** button. Notice that the teapot moves from left to right, but near the middle of the sequence it reverses direction back to the left, and then reverses direction a second time back to the right. This is because we changed the teapot's **X Position** interpolation curve. The X value of the teapot's position goes up initially (which makes the teapot move to the right), and then goes down near frame **40** (which makes the teapot move back to the left).

28. With key **2** selected, click each of the standard interpolation tangent buttons in the **Curve Editor** toolbar shown in the following image. This illustrates the effect of each tangent on the graphical representation of the teapot's interpolation.

This exercise demonstrated how to animate controllers for an object's position, but the procedures are identical for animating other controllers, such as those for an object's parameters. To animate the radius of a primitive, for example, locate the word **Radius** in the Controller window of the **Curve Editor** and you will be able to edit the animation of the object's radius.

Summary

This chapter revealed some of the power and versatility of controllers in 3ds Max. Through the use of the **Motion** panel and the **Curve Editor**, you learned how to assign and edit controllers in order to dictate precisely how your animations should take place. With just a few clicks of the mouse, you can assign complex action to an object and edit that action at any point along the sequence.

Compared to other industries, the number and type of animated objects in an architectural scene is relatively small, but, for objects that do require animation in our line of work (such as cameras), getting the animation right is just as important as it is in other industries. Knowing how to work with controllers is critical to great animation.

PART 6

Rendering

Someday, we may no longer have to be concerned with issues such as file sizes or face counts, but for the foreseeable future we should always try to use the tools available to allow for efficient work and prevent wasted time. I suspect that no matter how fast computers become, software developers will always fill your plates with more and more processor-hungry and memory-consuming programs and resources.

CHAPTER 16

Rendering Basics

THE WORD "RENDER" MEANS, AMONG other things, to cause to be or become. In 3ds Max, **rendering** is the process by which you create an image from the components of your scene. 3ds Max uses a program feature known as a **render engine** or **renderer** to perform the rendering process. 3ds Max ships with two unique render engines, although additional third-party renderers can be used. These are the default scanline renderer and the mental ray renderer.

The default scanline renderer provides a good mix of quality, speed, flexibility, and ease of use. The mental ray renderer, the other rendering option, offers the capability of producing higher-quality renderings with advanced lighting features. The mental ray renderer, however, is more difficult to use than the scanline renderer and can significantly increase render times. Although mental ray is used as the main rendering engine by a large percentage of veteran 3ds Max users, it is an advanced feature and therefore not covered in this book. This chapter focuses on the default scanline renderer and the critical settings that users in the visualization industry should be familiar with. The heart of the rendering process is the **Render Scene** dialog box—where most of the critical rendering settings lie.

In addition to the **Render Scene** dialog, this chapter also covers some great tools that can be a tremendous benefit to you during the rendering process. The RAM Player gives you the ability to load raw images into memory for playback at various rates, the **Print Size Wizard** helps you plan the rendering dimensions of a particular print size, and the Panorama Exporter lets you create and view 360-degree spherical panoramas.

The Render Scene dialog box

The **Render Scene** dialog box can be accessed by clicking the **Render Scene** icon on the **Main** toolbar, by using the **Rendering** menu, or by pressing F10. It contains five tabs when the default scanline renderer is used, as shown in Figure 16-1. The **Common** tab contains commands that are common to all renderers, while the **Renderer** tab contains commands that are specific to the selected renderer. The **Render Elements** tab contains features that allow you to render select elements of your scene, such as atmospheric effects, shadows, and alpha channels. The **Raytracer** tab controls advanced

1

settings for raytracing, and the **Advanced Lighting** tab contains settings that control radiosity and other advanced lighting features, including Light Tracer. The **Render Elements, Raytracer,** and **Advanced Lighting** tabs are all advanced areas of 3ds Max, and with the exception of Advanced Lighting, are not covered in this book.

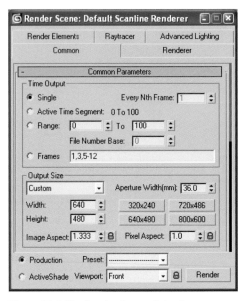

Figure 16-1. The Render Scene dialog box

Two buttons can initiate the rendering process. One is the **Render** button located at the bottom of the **Render Scene** dialog box, and the other is the **Quick Render** button located on the **Main** toolbar. The **Quick Render** button initiates the rendering process using the settings from the **Render Scene** dialog box, regardless of whether or not the dialog box is open.

The **Render** button in the **Render Scene** dialog box is visible at the bottom of the dialog box regardless of which tab is active. To the left of the **Render** button are some other handy features that are also always visible.

By default, all renders are set to **Production,** as shown in the bottom left corner of Figure 16-1. This means that your rendered images will be created in the best way possible, or as good as your work allows. The other option you can choose is **ActiveShade,** which gives you a preview of your rendering that shows you the effects of changing lighting or materials in your scene. If you change the lights or materials in your scene, the **ActiveShade** window automatically updates the rendering. This can be very useful and time-saving for large scenes that take a long time to render. You can also load a view-port with an **ActiveShade** display by right-clicking the viewport name and selecting **Views ➤ ActiveShade** from the drop-down list.

When you right-click an **ActiveShade** render window or viewport, a quad menu appears with various options, as shown in Figure 16-2. You can close the **ActiveShade** window or viewport by selecting **Close.** Several other options are available, and I invite you to explore them more if you find that the **ActiveShade** feature may benefit your work.

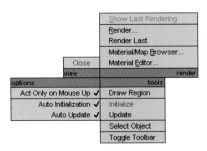

Figure 16-2. The ActiveShade quad menu

Another important feature at the bottom of the **Render Scene** dialog box is the **Lock View** feature. Few things in 3ds Max can be as frustrating as setting a time-consuming rendering in motion and leaving, only to come back and find that you've rendered the wrong viewport. You can render the wrong viewport by inadvertently activating a different viewport or by intentionally working in a different viewport and forgetting to reactivate the correct one when it's time to render. The active viewport displayed in the viewport drop-down list will always be the viewport that's rendered. To render the same viewport every time, regardless of which viewport is active, select the **Lock View** option.

Another feature at the bottom of the **Render Scene** dialog box is the **Preset** drop-down list. This feature lets you save several settings in numerous different categories, as shown in Figure 16-3. Saving these settings can be extremely handy and time-saving when you want to reuse settings that you've spent a great deal of time setting up. I find this feature particularly useful in saving and loading environment and render effects.

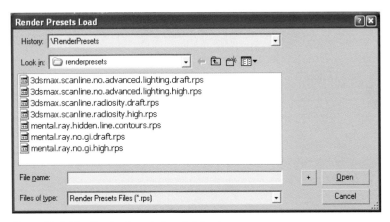

Figure 16-3. The Render Presets Load dialog box

The Common tab

The **Common** tab of the **Render Scene** dialog box, shown in Figure 16-4, contains three rollouts common to all render engines: **Common Parameters, Email Notifications,** and **Assign Renderer**. The **Assign Renderer** rollout is where you change the render engine type from the default scanline to any other type, such as mental ray or a third-party render engine.

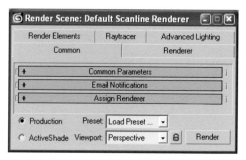

Figure 16-4. The three rollouts of the default scanline renderer

Time Output

The first section of the rollout, **Time Output** (Figure 16-5), deals with settings that control the specific frames to be rendered. The default **Single** option renders one frame—the current frame designated by the Time slider. The **Active Time Segment** option renders all of the frames shown in the Time slider. The **Range** option renders a range of frames designated in the two fields to the right of the option. The **Frames** option allows you to specifically designate the frames you want to render. You can specify individual frames or any range of frames using commas and hyphens. For example, if you want to render frames 1, 3, and 7 through 10, you would enter **1,3,5-12**.

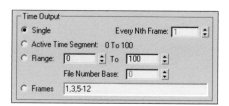

Figure 16-5: The Time Output section

When the **Active Time Segment** or **Range** option is used, you can render frames in selected increments using the **Every Nth Frame** option. If you have an animation with a large number of frames and want to perform a test render without spending the time to render each frame, you can render frames at regular intervals (that is, every nth frame) to get an overview of the entire sequence and find potential problems. Sometimes even rendering every fiftieth frame, if that's all you have time to render, can show you enough to know that your sequence is ready for a complete rendering.

When the **Active Time Segment** or **Range** options are used, you can also take advantage of the **File Number Base** setting. This setting allows you to designate the number given to the first rendered image file that is created during the rendering process. By default, whenever you render a sequence, the first file that is created is given the suffix of four zeros, or 0000. Each frame after that is followed by 0001, 0002, 0003, and so on, depending on the specific frames or range of frames you designate. With the File Number Base option, you can designate a different start suffix so that the first rendered file ends in some number other than 0000.

Output Size

You specify the dimensions, in pixels, of the final rendered output in the Output Size section, shown in Figure 16-6. The drop-down list provides standard categories of output such as high-definition, NTSC, PAL, and 35 mm. Selecting one of these categories causes 3ds Max to display the most common dimensions associated with the selected category in the four preset buttons to the right of the Width and Height fields. You can select from one of these preset buttons or type a specific width or height value yourself. The Image Aspect value shows the aspect ratio for the specified width and height values. The lock button to the right of the Image Aspect allows you to lock the aspect ratio, so that changing either the Width or Height value will cause the other value to change so that the aspect ratio is preserved. The Pixel Aspect ratio sets a value that can be changed to correct the way a rendering displays on a device other than your computer's display. If you change the pixel aspect ratio to something other than 1.0, the image might look squashed on your computer's display, but will look correct on a device with non-square-shaped pixels. You will probably never need to change this setting if your final product will be displayed on a computer or TV.

Figure 16-6: The Output Size section

Options

The **Options** section, shown in Figure 16-7, allows you to selectively include or exclude certain features in the rendering process. The options enabled by default are **Atmospherics, Effects,** and **Displacement.** This means that by default, any rendering you create will include all the active atmospheric and render effects that you created within your scene, as well as any applied displacement mapping. If you decide that you want to exclude atmospheric effects on a test render because of the added time it takes to complete the rendering, simply deselect the **Atmospherics** option.

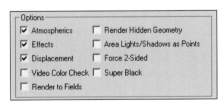

Figure 16-7: The Options section

Render Output

The **Render Output** section, shown in Figure 16-8, allows you to create an image or animation file during the rendering process. By default, the rendering output is set to **Rendered Frame Window** only. To save the output to a file, click the **Files** button, select a directory to save the file within, type a name, and select the file type from the **Save as type** drop-down list. When you save an output path with the **Files** button, the **Save File** option is automatically enabled.

Figure 16-8: The Render Output section

In the visualization industry, I have found that the only file types that I need to render on a regular basis are the .jpg, .tga, and .tif. The following are descriptions of each file type and its typical uses:

- **JPEG** (Joint Photography Experts Group): The .jpg file is the best file type to use when rendering images for general purpose or for rendering a sequence of images to be animated later. When rendering a long sequence of images, I prefer using a .jpg, because there is no significant loss in quality, and a .jpg usually requires only a fraction of the storage space of a .tif or .tga. Long sequences of images with large file sizes can require an enormous amount of disk space and a great deal of RAM for video editing. A .jpg uses an algorithm that allows for extremely high compression with a minimal loss of quality. When you save to the .jpg format, I recommend using a quality level of 95.

- **TIFF** (Tagged Image File Format): The .tif file is the best file type to use if your final product is a high-resolution print and file size is not important. The several classes of .tif files each have different purposes. If you send a .tif file to a professional printing service, you may need to get specific guidance as to the type of .tif file they want to use. I also recommend saving without compression to allow for the highest possible quality.

- **TGA** (Targa): The .tga file is the best file type to use if the final product is an image with an embedded alpha channel. An **alpha channel** is a type of data embedded in an image file that assigns transparency information for each pixel. A typical image file will contain three channels of information for each pixel, corresponding to the three colors used to determine the appearance of each pixel. An alpha channel is a fourth channel that contains an additional piece of information for each pixel—a value from 0 to 255 that determines whether or not the pixel will be transparent or opaque. A value of 0 represents black (complete transparency). A value of 255 represents white (complete opacity).

All rendered images are created with an alpha channel. However, not all file types have the ability to save it; the .tga file type is commonly used to store this extra channel of information. The left image in Figure 16-9 shows a rendered flower, and the image on the right shows the alpha channel that is created with the rendering. When you want to save an alpha channel with a .tga file, make sure that you enable the 32-bit option on the setup menu that appears during the **Save As** operation. If you do not save a .tga with the 32-bit option, the alpha channel is lost.

Figure 16-9. Rendering of a flower and the accompanying alpha channel

The **Net Render** option enables you to send your job to a network render manager so that you can use all of the computers at your disposal to help in the rendering process. Network rendering is discussed in detail later in this chapter.

The handy **Skip Existing Images** option skips the rendering process for files that have already been rendered. If you render a sequence of images and later find that a number of those images have problems that must be corrected, you can erase the problematic images and re-render the entire job without having to specify the exact frames to be rendered.

Using the Render Scene dialog box

This exercise demonstrates how to use some of the critical settings found within the **Render Scene** dialog box.

1. Reset 3ds Max.
2. In the Perspective view, create a teapot that rotates 360 degrees about the Z axis during 100 frames.
3. Click the **Render Scene** icon, or press F10.
4. In the **Time Output** section, select the **Active Time Segment** option.
5. Change the **Every Nth Frame** setting to **3**. This will cause every third frame to render.
6. In the **Output Size** section, click the **320x240** preset. This sets the aspect ratio to a desirable value. You can now lock the aspect ratio and then increase the overall size of the output while still maintaining this desirable aspect ratio.
7. Lock the image aspect ratio by clicking the icon to the right of the **Image Aspect** field.
8. Change the **Width** of the output to **500**. The **Height** value changes to **375**.
9. In the **Render Output** section, click the **Files** button. The **Render Output File** dialog box opens.
10. Select a location on your computer to create a new directory to save this temporary rendering output.
11. Change the file type to .jpg, name the file **Test,** and click the **Save** button.
12. Change the quality of the .jpg output to **95,** and select **OK** to close.
13. Under the **Assign Renderer** rollout, click the **Preset** drop-down list, and select **Save Preset**. The **Render Presets Save** window appears.
14. Name the preset **test,** and click the **Save** button to close. Having done this, you can load these settings later, even after closing and reopening 3ds Max.
15. Click the **Render** button to save the 33 rendered images to the specified directory.

Email Notifications

Besides the **Common Parameters** rollout, **Email Notifications** is the only other rollout that needs to be discussed. The **Email Notifications** rollout, shown in Figure 16-10, gives you the ability to send email notifications to and from any email address you specify. These notifications include progress notifications of every nth frame, failure notifications, and completion notifications. All you need to do is specify a **From** address, a **To** address, and your **SMTP Server.**

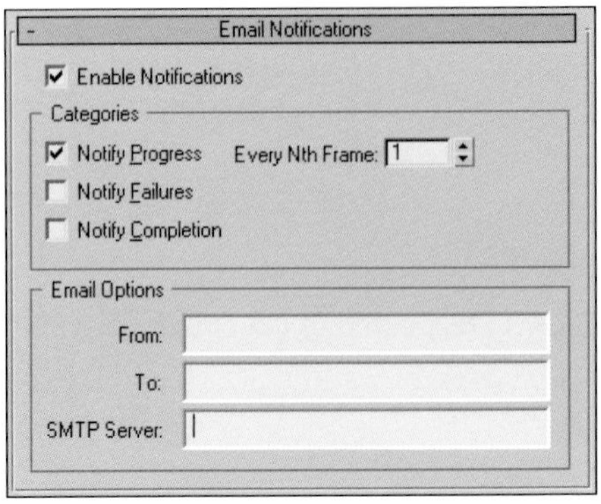

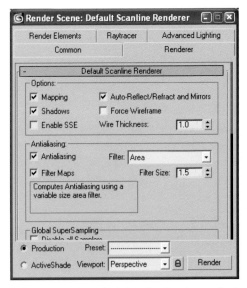

Figure 16-10. The Email Notifications rollout

If you work a typical work week—that is, from 8 a.m. to 5 p.m. Monday through Friday—weekends present the most useful times to render large jobs. In fact, you would have 63 hours from Friday at 5 p.m. until you return at 8 a.m. on Monday. By setting up 3ds Max to send progress or failure alerts from your office to your email account at home, you can save yourself a great deal of heartache by knowing about a failure when it happens instead of finding out about it Monday at 8 a.m. This gives you the opportunity to come back into the office to fix whatever problem caused the rendering failure before the entire weekend has come and gone with nothing to show for it. Of course, many veteran 3ds Max users might argue that they've never heard of an 8 a.m. to 5 p.m. 3ds Max job.

The Renderer tab

Up to this point, the discussion of the **Render Scene** dialog box has been limited to the **Common** tab. The next critical tab for users at the foundation level is the **Renderer** tab. When the assigned renderer is set to the default scanline, the **Renderer** tab contains only one rollout, the **Default Scanline Renderer** rollout (Figure 16-11). This rollout controls options and settings for the scanline renderer only.

Figure 16-11. The Default Scanline Renderer rollout

Options

The **Options** section gives you the flexibility to turn on and off certain features that greatly impact rendering times. These features include such things as mapping, shadows, auto-reflections, and refractions. When doing test renders, I find it very handy to be able to turn off these options for the entire scene with just a couple clicks of the mouse. Likewise, I find it very handy to be able to render the entire scene in wireframe by simply turning on the **Force Wireframe** option, which you can use as another way of conducting a quick test render of a scene. The **Wire Thickness** setting can be used to change the wire thickness (measured in screen pixels) so that the objects display better.

Antialiasing

The **Antialiasing** section gives you the option to turn off anti-aliasing, a topic discussed in Chapter 6. Like the options just discussed, the **Antialiasing** option can be disabled to speed up test renderings, but under no circumstances should it be disabled for a final render.

The **Filter** drop-down menu, shown in Figure 16-12, contains a list of anti-aliasing filters that allow you to sharpen or soften your final output, depending on your needs. I have found a consistent use for only two of these filters: the default **Area** filter and the **Video** filter. The **Area** filter is the default filter type, and of all the available filters, usually provides the best and most practical rendering appearance for still images. Some of the other options provide too much sharpness or blurring. The **Video** filter causes slight blurring in a rendered image, so you may not particularly care for the appearance of a single image rendered with the Video filter. However, by not using the Video filter, you risk producing animations with noticeable flaws, such as flickering and texture crawl (also covered in Chapter 6). Although a single image from an animation may look excessively blurred, the animation itself will usually look fine, especially if you render at a higher-than-needed resolution and convert down to your desired output size. As an additional note, the **Filter Size** value should be left at **1.5**.

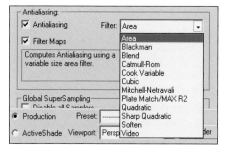

Figure 16-12. The available anti-aliasing filters

Global SuperSampling

This section allows you to enable **Global SuperSampling,** which is covered in chapter 6.

Object and Motion Blur

These sections control some of the parameters of Motion Blur, an effect covered in detail in chapter 18. These sections are likewise covered in chapter 18.

Auto Reflect/Refract Maps

The **Rendering Iterations** setting controls the number of interobject reflections with certain map types. Increasing this value may improve reflection quality, but can drastically increase rendering times. This value should remain at **1** until such time that you create scenes with advanced lighting methods.

Color Range Limiting

The options in this setting deal with advanced aspects of color management and are not covered in this book.

Memory management

3ds Max is a memory-hungry program, and as any veteran user will tell you, you should purchase as much memory as your budget allows. If you render a large scene that wants to consume more memory than is available, you risk crashing 3ds Max or your computer. If you simply don't have enough memory to render a particular scene, and you want to better your chances of avoiding such a crash, you can enable the **Conserve Memory** feature. This feature causes 3ds Max to render using 15 to 25% less memory, at the expense of render speed. Your scene may take a little longer to render, but you don't run as great a risk of crashing 3ds Max or your computer.

Choosing file dimensions

Whether your final product is a high-resolution print or a high-definition DVD, knowing what dimensions to use in your file output is critical. The standard computer screen displays approximately 72-130 pixels per inch (ppi), though your particular graphics card may allow you to alter this setting. While this range of resolution may look fine on a computer display, an image printed at the lower end of this range will look considerably pixilated and lack photographic quality. Learning the complexities of print and video resolution can be difficult and confusing, but the following discussion should give you a good understanding of the basics and the tools needed to produce high-quality presentations regardless of the format.

Before jumping into the details of video and print resolution, a discussion of what I refer to as the "final product" is warranted. In almost every visualization project I work on, the very first question I ask the client is "What is the final product?" The final product is the very thing that the client is paying you to create. It may be a single .jpg image that you send over the Internet, a high-definition DVD, a large-scale high-resolution print, or all of the above. Regardless of its form, the final product should drive your strategy towards completion of your project. If your final product includes a high-resolution image or high-definition DVD, you will need to incorporate a higher level of detail into your scenes than you will for an image to be viewed over the Internet or an animation to be viewed on a standard-definition TV. When it comes time to render your scene, the final product will dictate exactly what dimensions are needed for the file output. So let's see what the typical final products are and the dimensions that should be used for each.

Prints

Whether your image is going to be displayed in a magazine advertisement or on a street-side billboard, images that get printed need to be at a considerably higher resolution than for any other media type. When you create an image for print, you should always attempt to use a resolution of at least 300 dpi, but under no circumstances should you allow the resolution to fall below 150 dpi. If time and resources permit, resolutions up to 600 dpi are warranted, but anything above 600 dpi is unnecessary, because the human eye is incapable of discerning better resolutions. 300 dpi is about the minimum resolution necessary to achieve photographic print quality; however, for a large-scale print such as a street-side billboard, 300 dpi may not be feasible. This may be especially true if your scene incorporates advanced lighting, effects, high polygon counts, or other characteristics that require too much RAM or too much time to render at such high resolution.

The billboard image in Figure 16-13 is a 36x18-inch print image rendered at 150 dpi and subsequently blown up to 8x4 feet. This resolution suffices, because the billboard should be viewed from at least a few feet away, and any pixilation will be unnoticeable.

Figure 16-13. A rendered image used in a billboard

How do you know exactly what dimensions to use as the file output? All you need to do is determine the actual size of the printed final product in inches, and multiply the length of each side by the dpi you want. For example, if your image is going to be a 36-inch-wide and 24-inch-high print, and you need 300 dpi, your file output size should be 36x300 by 24x300, or 10,800 pixels wide and 7,200 pixels high. If you do not have the great deal of RAM required to render such a high-resolution image, you can render the image in segments and splice the segments together in a photo-editing program. This procedure will be discussed later in this chapter. If you need to print a 3x3-inch image for a magazine advertisement or a brochure, try for a 600 dpi image, since RAM and time should not be as big a factor, and because the image will be viewed at a distance of only a few inches.

Television

The resolution you need to render an animation at depends completely on the primary media through which your animations will be viewed. If the primary media is television, the exact resolution also depends on the region in the world in which your animations will be broadcast. For example, the standard resolution for North America is **NTSC** (National Television System Committee), which is **720x486**. In most European countries, the resolution is **PAL** (Phase Alternation Line), which is **720x586**. In time, both of these formats will probably become obsolete and make way for high definition TV.

High Definition DVDs

High-definition DVDs were introduced in 2006 with two competing formats; **HD-DVD** and **Blu-ray**. Both of these formats allow for dramatic improvements in how you can playback your animations on HDTVs and are slowing but surely becoming the standard for those of us in the visualization industry.

Standard DVDs use a video resolution of **640x480** dpi, but high definition far exceeds this with two much larger resolutions; **1920x1080** and **1280x720**. Creating an animation at a resolution of either type can be quite a challenge, but these resolutions are becoming more and more feasible with each passing year as computers become faster and integrate more RAM. The difference in play-back quality between standard definition and high definition is remarkable and if at all possible, you should strive to render your animations at a high resolution. Even if the final product is a standard DVD or if the final media is television, animations that are rendered at a higher resolution and con-verted down look dramatically better than animations that are just rendered at standard definition. A perfect example of this is a Hollywood CG film. Most Hollywood studios render their animations using the **2K Academy** resolution, which is **2048x1556**. For highly detailed sequences, they often increase this to the **4K Academy** resolution, which is **4094x3072**. They do this for the sole purpose of making the animations crisper and with fewer antialiasing side effects, such as 'pixel dancing', texture crawling, etc.

Standard Definition DVDs

If your final product is to be a standard DVD played on a standard definition television, you can ren-der at a resolution of 640x480 to yield acceptable results. However, if you're animation will also be played on television, you should render at the standard television resolutions and simply convert the animation to 640x480 during the DVD authoring process. You can either crop the additional width before authoring or allow the animation to be squeezed along its width automatically.

Internet Images

A good website will have a maximum pixel width of about 1,000 pixels because many computer users either do not have their monitors set beyond the standard 1024x768 resolution, or because most users don't typically view web pages in a maximized window. Because of this, images in web-sites are usually no larger than 1,000 pixels, and most of the time are much smaller than this. Therefore, renderings that you create for print or DVD will already be sufficient for displaying on the Internet. Although .jpg is the standard image type for Internet display, you always have the option of using the animated .gif file type to display animations.

Internet Video

Chances are, if you need to create an animation for viewing on the Internet, you already need to create an animation for DVD. If that's the case, creating a video for the Internet is just a simple mat-ter of using the raw images to create a video file. With each passing year, video compression gets better, and Internet connections get faster, giving you the ability to upload higher-quality videos with larger dimensions. Although 3ds Max comes with the ability to create decent video compres-sions, a professional video editor using top-of-the-line software can produce far better videos in much smaller files. If you don't have the resources to use a professional video editor, or if you would like to create a simple video to email your client for approval purposes, the following settings will allow you to create a high-quality video with decent video compression.

- File Type: MOV Quick Time File (*.mov)
- Compression Type: Sorenson Video 3
- Frames per second: 15
- Key frame every: 30 frames
- Quality: High

For more power and versatility in compressing your videos, you might want to try Autodesk's Cleaner software.

Additional rendering tools

3ds Max contains several handy rendering tools that suit the architectural visualization industry very well. The **Print Size Wizard** gives you an easy way to determine the size at which your rendering must be created to accommodate the print resolution you need. The **RAM Player** gives you the ability to quickly load, play, and save image and video files with your computer's available RAM. Finally, the **Panorama Exporter** lets you create panoramic images that can give your clients the interactive capability of looking around a scene in any direction.

The Print Size Wizard

If you want an easy way to figure out what dimensions you need to render, 3ds Max can help you out with the **Print Size Wizard.** The **Print Size Wizard,** shown in Figure 16-14, is a user-friendly interface that does the math for you. To use this feature, simply select a dpi (dots per inch) value and enter a value for either the paper dimensions or image dimensions. As you change either one of these dimensions, the other dimension updates accordingly. The wizard even tells you the uncompressed file size of the image. As the image dimensions change in the wizard, the rendering dimensions in the **Render Scene** dialog box change as well.

In the **Print Size Wizard,** shown in Figure 16-14, notice that the image width and height are the default rendering dimensions. With the dpi set to **300** (the minimum needed for photographic quality), the image will only print 2.1 inches wide and 1.6 inches high, because there simply aren't enough pixels to make the print any larger without losing quality. Although this limitation may be readily apparent to you, assume that your clients know nothing about pixels, dpi, or print quality. If you don't make it abundantly clear that a 640x480 dpi rendering can't be printed at large scale, you may get a call from your client wondering why the image you sent looks so bad after he or she spent a great deal of money getting it blown up and laminated. Furthermore, don't assume that if you send the client an image for review or approval, the client won't sign off on the image and get it printed before you have a chance to send him a high-resolution image.

Figure 16-14. The Print Size Wizard

The RAM Player

The RAM Player, shown in Figure 16-15, is an invaluable rendering tool that lets you load a sequence of images into your computer's RAM and play them back at various speeds, without the effect of reduced quality that comes from video compression. You can also load two separate sequences into the two available channels and compare them. Finally, once the sequence is loaded, you can quickly save multiple versions of the sequence using varying dimensions and video compressors.

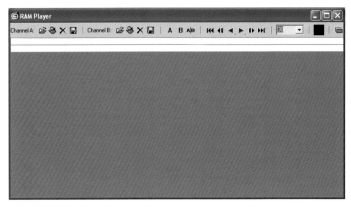

Figure 16-15. The RAM Player

To load a sequence of images, click the **Open Channel A** button (next to **Channel A**) and navigate through the explorer window, as shown in Figure 16-16, to locate the images. Select any numbered image, select the **Sequence** option at the bottom of the **Open File** dialog box, and click **Open.**

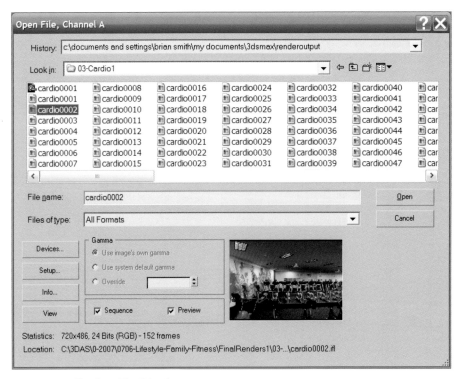

Figure 16-16. The Open File dialog box

The **Image File List Control** dialog box opens, as shown in the left image of Figure 16-17. Within this dialog box are options that let you load every nth frame, multiply the number of frames, or change the start and end frames. Click **OK** to load all of the frames. The final step is to confirm the settings in the **RAM Player Configuration** dialog box that opens (shown in the right image of Figure 16-17). In this dialog box, you can change the resolution dimensions or the total amount of memory used to load the images. To keep the default settings, click **OK**. The images will then load into the RAM Player.

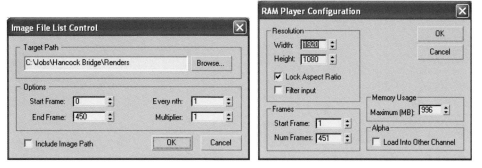

Figure 16-17. The Image File List Control dialog box (left) and the RAM Player Configuration dialog box (right)

As the images load into the RAM Player, you will see a status indicator appear, as shown in Figure 16-18. This indicator shows how many frames are loaded, the amount of memory used, and the amount of available memory remaining. In order for the images to play back smoothly, you must make sure that the memory doesn't run out before the images load. If the available memory runs out, the images will not load into RAM any longer and the sequence will probably not play back smoothly.

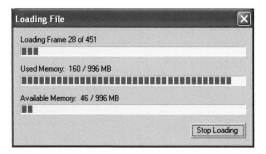

Figure 16-18. RAM status indicator

Once the images finish loading, you can play the sequence by clicking the **Playback Forward** button, or you can advance the images one frame at a time by clicking the **Next Frame** button.

A playback rate drop-down list, located to the right of the player controls, sets the number of frames that are played per second. Using a reduced frame rate is common for videos that play on websites. For example, reducing the playback rate of the typical animation from 30 fps to 15 fps means that you can halve the file size of animations that you load on your website. Videos at 15 fps still play well enough for most online purposes and load twice as fast as typical 30 fps animation. To see what your animations would look like at 15 fps, simply load every other frame in the RAM Player and change the playback rate to 15 fps using the drop-down list.

To the left of the play controls is the **Open Channel B** button. This is the same as the **Open Channel A** button except that any image loaded with this button is loaded into Channel B. By loading different images or sequences into the two channels, you can compare them during playback. Once you load both channels, you can use the **Channel A** and **Channel B** toggle buttons to hide or show the images in the two channels. By clicking and dragging in the channel display window, you can set the **A|B** divider between the two channels.

Finally, the **Open Last Rendered Image in Channel A** button does as its name implies. This tool is handy, because after using it, you can render the scene again with different settings, and click the **Open Last Rendered Image in Channel B** button to compare two different renderings of the same scene.

Using the RAM Player

This exercise demonstrates how to use the RAM Player to play a sequence of images and save the sequence as a movie file.

1. Reset 3ds Max.

2. In the **Rendering** menu, select **RAM Player.**

3. Click the **Open Channel A** icon, go to the directory **3dsMax2008\Images\3DATS\EntryNorth**, highlight any image in the sequence, enable the **Sequence** option, and click the **Open** button.

4. Click the **OK** button in the **Image File List Control** dialog box to accept the default settings.

5. Click the **OK** button in the **RAM Player Configuration** dialog box to accept the default settings. The sequence of images should begin to load in the RAM Player.

6. Click the **Save Channel A** icon.

7. In the **Save as type** drop-down list, select the **MOV** file type.

8. Name the movie **EntryNorth,** and click the **Save** button. The **Compression Settings** dialog box appears.

9. In the **Compression type** drop-down list, select **Sorenson Video 3,** and in the **Quality** section, use the slider bar to set the quality to **High.**

10. Click **OK** to save the movie. Depending on the number of frames and the image resolution, the saving process could take up to several minutes. This sequence, however, should take only a few seconds.

The Panorama Exporter

Here's another great tool that's as easy to use as any. The Panorama Exporter lets you create a 360-degree panorama from any camera and export the panorama as a QuickTime movie file. The Panorama Exporter works by rendering six separate views from a camera (Front, Back, Left, Right, Top, and Bottom) and splicing the images together to create one large image that is then wrapped around the camera spherically. The size of the wrapped image is determined by the dimensions you use to render the panorama. Since the typical camera only shows about a 45-degree section of that panoramic image (or one-eighth of a 360-degree view), the dimensions of the overall image must be about eight times larger than the dimensions of the final panorama. In other words, if you want your final panorama movie file to be displayed at 256x128 dpi and look every bit as clear and sharp as an image rendered at 256x128 dpi through the **Render Scene** dialog box, you must actually use dimensions of at least 2048x1024 dpi.

The Panorama Exporter feature is found under the **Rendering** menu, and once activated, can be found within the **Utilities** panel. When you select **Panorama Exporter,** the **Render Setup** dialog box opens, as shown in Figure 16-19, with a layout very similar to the **Render Scene** dialog box. The first rollout of the dialog box, **Interactive Panorama Exporter Common Parameters,** contains the only settings that are not featured in the **Render Scene** dialog box. At this point, you only have to tell 3ds Max the dimensions you want for the panorama movie file, but note that you must first have a camera in your scene to use the utility. Once the dimensions are set, click the **Render** button at the bottom of the dialog box.

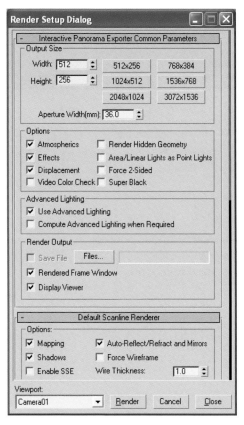

Figure 16-19. The Panorama Exporter

When the rendering process is finished, the Panorama Exporter Viewer opens, as shown in Figure 16-20. In the viewer, you can rotate your camera around the panorama by holding down the left or right button and moving the mouse, or you can rotate the panorama around your camera by holding down the right button and moving the mouse. You can also zoom in and out by holding down the middle (scroll) button and moving the mouse up and down.

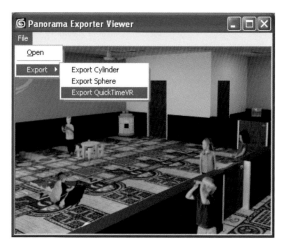

Figure 16-20. The Panorama Exporter Viewer

The Panorama Exporter Viewer contains only one menu item, the **File** menu, which allows you to export the panorama to a movie file. To export a movie, select **File ➤ Export ➤ Export QuickTimeVR,** and save the movie file. You can then open the movie file independently of 3ds Max.

Video Post

Whether you manage or work for an animation company, act as a freelancer, or simply use 3ds Max as a student, you have a great deal to benefit from learning Video Post operations. Video Post, as the name implies, involves creating or modifying video files after the rendering process is completed. With Video Post, you can perform basic video editing or complex compositing. The information about the available Video Post techniques could fill many chapters; however, as with all areas of 3ds Max, this book concentrates on the foundation-level features that are most practical to the architectural production environment, and covers basic video editing, one of the most practical and useful facets of Video Post.

Whether or not you hire a professional video editor to create your final animation product, using Video Post to perform basic video editing is beneficial in numerous ways. Video Post cannot replace professional editing software; however, you can use Video Post to create test animations for your own continued work, or as a reference for your video editor. Being able to perform basic video editing gives you the freedom to test numerous ideas for your final products without having to pay top dollar for hours of professional editing.

The Video Post interface, shown in Figure 16-21, is made up of four areas: the toolbar, the status bar/view controls, the queue, and the event tracks area. Video Post operations revolve around events, which are input elements that either provide the content for the final output (i.e., images) or change the final appearance of the content. There are seven different event types accessible through the seven rightmost icons in the Video Post toolbar: Scene, Image Input, Image Filter, Image Layer, Image Output, External, and Loop. Some are only selectable when certain other event types are highlighted.

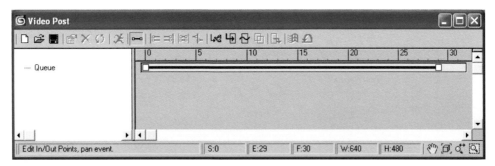

Figure 16-21. The Video Post interface

Image Layer events composite other images and scenes, while External events typically perform image processing with external programs. Both are advanced areas of Video Post and are not covered in this book.

The Scene event adds images to the queue by rendering a particular viewport. Essentially, the Scene event functions as a tool that lets you render multiple viewports or cameras in one operation, and send the output to a file. The Loop event causes other events to repeat over time.

The three events that this book focuses on are Image Input, Image Filter, and Image Output. The following list describes the functions of these three events;

- **Image Input event**: Adds already-rendered still or moving images to the queue
- **Image Filter event**: Performs image processing on another event
- **Image Output event**: Sends images processed by other Video Post events to a file

Video editing with Video Post

This exercise demonstrates how to perform basic video editing using Video Post.

1. Reset 3ds Max.
2. Select **Rendering ➤ Video Post**.
3. Click the **Add Image Input Event** icon on the Video Post toolbar (shown following).

4. Click the **Files** button, go to the directory **3dsMax2008\Images\3DATS\EntryNorth**, highlight any image in the sequence, enable the **Sequence** option, and click the **Open** button.
5. In the **Image File List Control** dialog box, click **OK** to accept the default options. This tells 3ds Max that you want to load all 31 images. Remember that 31 images (not 30) yield one second of animation.

6. Click **OK** to close the **Add Image Input Event** dialog box. There is now an Image Input event loaded in the event tracks area, as shown in the following illustration. Notice that the loaded event is identified as an **Image Input Event** by the icon located to the left of the first image name in the queue. Also, notice that the track associated with the loaded event extends outward by as many frames as there are images loaded. If you load 500 images, the track will extend out to 500 frames; however, you won't see all 500 frames unless you use the view controls in the bottom-right corner of the Video Post interface. To see all of the tracks, click the **Zoom Extents** icon. To pan the view, click the **Pan** icon.

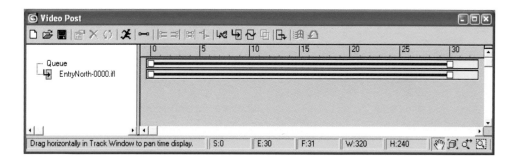

7. Click the **Add Image Input Event** icon again.

8. Click the **Files** button, go to the directory **3dsMax2008\Images\3DATS\EntrySouth**, highlight any image in the sequence, enable the **Sequence** option, and click the **Open** button.

9. In the **Image File List Control** dialog box, click **OK** to load all 31 images.

10. In the **Video Post Parameters** section of the **Add Image Input Event** dialog box, change the **VP Start Time** to **31** and the **VP End Time** to **61**. This tells 3ds Max that the first of the 31 images is loaded into frame 31, and the last image is loaded into frame 61.

11. Click **OK** to close the dialog box. This puts the second sequence of 31 images immediately after the first, as shown in the following illustration.

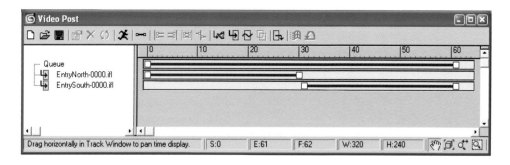

12. Click the **Zoom Extents** icon (shown following) to see all 61 frames of the sequences.

13. Click the **Image Filter Event** icon (shown following) on the Video Post toolbar. The **Add Image Filter Event** dialog box opens.

14. In the **Filter Plug-In** drop-down list, select **Fade** as the **Image Filter Event,** as shown in the following illustration.

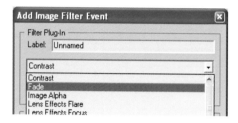

15. In the **Filter Plug-In** section, click the **Setup** button, select the **In** option, and click **OK** to close the **Fade Image Control** dialog box. This tells 3ds Max to perform a fade-in rather than a fade-out as the movie starts.

16. Click **OK** to close the **Add Image Filter Event** dialog box. Notice now that the **Fade Image Filter** event is loaded in the queue and its effects are spread from frame 0 to frame 60. This would produce a fade-in that lasts 60 frames, which would not look good. Let's change the effect so that it ends at frame 15.

17. Double-click the **Fade** event in the queue. The **Edit Filter Event** dialog box opens. Double-clicking any event in the queue or any event tracks area opens the corresponding dialog box.

18. Change the **VP End Time** to **15** so that the fade-in ends at frame 15, as shown in the following illustration. Select **OK** to close.

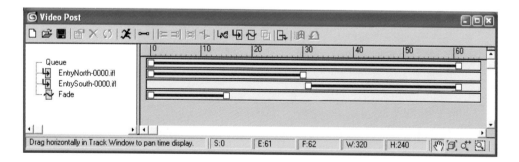

19. Click the **Add Image Output Event** icon (shown following) in the Video Post toolbar. The **Add Image Output Event** dialog box opens.

20. Click the **Image File** section, click the **Files** button, change the file type to **MOV,** name the movie file **test,** select a location on your computer to save the files, and click **Save.**

21. Set the compression type to **Sorenson Video 3** and the quality to **High.** Select **OK** to close.

22. In the **Add Image Output Event** dialog box, change the **VP End Time** to **61.**

23. Select **OK** to close the dialog box. The queue should now have four events loaded, as shown in the following illustration.

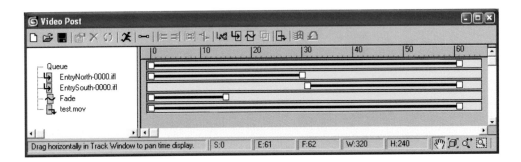

24. Click the **Execute Sequence** icon (shown following) in the Video Post toolbar.

25. In the **Time Output** section, select the **Range** option, and set the range from **0** to **61.** This ensures that all 61 frames of the sequences are included.

26. Click the **Render** button. Video Post now performs the video editing and produces a .mov file. You can play the file to see the results of combining the two video sequences and adding a fade-in.

You should also be aware of the following icons on the Video Post toolbar:

1. **Delete Current Event:** This icon deletes any selected event. By selecting the word **Queue** at the top of the event list within the queue, all events are highlighted. Clicking the **Delete Current Event** icon with all events highlighted will cause the entire queue to be deleted.

2. **Edit Range Bar:** If you are using the view control icons at the bottom-right of the Video Post interface, you can either right-click the mouse or click this icon to re-enter range edit mode. In range edit mode, you can move an event track by clicking the middle of its range bar (which turns red when selected) and dragging it left or right. You can also change the start or end frame of the range by dragging either end of the bar.

3. Edit Current Event: Selecting this icon opens the corresponding event dialog box. Double-clicking any event or track does the same thing.

Network rendering

Using one computer to produce a few renderings is not a problem, but when it comes time to create long animations of a complex scene, a single computer just won't do. Having multiple computers to produce these types of animations is critical, but just as critical is creating a system to divide the work among the computers. The network rendering capability of 3ds Max does just that.

Network rendering, simply enough, is the process of rendering with a network of computers. These rendering networks are sometimes called **render farms.** With network rendering, one computer must be set up to serve as the network manager, to farm out, or distribute, the work to other computers performing work as **rendering servers.** The entire process is monitored by a computer serving as the **queue monitor.** The queue monitor allows you to monitor the progress of the rendering job and each computer's contribution to finishing the job. It also allows you to edit job settings, start or stop a job, change the order of jobs, and much more. The same computer can serve simultaneously as the queue monitor, manager, and server.

To perform network rendering, enable the **Net Render** option at the bottom of the **Render Scene** dialog box, as shown in Figure 16-22.

Figure 16-22. The Net Render option in the Render Scene dialog box

Once you enable this option and click the **Render** button, the **Network Job Assignment** dialog box appears, as shown in Figure 16-23. At the top of the dialog box is the **Job Name** field, where you specify the name of the rendering job. You can name your jobs however you like, but each job name must be unique. Below this field is the **Description** field, where you can provide a description of your job.

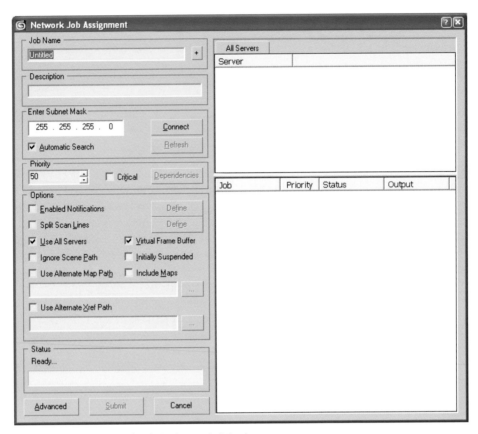

Figure 16-23. The Network Job Assignment dialog box

On the right-hand side of the dialog box is a listing of the servers that are available to receive network job assignments. However, before any servers can be available to receive job assignments, you must run the network Manager. The network Manager is one of the three components of a larger program named Backburner. The Manager, along with the Server and Monitor, is found in the Autodesk program directory, accessed through **Start ➤ Programs ➤ Backburner**, as shown in Figure 16-24.

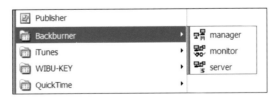

Figure 16-24: The Backburner components

Click the **manager** icon, return to the Backburner directory, and click the **server** icon. When you launch the Server, it immediately searches for the Manager, and when it connects to the Manager, it posts a statement saying **Registration to [IP address] accepted**. Likewise, the Manager will post a statement saying **Successful registration from [computer name]**. If either program is closed, a statement will be posted by the other program stating that closed program is "going down."

Figure 16-25. The Backburner Manager (left) and Server (right)

Now that both the Manager and Server are running, you can connect to the network through the **Network Job Assignment** window. Click the **Connect** button, and all of the computers running the Server program will appear in the **Server** listing, as shown in Figure 16-26.

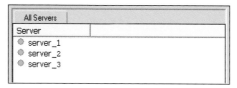

Figure 16-26: The connected Servers

Now, all you have to do is click the **Submit** button at the bottom of the **Network Job Assignment** dialog box. When you do, the **Network Job Assignment** dialog box will disappear, and an independent **Render Frame** window and the **Render Progress** dialog box will appear. They will both remain visible for the duration of the rendering process, after which they will disappear. You can close the 3ds Max program after the network rendering process is underway without interrupting the rendering. You should not attempt to work in 3ds Max on a computer that is being used as a server, because the computer will have much less RAM and processor power available while trying to render as a server in the background. You can, however, run the Manager and Monitor programs on a computer that you are working on.

The Manager will always assign frames in a way that maximizes the efficiency of the rendering network. If a server becomes idle, the Manager automatically detects it and no longer considers it for a frame assignment. If a server is disconnected, the Manager takes that server's current frame and reassigns it to another server.

Once rendering begins, you can monitor its progress with the Queue Monitor program, shown in Figure 16-27. But before the Queue Monitor will show the progress of any job, you must first connect it to the network using the **Connect** icon (shown right), found on the far left of the only toolbar in the interface.

Once you connect, all of the jobs past and present will be displayed in the **Show All** table. When you select a job, the details of its progress will appear in the table on the right-hand side of the dialog box. The tabs at the top of the table will take you to other tables displaying more details about the selected job. To delete a job permanently, select the job and click the **Delete Job** icon (shown right).

At the bottom of the **Queue Monitor** dialog box is a table that displays all of the computers that the program has recognized at some point in the past. Those that are currently connected will appear in green, and their status should be listed as busy.

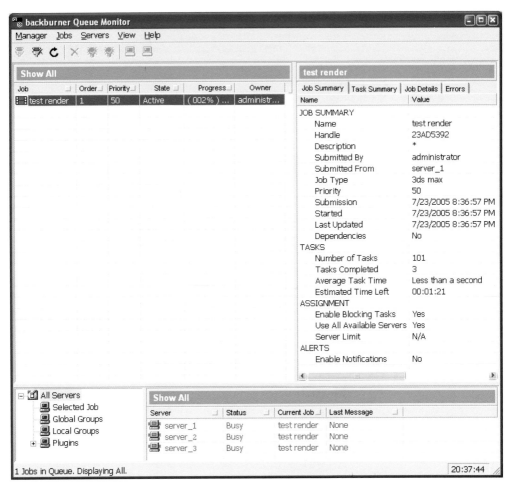

Figure 16-27. The Queue Monitor

Network rendering

This exercise demonstrates how to perform network rendering using a single computer.

1. Reset 3ds Max.

2. Start the Manager, Server, and Monitor programs from a single computer. For the sake of simplicity and training, this exercise demonstrates network rendering without having to place multiple computers on the network. The tutorial is the same regardless of the number of computers on the network.

3. In the Perspective view, create a teapot that rotates 360 degrees about the Z axis during 100 frames.

4. Click the **Render Scene** icon to open the **Render Scene** dialog box.

5. In the **Time Output** section, select the **Active Time Segment** option.

6. In the **Render Output** section, click the **Files** button.

7. Save the file as a .jpg, name the file, and click the **Save** button to close.

8. In the **JPEG Image Control** dialog box, select a quality of **95**, and click **OK** to close.

9. In the **Render Output** section, enable the **Net Render** option.

10. Click the **Render** button to begin the rendering process.

11. In the **Network Job Assignment** dialog box, click the **Connect** button. The name of the computer you are using should appear in the window on the right in the dialog box under **Server.**

12. Click the **Submit** button at the bottom of the **Network Job Assignment** dialog box. The dialog box disappears.

13. Maximize the **Monitor** program that is running in the background.

14. Click the **Connect** icon on the far left-hand side of the **Monitor** toolbar.

15. The current job being rendered is displayed in the table on the left-hand side of the dialog box.

Summary

This chapter has focused on the critical settings within the **Render Scene** dialog box and some of the great tools that enhance the rendering process. Though the **Render Scene** dialog box contains a large number of settings for advanced lighting and the mental ray renderer, advanced lighting was sufficiently covered in Chapter 12, and mental ray is not presented in this book. Other nice features covered include rendering tools like the Panorama Exporter, the RAM Player, Video Post, and network rendering.

Rendering is the last step in the production process, unless you do your own video editing or DVD authoring. The next two chapters both present features to use before you begin to render a scene. However, they are placed after this chapter, because the information covered in both chapters is better understood with knowledge of the basics of rendering. After learning the features discussed in these next two chapters, you will have all the tools needed to create photorealistic architectural visualizations from start to finish. The only things left to cover at that point will be some practical, real-world production tips and tricks, which can be found in Appendix B.

CHAPTER 17

Scene Assembly

IN THE IDEAL 3D WORLD, you could build all your scenes without regard to file size, available RAM, CPU speed, rendering times, or any number of things that complicate the design process. However, since most of us have to be aware of our computers' limitations, we have to manage the way we build objects and assemble our scenes. I've already discussed how creating objects with unnecessary detail results in longer rendering times and refresh rates. Likewise, assembling a scene improperly can result in unnecessarily long moments of waiting on your computer to update.

Creating a 3D scene is usually a long process—one that can take up to several months. Anything you can do to streamline your work should be considered. One practice that can save countless hours is building the major components of your scenes separately from each other. Your ability to work efficiently in 3ds Max can become significantly hindered when you allow too many highly detailed objects to reside unnecessarily in the background of your scene. Although it is usually necessary to have other objects visible in your scene as a reference, you should make an effort to prevent your scenes from becoming too large in file size or in polygon count.

This chapter covers the tools that allow you to assemble a scene from multiple files and work efficiently once the assembly process is complete. In addition, you will learn work practices that will reduce the time you wait on your computer to catch up with your commands. Knowing how to create the individual elements of a 3D scene is obviously important, but equally important is knowing how to assemble those elements without wasting countless hours waiting on your computer.

Computer power vs. scene complexity

Whether your project calls for a large golf course community with hundreds of homes or an individual single-family residence, great care should be taken in the methods you use to build and assemble your scenes. Whether your project requires the collective effort of dozens of individuals or you alone, your production process should be based on speed and efficiency. Someday, when computers are powerful enough, you may never have to worry about how complex your scenes become. But for the foreseeable future, you should employ practices and procedures that keep your wait time to a minimum. Before I cover some of the critical tools that allow you to assemble a scene from numerous individual elements, let's cover some of the realities of working in a 3D world.

There are several different situations in which the 3ds Max user is forced to wait on the computer. Three of these, in particular, are situations in which good procedures and practices can spare you from long and unnecessary waiting:

- Transferring files
- Refreshing viewports
- Rendering

Most other times, 3ds Max is waiting on the user for input, but for each of these you are forced to spend at least some time waiting on 3ds Max and your computer, depending largely on how you manage your scenes. So what are the attributes of a scene that affect each of these three situations, and what can you do to minimize your wait during each of these processes? In each case, I'll discuss how scene complexity affects the way 3ds Max transfers file data, and then I'll explain how it affects the time needed to refresh and render a viewport.

Transferring files

It goes without saying that larger files take more time to open, save, or merge. But what makes a file large, and what other characteristics of a scene cause the file commands to need more time to execute? If you were to open 3ds Max and save a file without having created any objects, you would notice that the file size is approximately 140K. As with any program, .max files saved with no user input still contain a certain amount of default data.

Except for the smallest scenes with virtually no objects, the vast majority of a scene's file size is dependent on the number of faces it has to keep track of. While most faces require a certain amount of data to be stored in order to define the normal and three vertices that make up a face, not all faces must be tracked. Parametric, instanced, and referenced objects are all examples of object types that contain faces whose data is not stored individually, but rather with the parent object. Let's look at a few examples of how all of this affects a scene's file size.

Figure 17-1 shows a single teapot with 25 segments and 40,000 faces. The file size for a scene that contains this object alone is 143K, only 3K more than a scene with no objects. Why is this? Because 3ds Max doesn't need to store the same amount of data for every face as it would if the scene were made up of 40,000 independent faces. The key information 3ds Max needs to store about this scene is that there is a single teapot with a particular radius value located at x, y, z, oriented x, y, z degrees, scaled a certain % along x, y, z, etc. There are, of course, numerous parameters and settings that go into defining the exact appearance and characteristics of this teapot, but this information only needs to be defined for the teapot, not all the individual faces that make it up.

Figure 17-1. The 40,000 faces of a teapot

Now let's see what happens if you collapse this teapot into an editable mesh or poly. This same scene with the teapot collapsed to an editable mesh results in a file size of 1.85MB; when collapsed to an editable poly the resulting file size is 2.23MB. Both of these files are significantly larger, and when this result is compounded with hundreds of objects, the result can be a file size that is simply too large to open or save with today's computers.

Being able to minimize file size by keeping objects in their original parametric form is ideal; however, it's usually not practical for most scene elements. But there are equally effective ways of keeping file sizes under control with object types that typically make up a scene. Continuing on with the teapot example, let's use the Clone feature to create a scene with 25 of these teapots as collapsed editable meshes.

Figure 17-2 shows a scene with 25 meshes collapsed from the original teapot. If you create these meshes using the Copy command, each object becomes independent of the others, and 3ds Max has to track each and every face on each mesh. The result is a file size of 61.8MB and a scene that takes approximately 10 seconds to open and save. This same arrangement of meshes created with the Instance command, however, results in a file size of only 1.89MB and a scene that takes a fraction of a second to open or save. Clearly, whenever you need to duplicate highly detailed objects, it's better to use the Instance command than the Copy command. The trick is determining the point at which it becomes necessary to use the Instance command. After using the Copy command, you can attach all the copies to each other to make a single individual mesh. Instanced objects cannot be collapsed or attached without losing the quality that makes them instanced objects. There are some advantages to having few objects in your scene, even if it means slightly larger file sizes. Fewer objects result in easier object management for both you and 3ds Max. With fewer objects, the "Preparing Objects" step of rendering can be greatly reduced because 3ds Max doesn't have to run through the same process for as many objects.

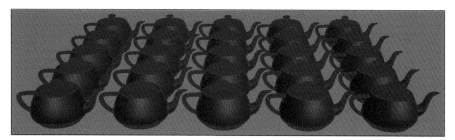

Figure 17-2. 25 objects and 1 million faces

Instance vs. copy

So when is it better to instance objects rather than copy and collapse them? Let's look at the example in Figure 17-3. This is a rendering of a medical office building that contains approximately 1 million faces. The blown-up area shows an area where the face count is substantially higher than other areas because of the curves needed to make the detailed balustrade. This is also an area that may be used for close-up shots, so the need for detail is even greater here. There are 20 small balusters and 2 large decorative column caps. To achieve the necessary level of detail, each baluster needed to contain approximately 10,000 faces and each column cap needed to contain approximately 20,000. These are both examples of objects that are suitable candidates for instancing. By creating instances of these objects, not only can you quickly change one and have the others update automatically, but 3ds Max only needs to store the face data for one object, thereby saving you from a much larger file size.

Figure 17-3. Using the Instance command to reduce file size

Once you instance objects like this, I highly recommend grouping them together to avoid seeing each individual instance displayed in the **Select by Name** dialog box, and so that you can quickly and easily change their display characteristics. Since objects like these increase your display refresh rates, it is often helpful to hide the objects or change their display to a box.

Let's look at one more example before moving on. Figure 17-4 shows a large condominium development with eight residential buildings and a clubhouse. In this development, there are six identical large residential buildings containing approximately 500,000 faces each, and two identical smaller buildings containing about 300,000 each. This is an example of when instancing objects would clearly be better than copying objects. The file size for a scene with just the larger building by itself is approximately 10MB, and a scene with the smaller building by itself is 8MB. If these buildings were copied rather than instanced, the file size for a scene with just the eight buildings alone would be almost 80MB.

Figure 17-4. A scene with instanced buildings to reduce file size

Using the Copy and Instance commands

This exercise demonstrates the differences between the Copy and Instance commands when used to populate a scene with multiple clones of a high face count.

1. Reset 3ds Max.

2. In the Perspective viewport, create a sphere of any radius, with **200** segments.

3. Save the file anywhere on your computer.

4. Using Windows Explorer, determine the size of the file you just saved. It should be approximately 180K. (Your file size may vary slightly from this value.)

5. Collapse the sphere to an editable mesh.

6. Resave the file and check the file size again. It should now be approximately 1.82MB, ten times the size of the previous save.

7. Hold down **Shift** and click the sphere. The **Clone Options** dialog box appears.

8. Select the **Copy** option and make **25** clones of the sphere.

9. Save the file and check the file size. It should be approximately 44MB.

10. **Undo** the Clone command.

11. Clone the sphere again using the **Instance** option and make **25** clones.

12. Save and check the file. It should now only be approximately 1.85MB (roughly 25 times smaller than the previously saved version). To summarize, instances reduce files size and use less RAM. Copies should be used when the individual objects need to retain unique appearances that aren't tied to the appearance of other objects.

Refreshing and rendering viewports

Everyone knows that the more faces that are displayed in a viewport, the longer it will take for the viewport to refresh. But what can be done to maximize the number of faces in your scene and minimize the amount of time it takes to refresh the viewports? Chapter 1 covered some of the great features that allow you to work in large, complex scenes without having to endure excessive refresh times. These included **Disable View, Rendering Levels,** and **Fast View.** Chapter 2 discussed the **Hide** feature, the **Display as Box** option, and the use of layers. All these features are critical to efficient work in 3ds Max. Now, let's cover some of the techniques of building and assembling scenes to minimize the time needed to refresh viewports.

Let's go back to the condominium example I just talked about. This project involved several sequences that went into the creation of a 4-minute animation. Numerous camera paths were set up throughout the site and not much was left out of the final animation. A scene with the entire project loaded contained approximately 1,000 objects and 4 million faces. Rendering a scene of 1,000 objects and 4 million faces can easily take 1 hour per frame, even without adding advanced lighting, rendering effects, or numerous other features that make an average rendering look photorealistic. If the final product were just a few individual images, the methods used to assemble the scenes would not be critical. However, since the animation needed to be 4 minutes long, or 7,200 frames, spending over an hour per frame was not an option. Even with a 10-computer render farm, the final animation could take over 720 hours of straight rendering time. These 7,200 frames don't even account for the numerous preview renderings and changes requested by the client. Needless to say, something needed to be done to make the project more manageable and allow for use of some of the advanced lighting and effects features.

The only solution was to break the project up into individual scenes of smaller size. On the set of a movie or TV show, scenes are created for filming from very specific camera angles so that the viewer doesn't see that just outside of the camera's view is the filming crew, the audience, and the studio walls. Just like the set of a movie, I assembled my scenes so that only those objects that would be seen by the camera were present. After developing a script, I created camera paths; and with the camera paths created, I knew exactly what I could leave out of each scene.

The sequence of images in Figures 17-5 through 17-8 show portions of a 30-second clip (900 frames) for the condominium project. In this particular scene, the camera moves around a virtual conference room and zooms into a set of architectural drawings resting on a table. As the camera moves closer, the first page is folded back, revealing a photo of the project. The camera continues to move closer, and the project is seen rising out of the photo. As the camera moves down to a street-level view, the conference room fades away and the viewer is led through the center of the project.

Frames 0 through 300 (Figure 17-5) only show the conference room objects, but in Figure 17-6 you can see the tops of the buildings rising out of the photograph. So for the first 300 frames, I was able to exclude the condominium objects, and the result was a very small file size of only 495K. Since the objects in the condominium project were not part of the scene for these first 300 frames, these frames rendered much faster. This was because the advanced lighting solutions did not have to take these objects into account; this is also because the RAM on the render farm computers was not completely expended loading this additional content. When you don't have enough RAM, your renderings may slow to a crawl because the processor will have to wait for information to move back and forth from the hard drive to the RAM before it can complete its work. If your RAM is completely expended and 3ds Max still wants more, your processor may work at as little as 10% efficiency, thereby increasing your rendering times as much as tenfold. Additionally, the cars in this project were RPCs. (**RPC** stands for Rich Photorealistic Content, a third-party plug-in from Arch-Vision—www.archvision.com—that I often use in my projects.) As the acronym implies, RPCs are a great source of content for architectural scenes. Available RPCs include vegetation, people, fountains, and in this case, vehicles. Since the cars were not visible in these frames, 3ds Max did not have to load the supporting plug-in files during the rendering process, which saved additional time. One final benefit to making the first scene this way was that these first 300 frames could be sent to Network Render while I continued to work on finalizing the condominium objects that were about to appear in the next sequence. By the time the second scene was ready for rendering, the first scene had already finished rendering.

 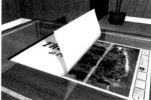 

Figure 17-5. Frames 0 through 300

I continued to break up the overall scene file into smaller files to take advantage of reduced file sizes, more available RAM, advanced lighting, and earlier final renders. In frames 301 through 400 (Figure 17-6), I was still able to exclude most of the site elements, such as streets, grass, and shrubs, but because the buildings and trees needed to be shown, the file size and face count jumped to over 40MB and 4 million, respectively.

Figure 17-6. Frames 301 through 400

Frames 401 through 600 (Figure 17-7) were the largest and most difficult to render, at over 5 million faces and 82MB. These frames showed the greatest number of objects and took much longer to render than any other frames in the clip.

Figure 17-7. Frames 401 through 600

In frames 601 through 900 (Figure 17-8), I was able to exclude two of the buildings and all their surrounding site elements. In addition, the conference room had faded away by this point, so these objects could also be excluded. The result was a significant reduction in file size, from 82MB to 58MB.

Figure 17-8. Frames 601 through 900

Figure 17-9 shows the final breakup of files for Scene 01. The files were named descriptively, with the scene name at the beginning (Conf.Rm) and the frame numbers at the end (0000-0300) so that I could easily keep track of them. Notice the varied file sizes involved. Even the largest file, at 82MB, contained only about half the objects used in all the scenes. Hundreds of objects that could not be seen from this scene's perspective were excluded from these files, such as the clubhouse pool objects, a small marina on the water, and much more. Had I not broken up the project into these smaller files, I would have had to work with a single file that contained all the project objects. This file would have been close to 200MB and required far more RAM than my computers had available.

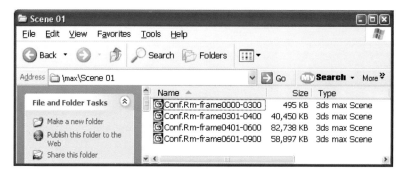

Figure 17-9. Files for Scene 01

Assembly tools

Now that we've covered some of the strategies for creating more manageable files, let's look at some of the tools in 3ds Max that make it possible to create these files. All the tools mentioned in this section are found in the File menu.

In addition to these tools, I'll cover some of the features that give you the ability to maintain an accurate picture of how complex your scenes become. These features will show you at any time exactly how many objects, faces, lights, plug-ins, and other elements your scene contains. They will also allow you to keep track of a scene's file size and the amount of RAM being used.

Save Selected

The Save Selected command is an important part of the scene-assembly process. It saves to a separate file any objects you have selected prior to executing the command. It's useful in a couple of different ways. If you open a file with numerous objects and want to save a particular object to a separate file as part of your library for future projects, select the objects and select the Save Selected command. This feature also works great when you simply want to break up a large file into smaller files for later assembly. While working in a scene, you may often find that you've just created some objects that contain a large number of faces, and these objects aren't needed until rendering time. Keeping these complex objects in your scene makes working in 3ds Max more difficult and places an unnecessary burden on your computer. Saving these select objects to a separate file makes it easier to continue working on the rest of the scene.

Figure 17-10 shows an example of a project in which several objects were saved to separate files because their face count became an issue. Keeping all these objects in the primary scene file made the file excessively large and consumed too much RAM. After saving these objects to separate files, they were later merged during scene assembly just prior to rendering. Notice the files in the Scene 04 folder are organized in a logical and easy-to-understand manner. The primary scene files are labeled Overhead-frame0000-0400 and Overhead-frame0401-0600, and the files to be assembled later are labeled with easy-to-recall names and the prefix x- so that Windows lists them together after the primary files.

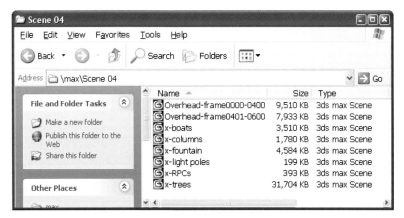

Figure 17-10. Using Save Selected to save smaller, high–face count files outside main scene file

Merge

The Merge feature lets you bring objects from another file into the file you are working on. When you merge objects, there is no link maintained between the two files involved, so changing the objects in either file has no effect on the other file. To perform a merge, select **File ➤ Merge** and select a file from the **Merge File** dialog box, as shown in Figure 17-11.

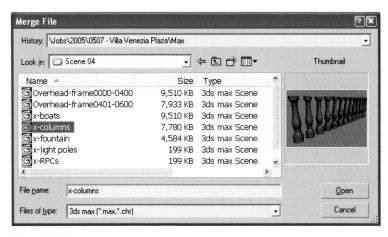

Figure 17-11. Merging files

After selecting the file, the **Merge** dialog box appears, as shown in Figure 17-12. This dialog box is nearly identical to the old **Select Objects** dialog box, and works in the same way. Once you select the object or objects you want to merge, click **OK** to complete the merge.

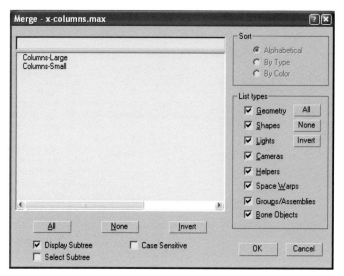

Figure 17-12. The Merge dialog box

Using the Save Selected and Merge commands

This exercise demonstrates how to use the Save Selected command to save select objects to separate files, and the Merge command to bring them back into the same file.

1. Reset 3ds Max.

2. In the Perspective view, create three spheres, three teapots, and three cylinders of any size.

3. Select the three teapots, and select **File ➤ Save Selected.** The **Save File As** dialog appears.

4. Name the file `Teapots` and save anywhere on your computer.

5. Select the spheres and use the Save Selected command to save them to a file with the name `Spheres`.

6. Select the cylinders and use the Save Selected command to save them to a file with the name `Cylinders`.

7. Reset 3ds Max.

8. Select **File ➤ Merge.** The **Merge File** dialog box appears.

9. Select the file named `Teapots`, highlight all three teapots, and click **OK** to complete the merge.

10. Run the Merge command again, select the file named `Spheres`, highlight any two spheres, and click **OK** to complete the merge.

11. Run the Merge command once more, select the file named `Cylinders`, highlight any one of the cylinders, and click **OK** to complete the merge.

Import

The Import command is similar to the Merge command, except that it works with file types other than the native .max file. Two file types you will become very familiar with in the visualization world are the .dwg and .3ds file types. The .dwg is the native AutoCAD file type that you will use for importing architectural drawings. The .3ds file is the old DOS 3D Studio mesh file format, which is still widely used as an exchange file format between various 3D software packages. Although you may never need it for exchange purposes, you may find it invaluable in its ability to create certain types of mesh objects, such as those from the polylines of a 2D CAD program. Figure 17-13 shows the **DWG Import** and **3DS Import** dialog boxes that appear when the command is executed. In most cases, you will want to click **OK** to merge the imported objects, rather than replace the entire scene.

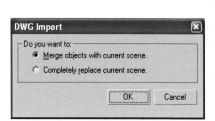

Figure 17-13. The DWG Import and 3DS Import dialog boxes

Export

The Export feature is used to export all the objects of your current file into another file type. Although you should rarely need to use this command, the most common file type you will probably need to export to is the native AutoCAD .dwg file type. One situation I have found this command very useful for is when I want to create linework in 3ds Max and export that linework into AutoCAD. I do this when I want to trace the exact position of 3D objects in a 3ds Max scene and use that linework as a reference to more work in AutoCAD.

Export Selected

The Export Selected feature works similarly to Export, except that it works only with those objects that are selected prior to executing the command.

XRef Objects

The XRef Objects feature, shown in Figure 17-14, is a great tool that allows you to load objects from other files and maintain a link to those files. You can maintain smaller working files by using the XRef command for select objects that contain a large number of faces. If changes are made to an object in the source file, the object is updated in the file that contains the XRef. These changes include any transforms, modifiers, an object's parameters. If you make any of these changes to objects in the source file, the XRef will update to show the change.

The XRef Objects feature is an alternative to the Merge feature. Which method you use is simply a matter of preference; however, breaking up large files into smaller, more manageable files is always a good choice.

To use the XRef Objects feature, select **File ➤ XRef Objects.** Click the **Create XRef Record from File** icon (most top-left icon), locate the file you want to XRef into your scene, click the **Open** button, and select the objects you want to place in your scene. Once you this, all the scene objects and materials will be displayed in the bottom half of the **XRef Objects** dialog box, and the new objects will appear in your scene. The objects are selected and can be transformed, but the parameters and modifiers that are available in the source file will not be available in your current file.

Within this dialog box are handy options that allow you to disable the XRef, merge the objects, and remove them from the XRef link. If you select one of the XRef objects and open the **Modify** panel, you can use a proxy object in place of the real object to reduce the number of visible faces in the viewport. This can help speed-up viewport navigation.

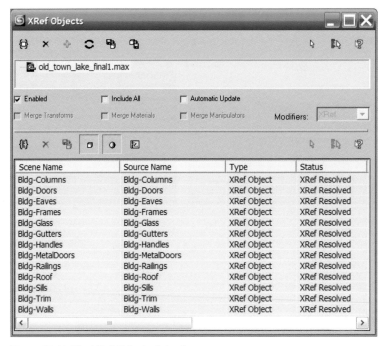

Figure 17-14. The XRef Objects dialog box

Using the XRef Objects command

This exercise demonstrates how to use the XRef Objects command to bring externally referenced objects into the current file, and how changing the objects in the source file causes the XRef to update automatically.

1. Reset 3ds Max.

2. In the Perspective view, create a teapot of any size.

3. Name the file **teapot**, and save anywhere on your computer.

4. Reset 3ds Max.

5. Select **File ➤ XRef Objects.**

6. Click the **Create XRef Record from File** icon and select the file you just saved.

7. Click the **Open** button to finish the command.

8. Save the file with the name **teapot XRef**.

9. Open the first file you created (**teapot**).

10. Increase the radius of the teapot twofold.

11. Save the file.

12. Open the second file you created (**teapot XRef**). The teapot in this file should now look twice the size it did before, as it does in the source file.

XRef Scenes

The XRef Scenes feature works the same as the XRef Objects feature, with two main exceptions. First, the XRef Scenes feature performs the XRef on all objects in the source file, rather than just the selected objects. Second, once the scene is XRef'd into the new file, the objects are not selectable or transformable.

File Link Manager

The File Link Manager creates XRef-like links to AutoCAD drawing files. Whenever I need to bring in linework from AutoCAD, however, I always use the Import feature rather than the File Link Manager. I do this because I prefer to import small, more manageable amounts of linework at a time, and then work on that imported linework immediately. In 3ds Max, when I finish modeling the objects I use the AutoCAD linework for, I delete the imported linework and start the process over again with a new area of the scene (and new linework). Because of this, I do not need linework to be continuously updated and reloaded. This method of work is a matter of preference, and like most areas of 3ds Max, there are numerous ways to accomplish the same thing. In this case, I prefer to import.

   An additional problem you might encounter with the File Link Manager is that if you file link a scene and assign materials, and then make changes to the .dwg file, all the material assignments are lost.

File Properties

This feature gives you a great snapshot of some of the important characteristics of your scene, such as the total number of faces, objects, lights, and cameras. This particular information is found on the Contents tab of the **File Properties** dialog box, and is only updated when you resave the file. Figure 17-15 shows the contents of the scene with the 25 teapots and 1 million faces (discussed earlier).

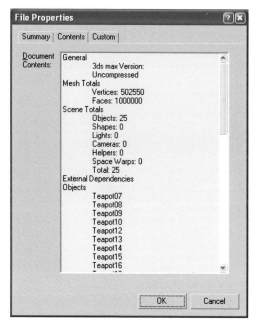

Figure 17-15. The File Properties dialog box

Summary Info

The Summary Info feature, shown in Figure 17-16, provides a more detailed view of the makeup of your scene than the File Properties feature. In addition to showing some of the information provided in the **File Properties** dialog box, the Summary Info feature also shows you important information such as how much RAM is being used. This information is updated as changes in the file occur, rather than only after the file is resaved.

In the **Summary Info** window (located at the lower half of the **Summary Info** dialog box) is detailed information that is shown only for the current frame that the Time slider is on. For example, if the number of faces in a teapot is changed from one frame to another, then the **Summary Info** dialog box will display the number of faces the teapot contains at the frame that the Time slider is on.

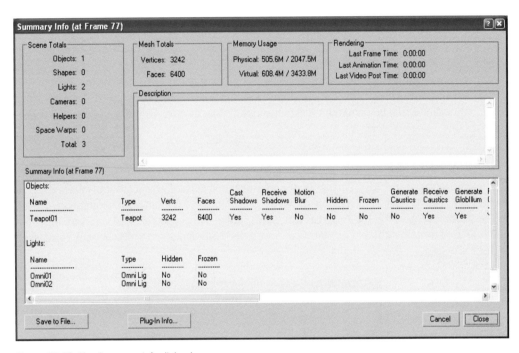

Figure 17-16. The Summary Info dialog box

Archive and Resource Collector

Although not completely related to scene assembly or other features covered in this chapter, the Archive feature and the Resource Collector are two additional features found within the File menu that are worth mentioning.

These tools are very handy in two particular situations. First, if you want to take a .max file and work with it on a different computer—maybe a laptop that you're taking on the road—the Archive and Resource Collector features are exactly what you need. Second, if you need to send your scene to someone else so that they can work on it, these features are invaluable.

The Archive feature creates a .zip file of every file 3ds Max needs to create your scene, including all image files used in materials and any plug-in resource files. To use the Archive feature, select **File ➤ Archive,** give the .zip file a name, and click **Save** to complete the command. You can only perform this command while in the 3ds Max file that you want to archive.

The Resource Collector feature does almost the same thing as the Archive feature; however, it does not automatically create a .zip file when it saves the files. To use the Resource Collector feature, go to the **Utilities** panel, open the **Utilities** rollout, and select **More** ➤ **Resource Collector.** The Command panel displays a **Parameters** rollout, as shown in Figure 17-17. Click the **Browse** button and select a location in which to save all the support files. Enable the **Include MAX File** option if you want a copy of the .max file to be saved along with the rest of the files.

Figure 17-17. The Resource Collector

Summary

This chapter has shown why it's so important to know how to build and assemble a scene without excessive file sizes or face counts. Someday, we may no longer have to be concerned with such issues, but for the foreseeable future we should always try to use the tools available to allow for efficient work and prevent wasted time. I suspect that no matter how fast computers become, software developers will always fill your plates with more and more processor-hungry and memory-consuming programs and resources. If this is true, then the topics covered in this chapter will always apply.

At this point, there's not much left to cover at the foundation level. The next chapter will cover the last major area of 3ds Max I have yet to discuss—effects. After this chapter, you'll have looked at all the major areas in 3ds Max that apply to users in the visualization industry.

CHAPTER 18

Effect Basics

IN 3DS MAX, THE WORD "effect" can have many different meanings, depending on whom you talk to and what industry you work in. For 3ds Max, the features that employ the term "effects" fall into two categories: **atmospheric effects** and **render effects**. Atmospheric effects simulate real-world conditions or elements and are incorporated during the rendering process. Render effects simulate the effect of viewing the world through the lens of a camera, and are added after the initial rendering process is complete. Both types of effects can significantly improve an architectural visualization, but they can also have a dramatic impact on the time it takes to render a scene, so they should be used with some discretion.

This chapter covers each of the available atmospheric and critical render effects, all of which can enhance the quality and realism of an architectural visualization. When you first begin to explore these features, you may be surprised at just how easy they are to use. Some require very little explanation, but all of them usually require some amount of experimentation to achieve the desired effect. After reading this chapter, you will be able to add a great deal of quality to your visualizations with the following effects.

Atmospheric effects:

- Fire Effect
- Fog
- Volume Fog Volume Light

Render effects:

- Lens Effect
- Depth of Field
- Motion Blur

Atmospheric effects

3ds Max contains four types of atmospheric effects: Fire Effect, Fog, Volume Fog, and Volume Light. To access these effects, select **Environment** from the **Rendering** menu, or press 8. Doing so opens the **Environment and Effects** dialog box, as shown in the left image of Figure 18-1. In the **Atmosphere** roll-out, click the **Add** button to open the **Add Atmospheric Effect** dialog box (right image), select the effect you want to add, and click **OK** to close.

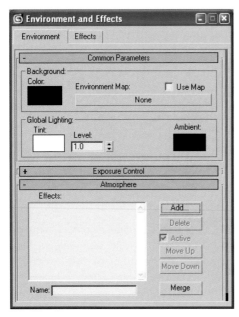

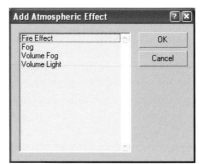

Figure 18-1. The Environment and Effects dialog box (left) and the Add Atmospheric Effect dialog box (right)

One of the first things to consider in adding an effect is where the effect is going to exist. Two of the effects, Fire and Volume Fog, require the use of an object called an atmospheric apparatus gizmo to define the space in which the effect is to exist. The Fog effect contains its own unique parameters to define its location, while the Volume Light effect uses a light's parameters to define its location.

The atmospheric effects will be discussed in alphabetical order, as they appear in the **Add Atmospheric Effect** dialog box—not in the order of their importance.

The Fire effect

Although not one of the more widely used effects in visualization, the Fire effect is very helpful in the simulation of one very important element of many visualizations. While you can use the Fire effect to create explosions, set things on fire, and numerous other things, the most useful application I have found for the Fire effect in visualizations is in the simulation of a simple fireplace. This one application alone makes learning the Fire effect worthwhile.

Before the Fire effect can be added to your scene, you must create an atmospheric apparatus gizmo. To access this type of gizmo, select the **Helpers** icon (shown right) from the Create panel.

The second helper type listed in the drop-down menu below the Create icons is **Atmospheric Apparatus,** as shown in the left image of Figure 18-2. Selecting this helper type opens a rollout with three gizmo types: **BoxGizmo, SphereGizmo,** and **CylGizmo** (right image). Although future releases of 3ds Max may contain more sophisticated types of volumes, currently you are limited to defining the area of the Fire and Volume Fog effects to the volume of a box, sphere, or cylinder. However, you can apply non-uniform scaling and position numerous gizmos throughout your scene to define more sophisticated volumes.

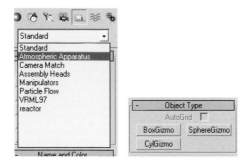

Figure 18-2. Accessing the Atmospheric Apparatus menu

To create a gizmo, select the gizmo type and click inside a viewport to define its volume, in the same way you would create the box, sphere, and cylinder primitives. Now when you add a Fire effect in the **Environment and Effects** dialog box, **the Fire Effect Parameters** rollout appears, as shown in Figure 18-3. In the **Gizmos** section, click the **Pick Gizmo** button; then, inside a viewport, click the gizmo you want to add the effect to.

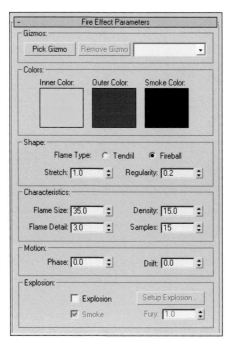

Figure 18-3. The Fire Effect Parameters rollout

The **Fire Effect Parameters** rollout contains numerous parameters to give you precise control over the appearance of the Fire effect. However, as I stated in the beginning of the chapter, most effects require some experimentation to achieve the desired look. The best way to learn the Fire effect is through the use of a practical exercise geared toward creating a typical fireplace.

Using the Fire effect

This exercise demonstrates how to use the Fire effect to simulate a typical fireplace.

1. Reset 3ds Max.

2. Click the **Helpers** icon in the **Create** panel and select **Atmospheric Apparatus** from the drop-down list.

3. Click the **SphereGizmo** button, and in the Perspective view, click and drag to define a gizmo with a radius of **50** units.

4. Enable the **Hemisphere** option, located directly below the **Radius** field. This changes the sphere into a hemisphere.

5. Perform a non-uniform scale by scaling the gizmo 300% along the Z axis. This will help stretch the flames of the fire.

6. Perform a Zoom Extents operation of the Perspective view.

7. Press **8** to open the **Environment and Effects** rollout.

8. In the **Background** section of the **Common Parameters** rollout, click the black color swatch to open the color selector.

9. Change the color to pure white, which will change the background to white.

10. In the **Atmosphere** rollout, click the **Add** button and select **Fire Effect.**

11. In the **Fire Effect Parameters** rollout, click the **Pick Gizmo** button, and click the **SphereGizmo** you created in the Perspective view. The effect is now added to the scene, and when rendered should look like the first fire on the left in the following illustration.

12. Within the **Shape** section, change the **Flame Type** to **Tendril.** This option creates pointed flames along the Z axis of the apparatus. Changing this option alone, however, will not produce the desired look—a few more adjustments must be made.

13. Change the **Stretch** value to **2.** The **Stretch** parameter scales flames along the Z axis of the apparatus. Values less than the default **1.0** cause the flames to appear shorter and thicker, while values greater than **1.0** cause the flames to appear longer and skinnier. The result should look like the second fire in the following illustration.

14. Next, change the **Flame Size** to **10.** Reducing the **Flame Size** makes more individual flames visible and keeps the effect from looking like a fireball. The result should look like the third fire in the following illustration.

15. Change the **Flame Density** to **30.** Increasing the **Flame Density** makes the fire less transparent and appear to burn hotter. The result should look like the fourth fire in the following illustration.

16. Finally, change the **Flame Detail** to **1** and render again to see the effect of changing this parameter. The result should look like the fifth fire in the following illustration, in which the fire appears blurred and less detailed. A **Flame Detail** value of **3** should work in most situations. Higher values increase render times, and may require an increase in the **Samples** values to produce a visible difference, which increases render times even further.

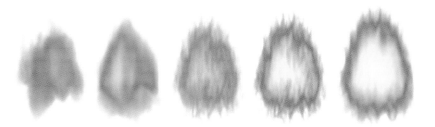

You can animate the fire by simply changing the phase over time. Over a 10-second period of time (i.e., 300 frames), try changing the **Phase** to **300**. This should produce a realistic animated fire.

The Fog effect

Fog is an extremely useful feature in 3ds Max that can give your work not only a greater sense of realism, but also inspire a greater sense of emotion. Adding fog to your scene can completely change the look of your visualization in numerous ways.

There are two types of fog effects in 3ds Max: **Fog** and **Volume Fog.** The Fog effect creates either a "standard" fog throughout the entire scene, which makes objects appear to fade with increasing distance from the camera, or a "layered" fog, in which the fog is confined to specific elevations. Image 1 in Figure 18-4 depicts a scene before fog is added. Image 2 shows the same scene with a standard fog that permeates everywhere. Image 3 shows the scene with layered fog, where the fog exists from the ground to approximately 5 feet above the ground. The Volume Fog effect creates fog in a volume defined by an atmospheric apparatus gizmo. Image 4 in Figure 18-4 depicts the scene with Volume Fog, where the gizmo occupies a volume confined to the first few feet above the lake. Because of this, the fog exists only above the lake in the foreground. I'll first cover the Fog effect and then move on to the Volume Fog effect.

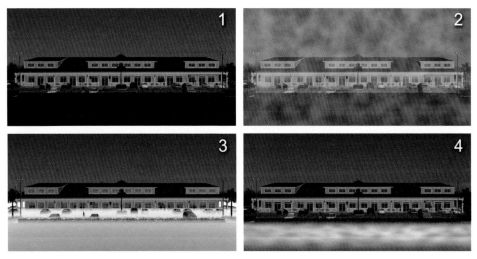

Figure 18-4. Examples of the Fog effect with various settings

The Fog effect contains only one rollout, **Fog Parameters** (shown in Figure 18-5). The color swatch sets the color of the fog, which can either be left as pure white or given a subtle amount of color to enhance the effect of penetrating light. You can also dramatically change the color of the fog to simulate something other than fog, such as the smoke from a fire.

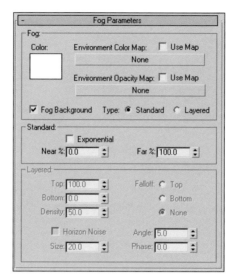

Figure 18-5. The Fog Parameters rollout

The Environment Color Map lets you use a map to determine the color of the fog. Though I don't use this feature much, I use the Environment Opacity Map (located directly below the Environment Color Map) with almost all fog effects. The Environment Opacity Map lets you use a map to assign opacity to the fog. Once you load a map, you then drag the loaded map into the **Material Editor**, at which point you can control the parameters of the map as you would with any other map.

Below the map buttons is the **Fog Background** option, which should always be enabled if the background is visible (i.e., if there is no mapped object that represents the background).

Standard fog

Enabling the standard fog option causes the entire scene to show fog. It acts like a filter causing all scene objects to fade from their normal appearance to whatever color the fog is. This fading increases with distance from the camera.

Within the **Standard** section of the rollout is the **Exponential** option. This option increases the density of the fog exponentially with distance, rather than linearly. I recommend always enabling this option because without it, transparent objects (such as vegetation created with opacity maps) will not render correctly.

The **Near %** and **Far %** values determine the strength of the fog at its beginning point and ending point. The beginning point is a distance from the camera defined by the **Near Range** value. This value is located in the **Environment Range** section of the **Parameters** rollout of a camera, as shown in Figure 18-6. The ending point is a distance from the camera defined by the **Far Range** value, which is located in the same place. Image 2 in Figure 18-4 used a **Near %** value of **0.0** and **Far %** value of **50.0**. I recommend leaving the **Near %** value at **0.0** and altering the **Far %** value to determine the overall strength of the fog for the entire scene. If the **Near %** value is set high, you might not see anything in your scene other than fog.

Figure 18-6. The Environment Ranges settings

Environment ranges

The **Environment Ranges** values allow you to specify the distance from the camera at which certain environment effects, such as Fog (standard), are to take place. By default, the **Near Range** is set **to 0.0** and the **Far Range** is set to **1000.00** (or **83'4"**, with units set to **US Standard**). This means that the effect will begin at the camera with a strength specified in the **Near %** field located in the **Environment and Effects** dialog box, and extend out to 1,000 units from the camera, where it will end at a strength specified in the **Far %** field.

In the example in Figure 18-7, numbers are placed at their specified distance from the camera to demonstrate the use of environment ranges.

In the top image, no environment effects are applied.

In the second image, a Fog effect is applied with the default settings. Since the Fog effect begins at the camera with 0% strength and reaches 100% strength at a distance of 83 feet, 4 inches from the camera, none of the numbers are visible.

In the third image, the fog still begins at the camera, but reaches 100% strength at a distance of 310 feet from the camera. For this reason, the numbers appear to fade as their distance from the camera increases. The objects 300 feet from the camera are barely visible.

In the bottom image, the fog still reaches 100% strength at a distance of 310 feet, but it doesn't begin until it is 150 feet away from the camera. For this reason, the objects 100 feet from the camera do not appear faded at all.

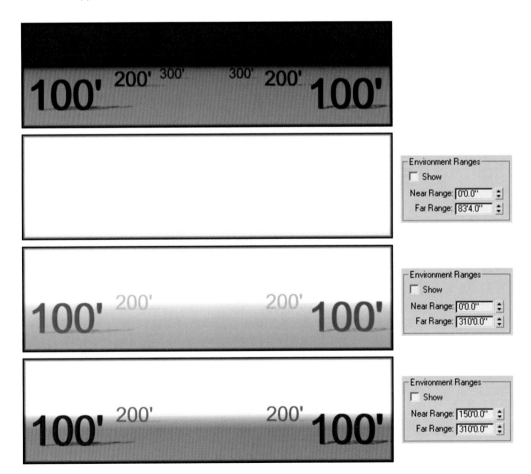

Figure 18-7. The effect of using environment ranges with Fog

Using environment ranges to control an effect

This exercise demonstrates how to use environment ranges to control a Fog effect.

1. Reset 3ds Max.

2. Press **8** to open the **Environment and Effects** dialog box.

3. In the **Atmosphere** rollout, click the **Add** button. This opens the **Add Effect** dialog box.

4. Select **Fog** and click **OK** to close. The Fog effect is now added to your scene.

5. While in the Perspective view, press **Ctrl+C** to turn the view into a Camera view.

6. In the Camera view, create a teapot with a radius of **25** units.

7. Move the camera so that it captures a view of the teapot from the side.

8. Render the scene. The fog that you added to the scene should make the background white, as shown in the left image of the following illustration.

9. Select the camera, and go to the **Modify** tab. In the **Environment Ranges** section of the **Parameters** rollout in the Command panel, enable the **Show** option to display the environment range cone.

10. Reduce the **Far Range** value to **500** and render the scene. Fog should appear to whiten the teapot because the far range—which is the distance at which the fog is 100%—is closer to the teapot. The middle and right images in the following illustration show the scene with reduced **Far Range** values.

11. Continue to reduce the **Far Range** value until the environment range cone no longer encompasses the teapot, as shown in the following illustration. When this happens, render the scene, and the teapot should completely disappear. The fog is at 100% at a distance that is closer than the teapot.

Layered fog

Layered fog uses a top and bottom value to establish the elevation at which the fog exists, as shown in Figure 18-8. You set the lower extent of the fog in the **Bottom** field and the upper extent in the **Top** field. The **Density** value sets the strength, or thickness, of the fog.

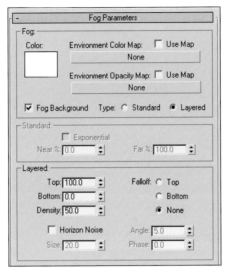

Figure 18-8. Layered fog settings

In the real world, fog does not instantly start and stop at certain elevations. Instead, it fades away. Likewise, 3ds Max does not automatically set the **Top** and **Bottom** values as the dramatic change between where fog exists and doesn't exist. You can, however, minimize the transition between fog and no fog using the **Falloff** option in the **Layered** section. Adding falloff at the bottom or top of the fog will cause the fog to fade away at an exponential rate rather than at a linear rate.

The **Horizon Noise** option can increase realism by adding noise to the fog in the area around the horizon. The **Size** value sets the size of the noise and the **Angle** value determines the angle from the horizon at which the noise begins to break up the fog. If the **Top** and **Bottom** values are so low that the fog crosses the horizon, the Horizon Noise feature will cause an undesirable effect in which the fog seems to be mirrored above and below the horizon. Although Horizon Noise is a great feature, you will probably have to experiment with the parameters in the **Layered** section to get just the look you want.

You can have multiple layers of fog by simply adding more Fog effects within the **Atmosphere** rollout.

The Volume Fog effect

The Volume Fog settings, shown in Figure 18-9, give you the flexibility of defining the limits of fog using an atmospheric apparatus gizmo, the same way as discussed for the Fire effect. The gizmos are created and used the same way for the Volume Fog effect as for the Fire effect. Furthermore, many of the settings discussed in the Fog effect work the same in the Volume Fog effect.

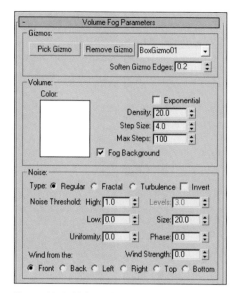

Figure 18-9. Volume Fog settings

The **Soften Gizmo Edges** value softens the fog around the edge of the gizmo. The default setting of 0.2 works fine in most cases, but even subtler edges can be achieved by increasing the value up to 1.0. A value of 0.0 will produce the undesirable effect of defining the gizmo with a harsh border.

The **Step Size** determines the coarseness of the fog. The smaller the value, the finer the fog becomes.

The **Max Steps** value sets the sampling of the fog. Increasing the value improves the sampling; however, it also increases the rendering time. The default value of 100 should work fine in most situations, and should not be set much higher without good reason, as high values could slow your computer to a crawl.

Within the **Noise** section of the **Volume Fog Parameters** rollout are settings to control the noise of the fog. The noise settings essentially control the design of the fog, and like so many of the effects discussed in this chapter, take a great deal of experimentation for the desired appearance to be achieved. The two settings I find particularly useful to control are **Size** and **Uniformity. Size,** as with the Fog effect, controls the puffiness of the fog. The **Uniformity** value, as the name implies, controls how similar the fog is throughout its volume. As you increase **Uniformity** to the maximum value of 1.0, the fog becomes less speckled.

By animating the **Phase,** you can make the fog appear to churn. By adding **Wind Strength,** you can make the fog appear to move in a direction defined by the **Wind from the** setting. Unless you animate the **Phase,** the **Wind Strength** setting will have no affect on the fog.

Creating Volume Fog

This exercise demonstrates how to create and modify the **Volume Fog** effect.

1. Reset 3ds Max.

2. Click the **Helpers** icon in the **Create** panel and select **Atmospheric Apparatus** from the drop-down list.

3. Click the **SphereGizmo** button, and in the Perspective view, click and drag to define a gizmo with a radius of **50** units.

4. Press **8** to open the **Environment and Effects** dialog box.

5. In the **Atmosphere** rollout, click the **Add** button. This opens the **Add Effect** dialog box.

6. Select **Volume Fog,** and click **OK** to close. The Volume Fog effect has now been added to your scene, but it hasn't yet been added to a gizmo.

7. In the **Volume Fog Parameters** rollout, click the **Pick Gizmo** button and then select the **Sphere-Gizmo** you just created in the Perspective view. Render the scene, and the result should look like image 1 in the following illustration.

8. Within the **Noise** section of the **Volume Fog Parameters** rollout, reduce the size from the default value of **20** to **10**. Render the scene and the result should look like image 2.

9. Increase the **Uniformity** to **0.2**. Render the scene and the result should look like image 3.

10. Decrease the **Density** to **5**. Render the scene and the result should look like image 4. This demonstrates how the settings can be altered to achieve just the right look.

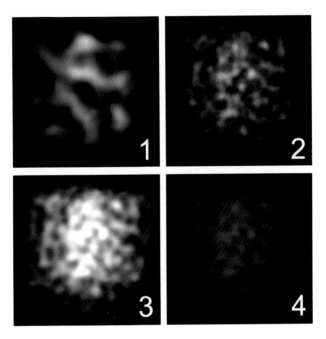

The Volume Light effect

Volume Light is probably the most widely used atmospheric effect, with numerous uses. It allows you to create the effect of light interacting with fog or other atmospheric particles. You can use it to simulate the glow around a light source, light coming through the windows of a building, or light shining from the headlights of a car, as shown in Figure 18-10.

Figure 18-10. Volume Light simulating the headlights of a car

To create a Volume Light effect, you must attach the effect to a light in your scene in the same way you attach Volume Fog to a gizmo. When you attach the effect to a light, a single rollout appears, as shown in Figure 18-11. Although the parameters in this rollout control most of the characteristics of the effect, they do not control the extent or intensity of the effect. These two characteristics are controlled through the light's settings within the Command panel.

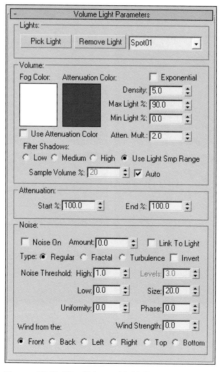

Figure 18-11. The Volume Light Parameters rollout

The Volume Light effect takes the shape of whatever light type is used, and is attenuated through the **Attenuation** parameters in the **Volume Light Parameters** rollout in the Command panel. In the example in Figure 18-10, a target spotlight is used with attenuation to create the light emitting from the headlights and attenuating after a certain distance. If the light type in this example were an omni light, the result would have been much different. The Volume Light would be cast in all directions, as shown in Figure 18-12.

Figure 18-12. Volume Light with an omni light source

Within the **Volume** section of the **Volume Light Parameters** rollout are several settings previously discussed in the sections on the Volume Fog and Fire effects. There are, however, several settings unique to Volume Light.

When enabled, the **Use Attenuation Color** option causes the Volume Light to attenuate from the **Fog Color** to the **Attenuation Color.** This option can be useful for creating unique effects. The **Atten. Mult.** option can be used to multiply the color change effect of the **Attenuation Color** feature.

The **Max Light %** is another way of controlling the intensity of the light. Although I recommend leaving this setting at the default value of 90, you can decrease this value to make the light appear less bright.

The **Min Light %** is a setting that should remain at 0 because any value other than 0 will cause the entire scene to be as bright as the **Fog Color,** unless the light is blocked by geometry. I highly recommend leaving both the **Max Light %** and **Min Light %** settings at their default values, and controlling the light through the other available settings.

The **Filter Shadows** settings control the blur applied to shadows cast within the volume of the Volume Light. These settings should work for almost any situation and should not have to be changed.

Just like the **Max Light %** and **Min Light %** values, the **Attenuation Start %** and **End %** values essentially perform the same function as other settings. In this case, you can change the start and end attenuation of the light as a percentage of the distance values specified in the settings found in the Command panel. I recommend leaving these settings alone to avoid confusion with the other settings that perform the same function.

The **Noise** section of the **Volume Light Parameters** rollout contains almost the same settings as the **Noise** section for the Volume Fog effect, with a couple exceptions. Noise is automatically enabled with Volume Fog; but with Volume Light, you must enable the **Noise On** option. Once it's on, you can control the amount of noise with the **Amount** value, which can be set from 0.0 (no noise) to 1.0 (full noise).

If you animate a light containing a Volume Light effect that also contains noise, you will almost always want the noise to remain linked to the world coordinates so that the noise doesn't move as the light moves. If you have a Volume Light attached to the headlights of a car, as in the example in

Figure 18-14, you would want the noise to remain stationary as the car moves. Otherwise, it would appear as if the air and all the particles causing the noise were moving along with the car. Enabling the **Link To Light** option links the noise to the light, rather than the world coordinate system. For certain special effects, this may be desirable; but for most every situation, this option should remain off.

Other atmospheric effects are available as third-party plug-ins, but the four effects discussed in this chapter all perform their designed function in a very acceptable manner. Although other plug-ins may provide more power and flexibility, which could be very useful in other industries, these effects can be made to do the job in almost any visualization project.

Creating Volume Light

This exercise demonstrates how to create and modify the Volume Fog effect. This example can be applied to numerous situations, such as the headlights of a car, light coming through a window, and even the light from a film projector in a movie theater.

1. Reset 3ds Max.
2. In the center of the Perspective view, create a free spotlight.
3. Press **8** to open the **Environment and Effects** dialog box.
4. In the **Atmosphere** rollout, click the **Add** button. This opens the **Add Effect** dialog box.
5. Select **Volume Light,** and click **OK** to close. Volume Fog is now an effect added to your scene, but it hasn't yet been assigned to a light.
6. In the **Volume Light Parameters** rollout, click the **Pick Light** button and then select the light you just created in the Perspective view.
7. Render the scene. The volume light is very dense and should be reduced.
8. Within the **Volume** section of the **Volume Light Parameters** rollout, reduce the **Density** value from **5.0** to **1.0.** This reduces the density of the volume light to a fifth of its previous value.
9. Render the scene again and notice that the volume light is much less intense.
10. Experiment with the various volume light parameters and the parameters in the Command panel to see what type of look you can apply to your volume light.

Render effects

The render effects available in 3ds Max include all those shown in the **Add Effect** dialog box (Figure 18-13). To access these effects, click the **Add** button on the **Effects** tab of the **Environment and Effects** dialog box. Each acts as a type of filter that changes the rendering after the initial rendering process has been completed; once a rendering is completed and these effects have been added, they cannot be removed. While some of the available effects are best suited to be added during the rendering process, I strongly recommend not incorporating certain effects during the rendering process. These effects can be added in the post-production process through 3ds Max's Video Post feature, or with another program such as Photoshop. The four effects that shouldn't be added are as follows:

  • Brightness and Contrast

  • Color Balance

  • Blur

  • Film Grain

Each of these are very simple effects to add in post-production, and it is better to have the option of adding them or not adding them after your rendering process is completed.

Two additional effects listed in Figure 18-13 that will not be discussed are Hair and Fur and AfterBurn Glow. AfterBurn Glow is simply a demo plug-in effect. The Hair and Fur effect is geared toward other industries, but you might find it worthwhile to experiment with simulating grass in an architectural scene. In this way, the Hair and Fur effect has been a tremendous benefit to many visualization users because of its ability to simulate 3D grass at a minimal cost to RAM and file size.

The three effects that will be discussed in this chapter are **Lens Effect, Depth of Field,** and **Motion Blur.** Each of these effects contains very powerful features that cannot be added as effectively or with as much realism in post-production or in other programs. Therefore, they will be discussed in detail.

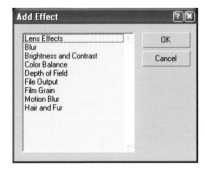

Figure 18-13. The Add Effect dialog box

The Lens effect

Lens effects simulate some of the real-world effects caused by sunlight hitting the camera at just the right angle. Lens effects are probably the most widely used of the render effects available in 3ds Max and, if not overdone, can add a great deal of realism to your scenes. There can be a tendency to put too much intensity into Lens effects, to the point that they don't look real and distract the viewer from the presentation's focus.

When you add the Lens effect to the effects list, two rollouts appear: **Lens Effects Parameters** and **Lens Effects Globals,** as shown in Figure 18-14. Within the **Lens Effects Parameters** rollout are effects for Glow, Ring, Ray, Auto Secondary, Manual Secondary, Star, and Streak. These effects each have their own unique rollouts, but also share the parameters within the **Lens Effects Globals** rollout. Changing a parameter for any loaded effect will change that parameter for all loaded effects. For example, if you double the **Size** value for Glow, the **Size** value is automatically doubled for Ring. If you want to double the size of the Glow without doubling the size of the Ring, you must use the **Size** parameter in the **Glow Element** rollout, rather than the **Size** parameter in the **Lens Effects Globals** rollout.

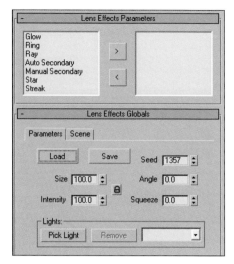

Figure 18-14. The Lens Effects Parameters and Lens Effects Globals rollouts

Because there are so many effects and so many unique parameters for each effect, I'll only cover the shared parameters found in the **Lens Effects Globals** rollout. You should explore each effect individually to get a feel for its function.

You can add and use as many effects as you want all at once by highlighting the effects in the left window of the **Lens Effects Parameters** rollout, and clicking the right arrow button to add them to the right window. You can unload them by moving them back to the left window using the left arrow button. You can also load effects by double-clicking them in the left window.

The **Lens Effects Globals** rollout contains two tabs: **Parameters** and **Scene**. The **Load** and **Save** buttons can be used to load existing parameter settings or save new ones for later use. This is very handy when you've spent a great deal of time to get an effect to look just right and want to use the same settings later without having to go through the same labor again.

Before an effect can be used, it must be attached to a light object. To attach an effect, click the **Pick Light** button and select the light in a view. You can attach the effect to multiple lights.

The **Size** is a percentage of the rendered frame.

The **Intensity** controls the brightness and opacity of the effect, with higher values yielding brighter, more opaque effects.

The **Angle** value can be used to rotate the effect around the viewer's perspective.

The **Squeeze** value changes the aspect ratio of the effect to compensate for various frame aspect ratios. The effect is stretched horizontally with positive values up to 100, and stretched vertically with negative values down to –100.

Creating a Lens effect

This exercise demonstrates how to create and modify various Lens effects.

1. Reset 3ds Max.

2. Create an omni light in the center of the Perspective view.

3. Press **8** to open the **Environment and Effects** dialog box.

4. On the **Environment** tab, change the Background color to a medium-blue color, similar to a mid-day sky.

5. Select the **Effects** tab, click the **Add** button in the **Effects** rollout, and select **Lens Effects** from the **Add Effect** dialog box.

6. In the **Lens Effects Globals** rollout, click the **Pick Light** button and select the light object in any view.

7. In the **Lens Effects Parameters** rollout, double-click the first effect in the window on the left (Glow) and render the scene. It should look like image 1 in the following illustration.

8. Next, double-click **Ring** to load this effect. Render the scene. It should look like image 2.

9. Double-click **Ray** to load this effect. Render the scene. It should look like image 3.

10. Double-click **Auto Secondary** to load this effect. Render the scene. It should look like image 4.

11. The effect you just loaded, Auto Secondary, is very faint and difficult to see, so let's increase the intensity of the effect. With the Auto Secondary effect highlighted in the right window of the **Lens Effects Parameters** rollout, scroll down to the **Auto Secondary Element** rollout and increase the **Intensity** to **50**. Render the scene. It should look like image 5. Notice that this effect becomes brighter without affecting any of the other three loaded effects.

12. Finally, let's reduce the size of all the effects. With any effect highlighted, reduce the **Size** value in the **Lens Effects Globals** rollout to **75.** Render the scene. It should look like image 6. Notice that all of the effects are reduced in size by 25%.

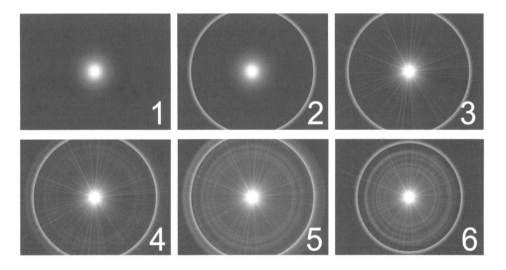

The Depth of Field effect

Depth of Field simulates the natural blurring effect of objects in the foreground and/or background when viewed through a camera. Adding Depth of Field in the right way can significantly increase the quality and realism of any scene. 3ds Max provides two ways to generate Depth of Field—as a render effect or a multi-pass effect. The multi-pass option will be discussed at the end of the chapter.

Depth of Field works by specifying a distance at which a camera is to focus. Anything closer to or farther away from the camera is blurred to some degree, depending on the distance from this specified distance, also known as the **target distance.** The farther an object is from the target distance, the greater the blurring effect.

When you load Depth of Field as a render effect, the **Depth of Field Parameters** rollout appears, as shown in Figure 18-15. Although you can apply the effect to a view without a camera, it is most practical to assign the effect to a specific camera. To do so, click the **Pick Cam.** button and select the camera. You must then tell the camera where to focus. There are two ways to do this. For one, you can click the **Pick Node** button and select an object in your scene that you want to have the camera focus on. The other option is to select the **Use Camera** option in the **Focal Point** section, select the camera in your scene with the applied effect, and set the **Target Distance** in the **Parameters** rollout of the Command panel.

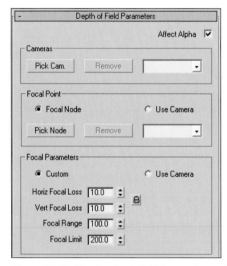

Figure 18-15. The Depth of Field Parameters rollout

The images in Figure 18-16 show an example of Depth of Field applied to a scene with two rows of teapots. Notice that in the image on the left, the target distance is set close to the teapots in the foreground. In the middle image, the target distance is set close to the teapots in the middle (third) row. Finally, the image on the right shows the target distance set near the teapots in the background.

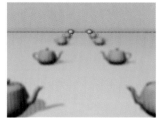

Figure 18-16. Depth of Field effects

Once you specify a target distance or a focal node, you must specify the range in which the camera will show objects in focus. This range is known as the focal range, and it is set in the **Focal Parameters** section of the **Depth of Field Parameters** rollout. Increasing the **Focal Range** value will make a greater area in your scene be in focus. You can also set the **Focal Limit** as the distance from the target distance at which blurring reaches a maximum value. If the blurring is too great too close to the target distance, simply increase the **Focal Limit** value until the blurring is acceptable. Finally, the **Horiz Focal Loss** and **Vert Focal Loss** values set the strength or intensity of the blurring. Reduce these values to reduce the overall blurring effect.

The Motion Blur effect

Motion blur adds a tremendous amount of realism to your scenes by simulating the effect of motion captured with a real camera. When an object moves in the short period of time that a camera shutter is open, the image of the object is blurred. This may be a result of the objects moving or the camera itself moving.

3ds Max generates motion blur in several different ways, but essentially there are two types of motion blur: Image Motion Blur and Object Motion Blur. **Image Motion Blur** creates the blur effect by smudging an object. **Object Motion Blur** renders multiple copies of an object and then superimposes them.

There are three primary means with which to add motion blur. One way is using **Scene Motion Blur,** a Video Post feature that blurs objects after the rendering process, and is generally less effective and realistic than the other two processes. Scene Motion Blur is not covered in this book. The two features that are covered are **Motion Blur,** found on the **Effects** tab of the **Environment and Effects** dialog box, and **Multi-Pass Effects,** found in the **Parameters** rollout of a camera object. Multi-Pass Motion Blur, along with Multi-Pass Depth of Field, will be discussed at the end of the chapter.

The Motion Blur effect is a render effect found on the **Effects** tab of the **Environment and Effects** dialog box. Before it can be used, it must first be activated for each individual object within the **Object Properties** dialog box. To activate it, select an object or group of objects to which you want to apply the Motion Blur effect, right-click inside the active viewport, select **Properties** from the quad menu, and select the **Image** option within the **Motion Blur** section, as shown in Figure 18-17. You can apply Motion Blur using either the **Object** or **Image** option; however, the **Image** option usually provides better results.

Figure 18-17. Motion Blur parameters within the Object Properties dialog box

You can deselect Motion Blur for any object or group of objects by deselecting the **Enabled** option. The **Multiplier** setting allows you to multiply the effect of the blur. However, I recommend just changing the basic settings that control the appearance of the blur to avoid confusion.

Those settings that control the appearance of the blur are found in the **Render Scene** dialog box, as shown in Figure 18-18. Here you can change the **Duration** of frames used to calculate the blur for either Object Motion Blur or Image Motion Blur. Within the **Image Motion Blur** section, there is an option to enable **Transparency.** If you don't enable this option, objects with transparent areas created with opacity maps will not show blurring behind the transparent areas. This option should always be enabled because visualizations usually have numerous uses of objects with transparent areas.

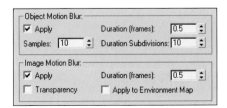

Figure 18-18. Motion Blur parameters within the Render Scene dialog box

As I mentioned before, you cannot use Motion Blur until you activate the option for each individual object; however, you can use Motion Blur without even loading it as an effect on the **Effects** tab of the **Environment and Effects** dialog box. In other words, as soon as you activate it in the **Object Properties** dialog box, Motion Blur will be used. If you do load Motion Blur into the effects list, the **Motion Blur Parameters** rollout appears, as shown in Figure 18-19. Only two settings are available, one to enable transparency and the other to control the duration of frames used to calculate the motion blur. When Motion Blur is added within the Environment and Effects dialog box, both of these settings override the same settings found in the **Render Scene** dialog box. Although not necessary, I recommend loading Motion Blur through the Environment and Effects dialog box and controlling the **Duration** setting here. This is the one central location you have to keep control and visibility over all your effects.

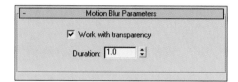

Figure 18-19. The Motion Blur Parameters rollout

Creating Motion Blur

This exercise demonstrates how to quickly and easily create a simple blur for any object.

1. Reset 3ds Max.

2. Create any object in the Perspective view.

3. Right-click the object in the active view and select **Properties** from the quad menu. The **Object Properties** dialog box opens.

4. In the **Motion Blur** section of the **Object Properties** dialog box, enable the **Image** option for the Motion Blur feature.

5. Animate the object so that it moves from one place to another during the course of the default 100-frame active time segment.

6. With the Time slider at frame 0, render the Perspective view. The image should look clear because at frame 0, the object hasn't begun moving yet.

7. Move the Time slider to frame **50** and render the Perspective view again. The object should look blurred now because it is moving at this point in time.

Multi-pass effects

Multi-pass effects are another more powerful option for the Depth of Field and Motion Blur effects. Multi-pass effects are found in the **Parameters** rollout of the Command panel when a camera object is selected. The available multi-pass effects include Depth of Field (mental ray), Depth of Field, and Motion Blur, as shown in Figure 18-20. Since Mental Ray is not covered in this book, the first option will likewise not be covered. In the following sections, I will cover Motion Blur and Depth of Field.

The Multi-Pass Motion Blur effect

The Multi-Pass Motion Blur effect is the most realistic means of adding motion blur to your scene—but it takes much longer to render than the Motion Blur effect because it renders the entire scene numerous times. 3ds Max achieves this effect by rendering several versions of the same frame with selective objects being offset from their normal locations. 3ds Max then combines these images with some processing to achieve the blurred effect. Although there is a process by which you can use layers to apply a multi-pass effect to only the objects to be blurred, this is an advanced process that is not always practical, and will not be covered in this book.

Figure 18-20. The available multi-pass effects

To enable Multi-Pass Motion Blur, select the **Enable** option (shown in Figure 18-20) and select **Motion Blur** from the drop-down list directly below it. When you select **Motion Blur,** the second rollout in the Command panel changes to the **Motion Blur Parameters** rollout, as shown in Figure 18-21. While each of the parameters in this rollout can have a dramatic effect on the overall appearance of the motion blur, there are only two parameters you should give specific attention to: **Total Passes** and **Duration (frames).** If you take the time to investigate the other parameters in this rollout, you will probably find that either their manipulation does nothing to significantly improve the quality of your work, or that their manipulation degrades the quality of your work to an unacceptable level.

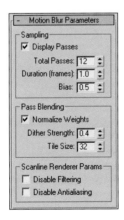

Figure 18-21. The Motion Blur Parameters rollout

The **Total Passes** value dictates how many times each individual frame will be rendered and, therefore, how many will be averaged to achieve the effect. Figure 18-22 shows the effect of changing the **Total Passes** value while leaving all other parameters at their default settings.

The top-left image shows a single frame of a car animation, but because Motion Blur is not enabled, the car appears to be motionless.

The top-right image shows the result of enabling Motion Blur and setting the **Total Passes** to its lowest possible value of 2. Close inspection of the blown-up image of the rear bumper shows two separate images combined into one. These are the two passes that 3ds Max uses to create one image in which only objects in motion are blurred.

The bottom-left image shows the result of increasing **Total Passes** to 3. The same blown-up image of the rear bumper shows three distinct passes; and because the passes are so distinct, the overall effect of motion blur is unrealistic. To achieve a believable effect, the number of passes should be high enough so that these distinctions can't be made.

The bottom-right image shows the result of increasing **Total Passes** to its default setting of 12. This image is much more realistic, but unfortunately 12 passes takes 12 times as long to render as a single frame with no motion blur. If your objects in motion are small enough or far enough away from the camera, you can achieve realism with much fewer than 12 passes. As with most effects, you should experiment adequately before settling on any particular setting. The **Preview** button directly above the **Multi-Pass Effect** drop-down list in the **Parameters** rollout allows you to preview the Motion Blur in Wireframe mode.

The other Motion Blur parameter that you should try experimenting with is **Duration (frames)**. This value tells 3ds Max how many total frames should be used to compute the blur for each individual frame. With a setting of 2, for example, 3ds Max uses one frame before and after an object's position to compute the blur. With a setting of 4, 3ds Max uses two frames before and two frames after, and so on. The more frames used, the more dramatic the blurred effect will be. Increasing this value may also require a greater number of total passes since the individual passes will be farther apart from each other and thus easier to see.

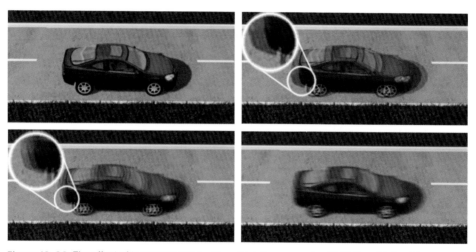

Figure 18-22. The effect of increasing the number of total passes using Multi-Pass Motion Blur

The Multi-Pass Depth of Field effect

Multi-Pass Depth of Field creates blurring based on distance from the camera. This effect simulates real-world cameras by allowing some objects to be in focus while objects at other depths are out of focus, as shown in Figure 18-23. Actually, in this case, it's people. That's me at the front-left and my long-time business partner Brian Zajac at the front-right.

Figure 18-23. An example of applying Multi-Pass Depth of Field to myself (front-left) and my cohort Brian (front-right)

To enable Multi-Pass Depth of Field, select the **Enable** option (shown in Figure 18-20) and select **Depth of Field** from the **Multi-Pass Effects** drop-down list directly below it. When you select **Depth of Field**, the second rollout in the Command panel changes to **Depth of Field Parameters**, as shown in Figure 18-24.

Figure 18-24. The Depth of Field Parameters rollout

To use Multi-Pass Depth of Field, you must determine where the camera should focus—everything closer to or farther from the camera will be blurred to some degree. That distance can be specified with one of two parameters: target distance and focal depth.

Target distance is the distance from the camera to the camera target. This parameter is the last in the **Parameters** rollout (partially shown at the top of Figure 18-24), and exists whether the selected camera is a target camera or a free camera. When a free camera is created, the target distance is set to the value of the last target camera created, even though a target doesn't exist.

Focal depth is the distance at which the camera is in focus. To use the **Focal Depth** parameter, you must disable the **Use Target Distance** option, which is enabled by default.

I prefer to use target distance to specify the point at which the camera should focus, because with this option, you can see at any time where in the scene the camera is focused. With the **Focal Depth** option, you don't have that visual clue, and unless you take a measurement or a test render, you don't know if the correct distance is specified. Figure 18-25 shows a perfect example of how the target distance option gives you the visual clue. The left image shows the Top view of a scene with several people at varying distances from the camera. Notice that the target of the camera is positioned exactly at the second set of people. The image on the right shows how this causes the second set of people to be in focus and the rest of them to be out of focus.

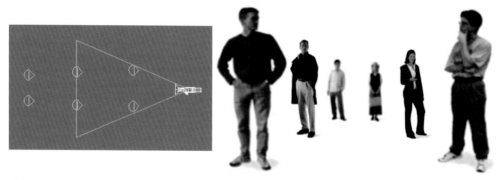

Figure 18-25. Using target distance to specify focus location on a camera

The only other two parameters I care about when using Multi-Pass Depth of Field are **Total Passes** and **Sample Radius. Total Passes** works the same here as with Motion Blur. Just as with Motion Blur, you will have to determine how many passes you can afford to spend your rendering time on, as well as the minimum number needed to produce a realistic effect.

The **Sample Radius** parameter is the other critical parameter that you should pay attention to when applying Multi-Pass Depth of Field. This parameter specifies the potential distance that the scene can move around the focus point. Larger **Sample Radius** values produce greater blurring. The default setting of 0'1.0" produces an almost unnoticeable effect, so you might try 1'0" or 1'6".

Figure 18-26 shows several examples of a scene rendered using different **Sample Radius** values. In the top-left image, Depth of Field is applied with the default **Sample Radius** of 0'1". In the top-right image, the **Sample Radius** is increased to 0'3". In the bottom-left image, the **Sample Radius** is increased to 0'6". In the bottom-right image, the **Sample Radius** is increased further to 1'0".

It is important to note, however, that the **Sample Radius** values needed to produce these results require a scene with similar scale. The teapots in this scene are 3 feet wide. Therefore, if the entire scene were scaled up to twice the size, and the teapots were 6 feet wide, the **Sample Radius** values would have to be twice as large to produce the same results. The bottom line is that you will probably have to experiment several times to find the **Sample Radius** value that produces the result you're looking for. Again, the **Preview** button located in the **Parameters** rollout is a great way to experiment without having to render the scene each time.

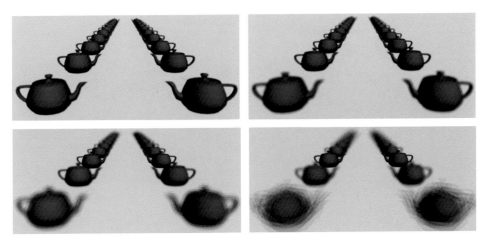

Figure 18-26. The effect of increasing Sample Radius with Multi-Pass Depth of Field

Summary

This chapter has covered many powerful effects that can drastically improve the quality and realism of your work with just a little effort. Each of these effects has a place in architectural visualization, and almost every award-winning image or animation has used at least one of the effects discussed in this chapter. When they are not used, it is much more difficult to pass off your work as a photo-realistic presentation—and for the amount of time they take to implement, they're certainly worth the effort.

Deciding which effects to implement based on the time it takes to render with them is a critical part of the rendering process. If time is available, you may want to consider the multi-pass effects to achieve the highest possible quality. If, however, time is short, you may have to reduce the number or quality of your effects. Making the right decision can mean the difference between meeting a deadline with a high-quality product and missing a deadline and losing a customer forever.

Appendixes

Customizing 3ds Max

3DS MAX CONTAINS POWERFUL CUSTOMIZATION features that enable you to streamline your work beyond those methods discussed throughout the chapters in this book. Customizing a program as complex as 3ds Max, however, is not effective unless you have a thorough understanding of the commands and features with which you arrange your interface. For this reason, I have placed an explanation of customization in this appendix. The first chapter in this book briefly highlighted some critical customization features that were necessary to mention during a discussion of the 3ds Max interface. This appendix picks up where Chapter 1 left off.

Although 3ds Max is used by numerous industries, its default interface layout is configured to provide the greatest efficiency for users in the entertainment industry. If you have finished reading this book, you now have a good foundation level understanding of 3ds Max and should take a look at some customization features that will make the interface more efficient and effective for your work in architectural visualizations.

The Customize menu

The bottom half of the **Customize** menu shown in Figure A-1 contains access to critical customization features in 3ds Max. These areas include **Configure User Paths, Units Setup, Grid and Snap Settings, Viewport Configuration,** and **Preferences.** The critical features of these areas were discussed in Chapter 1, and although they represent only a small fraction of all the customization features available, coverage of these areas is sufficient for the foundation level user. Playing around with these features and making numerous changes is easy and sometimes tempting, but exercise caution. Unless you read about a specific feature or explicitly understand what effect a particular change has on the program, you will probably be better off not to make the change. The next few pages discuss areas of customization in 3ds Max where change is much more justifiable.

UI schemes

When 3ds Max starts, it uses a file in the **3dsMax2008\UI** directory called **MaxStartUI.ui** to decide how to arrange the user interface. The very first time you run 3ds Max, that file is identical to the **DefaultUI.ui** file, but every time you close the program, the **MaxStartUI.ui** file is resaved with any changes made to any part of the user interface. If you move a toolbar or undock the Command panel, those changes will be saved in this file. To reload the original default user interface and revert back to the way 3ds Max appeared when you first installed it, click the **Customize** menu, select **Load Custom UI Scheme** (as shown in Figure A-1), and open the **DefaultUI.ui** file. If you make changes to the interface and want to revert back to the way 3ds Max was configured when you started your current session, simply select **Revert to Startup Layout** from the **Customize** menu, also shown in Figure A-1. To prevent the need of reverting to your startup layout because of inadvertent clicks of the mouse, you can lock the user interface by selecting **Lock UI Layout,** or use the keyboard shortcut **Alt+0**.

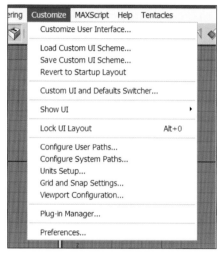

Figure A-1. The Customize menu

Custom UI and Defaults Switcher

Before going any further in the customization of 3ds Max, let's discuss the default user interface a little more. As I stated in the previous paragraph, 3ds Max is streamlined for the entertainment industry, not ours. Autodesk, however, kept the visualization industry in mind by preparing a way for us to make one simple customization change in our favor that has widespread effect over the entire program.

If you select **Custom UI and Defaults Switcher** from the **Customize** menu (see Figure A-1), a window appears which displays four different global configurations for 3ds Max. The default 3ds Max configuration shown at the top of the list provides a version of 3ds Max, as I mentioned, geared towards the entertainment industry. As the program clearly states in the center window, "The Max initial settings are configured to provide as much interactive performance as possible with small scenes, containing only a few shadow casting lights. Your application will be directed towards modeling, animating and rendering characters or models related to the entertainment industry."

Third in the list, the **DesignVIZ** configuration configures 3ds Max in a way that saves users in the visualization industry enormous amounts of time over the course of a project. Here the program states, "The DesignVIZ initial settings are configured to provide as much rendering performance as possible with large scenes, containing many lights. Your application will be directed towards photo realistic rendering of typical architectural models."

As an example, when you create a light with the default Max configuration, no shadows are cast unless you manually enable them. This lack of shadows suits the entertainment industry, however it does little to serve the visualization industry where lights almost always need to cast shadows. While changing this setting manually takes very little time, over the course of a project, you could easily make tens of thousands of similar changes that could otherwise be avoided by simply enabling the **DesignVIZ** configuration. I avoided a discussion of this feature in Chapter 1, because anyone missing this one area of discussion could be easily confused with what I would later call default settings. Because you are exploring more methods of useful customization, now would be a good time to begin using this feature. By reading the discussion of the **DesignVIZ** configuration in the center window, you can gain an understanding of just how broad the changes to the program are.

Figure A-2. A feature to globally change the UI to a design visualization configuration

Customize User Interface

The **Customize User Interface** feature, found at the very top of the **Customize** menu, provides access to another very large area of customization in 3ds Max. Selecting this first item in the menu opens the **Customize User Interface** dialog box. You can also access this dialog box by right-clicking certain icons in the **Main** toolbar, such as **Layer Manager,** or by right-clicking any empty space to the right of the toolbar.

When you open the **Customize User Interface** dialog box, shown in Figure A-3, five tabs appear at the top. With four of these tabs you can customize specific interfaces within the overall 3ds Max interface; the keyboard, toolbars, quads, and menu. The fifth tab provides a way to make color changes to just about any area of the program. Though users commonly change the viewport background from the default gray to black, you should take caution in doing so. Often changing one color causes a ripple effect which requires you to change another so that you can see the tools you need to use. You might find that making color changes is simply more trouble than it's worth, but it's all a matter of preference. If you want a dark background, you might be better off loading the **amedark.ui** interface.

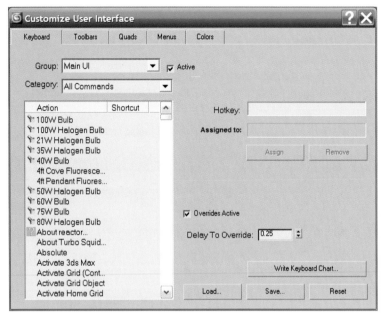

Figure A-3. The Customize User Interface dialog box

In each of the first four tabs, 3ds Max displays a list of commands by group type. These group types include many areas, such as **Material Editor** and **Video Post**. With some groups, the available commands (or features) can be further separated by categories. What is important here is that just about every command in 3ds Max can be found in these groups and linked to each of these four interface types. In the **Customize User Interface** dialog box, you can assign keyboard shortcuts, referred to here as **Hotkeys**. Within the **Toolbars** tab you can create, delete, or rename toolbars. Within the **Quads** tab, you can create, delete, and even edit quad menus. Finally, within the **Menus** tab you can create, delete, and edit not only the menus at the top of the program, but virtually every menu found in the program.

Use of each tab is fairly straightforward and takes little time to master. As an example, you can quickly assign hot keys by highlighting a command in the left scroll window, pressing a key on the keyboard and then clicking the **Save** button at the bottom of the dialog box. By holding down the Ctrl, Alt, or Shift keys while pressing any other key, you can create a shortcut from a combination of keys pressed simultaneously. Using the existing hot keys and setting up your own hot keys are good practices for speeding up your production time. It is always faster to use a hot key than to click on a menu item in the interface.

Summary

Once you have a strong foundation in 3ds Max, the **Customize User Interface** dialog box is truly an area worth exploring. The most beneficial way you can take advantage of this dialog box is to study how you work, figure out what commands you use most often and then customize the various interfaces around those commands. When you do, you'll find yourself working at top speed and efficiency.

Keyboard Shortcuts

Among the greatest time-saving features in 3ds Max are the keyboard shortcuts. Keyboard shortcuts allow you to execute a command by pressing a single key or a combination of keys on the keyboard. Using keyboard shortcuts saves enormous amounts of time over using interface elements such as menus, icons, or the Command panel. Instead of clicking in numerous places to execute a single command, you can use the keyboard to do it in a fraction of a second. Veteran 3ds Max users will usually keep one hand on the keyboard to quickly execute a command in less time than it would take to visually locate an icon.

While some commands are only accessible through certain menus or through the Command panel, the vast majority of all commands in 3ds Max can be executed with a keyboard shortcut. This appendix provides a list of 70 default keyboard shortcuts that I have found to be the most useful in my workflow as well as 30 additional shortcuts that I have set up for myself because of their frequency of use. Combined they provide shortcut access to what I consider 100 of the most useful 3ds Max commands available as shortcuts.

Default keyboard shortcuts

Table B-1 lists 70 handy default keyboard shortcuts. It is important to not try to learn every available default shortcut or to try to create a shortcut for every command that you find yourself using throughout the course of a project. Doing so will only confuse you. Instead, try to learn the default shortcuts for the commands you use most often and set up the additional shortcuts for the commands that you find yourself using most frequently. In this way, you will be able to recall the shortcuts quickly instead of pondering over a long list in your mind or on paper.

If a shortcut does not exist for a particular command, refer to Appendix A to learn how to create your own.

Table B-1. 70 default keyboard shortcuts in 3ds Max

Command	Shortcut
Adaptive Degradation	O
Advanced Lighting Panel	9
Align	Alt+A
Auto Key Mode Toggle	N
Camera View	C
Clone	Ctrl+V
Create Camera From View	Ctrl+C
Cycle Active Snap Type	Alt+S
Default Lighting Toggle	Ctrl+L
Disable Viewport	D
Display as See Through Toggle	Alt+X
Environment Toggle	8
Fetch	Alt+Ctrl+F
Front View	F
Go to Start Frame	Home
Go to End Frame	End
Hide Cameras Toggle	Shift+C
Hide Geometry Toggle	Shift+G
Hide Grids Toggle	G
Hide Lights Toggle	Shift+L
Hide Shapes Toggle	Shift+S
Hold	Alt+Ctrl+H
Isolate Selection	Alt+Q
Isometric User View	U
Left View	L
Material Editor	M
Maximize Viewport Toggle	Alt+W
New Scene	Ctrl+N
Open File	Ctrl+O
Percent Snap Toggle	Shift+Ctrl+P
Perspective User View	P
Place Highlight	Ctrl+H
Play Animation	/
Show Statistics Toggle	7
Quick Align	Shift+A

Command	Shortcut
Quick Render	Shift+Q
Redo Scene Operation	Ctrl+Y
Redo Viewport Operation	Shift+Y
Render Last	F9
Render Scene Dialog Toggle	F10
Restrict to Plane Cycle	F8
Restrict to X	F5
Restrict to Y	F6
Restrict to Z	F7
Save File	Ctrl+S
Select All	Ctrl+A
Select and Move	W
Select and Rotate	E
Select and Scale	R
Select By Name	H
Select Invert	Ctrl+I
Select None	Ctrl+D
Selection Lock Toggle	Space
Set Key Mode	`
Set Keys	K
Showing Floating Dialogs	Ctrl+`
Show Safeframes Toggle	Shift+F
Snaps Toggle	S
Spot/Directional Light View	Shift+4
Top View	T
Transform Gizmo Size Down	-
Transform Gizmo Size Up	=
Transform Type-In Dialog Toggle	F12
Undo Scene Operation	Ctrl+Z
Undo Viewport Operation	Shift+Z
View Edged Faces Toggle	F4
Wireframe/Smooth+Highlights Toggle	F3
Shade Selected Faces	F2
Zoom Extents All Selected	Z

Additional keyboard shortcuts

The shortcuts in Table B-2 are 30 additional ones that I have set up for commands that are used often or require numerous mouse clicks to access. Some of these shortcuts override default short-cuts, and whenever possible, I have used single keys for the shortcuts to make executing the commands as easy as possible. As with many of the default shortcuts, creating a shortcut with the first letter of the command the shortcut represents is not always possible.

When making your own shortcuts, you might want to consider matching your 3ds Max short-cuts to the shortcuts for commands found in Photoshop. Doing so might help you learn them more easily and prevent you from having to remember two different shortcuts for the same command.

In addition to the shortcuts discussed in this appendix, several companies manufacture keypad devices that allow you to program hundreds of keys as shortcuts to commands or to replace fre-quently typed words and phrases. This type of device, similar to a computer tablet, can save a tremendous amount of time, and I highly recommend its use.

Table B-2. 30 additional 3ds Max keyboard shortcuts

Command	Shortcut
Affect Pivot Only Mode Toggle	0 (zero)
Array	Alt+Shift+A
Asset Browser	J
Backface Cull	Alt+B
Boolean	Ctrl+B
Convert to Editable Mesh	[
Convert to Editable Polygon	]
Convert to Editable Spline	\
Curve Editor (Open)	Y
Display Floater	I
Edit Mesh Modifier	Page Up
Edit Spline Modifier	Page Down
Group	1
Group Attach	2
Group Close	3
Group Detach	4
Group Explode	5
Group Open	6
Hide Selection	Up Arrow
Hide Unselected	Down Arrow
Light Lister	Alt+L
Mirror	Ctrl+M
RAM Player	Alt+R
Tape Measure	Q

Command	Shortcut
Unfreeze All	, (comma)
Unfreeze by Hit	. (period)
Unfreeze by Name	/
Unhide All	Left Arrow
Unhide by Name	Right Arrow
UVW Map Modifier	Ctrl+U

Index

Gallery of Images

The following pages showcase work from 18 of the top visualization artists in the business. Rather than simply feature their best work, I wanted this unique gallery to highlight imagery from both the beginning of their career, as well as their work today. Accompanying each set of images is advice about improving the quality of your work and how with dedication and hard work, you too can vastly improve the level of your imagery.

"My best advice to anyone at any skill level is to build a good network of sub contractors. Whether you're a freelancer or the owner of a large visualization company, employing sub contractors has so many advantages that can completely change your final product and your workflow for the better. By subcontracting work out to others, you can accept larger jobs and complete any job in a shorter amount of time. Projects will always come along that are too large or have a deadline too soon for you or your firm to handle. Turning away any visualization project can be disheartening, especially when a large amount of money is involved. Also, by sending work to others in the industry, you automatically give yourself access to an extremely large wealth of knowledge. A large portion of what I have learned in this business has come as a result of sharing ideas and advice with some of the best in the industry... which all started when I began sending work to others."

Brian Smith, 3DAS
brian.smith@3das.com

"The easiest way to make your pictures look better and more realistic is to find nice photos in architectual magazines and try to duplicate them in 3D. By doing this, you will learn how to use colored lighting, how the light behaves in various types of spaces, and how it interacts with different types of surfaces. Add a few dramatic effects to your work whenever possible and try not to use the same approach to set up your scenes each time. You don't have to reinvent the wheel with each new project, but when time allows practice with different lighting, different materials, and different render settings."

Serge Vasilev, cat-a-pult
caesar@cat-a-pult.com

"Be an unrelenting student of your surroundings. The best lessons in lighting, materials, and composition come from things we are immersed in every day, every moment. The most striking 3D images are those that are able to make us feel something beyond the ink on the page, images that convey the sensations one would actually experience if the scene were reality."

Padhia Romaniello, Avocado Digital Design Inc / 3DAS
padhia@avocado3d.com / padhia@3das.com

"Plan your scene right from the start and choose your camera position very early on in the process so that way you can spend time just modeling what's important and visible in your camera. Then find your sky and lots of photo references of the kind of light you want to achieve in your image. Light and composition is what are going to make your image stand out from the rest."

Gustavo Capote
gcapotef@hotmail.com

"If you want to learn 3D quickly, you have to be prepared to dedicate an enormous amount of free time to self-education and practice. Use as many different sources of information as you can find, such as books, online tutorials, chat forums, and peers to name just a few. Understand techniques others have had success with and then try to develop your own new techniques for faster, more efficient workflow. Be innovative...experiment a little with each new project and try to learn something new with each project. If your renderings are disappointing to you, keep trying because every veteran user has been disappointed with their work more times than they can remember and with practice you can only get better."

Alexander Gorbunov, Intero Visuals
alexg@interovisuals.com

"If you're just starting in the 3d visualization field, I would definitely recommend paying a lot of attention to other people's work and techniques. Try to learn from the experiences of others and then develop your own workflow. Lot's of practice will lead you to a good level if you keep trying to improve your techniques and testing different possibilities. I'm pretty sure the most important thing though, is to enjoy what you're doing. The 3d work can be quite demanding. It'll be hard to reach your best if you think only about the final result and do not enjoy the whole process in itself."

Maurício Santos, Hype Studio
mauricio@hypestudio.com.br

"*Always expect your visualizations to take at least twice as long as you first project. The quickest way to lose a client is to miss a deadline and it's far better to set a late deadline and finish early than to set a quick deadline and finish late. You can always charge extra for quick turn-arounds or you can simply turn down a project, but being late is simply unacceptable in this business.*"

Nadiya Tarasyuk, Visarty
nt@visarty.com

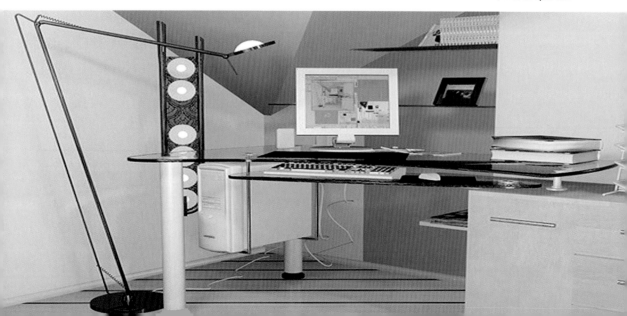

"*Surround yourself with people that are as hard-working and dedicated as you are... whether in the same office or as strategic partners in a distant country. This business demands late hours and self-sacrifice, especially for new business owners, so working with others that share this philosophy is absolutely critical. Create a good business plan from the start and stick to it!*"

Volodymyr Kvasnytsya, Visarty
vkvasnytsya@visarty.com

"Study the everyday environments around you...materials, objects and the way they react to light, the color of the sunlight at different times of the day, and the reflections in the glass of the buildings you pass on your way to work. Learn about photography; learn how cameras work and study great architectural photographs and how they are composed. Make the most of the people around you; learn and share!"

Martin Drake, Preconstruct
mdrake@preconstruct.com

"Always view your work with an artistic eye, considering composition and color of the piece from the very outset. Good composition, color and lighting can turn a dull, uninspiring image into a vibrant, memorable one. Study composition and mood in other media (painting, photography, film, etc.), look closely at the images that stick in your mind and try to figure out why. Before starting a piece, create some hand sketches or test renders to try out different camera angles. Make notes on the mood and feelings you want to convey with your work and at different stages in your work get critiques and advice from others (especially peers) as much as possible."

Derek Jackson, LSI Architects
derek.jackson@LSIarchitects.co.uk

"The advice I would like to give to beginners is to always follow your heart! What works for someone else, might not be right for you. You'll see a lot of workflows and software, etc., so try to read between the lines. Don't forget that if you are trying to make your work like the real world, keep looking around you look at things like shadows and light...look closely at how buildings are put together...read about construction and materials. Good modeling and lighting is about of 50% of good still image while the other 50% belongs to your perception of camera angle, atmosphere, composition, color scheme ...etc. Don't lose your nerves if something goes wrong, there must be an answer, maybe closer than you think. And finally, keep your hardware up-to-date... if your viewport is orbiting to slowly or you wait too long for a render, then upgrade as soon as possible. There is no reason to punish yourself with slow machines because nothing can buy your time. Good luck and keep rendering!"

Zdravko Barisic, TrideVAL
trideval@yahoo.com

"Our best advice would be to learn to be an effective team member. Often this involves checking your ego at the door, working in a way that will make sense to other people and learning to give and receive criticism effectively and objectively. Some of the most rewarding projects we have had the privilege to be a part of have been true collaborations. By utilizing the best talents of a team, we have been able to accomplish more in shorter time frames, and the result is always better than any one of us could have accomplished individually. Secondly, know your objective. An image is always much more successful when it is in line with what your client is trying to accomplish. There's nothing more frustrating than spending hours making the architecture look perfect only to discover that the model is meant to be conceptual, and that the client really wanted more life and people in the image."

Craig Jolly and Kirk Headley, Tin Cactus Studios
cjolly@tincactus.com, kheadley@tincactus.com

"If you are trying to make photorealistic renderings, you should include as much detail as time allows. Very few photorealistic renderings will lack the little things that make a big difference. For an exterior rendering, take the extra time to add little things like street signs, light poles, and benches. For interior renderings, add things like plates and knapkins to a dining table, picture frames to a dresser, or a bowl of fruit to a kitchen counter. These details are in the real world and should be in the 3D world as well. Try to learn as much as you can about photography, lighting, and composition. Finally, always solicit help, advise, and opinions from your peers and partners… they can often spot things that you simply can't see."

Sergio Molina, Rise Studios
sergio@risestudio.com

"While all artists have egos, over the years it's been necessary for me to shed the desire for total ownership of the image. When starting out, I worked mostly on my own and took pride in crafting each model and material, then lighting and rendering every image by myself. Now as a lead artist on a team that handles projects infinitely more complex, that hermitic workflow is now not only unhealthy but impossible. While I do miss many of those tasks, the speed at which the team is able to pull together incredibly complex scenes has made the work all the more exhilarating. Now I'm proud to say that every image and animation I work on is a fully collaborative effort, and the rewards continue to multiply every time we grow our team."

Shaun Donnelly, Tangram 3DS
sdonnelly@tangram3ds.com

"The best advice I could give is to get the best equipment you can afford. Software and plugins become more complex and clients demand more detail with each passing year. If you are not properly equipped you are often forced to rely on photo editing software and you risk missing your deadlines. The ability to render cars, trees, people, as well as things like realistic shadows, reflections or refractions is what it's all about. Concentrate on lighting and don't believe in universal settings for all the future projects. You should experiment a little with each new project to see what new emotions you can create with your materials and lighting. There are no magical settings that will always make your scenes look good...it takes a lot of hard work. Modeling is straight forward and doesn't require any artistic interpretation... however, materials and lighting do and are therefore the keys to beautiful images."

Reza Bahari, Visual 3D
visual3d@streamyx.com

"The best advice we can give is that every time you don't know how to do something in your renderings, don't panic. Just post your problem on one of the many forums out there. Even if you don't have a problem, reading posts from time to time will constantly teach you great solutions and new techniques. For large projects, write out a plan of attack and follow the plan...especially when multiple artists are involved. When teamwork is needed, a good strategic plan can make a world of difference. Never model more than the camera can see, unless you are expecting to take more shots from other vantage points. Pay careful attention to reflections as almost all materials have at least some reflection. Look at every detail in your drawings and if it's in the drawings, assume your clients want to see it in the visualization. And finally, if your first renders are not good enough, keep your head up! Future renderings and future projects will almost always be better!"

Martin Di Stasi, Adrian Moreno
& Juan Pablo Parodi, Panorama01
info@panorama01.com

"Attention to detail is vital for a photo realistic rendering. If the detail is in the architectural drawings, it should be in your 3D scene unless the client specifically says otherwise. Combining that drive for attention to detail with my collegiate degree in the arts, I always try to mimic the properties of the world—how it is designed, colored, and lit. So the next time you get stuck in the virtual world, take a five minute break and see how Mother Nature did it. With a little bit of extra effort, exploration and education, you can always surpass your last project in photorealism."

Brian Zajac, 3DAS
brian.zajac@3das.com

"Detail truly makes the difference between a good render and a great render. I would also say that a good knowledge of basic art, design and photography has helped me in ways that just knowledge of 3D software simply could not. Understanding how buildings are created in the real world and how the materials are used is a tremendous help. Knowing how to read architectural drawings and intelligently fill in missing information is critical to efficient workflow."

Nick Smith
ncjsmith@gmail.com